시사 Books

초판 발행	2016년 7월 11일
개정판 발행	2025년 5월 20일
저자	이지영
편집	권이준, 김아영, 윤상희
펴낸이	엄태상
디자인	김지연
조판	이서영
콘텐츠 제작	김선웅, 장형진
마케팅	이승욱, 노원준, 조성민, 이선민
경영기획	조성근, 최성훈, 김로은, 최수진, 오희연
물류	정종진, 윤덕현, 신승진, 구윤주
펴낸곳	시사북스
주소	서울시 종로구 자하문로 300 시사빌딩
주문 및 교재 문의	1588-1582
팩스	0502-989-9592
홈페이지	http://www.sisabooks.com
이메일	book_english@sisadream.com
등록일자	1977년 12월 24일
등록번호	제300-2014-92호

ISBN 978-89-402-9444-4 13740

* 이 책의 내용을 사전 허가 없이 전재하거나 복제할 경우 법적인 제재를 받게 됨을 알려 드립니다.
* 잘못된 책은 구입하신 서점에서 교환해 드립니다.
* 정가는 표지에 표시되어 있습니다.

저자 이지영

감수자 Miles Meili

저자 서문

반복의 미학 (The Aesthetics of Repetition)

영어 학습에 있어 어휘의 중요성은 아무리 강조하여도 지나치지 않다. 하지만, 대부분의 영어 학습자들은 종종 어휘의 학습을 영어 학습의 일부 또는 부담스러운 일 정도로 치부하는 경향이 있는 것 같다. 특히, TOEIC, TEPS, TOEFL 등을 공부하는 대다수의 영어 학습자들은 단시간 내에 공인영어인증시험의 특정 점수 이상을 얻어 내기 위해 고군분투하며 고득점을 위한 획기적인 영어 학습법을 끊임없이 갈구하면서도 정작 언어 학습의 기본이 되는 언어의 기초 단위인, 어휘의 형태와 의미 그리고 그것의 사용에 대해서는 무관심하다. 이러한 안타까운 상황의 악순환은 영어 학습자들에게 많은 시간의 낭비와 불만족스러운 점수라는 결과로 돌아오게 되며, 뒤이은 영어 학습에의 흥미 상실, 때로는 '포기'라는 단어를 머리 속에 떠올리게 하기도 한다. 다년간 학습 현장에서 이러한 과정을 겪어온 학생들을 만나오면서 참으로 안타까운 마음을 감출 수 없었으며, 그렇다면 과연 그들에게 지금 필요한 것은 무엇이며 어떻게 하면 그들의 어려움을 조금 더 수월하게 해결해 줄 수 있을까에 대해 진지하게 생각해 보는 계기를 갖게 되었다.

사회가 현대의 영어 학습자들에게 요구하는 영어 실력은 단순히 듣기 및 읽기 능력의 탁월함 만을 의미하지는 않는다. 이제는 타인의 지식이나 의견을 명확하게 이해하는 수준을 넘어 자신의 지식과 의사를 명확하게 전달하고 표현할 수 있는 유창한 말하기 및 쓰기 능력을 요구한다. 따라서 그 요구 조건을 충족시키기 위해서 영어 학습자들은 언어의 하나의 영역에 집중할 것이 아니라 듣기, 읽기, 말하기, 쓰기와 같은 4개의 영역을 고루 향상시켜야 한다는 결론이 나오며, 이 네 개 영역의 능력 향상을 위해서는 언어 학습의 첫 단계이자 그 언어 자체의 의사 전달을 위한 매개가 되는 어휘와 그 어휘의 효율적인 활용을 위한 문법의 학습이 필수적으로 이루어져야 함은 너무나도 명백하다. 이러한 기초가 잘 다져져야 영어 학습자들이 그토록 간절히 원하는 빠르고 효과적인 영어 성적 및 실력의 향상을 기대해 볼 수 있다.

반복의 힘

미술 교사였던 피카소의 아버지는 어린 시절 피카소가 처음 미술을 배울 때 그에게 비둘기의 발만 반복해서 그리도록 하였다. 하나의 특정 사물을 반복적으로 관찰하고 연습한 그는 15세가 되자 사람의 얼굴뿐만 아니라 몸체 등과 같은 다른 대부분의 사물들을 그릴 수 있게 되었다. 이는 기본기에 충실하여 한 가지를 제대로 할 수 있게 되었을 때 다른 것에의 올바른 응용도 가능함을 보여주는 대표적인 일화라 할 수 있겠다. 또한 궁수들은 궁술을 연마할 때 수백 수천 번 과녁을 향해 활을 쏘는 연습을 함으로써 정확하게 원하는 목표점에 활을 쏠 수 있게 되며 그 때가 되어서야 다른 궁술도 터득할 수 있게 된다고 한다. 여기서 우리가 주목해야 할 것은 "반복의 힘"이 아닐까 한다. "무엇이든 지속적으로 반복하여 연습하면 완벽해진다(Practice makes perfect)"는 것을 우리는 알고 있다. 특히, 언어 학습에 있어서 반복 학습 없이 어휘의 습득은 불가능하다. 그렇다면 그 실천은 어떻게 해야 할 것인가? 한번 외운 것은 최소한 7번 이상 반복하여 복습해야 한다. 인간의 뇌는 한번 학습한 내용을 대략 1시간이 지나면 절반은 잊어버리는 망각 습성을 갖고 있다. 따라서 단기 정보를 장기 기억으로 전환하려면 복습이 적절한 시기에 이루어져야 한다. 다시 말하면, 어휘의 복습이 최초 어휘에의 노출 후 한 시간 이내에, 잠자리에 들기 전에, 그 다음 날 아침에, 그리고 주말에 재차 복습이 이루어져야 하며 그 이후로도 시간 날 때마다 틈틈이 암기한 어휘들의 복습이 이루어져야 한다. 어휘 습득 과정은 그렇기 때문에 상당한 시간과 노력을 요구하는 과정임을 늘 염두에 두고 목표를 이루기 위해 좀 더 장기적인 계획을 세우고 끈기 있게 그 계획을 실천해 나아가야 한다.

저자 서문

통합 학습 전략을 담은 어휘집 (언어의 4개 영역과 어휘를 한번에 잡자!)

토플을 준비하는 영어 학습자들을 위한 어휘집들은 비슷한 양과 수준의 어휘를 수록하고 있다. 하지만 이러한 어휘들을 학습자가 얼마나 효과적으로 암기하여 영어 실력 향상에 도움을 주는가는 또 다른 문제이다. 이러한 측면에서 본 교재는 어휘와 유의어, 그리고 그에 따른 짧은 예문만을 제시하는 여타의 어휘집과는 달리, 토플에 자주 출제되는 어휘를 담고 있는 까다로운 빈출 주제문을 제시하고 이 문장과 같은 의미를 전달하기 위해 활용될 수 있는 유의어 및 표현을 사용한 2-3개의 재진술 문장들을 제시하고 있다. 이는 영어 학습자들로 하여금 실전과 유사한 어휘와 문장 구조에의 노출을 용이하게 하며, 문장 안에서의 그것들의 활용에 대한 모범적인 예시를 얻도록 하고, 이를 통해 어휘와 문법의 자연스러운 습득 및 그 어휘의 다른 문장 안에서의 적절한 활용에 대한 감을 잡을 수 있도록 한다. 또한 대부분의 어학 시험들이 영어 학습자들에게 요구하는 생각과 의견을 재진술하기(paraphrase) 및 요약하기(summarize) 능력의 향상을 위해 다양하고 적극적인 예문을 제시하여 복잡한 문장의 빠른 이해를 돕는다. 온라인 상에서 제공하는 MP3 파일은 제시된 어휘와 문장을 반복적으로 듣게 함으로써 영어 학습자들의 어휘에 대한 인식과 속도를 향상시킬 수 있도록 하면서 더불어 따라 말하기를 함으로써 듣기 및 말하기 실력 향상에도 도움을 주도록 구성하였다. 각각의 주제문의 재진술 문장들 하단에는 개별적으로 영어 학습자가 문장을 만들어 보는 공간을 만들어 둠으로써 쓰기 실력도 함께 향상시킬 수 있도록 구성하였다. 따라서 교재에서 제시하는 여러 어휘들과 문장들의 반복적인 학습은 어휘와 문법의 자연스러운 습득뿐만 아니라 영어의 4개 영역의 향상을 동시에 이룰 수 있는 효과를 보장해 줄 것이고, 더 나아가 새로운 문장들 또는 지문들을 접했을 때 응용력과 유연성을 갖도록 하여 더 심층적이고 구조화된 이해를 할 수 있도록 많은 도움을 줄 것이다.

유학을 준비하는 영어 학습자들에게

유학을 준비하는 학생들이 반드시 숙지해야 할 사항 중 하나는 영어권 국가들은 타인의 창작물의 표절에 대해 상당히 엄정한 기준을 갖고 있다는 것이다. 영어권 국가의 학교들은 이를 알리기 위해 처음 유학을 온 학생들에게는 특히 별도로 세미나를 열어 표절은 무엇이며, 표절을 왜 기피해야 하고, 표절에 따른 처벌은 무엇인지에 대해 상세하게 교육한다. 뿐만 아니라 각각의 수업에서도 교수님들은 이 표절 규정에의 엄정한 준수를 학생들에게 재차 강조한다. 이러한 영어권 국가들의 문화적 특성과 타인의 지식이나 생각을 자신의 언어로 바꾸어 말하거나 요약한 후 자신의 의견을 개진하는 영어의 언어적 특성을 고려할 때 유학을 준비하거나 여하간의 목적으로 토플을 준비하는 여러분들에게 이 교재는 가장 필수적인 지침서이자 최고의 선택이라고 말 할 수 있겠다.

처음에는 무엇이든 당연히 힘들고 어려우며 받아들이는데 많은 시간과 노력이 요구된다. 하지만 포기하지 않고 지속적으로 그것을 반복한다면 처음보다는 그 다음이 조금 더 수월해질 것이고, 또 처음에는 보이지 않던 것들이 눈에 들어오게 될 것이다. 또한 만일 너무 어렵고 힘들어서 포기하고 싶다면, 그것은 지금까지 나 자신이 영어 학습에 다른 사람들보다 소홀하였기 때문에 나오는 당연한 대가임을 인정하고, 이것 말고 다른 방법이 있을 것이라는 막연한 생각은 이제 그만 접어두고 스스로 하고자 하는 굳건한 의지를 갖고, 마음을 열어 좀 더 노력하고 인내해야 할 것이다. 단언컨대, 이 교재의 철저한 활용은 여러분들로 하여금 토플 시험에의 최적화를 가능하게 하여 TOEFL, TEPS, TOEIC 등을 포함하는 여타의 시험에서의 고득점뿐만 아니라 유창한 영어 실력의 획득을 확실하게 보장해 줄 것이다.

저자 이지영

이 책을 공부하는 법

TOEFL VOCABULARY STUDY PLAN

The Teacher's Guide to How to Teach TOEFL Vocabulary to Students

TOEFL, TEPS, TOEIC을 포함하는 대부분의 공인영어인증시험에서의 성적 및 영어 실력 그 자체의 향상을 목표로 하는 많은 영어 학습자들을 대상으로 영어교육을 담당하는 선생님들을 위해 도움을 주고자 교재를 최대한 활용할 수 있는 지침을 간략하게 적어 본다. 본 교재는 1과 당 10개의 표제어와 그에 따른 유의어 군(대략 1과당 총 100 단어)으로 이루어져 있는 30개의 과(총 300개의 표제어)로 구성되어 있다. 따라서 학습자의 영어 실력에 따라 토플 초급자들을 대상으로 할 경우 1개월 20강 기준 3개월 (1강 5개의 표제어와 그에 따른 유의어 묶음) 과정으로 문법적인 부분과 어휘적인 부분에 대한 상세한 해설을 포함하여 수업을 진행할 수 있으며, 중급자를 대상으로 할 경우 2개월(1강 10개의 표제어와 그에 따른 유의어 묶음 30강, 5과 마다 출제되는 Review Test를 활용한 토플 실전 학습 총 6강 및 2주 단위 복습 총 4강)의 과정으로, 고급자를 대상으로 할 경우 1개월(1강 20개의 표제어와 그에 따른 유의어 묶음 15강 및 10강 마다 Review Test를 활용한 토플 실전 학습 총 3강 및 MP3 파일을 활용한 2주 단위 복습 총 2강)의 과정으로 강의를 진행할 수 있다. 좀 더 효과적인 학습을 위해 아래와 같은 강의의 흐름을 참고해보도록 한다.

1. 각 표제어마다 제시되어 있는 토플 빈출 대표 문장의 심층적인 분석 및 해설을 한다. 이 과정에서는 중요한 문법적 지식 및 표제어를 제외한 나머지 핵심 어휘를 짚고 넘어가도록 한다.
2. 대표 문장을 완벽하게 숙지하였다면, 표제어를 소개하고 그 표제어 대신에 활용할 수 있는 유의어들을 소개하도록 한다. 이는 기본 단어 실력의 향상을 도울 뿐만 아니라 표제어와 유의어 사이의 호환 가능성에 대한 감을 잡을 수 있도록 도와줄 것이다. 또한, 단순히 단어와 그에 해당하는 짤막한 예문 만을 제시하는 여타 어휘집과는 달리 핵심 어휘를 포함하는 문장들을 제시하고 그 문장들 안에서 핵심 어휘들이 어떻게 활용되고 있는지를 학습하도록 함으로써 살아있는 영어, 실전에 대비하는 영어 학습을 가능하게 한다.
3. 각 표제어와 토플 빈출 대표 문장을 명확히 숙지한 후, 앞에서 제시한 각 표제어의 유의어 또는 유의 어구를 활용하여 학습자들로 하여금 재진술 문장을 스스로 만들어 보도록 한다. 이는 학습자 스스로 PARAPHRASE 또는 SUMMARY 과정을 경험하도록 하는 기회를 제공해 줄 것이다. 이 과정에서 교재에 제시된 각 표제어와 그에 따른 재진술 문장 1과 2에 사용된 표제어의 유의어 1과 2는 토플 단어 시험에 일반적으로 함께 출제되는 단어들로 표제어와 함께 반드시 숙지해야 하는 단어들이므로 묶음 암기를 강조하고 이를 완벽히 숙지하도록 재진술 문장을 만들 때 문장 안에서 적극 활용해 보도록 학습자들에게 권한다.
4. 재진술 문장 1과 2를 모범 답안으로 학생들에게 제시 및 설명한다. 대표 문장과 재진술 문장의 학습은 토플의 SIMPLIFICATION 문제 유형의 적극적인 학습을 도와주며 또한 더 나아가 SUMMARY 문제에 대한 감을 잡을 수 있게 해 줄 뿐만 아니라 토플에 등장하는 여타 다른 문제 유형이 요구하는 올바른 답안을 찾아내는데 있어서도 가장 효과적인 학습 방법이 될 것임을 학생들이 인지하도록 한다. 때로는 이에 대한 예를 Review Test의 문제들을 활용하여 제시할 수 있다.
5. 시간이 허락할 경우 또 다른 재진술 문장을 만들어 보도록 한다. 재진술 문장을 만들 때에는 자신의 언어를 활용하여 좀 더 쉬운 단어들과 좀 더 적은 수의 단어로 만들어 볼 것을 학습자들에게 권한다. 재진술 문장을 만드는 이러한 과정은 학습자들로 하여금 말하기와 쓰기 영역에서 요구하는 다른 말로 바꾸어 표현하기 및 요약하기 능력을 체계적으로 향상시키도록 도와 줄 것이다.
6. MP3 파일을 활용한 대표 문장 및 재진술 문장 따라 읽기를 통해 토플의 끼다로운 핵심 문장 및 핵심 어휘를 완벽하게 본인의 것으로 만들도록 유도한다. 또한 이 따라 읽기 과정은 시간이 날 때마다 반복해 줄 것을 강조한다. 본 교재의 모든 문장들 및 어휘들은 토플에 등장하는 문장들 중 빈출 주제를 다루고 있으며, 특히 까다로운 문장들로 구성되어 있기 때문에 따라 읽기 과정을 통한 발음, 어휘, 문법 및 의미의 자연스럽고 완벽한 숙지는 읽기 및 듣기 영역에 있어서 문장의 읽기 및 듣기 속도 및 이해도 향상을 도와줄 뿐만 아니라 말하기 영역을 위한 가장 효과적인 연습도 가능하게 하여 한번에 여러 영역의 실력 향상을 꾀할 수 있는 가장 빠르고 효과적인 방법임을 학습자들에게 강조한다.

이 책을 공부하는 법

The Guide to How to Study
TOEFL Vocabulary Without a Teacher

TOEFL, TEPS, TOEIC을 포함하는 대부분의 공인영어인증시험에서의 성적 및 영어 실력 그 자체의 향상을 목표로 하는 많은 영어 학습자들 중 여러 가지 이유로 선생님의 도움 없이 독학을 해야 하는 학습자들을 위해 도움을 주고자 교재를 최대한 활용할 수 있는 지침을 간략하게 적어 본다. 본 교재는 1과 당 10개의 표제어와 그에 따른 유의어군(대략 1과당 총 100 단어)으로 이루어져 있는 30개의 과(총 300개의 표제어)로 구성되어 있다. 따라서 학습자의 영어 실력에 따라 토플 초급자의 경우 3개월의 기간을 잡고 하루1과 중 5개의 표제어와 그에 따른 유의어 묶음을 문법적인 부분과 어휘적인 부분에 집중하여 완벽히 숙지하도록 하며, 중급자의 경우 2개월의 기간을 잡고 하루 1과 10개의 표제어와 그에 따른 유의어 묶음을 완벽히 숙지하도록 하며, 고급자의 경우 단기적으로 어휘를 마친다는 각오로 1개월 동안 하루 2과 분량의 20개의 표제어와 그에 따른 유의어 묶음을 완벽히 숙지하고, MP3 파일을 활용한 따라 읽기 학습 과정을 매일 매일 꾸준히 반복함으로써 실전에 철저하게 대비할 수 있도록 한다. 좀 더 효과적인 학습을 위해 아래와 같은 학습의 흐름을 참고해보도록 한다.

1. 각 표제어마다 제시되어 있는 토플 빈출 대표 문장을 해석을 참고하여 정확하게 이해하도록 한다. 이 과정에서는 중요한 문법적 지식 및 표제어를 제외한 나머지 핵심 어휘를 찾아 완벽하게 숙지한다.

2. 대표 문장을 완벽하게 숙지하였다면, 표제어의 발음 및 뜻을 암기하고 그 표제어 대신에 활용할 수 있는 유의어들도 함께 암기하도록 한다. 이는 기본 단어 실력의 향상을 도울 뿐만 아니라 표제어와 유의어 사이의 호환 가능성에 대한 감을 잡을 수 있도록 도와줄 것이다.

3. 각 표제어와 토플 빈출 대표 문장을 명확히 숙지한 후, 제시된 각 표제어의 유의어 또는 유의 어구를 활용하여 재진술 문장을 스스로 만들어 보도록 한다. 이 과정에서 교재에 제시된 각 표제어와 그에 따른 재진술 문장 1과 2에 사용된 표제어의 유의어 1과 2는 토플 단어 시험에 일반적으로 함께 출제되는 단어들로 표제어와 함께 반드시 숙지해야 하는 단어들이므로 묶음 암기하며 이를 완벽히 숙지하도록 재진술 문장을 만들 때 문장 안에서 적극 활용해 보도록 한다.

4. 모범 답안인 재진술 문장 1과 2를 본인이 만든 재진술 문장들과 비교해 본다. 대표 문장과 재진술 문장의 학습은 토플의 SIMPLIFICATION 문제 유형의 적극적인 학습을 도와주며 또한 더 나아가 읽기 영역의 마지막 문제로 일반적으로 출제되는 SUMMARY 문제 유형에 대한 감을 잡을 수 있게 해 줄 뿐만 아니라 토플에 등장하는 여타 다른 문제 유형이 요구하는 올바른 답안을 찾아내는데 있어서도 가장 효과적인 학습 방법이 될 것임을 인지한다.

5. 재진술 문장 1과 2를 참고하여 또 다른 재진술 문장을 만들어 보도록 한다. 재진술 문장을 만들 때에는 자신의 언어를 활용하여 좀 더 쉬운 단어들과 좀 더 적은 수의 단어들로 만들어 보도록 한다. 재진술 문장을 만드는 이러한 과정은 학습자들로 하여금 말하기와 쓰기 영역에서 요구하는 다른 말로 바꾸어 표현하기 및 요약하기 능력을 체계적으로 향상시키도록 도와 줄 것이다.

6. MP3 파일을 활용한 대표 문장 및 재진술 문장 따라 읽기를 통해 토플의 까다로운 핵심 문장 및 핵심 어휘를 완벽하게 본인의 것으로 만들도록 한다. 또한 이 따라 읽기 과정은 시간이 날 때마다 반복한다. 본 교재의 모든 문장들 및 어휘들은 토플에 등장하는 문장들 중 빈출 주제를 다루고 있으며, 특히 까다로운 문장들로 구성되어 있기 때문에 따라 읽기 과정을 통한 발음, 어휘, 문법 및 의미의 자연스럽고 완벽한 숙지는 읽기 및 듣기 영역에 있어서 문장의 읽기 및 듣기 속도 및 이해도 향상을 도와줄 뿐만 아니라 말하기 영역을 위한 가장 효과적인 연습도 가능하게 하여 한번에 여러 영역의 실력 향상을 꾀할 수 있는 가장 빠르고 효과적인 방법이므로 매일매일 꾸준히 실천해 나가도록 한다.

영어 수준에 따라 하루에 5-20개의 표제어와 그에 따른 유의어(대략 하루에 50-200단어)를 완벽하게 학습하도록 한다. 처음에는 새로운 단어가 많아 조금 부담스러울 수 있으나 뒤로 갈수록 겹치는 단어가 많으므로 앞쪽에서 조금만 힘을 내어 준다면 뒤로 갈수록 조금 수월하게 학습을 할 수 있을 것이다. 어휘 학습은 반복의 과정 없이는 본인의 것이 되기 어려우므로 가능한 한 여러 번 핵심 어휘에 노출될 수 있도록 보고, 듣고, 말하고, 쓰기를 적극적으로 해야 함을 잊지 않도록 한다.

목차

Day 30

Day 1   vulnerable, meticulously, prone to, complicated, rudimentary, dwindle, distinguish, widespread, pronounced, penetrate   26

Day 2   buffer, marvelous, decimate, fatal, counterbalance, exclusively, extract, copious, unlikely, predecessor   38

Day 3   considerable, heyday, epitomize, consistent, staggering, obscure, recovery, bizarre, decoration, harness   50

Day 4   erratic, magnitude, prevent, disseminate, absurd, paradox, claim, remains, mechanism, excessive   62

Day 5   inevitable, fluctuations, rough, notably, prominent, breakthrough, adjacent, vibrant, demise, domesticated   74

review test   86

Day 6   precarious, integrate, spectrum, clue, intentional, contemplate, ensuing, stringent, tremendous, haphazard   96

Day 7   far-reaching, abhor, devise, brilliance, segregate, fragile, emergence, confined, perpetual, involve   108

Day 8   thrive, comparatively, afford, simultaneously, outstanding, barren, barrier, profound, inhospitable, adaptable   120

Day 9   propagate, precious, relevant, routinely, intact, deluxe, boundary, estimate, enhance, encroachment   132

Day 10   set, attribute, barely, assort, collide, collaboration, important, mundane, phenomenon, intermittently   144

review test   156

Day 11 outcome, arrangement, emerge, competitor, trigger, drawback, follow, consensus, conventional, inundate   166

Day 12 expand, distribution, portion, explain, be made up of, crude, fascinate, abandon, chief, consciousness   178

Day 13 artisan, exceptionally, proponent, accessible, exaggerate, consume, show, abrupt, inborn, locale   190

Day 14 mimic, lacking in, utterly, shatter, indigenous, participate in, divert, readily, motivation, extinct   202

Day 15 scorching, preoccupied, various, assess, despite, allocate, adroit, evade, trivial, accumulate   214

review test 226

Day 16 depict, drastically, solitary, vagarious, equilibrium, mixed, comprehend, advantageous, with regard to, elegant   236

Day 17 reflection, discover, original, implant, misleading, melt, suitable, surmise, withstand, procure   248

Day 18 foundation, protrude, task, utilization, antiseptic, arduous, arise from, fame, dreadful, chaos   260

Day 19 consume, terminal, progressively, similar to, deny, ancient, stimulate, product, controversy, inauspicious   272

Day 20 empty, depend on, govern, subsidize, capability, tend, symbolize, retain, contaminate, implement   284

review test 296

목차

Day 21 monotonous, actually, apprehension, aggravate, commence, enthusiastic, emphasize, sparse, conceal, even though　306

Day 22 bombard, feasible, investigate, position, compact, placid, predict, excavate, motionless, luminous　318

Day 23 contradictory, impending, approximately, effect, compressed, raise, bond, banish, staunch, supervise　330

Day 24 characteristic, unintentionally, alternative, roam, unparalleled, perspective, struggle, favorable, prudent, diligently　342

Day 25 perplexing, acute, respect, extant, extol, obstinate, pragmatic, overwhelm, initial, disrupt　354

review test　366

Day 26 surplus, release, immediately, persuasive, above and beyond, place, potential, delay, doctrine, substitute　376

Day 27 grant, difference, chaotic, qualification, weaken, require, covetous, potent, repair, misconception　388

Day 28 distinctive, evidence, ultimately, surprise, surpass, authenticate, additional, accelerate, ephemeral, satisfy　400

Day 29 absence, corrupt, recollect, indignation, obsolete, exercise, force, unbiased, tangible, transport　412

Day 30 repulsion, blame, inclination, declare, grab, nourishment, sequence, manipulate, brave, contemptible　424

review test　436

주제별 표현

Anthropology 인류학	446		Law 법학	466
Archaeology 고고학	446		Linguistics 언어학	468
Architecture 건축학	447		Literature 문학	469
Art History 예술사	448		Mathematics 수학	470
Astronomy 천문학	450		Marine Biology 해양 생물학	471
Biology 생물학	451		Medical Science 의학	471
Botany 식물학	452		Meteorology 기상학	472
Chemistry 화학	453		Music 음악	474
Communication 커뮤니케이션	455		Oceanography 해양학	475
Computer Science 컴퓨터 공학	455		Paleontology 고생물학	476
Economics 경제학	456		Philosophy 철학	476
Ecology 생태학	458		Physics 물리학	477
Energy 에너지	459		Physiology 생리학	478
Engineering 공학	459		Politics 정치학	479
Entomology 곤충학	460		Psychology 심리학	480
Environmental Science 환경학	461		Religion 종교	481
Film 영화	462		Sociology 사회학	482
Geography 지리학	463		U.S. History 미국사	483
Geology 지질학	464		Zoology 동물학	485
Health Science 건강의학	465			

PARAPHRASE & SUMMARY

주어진 문장의 핵심 내용을 자신의 언어로 풀어서 설명(PARAPHRASE)하거나 간략하게 요약(SUMMARY)하는 문장 재구성 능력은 학습자의 영어능력을 평가하는데 있어 상당히 중요한 척도이다. 이러한 이유로 TOEFL, TEPS, TOEIC을 포함하는 대부분의 공인영어인증 시험들은 영어 학습자의 이러한 능력을 직접적으로 또는 간접적으로 평가하는 데 주안점을 두고 있다. TOEFL에서 이러한 능력의 평가를 위해 활용하고 있는 몇 가지의 문제 유형을 간략하게 살펴보도록 하자.

TYPE 1. 직접 평가 유형

1. SENTENCE SIMPLIFICATION

TOEFL의 SENTENCE SIMPLIFICATION 문제는 복잡한 구조의 문장 이해도 및 재구성 능력을 직접적으로 평가하는 대표적인 문제 유형이다. 지문 중 다소 복잡한 구조와 단어로 이루어진 음영 처리된 문장을 제시하고 가장 간략하고 명확하게 이 원문을 재구성한 선택지의 문장을 고르면 된다.

EXAMPLE

<mark>Many ecologists today believe that climax communities that remain relatively stable for a long time result not from diversity but from the patchy structure of the environment and this kind of environment which varies in different localities can sustain a wider variety of organisms compared with an almost identical environment.</mark> As a local population becomes extinct, immigrants from a nearby community are rapidly substituted for it. Although the newly replaced species is totally different from the pre-existing one, it can nearly make up a gap caused by the extinct population and leave the food chain undamaged.

[SENTENCE SIMPLIFICATION] Which of the sentences below best expresses the essential information in the highlighted sentence in the passage? Incorrect choices change the meaning in important ways or leave out essential information.

ⓐ It is believed that the relative stability of climax communities arises from diversity, not from the environmental patchy structure which supports fewer organisms than a uniform environment.

ⓑ The patchiness of the environment is believed to lead to ecological communities that have been comparatively stabilized as a wide range of organisms are capable to be supported by it.

ⓒ Diversity results in climax communities that have been comparatively stabilized and a patchy environment sustains more organisms than an environment that is identical.
ⓓ Most ecologists now think that ecologically stable communities are generated from uniform environments.

해석

오늘날 많은 생태학자들은 오랫동안 상대적으로 안정을 유지하는 극상 군락은 다양성이 아니라 고르지 못한 환경으로부터 발생하며 이 환경은 지역마다 다르고 거의 고른 환경과 비교할 때 더 다양한 종류의 유기체를 지지한다고 믿는다. 기존에 존재하던 개체가 멸종하게 됨에 따라 인접 지역으로부터 온 종들이 빠르게 토착종을 대체한다. 비록 새롭게 대체된 종은 기존에 존재하던 종과 완전히 다름에도 불구하고, 새로운 종은 멸종 종에 의해 야기된 틈을 메우며 먹이 사슬을 안정적으로 남겨둔다.

해설 정답 ⓑ

Many ecologists today believe that ① climax communities that remain relatively stable for a long time result not from diversity but from the patchy structure of the environment and ② this kind of environment which varies in different localities can sustain a wider variety of organisms compared with an almost identical environment.

→ ① The patchiness of the environment is believed to lead to ecological communities that has been comparatively stabilized as ② a wide range of organisms are capable to be supported by it.

원문의 주요 내용인 ①은 '결과는 A가 아니라 B가 원인이다'라는 의미의 '결과(주어) result not from A but from B.'라는 문장 구조를 취하고 있다. 이는 'B(원인)는 ~라는 결과를 이끈다'라는 의미의 'B(원인) lead to 결과'라는 문장 구조로 재구성될 수 있다. 또한 원문의 ②는 등위 접속사 'and' 앞 절에 대한 부연 설명이므로 접속사 'as'를 활용하여 주요 내용의 종속절의 형태로 덧붙여질 수 있다. 이 때에 원문 ②의 문장 구조는 태의 전환을 통해 원문 ②의 주어가 재진술 문장의 'by + 목적어'로 원문 ②의 목적어가 재진술 문장의 '주어'로 자리를 바꾸어 문장을 재구성할 수 있다. 이 때에 동사의 형태는 'be 동사 + p.p.(과거분사)'가 된다.

오답의 근거

ⓐ It is believed that the relative stability of climax communities arises from <u>diversity</u>, not from <u>the environmental patchy structure</u> which supports <u>fewer</u> organisms than a uniform environment.
 → 밑줄 친 부분에 제시된 정보가 잘못된 오답 (diversity ↔ the environmental patchy structure; fewer → more)

ⓒ <u>Diversity</u> results in climax communities that have been comparatively stabilized and a patchy environment sustains more organisms than an environment that is identical.
 → 밑줄 친 부분에 들어갈 극상 군락 발생의 원인이 잘못 제시된 오답 (diversity → the patchy structure of the environment)

ⓓ Most ecologists now think that ecologically stable communities are generated from underline{uniform environments}.
→ 극상 군락의 발생 원인이 잘못 제시되었으며, 원문에 제시된 patchy environment와 identical environment에 대한 비교를 언급하는 중요한 부분의 정보가 누락된 오답 (uniform environments → the patchy structure of the environment)

2. VOCABULARY

TOEFL의 VOCABULARY 문제는 문장 안에 음영 처리된 단어 또는 어구와 의미상 가장 유사한 선택지를 고르는 문제 유형이다. 일반적으로 TOEFL의 어휘 문제는 주어진 전체 또는 일부 지문의 이해에 중요한 역할을 하는 어휘 중심으로 출제되어 학습자가 지문의 문맥을 정확하게 이해하고 있는지의 여부를 평가한다. 한 지문당 3-5개의 문제가 출제되며 이는 전체 문항 수의 대략 1/3 정도의 비중을 차지한다. 따라서 동의어 중심으로 어휘를 학습해 두면 비교적 쉽게 상당 수의 문제를 해결할 수 있다.

EXAMPLE

The primary causes of desertification have come from specific activities such as firewood gathering, overgrazing, overcultivation and overirrigation. As population densities have increased, crop cultivation has extended into increasingly more arid areas. These regions are conspicuously inclined to go through dry spells, so that poor harvest is prevalent. Since the removal of the natural vegetation should take precedence to raise crops, crop failures give rise to a lack of vegetal cover in large areas of land and leave these regions more vulnerable to water and wind erosion.

[VOCABULARY] 1. The word increasingly in the passage is closest in meaning to

ⓐ progressively
ⓑ subjectively
ⓒ intermittently
ⓓ convincingly

[VOCABULARY] 2. The phrase vulnerable to in the passage is closest in meaning to

ⓐ inhospitable to
ⓑ conscious of
ⓒ susceptible to
ⓓ detrimental to

> **해석**

사막화의 주요한 원인은 장작 수집, 과도한 방목, 지나친 경작, 지나친 관개와 같은 특정 활동에서 비롯된다. 인구 밀도가 높아짐에 따라, 작물 재배는 점점 더 건조한 지역으로 확장된다. 이 지역들은 건조 기간을 눈에 띄게 겪는 경향이 있으며 결과적으로 흉작이 만연하게 된다. 자연 식생의 제거는 작물을 재배하기 위해 선행되어야 하므로 흉작은 광대한 토지 지역에 식물 커버의 부족을 야기시키고 이러한 지역들을 침식 및 풍식 작용에 더 취약하게 만든다.

1. 해설 정답 ⓐ

음영 처리된 단어 'increasingly'를 포함하고 있는 원문은 '~함에 따라'라는 의미의 접속사 'as'로 연결되어, 'as'가 이끄는 종속절과 주절이 인과 관계에 있음을 알 수 있다. 문맥상 '인구 밀도가 높아짐에 따라, 작물 재배는 ~ 더 건조한 지역으로 확장된다.'라고 해석하는 것이 적절하므로 'more arid areas' 앞에 놓여 있는 부사 'increasingly'는 '점점 더' 또는 '갈수록 더'라는 의미를 갖고 있음을 유추할 수 있다. 따라서 'increasingly'와 의미상 가장 유사한 'progressively'가 정답이 된다.

2. 해설 정답 ⓒ

음영 처리된 어구 'vulnerable to'를 포함하고 있는 원문은 '~이므로'라는 의미의 접속사 'since'로 연결되어, 'since'가 이끄는 종속절과 주절이 인과 관계에 있음을 알 수 있다. 문맥상 '자연 식생의 제거는 작물을 재배하기 위해 선행되어야 하므로, 흉작은 광대한 토지 지역에 식물 커버의 부족을 야기하게 되며 야기시키고 이러한 지역들을 침식 및 풍식 작용에 더 ~하게 만든다.'라고 해석하는 것이 적절하므로 논리 구조상 흉작으로 식물 커버가 부족하게 되면 이 지역들은 침식 작용과 풍식작용에 'vulnerable to', 즉 '취약하게 됨'을 쉽게 유추할 수 있다. 따라서 'vulnerable to'와 의미상 가장 유사한 'susceptible to'가 정답이 된다.

TYPE 2. 간접 평가 유형

TOEFL의 FACT/NEGATIVE FACT 문제는 지문의 주요 내용과 관련된 세부적인 부분의 내용에 대한 이해도를 평가하는 문제 유형이다. 기본적으로는 이해도 평가를 목적으로 하나 더불어서 이해한 내용을 올바르게 재진술한 선택지를 고르게 함으로써 간접적으로 PARAPHRASE 또는 SUMMARY 능력을 평가한다. 좀 더 자세히 설명하자면, FACT 문제는 주어진 지문에 제시된 내용과 일치하는 내용을 담고 있는 선택지를, NEGATIVE FACT 문제는 지문에 제시된 내용과 상반되는 또는 언급되지 않은 내용을 담고 있는 선택지를 고르면 된다. 한 지문당 FACT 문제는 3-5개의 문제가 출제되고, NEGATIVE FACT 문제는 0-1개 정도 출제되어 출제 빈도가 상당히 높다.

> **EXAMPLE (FACT)**
>
> Petroleum, which is made up of crude oil and natural gas, appears to be produced from organic bodies in marine deposition. Microorganisms which sink to the ocean floor and pile up in sea mud may partly decay, exhausting the dissolved oxygen in the marine sediment. Once the oxygen disappears, the decomposition process is halted, and the residual organic matter is maintained.

[FACT] According to paragraph 1, which of the following is true about how petroleum is formed?

ⓐ Petroleum seems to originate in marine sediment where organic material exists.
ⓑ Decaying marine organisms form petroleum in combination with organic matter in marine deposition.
ⓒ Crude oil and natural gas arise from microorganisms that are present in marine mud.
ⓓ Petroleum formation needs huge amounts of oxygen to begin.

해석

원유와 천연가스로 이루어진 석유는 해양 퇴적물에 존재하는 유기 물질에서 생산되는 것 같다. 해저에 가라앉아 바다 진흙에 축적되는 미생물은 부분적으로 부패하고 해양 퇴적물의 용존 산소량을 다 써버리게 된다. 그 산소가 사라지게 되면, 부패 과정은 중단되며 남은 유기 물질은 남아있게 된다.

해설 정답 ⓐ

Petroleum, ~~which is made up of crude oil and natural gas~~ (← minor idea: 생략가능), appears to be produced from organic body in marine deposition.
→ Petroleum seems to originate in marine sediments where organic material exists.
Paraphrase할 때에는 동의어 또는 동의어구를 활용할 수 있다. 예를 들어, 위의 원문의 'appear to'는 동의 어구인 'seem to'로 '~로부터 생산된다'라는 의미의 'be produced from'은 '~에서 비롯하다', '~이 원인이다'라는 의미의 'originate in'으로 'organic bodies'은 'organic material'로 'marine deposition'은 'marine sediment'로 전환할 수 있다. 또한 문장을 재진술 할 때에는 중요하지 않은 내용들은 생략 가능하다.

> **EXAMPLE (NEGATIVE FACT)**
>
> The islands of the central and South Pacific, generally known as Oceania, are composed of three cultural regions including Melanesia, Micronesia, and Polynesia. Located in the southwest Pacific Ocean, Melanesia comprises various island groups such as the Solomon Islands, Vanuatu, and New Caledonia. Micronesia is mainly made up of small islands scattered over the northwest area of Oceania. Polynesia, defined as the islands within the Polynesian triangle, contains Hawaiian Islands and Samoa, Easter Island, and New Zealand. The entire population of the islands diffused throughout the two largest cultural areas, Polynesia and Micronesia, was calculated at 700,000 before the arrival of European settlers.

[NEGATIVE FACT] According to paragraph 2, all of the following are true statements about each subregion of Oceania Except

ⓐ The islands of Micronesia are small and diffused throughout the area northwest of Oceania.
ⓑ Melanesia is located in northern Micronesia.

ⓒ Hawaiian Islands and Samoa, and Easter Island belong to the cultural boundaries of Polynesia.
ⓓ These three regions are commonly called Oceania.

> 해석

일반적으로 오세아니아로 알려진 중앙태평양과 남태평양의 섬들은 멜라네시아, 미크로네시아, 그리고 폴리네시아와 같은 세 개의 문화 지역으로 이루어져 있다. 남서 태평양 지역에 위치한 멜라네시아는 솔로몬 제도, 바누아투 그리고 뉴칼레도니아와 같은 다양한 군도들로 이루어져 있다. 미크로네시아는 주로 오세아니아의 남서부 지역에 흩어져 있는 작은 섬들로 이루어져 있다. 폴리네시아 삼각지대 내에 섬들로써 정의되는 폴리네시아는 하와이 제도, 사모아 제도, 이스터 섬 그리고 뉴질랜드를 포함한다. 두 개의 거대 문화 지역들인 폴리네시아와 미크로네시아를 걸쳐 퍼져 있는 섬들의 전체 인구는 유럽의 정착자들의 도착 이전에 70만 명으로 추산되었다.

> 해설 정답 ⓑ

ⓑ Melanesia is located in northern Micronesia.
본문에서는 'Located in the southwest Pacific Ocean, Melanesia comprises various island groups ~.'라고 언급하고 있으므로 보기 ⓑ의 밑줄 친 부분은 본문으로부터 유추할 수 없는 정보이다. 따라서 문제에서 묻고 있는 '오세아니아의 하부 지역에 대한 진술이 아닌 것'이므로 정답이다.

> 오답의 근거

ⓐ The islands of Micronesia are small and diffused throughout the area northwest of Oceania.
→ 본문에서 'Micronesia is mainly made up of small islands scattered over the northwest area of Oceania.'라고 언급되었으며 이는 보기의 내용과 일치하므로 오답이다.

ⓒ Hawaiian Islands and Samoa, and Easter Island belong to the cultural boundaries of Polynesia.
→ 본문에서 'Polynesia, defined as the islands within the Polynesian triangle, contains Hawaiian Islands and Samoa, Easter Island, and New Zealand.'라고 언급되었으며 이는 보기의 내용과 일치하므로 오답이다.

ⓓ These three regions are commonly called Oceania.
→ 본문에서 'The islands of the central and South Pacific, generally known as Oceania, is composed of three cultural regions including Melanesia, Micronesia, and Polynesia.'라고 언급되었으며 이는 보기의 내용과 일치하므로 오답이다.

PARAPHRASE & SUMMARY 하기

다른 말로 바꾸어 설명하기PARAPHRASE와 요약하기SUMMARY는 일반적으로 따로 또 같이 이루어지는 언어 사용 과정이다. 즉, 지문이나 대화 또는 강의가 주어졌을 때 그 원문이 담고 있는 내용을 있는 그대로가 아니라 핵심이 되는 내용만을 명확하게 파악하여 간략하게 기술하는 것SUMMARY으로 선별된 중심 내용은 보다 효과적이고 간결하게 다른 말로 바꾸어 표현PARAPHRASE되어야 한다. 다음에 제시된 몇 가지 방법들을 활용해 보도록 하자.

STRATEGY 1. | 동의어 사용하기

원문에서 사용한 표현과 유사한 뜻을 가진 동의어 또는 동의 어구를 활용할 수 있다. 또한, 명사의 반복을 피하기 위해 명사를 재언급할 때는 대명사로 대체할 수 있다.

원문	바꾸어 쓰기
One of the most broadly accepted theories, which has been supported by anthropologists in the late nineteenth and early twentieth centuries, suggests that theater arises from myth and ritual.	The most established theory, (which have been) endorsed by anthropologists in the late 1800s and early 1900s, indicates that theater originates from myth and fixed ceremonies.

→ 'One of the most broadly accepted theories → The most established theory,' 'supported → endorsed,' 'in the late nineteenth and early twentieth centuries → in the late 1800s and early 1900s,' 'suggests → indicates,' 'arises from → originates from'과 같이 원문의 표현을 같은 뜻을 지닌 다른 표현으로 바꾸어 쓸 수 있다.

STRATEGY 2. | 태 전환하기: 능동태 ↔ 수동태

원문의 문장이 능동태인 경우 주어와 목적어의 자리를 바꾸어 수동태로, 수동태의 문장도 마찬가지 방식으로 능동태로 바꿀 수 있다.

원문	바꾸어 쓰기
The dust cloud that rises from an asteroid impact blocked out the sunlight, causing the extinction of plants and animals on Earth.	The sunlight was blocked out by the dust cloud rising from an asteroid impact, leading to the extinction of plants and animals on Earth.

→ 원문의 주어 'The dust cloud that rises from an asteroid impact'는 재진술 문장에서 'by+목적어(the dust cloud rising from an asteroid impact)'의 형태로 동사 뒤에 놓이며, 원문의 목적어 'the sunlight'는 재진술 문장의 주어의 자리로 옮겨짐으로써 태의 전환이 가능하다. 또한 태 전환시에는 동사의 형태가 'be 동사 + p.p(과거분사)'의 형태로 바뀐다.

STRATEGY 3. | 주어 바꾸기

원문 문장의 의미상 중심 내용을 주어로 사용하여 문장의 구조를 바꿀 수 있다.

원문	바꾸어 쓰기
In Great Britain, one of the most drastic shifts of the Industrial Revolution was the use of power.	The use of power was the most dramatic change of the Industrial Revolution in Great Britain.

→ 원문에서 내용상 중심이 되는 'the use of power'를 주어의 자리에 놓음으로써 문장 구조를 바꿀 수 있고 문장의 의미도 더욱 명확하게 할 수 있다.

STRATEGY 4. | 관용구문 사용하기

관용구문의 적절한 사용은 문장의 다양성을 높일 수 있다. 단, 빈번한 사용은 피하는 것이 좋다.

1) '~이 있다'라는 의미의 there is와 there are 표현 사용하기

원문	바꾸어 쓰기
A variety of moral issues associated with human rights should still be taken into account before the national law.	There are still many moral issues related to human rights which should be considered first before the national law.

2) 가주어 it 활용하기

원문	바꾸어 쓰기
Not until the middle of the 1900s did forecasters begin to develop a comprehensive understanding of global climate dynamics with some extent of precision.	It is not until the middle of the twentieth century that weather forecasters started to better understand global climate dynamics with some degree of accuracy.

원문	바꾸어 쓰기
To explain why only a few show signs of having been speared would be hard if improving their hunting luck was the chief motivation for the paintings.	If the drawings were created in hopes of a successful hunt, it would be difficult to explain why only a few chips are found.

STRATEGY 5. | 다른 품사로 바꾸어 쓰기

명사는 동사로, 형용사는 부사로 바꾸어 쓸 수 있다.

원문	바꾸어 쓰기
According to cognitive psychologists' assertion, our values, decisions, and the ways of analyzing our situations have a great impact on our behavior.	Cognitive psychologists assert that our values, decisions, and the ways of analyzing our situations greatly influence our behavior.

→ 명사 assertion은 동사 assert로 형용사 great은 부사 greatly로 그리고 명사 impact는 동사 influence로 대체될 수 있다.

STRATEGY 6. | 문장 구조 바꾸기

절을 구로 구를 절로, 단문을 복문으로 복문을 단문으로 전환하거나, 문장을 나누거나 결합함으로써 문장 구조의 다양성을 높일 수 있다.

1) 절(Clause)과 구(Phrase)의 전환

원문	바꾸어 쓰기
Although most of their scales have been lost, tunas and mackerels retain a patch of coarse scales near the head called the corselet.	Tunas and mackerels maintain a part of rough scales around the head called the corselet despite the loss of most scales.

→ 같은 의미를 갖고 있음에도 불구하고 although는 절을 이끄는 접속사인 반면 despite는 구를 이끄는 전치사이므로 문장의 재구성을 위해 효율적으로 활용될 수 있다.

2) 단문과 복문의 전환

원문	바꾸어 쓰기
Since ① the new markets brought in big fortunes for the few, ② the factory system separated labor into smaller, less skilled tasks, ③ which reduces the salaries of workers.	① The new markets which brought in big fortunes for the few ② made labor under the factory system smaller and less skilled tasks, ③ causing cut down of wages.

→ 원문의 세 개의 절은 하나의 절로 이루어진 문장으로 바꾸어 표현될 수 있다. 원문의 ①은 전환된 문장의 주부가 되었고 ②는 술부로 관계대명사절 ③은 결과를 나타내는 현재 분사 구문으로 전환될 수 있다.

3) 문장을 분할 또는 결합

원문	바꾸어 쓰기
The valleys in tropical regions seem to be a lot more hospitable to trees because not only are they less prone to dry out, but they have less frost and deeper soil layers.	In the tropics, the valleys appear to be much more suitable for trees. This is because they have less frost and deeper soil layers as well as are less likely to become parched.

→ 원문의 접속사 'because'가 이끄는 종속절은 문장을 분할하여 'This is because'의 다음 문장의 형태로 덧붙여질 수 있다. 이 때에 지시대명사 'This'는 앞 문장 전체의 내용을 받으며 문장 안에서 주절의 주어의 역할을 하며 문법적으로 완성된 문장을 만들기 위해 be 동사 'is'가 사용된다.

    지금까지 언급된 다른 말로 바꾸어 설명하기PARAPHRASE와 요약하기SUMMARY와 관련된 6가지의 전략들을 따로 또 같이 문장 안에서 활용한다면 같은 의미를 매우 다양한 방식으로 표현할 수 있을 뿐만 아니라 다양한 방식으로 표현되어 있는 문장을 이해하는 데에도 많은 도움을 얻을 수 있을 것이다. 단, 이러한 전략들이 적용되려면 기본적으로 풍부한 어휘 실력이 밑바탕 되어야 한다는 것을 기억하도록 하자.

001 vulnerable

Day 01
Ornithology

| SYNONYMS | adj. | susceptible, easily damaged, sensitive, weak | (영향을) 받기 쉬운, 취약한 |

vulnerable
[vʌ́lnərəbəl]

Songbird species that are **vulnerable** to predators have developed adaptation strategies which help them to protect themselves from the threats posed by begging calls.
포식자들에게 취약한 맹금 종들은 어미에게 먹이를 달라고 조르는 소리가 야기하는 잠재적인 위험을 피하기 위한 자신들만의 방법들을 발달시켜왔다.

PARAPHRASE 1

Songbird species are particularly **susceptible** to predators, so they have developed their own way of avoiding the potential dangers created by begging calls.

PARAPHRASE 2

Since songbird species are **easily damaged** by predators, they have evolved ways not to be affected by the possible dangers begging calls cause.

002 meticulously

Day 01 — Geology

| SYNONYMS | adv. | carefully, scrupulously, precisely, thoroughly, conscientiously | 주의 깊게, 꼼꼼하게 |

meticulously
[mətíkjələsli]

The first large scale geological map of Britain covering the entire country that William Smith ultimately created in 1815 was so **meticulously** prepared that many people still use it today.

1815년에 윌리엄 스미스는 마침내 최초의 영국 전역의 지질 지도를 만들었고 이는 매우 세심하게 만들어져서 오늘날에도 여전히 사용된다.

PARAPHRASE 1

William Smith finally devised the first nationwide geological map of Britain in the early 19th century. Since the map was so **carefully** researched, it is still in requisition today.

PARAPHRASE 2

In 1815, William Smith eventually produced the first nationwide geological map of Britain, which was so **scrupulously** created that it is still in use today.

003 prone to

Ecology

| SYNONYMS phr. | apt to, liable to, likely to, inclined to, disposed to, tending to, subject to, predisposed to | ~의 경향이 있는, ~할 것 같은 |

prone to

The individuals with characteristics that claim the high ground in the fight for existence are more prone to survive to the last and pass down their genes to the future generation.

생존경쟁에서 우위를 점하는 특징을 가진 개체들은 끝까지 살아남아 다음 세대에게 그들의 유전자를 물려주는 경향이 있다.

PARAPHRASE 1

Some individuals possess genes with higher probability for survival and reproduction. That is to say, they are more apt to survive and have offspring with the same advantages.

PARAPHRASE 2

The individuals who have traits that give them an advantage over their competition are more liable to survive and transmit the same traits to the next generation.

PARAPHRASE 3

The individuals with features that are crucial for survival are more likely to survive and produce offspring which possess the same genes.

004 complicated

Day 01
Psychology

SYNONYMS *adj.* complex, elaborate, intricate, involved, sophisticated, compound, detailed

복잡한, 정교한

complicated
[kάmplikèitid]

The process of encrypting information is more **complicated** for young adults and infants than it is for adults.

청소년들과 유아들은 성인들 보다 정보를 암호화하는 더 복잡한 과정을 갖고 있다.

PARAPHRASE 1

In comparison with young adults and infants, the process of putting information into a code is less **complex** for adults.

PARAPHRASE 2

Adults have a less **elaborate** process of encoding information compared to young adults and infants.

PARAPHRASE 3

Young adults and infants have a more **intricate** process of encoding information than adults.

005 rudimentary

Day 01

Agriculture

SYNONYMS adj. elementary, fundamental, indispensable, essential, crucial, vital, primary, underlying, basic, necessary, critical, integral

기초적인, 필수적인

rudimentary
[rùːdəméntəri]

Since water culture makes it easier to cultivate greenhouse vegetables in the harsh winter season, it is utilized in many different fields beyond rudimentary research.

수경재배는 겨울 동안 온실 채소의 성장을 용이하게 한다는 점에서 기초 연구를 넘어 다양한 영역에 적용된다.

PARAPHRASE 1

In a wide range of areas, aquaculture has applications beyond elementary study in the respect that it facilitates the growth of vegetables in greenhouses during winter.

PARAPHRASE 2

Hydroponics is applied in various fields beyond fundamental study in that it enables vegetables to grow during the cold season.

006 dwindle

Day 01
Forestry

SYNONYMS v. diminish, curtail, decrease, reduce, shrink, lessen, decline, lower, minimize, abate, scant, drop

줄다, 줄이다, 감소시키다

dwindle
[dwíndl]

As soon as a redwood forest develops, the types of species and the number of individuals growing on the floor of the forest dwindle.

삼나무 숲이 발달하게 되면, 숲의 바닥에서 자라는 종의 종류와 개체의 수는 감소하게 된다.

PARAPHRASE 1

A mature redwood forest diminishes the number of individuals as well as the kinds of species which grow on the floor of the forest.

PARAPHRASE 2

Once a redwood forest reaches maturity, both number and diversity of species inhabiting the forest floor are curtailed.

007 distinguish

Day 01
Sociology

SYNONYMS v. differentiate, separate, discern, discriminate, perceive, notice

구별하다, 식별하다

distinguish
[distíŋgwiʃ]

Unlike artisans' workplaces where the relationship between apprentices and their masters who manage and oversee them was intimate, factories clearly **distinguish**ed workers from management.

견습공과 그들을 관리 감독하는 장인들 사이의 관계가 긴밀했던 장인의 작업장과는 달리, 공장은 뚜렷하게 노동자를 경영진으로부터 분리하였다.

PARAPHRASE 1

In contrast with artisan's workrooms in which apprentices cooperated closely with the masters managing and overseeing them, factories sharply **differentiate**d workers from management.

PARAPHRASE 2

Workers and management were squarely **separate**d in factories, while the relationship between apprentices and the masters who supervise them were close in artisans' workshops.

008 widespread

Zoology

SYNONYMS adj. prevalent, dominant, prevailing, common, pervasive, popular, omnipresent, ubiquitous, universal, existing everywhere

일반적인, 지배적인, 널리 퍼진

widespread
[wáidspréd]

Now the most **widespread** species in the Puget Sound area in Washington State, the Sitka black-tailed deer particularly live in coniferous forests along the Pacific Coast that have a temperate climate.

시트카 검은 꼬리 사슴은 오늘날 퓨젯 사운드 워싱턴 지역에 가장 널리 퍼져 있으며, 특히 태평양 해안을 따라 기후가 온화한 침엽수림 지역에 서식한다.

PARAPHRASE 1

The Sitka black-tailed deer, largely inhabiting in temperate coniferous forests along the Pacific Coast, is now the most **prevalent** species in the Puget Sound area of Washington.

PARAPHRASE 2

The Sitka black-tailed deer is the most **dominant** species today in the Puget Sound region of Washington, particularly in temperate coniferous forests along the Pacific Coast.

009 pronounced

SYNONYMS *adj.* noticeable, obvious, striking, conspicuous, notable, evident, marked, clear, definite, distinct, apparent, plain, explicit, transparent, lucid, limpid, unambiguous, manifest

명백한, 뚜렷한

pronounced
[prənáunst]

Religious sculptures were created in most historical periods, but less **pronounced** explanation on their conventions is provided compared with that of porcelain or earthenware.

종교적인 조각은 역사의 대부분의 시기에 만들어졌지만 그 전통에 관한 묘사는 사기 그릇이나 자기의 전통에 대한 묘사보다 덜 명백하다.

PARAPHRASE 1

Although religious sculptures were produced in most periods of history, the delineation of their traditions is not as **noticeable** as that of porcelain or stoneware.

PARAPHRASE 2

While religious sculptures appeared throughout most historical periods, the descriptions of their traditions are less **obvious** than those of porcelain or earthenware.

010 penetrate

Ecology

SYNONYMS v. permeate, percolate, infiltrate, pierce, puncture, enter, go through, perforate, seep

관통하다, 스며들다

penetrate
[pénətrèit]

A plentiful source of water located beneath the earth's surface **penetrates** soil and rock layers and can be found at nearly every point in the earth's ecosystems, encompassing deserts, mountains, and grasslands.

지구 표면 아래에 존재하는 풍부한 수분 공급원은 토양과 암석층에 스며들어가며 산, 사막, 그리고 초원과 같은 지구 생태계의 거의 모든 지점에서 발견된다.

PARAPHRASE 1

Occurring below the surface of the earth, an abundant source of water **permeates** layers of soil and rock and can be found just about everywhere, in all ecosystems, such as mountains, deserts, and plains (←minor idea).

PARAPHRASE 2

Beneath the earth's surface occurs a rich source of water, which **percolates** through soil and rock formations and can be seen almost anywhere on earth.

DAILY CHECK-UP

A. Find the answer that is closest in meaning to the highlighted word or phrase in the sentence.

01. Dixie Alley running from Louisiana to Georgia into Tennessee, is **apt to** be affected by violent thunderstorms.
    (A) object to
    (B) inclined to

02. Hazardous chemicals can **permeate** through the soil.
    (A) go through
    (B) obstruct

03. Generally, a more **intricate** system is more liable to break down than a simple system.
    (A) prone
    (B) complicated

04. Today's creatures are more **sensitive** to climate changes than they were in the Cretaceous period.
    (A) vulnerable
    (B) prevailing

05. Humans' ability to gain an advantage over other species seems to be one of the most **noticeable** elements in human survival.
    (A) conspicuous
    (B) tamed

06. The eyes of tunas are covered with a smooth and transparent lid that **curtail**s water resistance.
    (A) augment
    (B) reduce

07. What varies is not the **fundamental** form but the additional details that do not impede the object's **vital** function.
    (A) essential
    (B) erratic

08. Infants are able to perceive and **differentiate** between stimuli.
    (A) discriminate
    (B) diminish

09. The new type of medicine has a **pronounced** effect on younger patients.
    (A) spontaneous
    (B) striking

10. Fragile goods should be **carefully** packed using plenty of wrapping.
    (A) considerably   (B) meticulously

B. Complete each sentence using one of the words or phrases given.

11. Strong animals are more _____ survive a struggle for life.
    (A) weak to   (B) liable to

12. If it were not for _____ evidence, no one should be punished.
    (A) apparent   (B) equivocal

13. Life put us in an _____ network of human relationships.
    (A) elaborate   (B) ordinary

14. The explosion resulted in _____ fires that have burned away most of the grassland areas.
    (A) repulsive   (B) widespread

15. In a specific region, a decrease in trees and plants significantly _____ absorption of water.
    (A) bears   (B) lessens

16. It is _____ to consider whether suitable materials are available when constructing a building.
    (A) indispensable   (B) superfluous

---

01. (B) 02. (A) 03. (B) 04. (A) 05. (A) 06. (B) 07. (A) 08. (A) 09. (B) 10. (B)
11. (B) 12. (A) 13. (A) 14. (B) 15. (B) 16. (A)

011 buffer

Biochemistry

Day 02

| SYNONYMS | v. | protect, conserve, preserve, save, guard, shield, keep, safeguard, shelter | 보호하다, 보존하다 |

buffer
[bʌ́fə(r)]

The oxygen depletion leads to the cessation of decomposition and allows the remaining matter to be **buffer**ed.

산소가 고갈되면, 부패의 과정은 중단되고 남아있는 유기 물질들은 보존된다.

PARAPHRASE 1

The process of decomposition stops and the remaining organic elements are **protect**ed as soon as the oxygen is exhausted.

PARAPHRASE 2

Once the oxygen is depleted, the process of decay is halted and the remaining organic substances are **conserve**d.

012   marvelous

Biology — Day 02

| SYNONYMS | adj. | miraculous, wonderful, superb, astonishing, incredible, remarkable, significant, noteworthy, awesome, phenomenal, tremendous, extraordinary, spectacular, sublime, magnificent, grand | 경이로운, 놀랄만한 |

marvelous
[mάːrvələs]

The evolution of plants that produce seeds on Earth, millions of years after ferns developed, began and this was considered the most **marvelous** invention in the field of biology.

양치식물의 진화가 이루어진 후 수 백만 년이 지나 또 다른 종류의 씨앗을 맺는 식물군이 지구상에서 발달하기 시작했고, 이는 생물학에 있어 놀라운 발명이었다.

PARAPHRASE 1

Millions of years after the evolution of ferns, another type of flora that bears seeds started to develop on Earth, which was a **miraculous** invention in biology.

PARAPHRASE 2

Seed-bearing plants began to evolve on Earth, millions of years after ferns developed, which was a **wonderful** biological invention.

013 decimate

Day 02
Ecology

| SYNONYMS | v. | destroy, **obliterate**, destruct, annihilate, extinguish, eradicate, devastate, wipe out | (동식물·사람을) 대량으로 죽이다, 말살시키다 |

decimate
[désəmèit]

Extensive areas of deciduous forests found in Europe have been **decimated** in order to use them for other purposes, including for houses and farmsteads.

유럽의 국가들은 주거나 농지와 같은 인간 욕구를 위한 이용을 위해 방대한 낙엽수림 지역을 파괴해왔다.

PARAPHRASE 1

European countries have **destroyed** vast areas of deciduous forests to use them for human needs such as housing and farming.

PARAPHRASE 2

In European countries, most deciduous forests have been **obliterated** for the purpose of making room for houses and farmsteads.

014 fatal

Health Science — Day 02

SYNONYMS adj. lethal, deadly, mortal, hazardous, harmful, detrimental, toxic, noxious, poisonous, disastrous, destructive, malignant, dangerous, toxicant, adverse

치명적인, 유해한, 해로운

fatal
[féitl]

It is commonly known that typhoid fever, which is one of the worst epidemics has pestered humankind. However, what makes it so fatal has been wrapped in a shroud of mystery through the centuries.

전염성이 강한 질병 중 하나인 장티푸스가 인류를 괴롭혀 왔음은 널리 알려져 있지만, 무엇이 그것을 그렇게 치명적으로 만들었는지는 수세기 동안 미스터리로 남아 있다.

PARAPHRASE 1

Even though one of the most contagious diseases, typhoid, is widely known to have plagued humanity, what makes it so lethal has remained unsolved for centuries.

PARAPHRASE 2

Typhoid, one of the most infectious diseases, is generally considered to have afflicted humanity, but what makes it so deadly has still been shrouded in mystery for centuries.

015 counterbalance

Day 02
Archaeology

SYNONYMS v. offset, counteract, balance, compensate, countervail, cancel out

상쇄하다, 상쇄시키다

counterbalance
[káuntərbæləns]

Merchants transported rigidly selected goods such as noble metals, silks and various artworks (←minor idea) **to counterbalance** any financial losses incurred as a result of the dangers intrinsic in traveling along the Silk Road.

상인들은 실크로드를 따라 이동함으로써 발생하는 위험으로 인한 재정 손실을 상쇄하기 위해 귀금속, 실크 그리고 다양한 예술품들과 같은 엄선된 상품들을 운반했다.

PARAPHRASE 1

Precious items that traders carefully chose were carried, which enabled them to **offset** the financial losses due to hazards intrinsic in moving along the Silk Road.

PARAPHRASE 2

Any financial losses incurred because of the risks associated with the journey along the Silk Road were **counteract**ed by valuable merchandise merchants carried.

016 exclusively

Day 02
Geology

SYNONYMS adv. solely, entirely, totally, only   오로지

exclusively
[iksklú:sivli]

The fossilized remains discovered in the Ediacara Hills in Australia include the oldest known animal fossils that are made up **exclusively** of soft-bodied creatures from the Precambrian.

호주 에디아카라 구릉 지대에서 발견된 화석화된 유적은 선캄브리아대의 연조직 생물들로만 구성된 가장 오래된 것으로 알려진 동물 화석을 포함한다.

PARAPHRASE 1

Found in the Ediacara Hills in Australia, the fossilized remains contain the oldest known animal fossils that are composed **solely** of soft-bodied organisms from the Precambrian.

PARAPHRASE 2

The fossilized remains from the Ediacara Hills in Australia encompass the oldest animal fossils consisting **entirely** of soft-bodied creatures.

43

017 extract

| SYNONYMS | v. | withdraw, remove, eliminate, discard, eradicate, abolish, deprive, divest, strip, take out, pull out, get rid of, throw away | 끌어내다, 제거하다 |

extract
[ikstrækt]

Even when the best techniques are used, only approximately 30 to 40 percent of the world's oil supply can be extracted, while the rest is too demanding to be brought to the surface, consequently staying under the ground.

최첨단 기술이 사용될 때에도, 전세계 석유 매장량의 대략 30-40%만이 추출될 수 있다. 하지만 나머지는 추출되기 훨씬 어려워서 땅속에 머물러 있게 된다.

PARAPHRASE 1

Although the use of state-of-the-art techniques allows about 30 to 40 percent of the entire oil deposits to be withdrawn, the extraction of the rest is still too difficult and thus it stays deep inside the Earth.

PARAPHRASE 2

Even using the most advanced techniques, only about 30 to 40 percent of the world's oil reserves can be removed, but the rest is a lot tougher to obtain and remains underground.

018 copious

Day 02
Hydrology

SYNONYMS *adj.* abundant, plentiful, ample, bountiful, profuse, lavish, affluent, prolific, opulent, luxuriant, sufficient,

풍부한

copious
[kóupiəs]

Groundwater refers to water that has permeated through the ground and become trapped in the fractures of rocks, and far and away the most copious type of groundwater is meteoric water which circulates as part of the water cycle.

지하수는 땅속으로 스며들어 암석의 균열부에 머물러 있게 되며, 단연코 가장 풍부한 지하수의 종류는 물의 순환의 일부로써 순환하는 천수이다.

PARAPHRASE 1

The water that has saturated the ground and filled open cracks in rocks is classified as groundwater, and meteoric water is by far the most abundant type of groundwater that circulates as part of the circulation of the earth's water.

PARAPHRASE 2

Groundwater is water that has passed down through the ground, staying in fractured rocks, and meteoric water is definitely the most plentiful type of groundwater rotating as part of the hydrologic cycle.

45

019 unlikely

Day 02
Anthropology

SYNONYMS *adj.* implausible, improbable, unbelievable, questionable, incredible, impossible

그럴 듯 하지 않은, 믿기지 않는

unlikely
[ʌnláikli]

According to the research on winds and currents by computer simulations, it was highly **unlikely** that drifting canoes would have been the primary way to make a conquest of the Pacific Ocean.

컴퓨터 시뮬레이션을 사용한 바람과 해류에 관한 연구에 따르면, 카누를 타는 것은 태평양을 정복하기위한 가장 가능성 없는 수단이었을 것이다.

PARAPHRASE 1

The study of winds and currents, with the help of computers, showed that drifting canoes was an extremely **implausible** means by which the Pacific was colonized.

PARAPHRASE 2

The computer simulation study on winds and currents indicated that drifting canoes would have been a most **improbable** way of conquering the Pacific.

020 predecessor

Paleontology

SYNONYMS n. forerunner, ancestor, forefather, forebear, antecedent

선조, 조상

predecessor
[prédisèsər]

Despite the fact that the fossil officially named Pakicetus unearthed in northern Pakistan includes only a skull of an archaeoceti, an extinct genus of predecessors of modern cetaceans encompassing whales, porpoises and dolphins (←minor idea), it provides experts with valuable insights into the origins of cetaceans.

파키스탄 북부에서 발굴된 파키세투스 화석은 고래, 돌고래, 알락 돌고래를 포함하는 현대 고래류의 선조들 중 멸종 속인 구고래아목의 두개골만을 포함함에도 불구하고, 전문가들에게 고래의 기원에 대한 가치 있는 통찰력을 준다.

PARAPHRASE 1

Although restricted to an Archaeoceti's skull, belonging to an extinct sub-order of forerunners of modern cetaceans, the fossil remains of Pakicetus uncovered in northern Pakistan give precious clues about the origins of cetaceans.

PARAPHRASE 2

Excavated in northern Pakistan, the Pakicetus fossil is limited to a skull of a prehistoric family of ancestors of extant cetaceans, known as Archaeoceti but it furnishes crucial information concerning cetacean origins.

DAILY CHECK-UP

A. Find the answer that is closest in meaning to the highlighted word or phrase in the sentence.

01. Whether a city has **bountiful** tourism resources is directly related to its competitiveness.
    (A) abundant   (B) deficient

02. Historic buildings should be **preserved** because they have great economic value.
    (A) exhumed   (B) conserved

03. It seemed pretty **questionable** that the hard ground under foot can have enough room for all this water.
    (A) unbelievable   (B) reliable

04. As ancient **forefathers** or guardians of a certain tribe, particular animals had taken on mythical significance.
    (A) antecedents   (B) descendants

05. If the election campaign of a political party is **only** targeted at a specific group of people, the party can never win an election.
    (A) copiously   (B) exclusively

06. Analysts argue that human developments are much more **detrimental** to farmland birds than wind turbines.
    (A) dangerous   (B) implausible

07. Anyone or anything regarded as a threat to the authority of Rome would be totally **destroyed**.
    (A) wiped out   (B) taken over

08. During the main sequence, the longest phase of stellar evolution occurs when gravity is **offset** by energy outflow.
    (A) withdrawn   (B) balanced

09. Pasteurization **removes** or reduces essential nutrients from milk.

   (A) buffers (B) eliminates

10. The Grand Canyon is well known for its **superb** natural scenery.

   (A) malignant (B) spectacular

B. Complete each sentence using one of the words or phrases given.

11. Ecotourism allows developing countries to _____ the environment as well as maximize economic growth.

   (A) countervail (B) preserve

12. Researchers realize the seriousness of the problem and find ways to _____ or decrease the problem.

   (A) extinguish (B) counteract

13. Raw milk causes _____ diseases to people.

   (A) lavish (B) lethal

14. By operating effective pumps, water in the mines was _____ with the help of Watt's steam engine.

   (A) decimated (B) eliminated

15. The short-lived plants, dandelions, are propagated from seed _____.

   (A) plentifully (B) deadly

16. Pest control has superseded other means that depend _____ on commercial fertilizers.

   (A) exclusively (B) hazardously

---

01. (A) 02. (B) 03. (A) 04. (A) 05. (B) 06. (A) 07. (A) 08. (B) 09. (B) 10. (B)
11. (B) 12. (A) 13. (B) 14. (B) 15. (A) 16. (A)

021 considerable

Day 03
Pedagogy

SYNONYMS **adj.** significant, substantial, marked, appreciable, noticeable, sizable, goodly, discernible, detectable, observable, perceivable

상당한, 인식할 수 있는

considerable
[kənsídərəbəl]

Wildman and Niles concluded that to ensure a comprehensive understanding of the classroom situations, teachers needed to receive instructional training for a **considerable** amount of time.

와일드맨과 나일스는 수업 상황에 대한 포괄적인 이해를 보장받기 위해 교사들 상한 시간 동안 교육 훈련을 받을 필요가 있다는 결론을 내렸다.

PARAPHRASE 1

The results from research conducted by Wildman and Niles suggested that instructors should undergo training for a **significant** amount of time in order to fully appreciate the classroom events.

PARAPHRASE 2

Wildman and Niles came to a conclusion that instructional training for a **substantial** time was required for teachers to grasp classroom situations wholly.

022　heyday

Day 03 Art History

| SYNONYMS | n. | the highest point, golden age, prime, zenith, peak, height, apex, crest, acme, crown, summit, pinnacle, top | 정상, 전성기 |

heyday
[héidei]

In the Tang Dynasty, white porcelain created in the provinces of Hebei and Henan developed into the exclusive ceramics of the Song dynasty, long considered one of the heydays in the history of China's ceramic industry.

7-10세기에 이르는 시기에 허베이와 허난 지방에서 만들어진 백자는 송대의 고급 도자기로 발달하였고, 이는 오랜 동안 중국 도자기 산업 역사의 전성기로 간주되었다.

PARAPHRASE 1

Whitewares made in Hebei and Henan provinces during the Tang Dynasty and matured during the Song Dynasty are believed to mark the highest point in the history of China's pottery for a long time.

PARAPHRASE 2

Produced in Hebei and Henan provinces, Chinese Tang Dynasty white porcelains evolved into the expensive Song ceramics, long deemed a golden age in the history of Chinese pottery.

023 epitomize

Day 03 | Anthropology

SYNONYMS v. summarize, outline, condense, encapsulate, abridge, nutshell, sum up

요약하다, 집약하다

epitomize
[ipítəmàiz]

Anthropologists suggested the most common theory that theater originated from stories and rites and **epitomize**d the formation process of theater.

인류학자들은 극은 신화와 의식으로부터 생겨났다는 가장 일반적인 이론을 제안했고 극이 어떻게 형성되었는지 요약했다.

PARAPHRASE 1

Upholding the most widely accepted theory that theater emerged from myths and rituals, anthropologists **summarize**d how theater was formed.

PARAPHRASE 2

Anthropologists supported the most popular theory that stories and rites affected theater and **outline**d how theater developed.

024 consistent

Cultural Anthropology

SYNONYMS **adj.** uniform, constant, coherent, invariable, even, unchanging, unchangeable, unvarying, sustained, steady, steadfast, stable, prolonged, continued

한결같은, 일관된 지속적인

consistent
[kənsístənt]

In a factory, a more regimented schedule was necessitated to make workers begin work at the ring of a bell and get machines going at a **consistent** speed.

공장 생활에 요구되는 더 엄격한 스케쥴 하에서 노동자들은 벨소리와 함께 일을 시작했고, 기계들은 일관된 속도로 작동 되었다.

PARAPHRASE 1

Factory life called for a more strict schedule, in which work was initiated at the ring of a bell and machines were kept going at a **uniform** rate.

PARAPHRASE 2

In the more rigid schedule required in factory life, workers started work at the sound of a bell and kept machines working at a **constant** pace.

025 staggering

Day 03

Zoology

SYNONYMS adj. shocking, disturbing, affecting, lurid, startling, frightening, stunning, distressing, surprising

믿기 어려운, 충격적인, 놀라운

staggering
[stǽgəriŋ]

David Douglas, Scottish explorer, discovered a **staggering** reduction in the number of deer around Fort Vancouver during the period of eight years between 1825 and 1832.

스코트랜드의 탐험가 데이비드 더글라스는 1825년에서 1832년 사이의 10년동안 포트 밴쿠버 주변 사슴 수의 극적인 감소를 발견했다.

PARAPHRASE 1

A **shocking** decrease in deer numbers throughout the Fort Vancouver area was found by Scottish explorer, David Douglas during the period between 1825 and 1832.

PARAPHRASE 2

Around Fort Vancouver, Scottish explorer, David Douglas noticed a **disturbing** change in deer numbers for eight years from 1825 to 1832.

026 obscure

SYNONYMS adj. ambiguous, vague, equivocal, uncertain, imprecise, blurry, nebulous, unclear, opaque, inexact, inaccurate, loose, indistinct

모호한, 불명확한

Day 03 Hydrology

obscure
[əbskjúər]

As the extent of groundwater resources is **obscure** in many arid lands, research programs are desperately needed to scrutinize the groundwater of these areas and to develop proper extraction technologies.

지하수의 규모가 여러 건조 지역에서 불명확하기 때문에, 이 지역의 지하수를 조사하고 적절한 추출 기술을 개발하기 위해 연구 프로그램이 절실히 요구된다.

PARAPHRASE 1

Programs for the exploration of groundwater and the development of extraction techniques are urgently needed because how much groundwater is stored is **ambiguous** in many dry regions.

PARAPHRASE 2

Since the degree of groundwater in many arid areas is **vague**, research programs are in urgent need of investigating groundwater and developing extraction techniques.

027 recovery

Day 03 — Ecology

SYNONYMS *n.* restoration, recuperation, rebound, revival, resuscitation — 회복

recovery
[rikʌ́vəri]

The causes for the **recovery** of Atlantic cod population numbers are attributed to other human activities such as controlling main predators and restricting types of and times for fishing.

대서양 대구의 개체 수 회복에 대한 원인들은 주요 포식자들의 개체 수를 통제하고 사냥의 형태와 시간을 제한하는 등의 다른 인간 활동 때문으로 여겨진다.

PARAPHRASE 1

The **restoration** of Atlantic cod populations results from other human actions: the regulation of principal predators and the restriction of times for and types of fishing.

PARAPHRASE 2

Other human actions, such as reducing predators and limiting fishing, resulted in the **recuperation** of Atlantic cod populations.

028 bizarre

Meteorology

SYNONYMS *adj.* eccentric, odd, strange, peculiar, eerie, weird, unusual, exotic, unconventional, mysterious, quaint, erratic

기이한, 특이한

bizarre
[bizάːr]

Climate fluctuation is caused by combined reasons, including global atmospheric changes, slower but evenly **bizarre** ocean currents, alterations of the ground surface of lands, and variations in the amount of ice and snow.

기후 변화는 전체적인 대기 변화, 그보다는 느리지만 역시 기이한 해류, 지표의 변화, 얼음과 눈의 양의 변화를 포함하는 모든 통합된 요소들에 의해 야기된다.

PARAPHRASE 1

The integrated reasons of climate fluctuation contain global atmospheric changes, slower but equally **eccentric** ocean currents, alterations of the ground surface of lands, and variations in the amount of ice and snow.

PARAPHRASE 2

The natural factors that include the chaotic atmosphere, **odd** oceanic circulation, unpredictability of land surfaces, and ice and snow give rise to the alteration of global weather patterns.

029 decoration

Day 03
Art History

SYNONYMS n. ornamentation, adornment, embellishment, decoration, garnishment

장식, 장식품

decoration
[dèkəréiʃən]

The most predominant themes in cave paintings are large wild animals, such as bison, horses and deer (←minor idea), depicted on bare walls without backgrounds or environmental decoration.

동굴 벽화의 가장 두드러진 주제는 들소, 말, 사슴과 같은 거대 야생 동물들이었으며, 배경이나 환경적인 장식이 전혀 없이 빈 벽에 그려졌다.

PARAPHRASE 1

Large wild animals are the most conspicuous subjects in cave paintings and are portrayed on bare walls with no backgrounds or environmental ornamentation.

PARAPHRASE 2

The paintings on bare walls in caves focus exclusively on predatory animals without unnecessary adornment related to the surrounding landscape.

030 harness

Motion Picture History

SYNONYMS v. employ, utilize, exploit, capitalize on, make use of, put into use, take advantage of

이용하다

harness
[hάːrnis]

It was not until the 1950s that color became a standard though **harness**ed over the following twenty years for special productions and the advent of the new screen formats was postponed for twenty-five years.

다음 20년에 걸쳐 특수 제작에 사용되었음에도 불구하고, 컬러는 1950년대가 되어서야 표준이 되었으며 새로운 스크린 구성방식의 도입은 25년 동안 지연되었다.

PARAPHRASE 1

Even though **employ**ed for the next twenty years for special productions, color did not become a norm until the 1950s and the introduction of the new formats for screen was delayed for a quarter century.

PARAPHRASE 2

Although they were **utilize**d for two decades for special productions, color has become a standard since the 1950s, the new screen formats were finally introduced after twenty-five years.

DAILY CHECK-UP

A. Find the answer that is closest in meaning to the highlighted word or phrase in the sentence.

01. Cave paintings showing evidence of a **considerable** degree of skill were found in France and Spain.
    (A) appreciable   (B) bustling

02. The most crucial reason for bird population **restoration** has been closely linked with the forests.
    (A) recovery   (B) demise

03. Woolen and textile manufacturers **used** the cheap and abundant labor pool in rural areas.
    (A) mingled   (B) exploited

04. Cave art does not seem to have reached an **apex** until the end of the Upper Paleolithic era, when the number of game decreased.
    (A) peak   (B) metamorphosis

05. **Peculiar** islands with a teardrop shape have been discovered on the plains around the edge of the outflow channels.
    (A) formidable   (B) odd

06. Had it not been for a new source of movable and **constant** power, the new generation of machinery might not have opened.
    (A) inexorable   (B) consistent

07. The **stunning** discovery was that subatomic particles that form an atom were neutrons, protons, and electrons.
    (A) startling   (B) adjoining

08. Weather forecasting prior to the introduction of current methods is **epitomized** by the old saying "Red sky at night, sailors delight. Red sky in morning, sailors warning".
    (A) distinguished   (B) encapsulated

09. If foreign cultures had not affected China, the significance of **embellishment** on pottery may have remained clear.

    (A) luminosity (B) adornment

10. The research results were **vague**, and needed to be clarified.

    (A) perilous (B) ambiguous

B. Complete each sentence using one of the words or phrases given.

11. Hunter gathers who still _____ stone implements were conquered by the Bantu peoples using iron weapons.

    (A) employed (B) shielded

12. The landscape is considered to be _____, but Earth's surface is constantly changing.

    (A) unvarying (B) nebulous

13. _____ wind-farm projects are being planned by some electricity generators in states except California.

    (A) Eccentric (B) Sizable

14. Scholars advance three distinctive but deeply involved opinions about the _____ origin of these paintings.

    (A) substantial (B) quaint

15. While Chinese pottery seems ornate from a modern perspective, to the Chinese the configuration of each object and its _____ had fairly important meaning.

    (A) adornment (B) recuperation

16. The _____ of succession is the species that dominate the area during a specific period and will exist only until intruded upon again.

    (A) demise (B) pinnacle

---

01. (A) 02. (A) 03. (B) 04. (A) 05. (B) 06. (B) 07. (A) 08. (B) 09. (B) 10. (B)
11. (A) 12. (A) 13. (B) 14. (B) 15. (A) 16. (B)

031 erratic

Day 04

Biology

SYNONYMS *adj.* unpredictable, irregular, variable, unstable, inconsistent, uneven

예측할 수 없는, 예측 불가능한

erratic
[irǽtik]

If the population of an opportunist species is observed over a long period of time, it will be considered particularly precarious as it has a tendency to soar and nosedive in erratic cycles.

오랜 시간에 걸쳐 관찰된 기회주의 종의 개체는 예측할 수 없는 주기로 증가하고 감소하는 경향이 있기 때문에 특히 불안정하게 여겨진다.

PARAPHRASE 1　Tracked over a long period of time, the population of an opportunist species is seen to be notably unsettled in the respect that it increases and decreases in unpredictable intervals.

PARAPHRASE 2　The population of an opportunist species observed through time is regarded as especially unstable because it tends to skyrocket and plummet in irregular cycles.

032 magnitude

Astronomy

SYNONYMS n. proportion, amount, immensity, size, volume, amplitude, dimension, scale

규모, 크기

magnitude
[mǽgnətjùːd]

Outflow channels on Mars seem to be the routes which are taken by water of great **magnitude** that flows out steadily from the southern mountainous areas into the northern plains.

화성의 유출 수로는 남부 산악 지대로부터 북부 평원 지역으로 끊임없이 흐르는 엄청난 양의 물이 지나는 통로인 것 같다.

PARAPHRASE 1 Outflow channels on Mars are possibly the courses allowing epic **proportions** of water to drain constantly from the southern mountainous areas into the northern plains.

PARAPHRASE 2 It is outflow channels on Mars that are probably the paths of huge **amounts** of water running from the southern highlands to the northern plains.

033 prevent

Day 04
Environmental Science

SYNONYMS v. deter, block, preclude, inhibit, avert, hinder, forestall, impede, restrict, obviate, obstruct, bar, avoid, stop, prohibit, restrain, forbid, ban, hamper, rule out

막다, 방해하다, 금지하다

prevent
[privént]

On the contrary, loosely fragmented soil is held together by the roots of grasses and other small plants, which helps to **prevent** wind erosion.

반대로, 잔디와 다른 작은 식물들의 뿌리는 헐겁게 분열된 토양을 꽉 잡아 풍식을 막도록 도와준다.

PARAPHRASE 1

In contrast, grasses and other small plants grasp loose soil tightly with their roots, thereby allowing erosion by the wind to be **deter**red.

PARAPHRASE 2

Conversely, by holding loose soil with plant roots, wind erosion is **block**ed.

034 disseminate

Day 04
Hydrology

SYNONYMS v. scatter, disperse, dissipate, distribute, diffuse, pervade, strew, spread out

퍼뜨리다, 흩어지다

disseminate
[dísémənèit]

Icebergs separated from the ice shelf drift in the ocean currents and wind systems around Antarctica and are disseminated among less colorful bergs in this area.

빙붕에서 떨어져 나온 빙하는 남극 주변의 해류와 풍계를 떠다니며 이 지역의 덜 화려한 빙하들 가운데 흩어져 있다.

PARAPHRASE 1

Once separated from the ice shelf, floating masses of ice in the currents and wind systems surrounding the South Pole are scattered among other bergs.

PARAPHRASE 2

Detached from glaciers, small icebergs floating near Antarctica are dispersed over the area.

65

035 absurd

Day 04
Performing Art

SYNONYMS **adj.** ridiculous, preposterous, foolish, outrageous, ludicrous, groundless, unreasonable, irrational, illogical, inconsistent, grotesque

우스꽝스러운, 터무니 없는

absurd
[ǽbsəːrd]

Using ironic comedy, satire portrays people or social institutions as **absurd** or depraved, which enables the audience to be excluded from the object of humor.

풍자는 반어적인 희극을 사용하여 사람이나 사회 제도를 우스꽝스럽거나 타락한 것으로 묘사하며, 이는 청중을 해학의 대상으로부터 제외시킨다.

PARAPHRASE 1　Satire depicts people or social systems as **ridiculous** or corrupt by making use of ironic comedy, consequently excluding the audience from the target of humor.

PARAPHRASE 2　Satire utilizes ironic comedy to describe the public or social systems as **preposterous** or vicious, not making the audience the target of humor.

036 paradox

Motion Picture History

SYNONYMS n. contradiction, inconsistency, enigma, incongruity, unconformity, dissonance, disharmony, variance

모순, 불일치

paradox
[pǽrədɑ̀ks]

Although films that are mute and films that speak are believed to be the most rudimentary division in movie history, the standard of periodization in history covers up many paradoxes.

영화 역사의 가장 기본적인 구분은 무성 영화와 발성 영화 사이에 놓이지만 이 시대 구분의 기준은 다수의 모순을 숨기고 있다.

PARAPHRASE 1

While the classification between silent pictures and sound pictures in cinema history are the most basic, a host of contradictions exist in this division.

PARAPHRASE 2

The most fundamental separation in the history of film lies between silent films and sound films, but this criterion hides multiple inconsistencies.

037　claim

Day 04
Psychology

| SYNONYMS v. | uphold, assert, declare, affirm, allege, insist, maintain, contend, support, urge, advocate, argue | 주장하다 |

claim
[kleim]

Cognitive psychologists **claim** that the way we behave is decided by what we really value, what we choose, and how we understand circumstances.

인지 심리학자들은 우리의 선택, 가치관, 그리고 상황을 이해하는 방식과 같은 여러 가지 요소들이 우리의 행동에 영향을 준다고 주장한다.

PARAPHRASE 1

Cognitive psychologists **uphold** that several factors such as our decisions, values and ways of interpreting situations have an effect on our behavior.

PARAPHRASE 2

Cognitive psychologists **assert** that our behavior is affected by choices, by our values and by our ways taking in situations.

038 remains

Architecture

SYNONYMS **n.** relics, ruins, remnants, debris, dregs, wreckage

(건물의) 잔해, 폐허, 유적(지)

remains
[riméinz]

There are some of the most striking stone buildings in the remains of the ancient city of the Inca Empire, Machu Picchu, located on a ridge of the eastern slope of the Andes Mountains of Peru.

가장 훌륭한 석재 건축물들 몇몇은 페루 동부 안데스 산맥 꼭대기에 위치한 잉카 유적지의 가파른 언덕에 놓여 있다.

PARAPHRASE 1

The relics, representing some of the most brilliant stone architecture, seem to cling to the steep hillside of the Incan site, Machu Picchu, high up on the eastern Andes Mountains of Peru.

PARAPHRASE 2

Situated on a ridge in the Andes Mountains of Peru, the ruins of the ancient Inca city named Machu Picchu allow people to find some of the most magnificent stone structures.

PARAPHRASE 3

Some of the finest masonry constructions can be seen among the remnants of Machu Picchu, the Incan site perched among steep mountain ridges of the Andes in Peru.

039　mechanism

Day 04
Agriculture

| SYNONYMS | n. | method, means, technique, way, process, instrument, approach, avenue, mode, vehicle, fashion, manner, channel, medium, route, course, path | 과정, 수단, 방법 |

mechanism
[mékənìzəm]

Aeroponics, an alternative **mechanism** for plant cultivation with no help of soil, is one of the cultivation techniques in which vegetation is nourished by a nutrient solution that is misted onto its roots.

토양의 도움 없이 식물을 재배하는 하나의 방법인 공중재배는 배양액을 뿌리에 뿌리는 방식으로 식물에 영양분을 공급하는 기술이다.

PARAPHRASE 1

A **method** of growing vegetation without soil named aeroponics is a **technique** that sprinkles the roots of plants with water and nutrients in order to feed the plants.

PARAPHRASE 2

A growing technique called aeroculture is another **means** of cultivating vegetation by spraying nutrients directly onto the roots of plants without the use of soil.

040 excessive

Environmental Science — Day 04

SYNONYMS *adj.* formidable, extreme, exaggerated, undue, exorbitant, inordinate, immoderate, extravagant

지나친, 과도한

excessive
[iksésiv]

The decline of grasses and trees is the consequence of the excessive increase in cattle numbers and the growing demand for firewood, making the ground defenseless and delicate.

풀과 나무의 감소는 소 개체수의 지나친 증가와 장작에 대한 수요 증가의 결과이며, 이는 토양을 무방비의 연약한 상태로 만든다.

PARAPHRASE 1

The formidable increase in the demand of cattle grazing and firewood for fuel results in the reduction of grasses and trees, causing the land to become weak and fragile.

PARAPHRASE 2

Grasses and trees have decreased as a result of the need for firewood as well as extreme numbers of cattle, which gives rise to deterioration of the land quality.

DAILY CHECK-UP

A. Find the answer that is closest in meaning to the highlighted word or phrase in the sentence.

01. Regardless of whether it is loose or cemented, a part of the entire **amount** of any sedimentary rock is made up of empty space.

    (A) volume　　　　　　　　(B) dregs

02. The huge areas of land and the enormous numbers of people bring about **excessive** desertification.

    (A) outrageous　　　　　　(B) immoderate

03. The organic **debris** is transformed into petroleum by the rising heat and pressure from the weight of the sediment.

    (A) remnants　　　　　　　(B) enigma

04. The Whig party **asserted** against Jackson's policies and his party in a lot of crucial fields.

    (A) obviated　　　　　　　(B) argued

05. The helium-filled weather balloon is the most often used **technique** for gauging detailed upper-atmospheric conditions.

    (A) dissonance　　　　　　(B) instrument

06. Comedy requires sufficient objectivity not to consider some deviations from social regulations as **preposterous** threats.

    (A) ridiculous　　　　　　(B) exorbitant

07. Encouraging less aggressive behavior is the best way to **hinder** violence in reality.

    (A) perforate　　　　　　　(B) impede

08. Unlike Rome which evolved from one single structure, Greece developed from dozens of **distributed** cities.

    (A) forestalled　　　　　　(B) scattered

09. In the case of **variance** between state law and federal law, state adjudicators will judge the case on the basis of federal law.
   (A) contradiction   (B) resuscitation

10. The drawings include animals that the artists have been most afraid of due to their size, speed or **unpredictable** behavior.
    (A) variable   (B) conscientious

B. Complete each sentence using one of the words or phrases given.

11. Small islands are _____ over a great distance of Micronesia, the northern area of Melanesia.
    (A) dispersed   (B) annihilated

12. The facial-feedback hypothesis _____ that emotions work in the opposite direction of facial expressions.
    (A) abridges   (B) maintains

13. Spartina was highly appreciated for its capability to _____ erosion and the degradation of the wetlands.
    (A) stop   (B) sustain

14. The new _____ of business were associated with a stricter sense of time.
    (A) processes   (B) incongruities

15. The massive ice sheets covering North American ceaselessly thawed and copious _____ of water trickled out from them.
    (A) wreckage   (B) amounts

16. Some archaeologists _____ that large animals offering food and materials were portrayed in the cave paintings.
    (A) alleged   (B) harnessed

---

01. (A) 02. (B) 03. (A) 04. (B) 05. (B) 06. (A) 07. (B) 08. (B) 09. (A) 10. (A)
11. (A) 12. (B) 13. (A) 14. (A) 15. (B) 16. (A)

041　inevitable

Day 05
Psychology

SYNONYMS **adj.** unavoidable, certain, sure, fixed, inescapable, ineluctable, inexorable

불가피한, 피할 수 없는

inevitable
[inévitəbəl]

According to Sigmund Freud, **people exhibit aggressively impulsive behavior** as an **inevitable** response to the **discouragement of daily life**.

지그문트 프로이드에 따르면, 사람들은 일상의 좌절에 대한 불가피한 반응으로 공격적이고 충동적인 행동을 나타낸다.

PARAPHRASE 1

Sigmund Freud argued that **people show impulsive aggression** in an **unavoidable** response to the **frustration of daily life**.

PARAPHRASE 2

Sigmund Freud said that a **certain** reaction to the **despair of daily life** is **aggressive impulses**.

042 fluctuations

Zoology

SYNONYMS n. variation, change, variance, alteration, modification, transformation, shift, mutation, conversion, metamorphosis, transition

변화, 변동

fluctuation
[flʌ́ktʃuèiʃən]

In addition to **significant fluctuations** in deer populations attributable to the seasonal migration pattern, **the numbers of deer have changed considerably** since the arrival of European explorers in Puget Sound.

계절에 따른 이동 양식이 원인이 되는 사슴 개체 수의 상당한 변화 이외에도, 사슴 개체 수는 유럽의 탐험가들이 휫젯 사운드 지역에 도착한 이래로 상당히 변화해 왔다.

PARAPHRASE 1

Not only **do considerable variations** in deer populations arise from the seasonal migration, but **the numbers of deer have significantly changed** since European explorers arrived in Puget Sound.

PARAPHRASE 2

Deer numbers in Puget Sound have undergone substantial **changes** due to **the arrival of European explorers** as well as the seasonal migration pattern.

043　rough

Day 05
Zoology

| SYNONYMS | adj. | rugged, rocky, uneven, jagged, stony, craggy, bumpy, irregular, patchy, erratic, ragged, toothed | 울퉁불퉁한, 고르지 않은 |

rough
[rʌf]

The animals dwelling in a mountain biome including the mountain goat, wild goat, sheep, and yak (←minor idea) have oriented themselves to their harsh surroundings such as the freezing weather, the oxygen deficiency, and the **rough** landscape.

산양, 들염소, 양, 야크를 포함하는 산악 생물군계에 서식하는 동물들은 추운 날씨, 산소 결핍, 그리고 험준한 자연 경관과 같은 혹독한 환경에 적응해 왔다.

PARAPHRASE 1

The cold, the oxygen depletion, and the **rugged** environment are the major natural conditions to which the animals in a mountain biome have adapted.

PARAPHRASE 2

The animals of a mountain biome have adapted to the hard freeze, the oxygen deprivation, and the **rocky** landscape.

044 notably

Sociology

| SYNONYMS adv. | particularly, remarkably, especially, specifically, uniquely, specially | 특히 |

notably
[nóutəbəli]

As leaders of the union movement, skilled craftsmen did not think that a **notably** strong connection existed between themselves and other laborers such as semiskilled and unskilled workers.

연합 운동을 진두 지휘했던 장인들은 그들과 반숙련공 또는 비숙련공과 같은 노동자들 사이에 특별히 강한 연대가 존재한다고 생각하지 않았다.

PARAPHRASE 1

Master artisans spearheading the union movement hardly felt that there was a **particularly** firm bond between themselves and laborers who were semiskilled and unskilled.

PARAPHRASE 2

Leading the union campaign, master craftsmen barely felt that they had a **remarkably** strong tie with semiskilled and unskilled workers.

045 prominent

Day 05
Paleontology

SYNONYMS *adj.* renowned, famous, well-known, distinguished, eminent, notable, celebrated, noted

유명한

prominent
[prάmənənt]

Sidneyia, a **prominent** animal found in the Cambrian-age Burgess Shale, which includes a lot of invertebrate fossils, is a typical example of the extinct arthropods, a previously unknown group of animals.

여러 무척추 동물의 화석을 포함하는 캄브리아기의 버제스 혈암에서 발견된 유명한 동물인 시드네이아는 이전에는 잘 알려지지 않았던 동물 집단인 멸종 절지 동물들의 전형적인 예이다.

PARAPHRASE 1

A **renowned** animal discovered from the Cambrian Burgess Shale called Sidneyia belongs to a group of the extinct arthropods that was hardly known before.

PARAPHRASE 2

Sidneyia, a **famous** Burgess Shale animal of the Cambrian period, falls under a previously obscure category of extinct arthropods.

046 breakthrough

Day 05

Energy

SYNONYMS n. advance, progress, stride, development, improvement

진보, 발전, 성장

breakthrough
[bréikθrùː]

Cost reductions anticipated with the help of new technological **breakthrough**s and production on a large scale made wind power one of the world's cheapest methods to generate electricity.

신기술의 발달과 대량 생산으로 예상되는 비용 절감은 풍력을 전력 생산의 세계적으로 가장 비용 효율적인 방법 중 하나로 만들었다.

PARAPHRASE 1

Wind power became the world's most cost-effective means of producing electricity as cost declines were projected because of technological **advance**s and mass production.

PARAPHRASE 2

Thanks to **progress** in new technology and high volume production, cost cutbacks were expected, which made wind power the cheapest way of electric power production.

79

047 adjacent

Day 05
Geology

SYNONYMS *adj.* nearby, neighboring, immediate, adjoining, close to, contiguous to, in proximity to, in the vicinity of

가까운, 인접한

adjacent
[ədʒéisənt]

As gas pressure vanishes progressively, water or steam may be forced to flow in the direction of **adjacent** wells in order for the oil to be pumped from the well.

기체 압력이 점차적으로 사라짐에 따라 물 또는 증기는 기름을 우물 밖으로 밀어내기 위해 인접한 우물로 흘러 들어갈 수 있다.

PARAPHRASE 1

A progressive reduction in gas pressure may require water or condensation to be pumped down **nearby** wells to press the oil out of the well.

PARAPHRASE 2

Water or vapor may be pumped down **neighboring** wells to push the oil out of the well as gas pressure gradually lowers.

048 vibrant

Ornithology

SYNONYMS adj. vigorous, active, energetic, vivid, lively, brisk, bustling, dynamic, spirited, animated

활기찬

vibrant
[váibrənt]

Using begging intensity to deliver food to stronger chicks capable of **vibrant** begging, parent birds should make decisions on the matters of food delivery based on offspring's calls.

활기찬 소리로 먹이를 달라고 보채는 보다 강한 새끼들에게 먹이를 전달하기 위해 새끼들이 내는 소리의 강도를 참조하는 어미새들은 새끼들이 먹이를 달라고 보채는 소리에 기반하여 먹이 전달에 대한 결정을 내린다.

PARAPHRASE 1

In order to feed healthier offspring, parent birds should take into account which nestlings beg in a more **vigorous** way.

PARAPHRASE 2

Food delivery from parent birds to young birds is decided on the basis of how **active** each youngster's begging is.

049 demise

Paleontology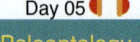

| SYNONYMS | n. | death, end, fall, decrease, downfall, collapse | 멸망, 죽음 |

demise
[dimáiz]

Paleontologists have advocated that the **demise** of the **dinosaurs** resulted from **climatic fluctuations related to progressive movements in the locations of continents and oceans caused by plate tectonics.**

고생물학자들은 공룡의 멸망은 판 구조론에 의해 야기된 대륙과 해양 위치의 점진적인 이동과 관련된 기후 변화에 의해 초래되었다고 주장해왔다.

PARAPHRASE 1

According to the paleontologists' assertions, gradual motions of continents and oceans caused by plate tectonics played a decisive role in climatic alterations, bringing about the **death** of the dinosaurs.

PARAPHRASE 2

Climatic changes associated with the slow activity of continents and seas that plate tectonics cause lead to the **end** of the dinosaur age.

050 domesticated

World History — Day 05

SYNONYMS adj. tame, domestic, trained

길들여진, 사육되는

domesticated
[douméstəkèitid]

The rudimentary cultural qualifications for the successful colonization of the Pacific region contain not only the proper boatbuilding and navigation skills to arrive at the islands, but also domesticated livestock and cultivation techniques suitable for marginal conditions.

태평양 지역의 성공적인 식민지화를 위한 문화적인 요건들은 섬에 도달하기 위한 적절한 배 제작 및 조종술뿐만 아니라 주변 상황에 적합한 가축과 경작 기술을 포함한다.

PARAPHRASE 1

The success of colonization in the Pacific islands was achieved by tame animals and cultivation technologies suited to marginal conditions as well as boatbuilding and navigation skills to reach the islands.

PARAPHRASE 2

There are some prerequisites for the colonization of the Pacific areas: boatbuilding and navigation skills for discovery and domestic animals and cultivation skills fit for settlement.

DAILY CHECK-UP

A. Find the answer that is closest in meaning to the highlighted word or phrase in the sentence.

01. Both these physical **transformations** have a noteworthy effect on the climate.
    (A) shifts   (B) demise

02. There are diverse reactions of farmers to **inescapable** depletion of the Ogallala aquifer.
    (A) profuse   (B) inexorable

03. Icebergs are **uneven** in shape and only a small portion of their mass is exposed above the sea surface.
    (A) irregular   (B) bustling

04. Basaltic rocks support springs of groundwater, **especially** at the Jabal Druze on the border between Jordan and Syria.
    (A) notably   (B) exclusively

05. Other forms of entertainment relied on either live performance or the **brisk** participation of a master of ceremonies.
    (A) active   (B) ludicrous

06. The tundra **contiguous to** the timberline is composed of a pretty complete cover of lowland shrubs, herbs, and grasses.
    (A) on the verge of   (B) in the vicinity of

07. The Romans did not make **strides** early in the field of speculative philosophy and science.
    (A) modifications   (B) improvements

08. Historians have regarded the **fall** of the Roman Empire to mark the end of the Ancient Era and the beginning of the Middle Age.
    (A) end   (B) dimension

09. The corpses of a massive number of animals were discovered in the grave, but **domestic** animals were not there.

(A) obviated (B) domesticated

10. The Emperor penguins are **distinguished** animals that inhabit the open ice of Antarctica during the winter.
    (A) patchy (B) well-known

B. Complete each sentence using one of the words or phrases given.

11. The deciduous forest is a _____ place where various species of flora and fauna flourish.
    (A) dynamic (B) jagged

12. Ample amounts of adorned Chinese ceramics running into Europe affected the work of various wares, _____ Delft pottery.
    (A) coherently (B) specifically

13. Immigrants from a _____ community swiftly replace a local population that dies out.
    (A) neighboring (B) distressing

14. In reactions to the _____ strife, the U.S. armed forces launched a military operation to eliminate the Native Americans.
    (A) ineluctable (B) implausible

15. The composition of ecosystems undergoes a lot of _____ before attaining a height of biological diversity.
    (A) garnishment (B) modification

16. _____ in construction materials and techniques can be gauged by the distinction in weight between current structures and those of similar size one hundred ago.
    (A) Progress (B) Decimation

---

01. (A) 02. (B) 03. (A) 04. (A) 05. (A) 06. (B) 07. (B) 08. (A) 09. (B) 10. (B)
11. (A) 12. (B) 13. (A) 14. (A) 15. (B) 16. (A)

REVIEW TEST (DAY 01-05)

A. The word _____ in the passage is closest in meaning to

01. The ice cores which reached approximately 215 meters in length were so long that they could **pierce** through glacial ice formed from compacted snow with air bubbles. They continuously kept the form of the clear, bubble-free ice generated from saltwater sticking to the base of the glacier. The features of this clear ice of sea were fairly similar to those of the ice from the green iceberg shown in Antarctic ocean.

(A) eliminate
(B) penetrate
(C) discriminate
(D) stretch

02. In 1815, William Smith eventually created the first nationwide geological map of Britain covering the whole of England and Wales and parts of Scotland, which was so **meticulously** prepared that it is still in use today.

(A) dramatically
(B) carefully
(C) fairly
(D) hardly

03. According to the Darwin, if the food available in a specific area is not able to support all individuals that inhabit in this area, these individuals will compete for survival. Those individuals with traits that allow them to get the upper hand in the fight for life are more **inclined to** maintain their existence and hand down their genes to the subsequent generation.

(A) likely to
(B) opposed to
(C) reluctant to
(D) inhospitable to

REVIEW TEST [DAY 01-05]

04. Hydro power which was derived from the energy of running or falling water has been **utilized** for practical purposes such as irrigation systems since ancient times. However, although water power was the major source of power to open the age of new inventions at the beginning of the Industrial Revolution, it had to give place to steam power **harnessed** in a lot of large scale factories and mills.

(A) upheld
(B) exploited
(C) decimated
(D) counteracted

05. If additional food, which is enough to support more people, cannot be produced in the rural economy, it would be hard to expect a swell in population. In this sense, more land was cultivated for food production by farmers at a great sacrifice of forests as well as marshlands in the sixteenth century. The most **miraculous** example of the expansion of agricultural land is the land reclamation works in Netherlands, which cleared more than 36,000 acres of land for cultivation during the sixteenth and seventeenth centuries.

(A) detrimental
(B) remarkable
(C) nebulous
(D) quaint

06. Scientists assumed that a huge asteroid which came into collision with Earth blocked sunlight by a dust cloud which was stirred up and hindered photosynthesis for several months. Also, surface temperatures fell below degree of frost, but global temperatures fairly increased in the long run due to the greenhouse effect. Moreover, many living things including dinosaurs were **exterminated** by dramatic global climate change and the disruption of food chain.

(A) eradicated
(B) affirmed
(C) flourished
(D) ameliorated

87

07. The first benefit biopolymers offer is that they are biodegradable and compostable. Generally, abandoned traditional plastics do not decay naturally and remain in the same area for several decades, causing environmental problems such as the emission of **lethal** pollutant and greenhouse gas.

(A) shabby
(B) sinister
(C) noxious
(D) idiosyncratic

08. From an early age, roaming his uncle's farm, William Smith explored and collected the fossils **ample** in the limestone of the Cotswold Hills. He also educated himself geometry, mapping and surveying through books. At the age of eighteen, he became an assistant to the master surveyor, Edward Webb, in order to learn surveying technique.

(A) compound
(B) susceptible
(C) conspicuous
(D) plentiful

09. Geologic research shows that ice barely covered **substantial** areas of southeastern Alaska along the inner continental shelf at the end of the last Ice Age. According to one study, by roughly 16,000 years ago, the northwest coast of North America was predominantly ice free but for the coastal region between Washington State and British Columbia.

(A) sizable
(B) inconsistent
(C) outrageous
(D) malignant

REVIEW TEST [DAY 01-05]

10. Fluoridated water provokes controversy between working for the common good and violating individual rights. Fluoridation can be regarded as a violation of ethical or legal rules that **prohibit** medical treatment without medical supervision or informed consent, and that **prevent** administration of unauthorized medical substances.

(A) forbid
(B) infiltrated
(C) buffered
(D) replenished

11. As a **method** of inquiry, qualitative research has been used in various academic fields. Researchers concentrate on gaining insight into people's attitudes, behaviors, concerns, motivations, cultures or lifestyles. To gather information, they utilize many **approaches** such as participant observation, non-participant observation, field notes, in-depth interview, and analysis of documents and materials.

(A) instrument
(B) venue
(C) recuperation
(D) incongruity

12. At the end of the 1920s, the most vital **transition** in the history of motion picture was the **conversion** from silent to sound movie. Even though all the extremely observable technological advances in home and theatrical delivery of the moving image have took place over the decades since then, there has been no other single **alteration** regarded as a similar sort of watershed.

(A) surveillance
(B) antecedent
(C) incongruity
(D) transformation

13. When it comes to the migratory birds' magnetic compass, many **prominent** biologists assure that birds have trouble detecting the earth's magnetic field as it is too weak to sense. Besides, some researchers argue that although birds can orient themselves to biological compasses, their ability to sense magnetic fields has not been fully explained.

(A) audacious
(B) eminent
(C) contemptible
(D) petty

14. Catholic leaders believe that the most essential gift from God is life and people have not absolute dominion but stewardship over the gift. In other words, as responsible stewards of life, people must on no accounts cause their own **death**, or the death of an innocent victim.

(A) repugnance
(B) attachment
(C) breakthrough
(D) demise

답안

01. (B) 02. (B) 03. (A) 04. (B) 05. (B) 06. (A) 07. (C)
08. (D) 09. (A) 10. (A) 11. (A) 12. (D) 13. (B) 14. (D)

REVIEW TEST [DAY 01-05]

B. Which of the sentences below best expresses the essential information in the highlighted sentence in the passage? Incorrect choices change the meaning in important ways or leave out essential information.

15. In addition to the difficulty of slowing down the process, the huge numbers of people and the extensive areas of land influenced results in the formidable seriousness of desertification.

(A) Desertification is in extreme decline since not only is it difficult to slow its speed, but it influences massive numbers of people and vast areas of land.
(B) The difficulty of delaying the speed of desertification as well as the tremendous numbers of people and the extensive areas of land affected result from the excessive expansion in desert areas.
(C) Desertification becomes serious unless it is affected by the great numbers of people and the large areas of land, which make it hard to slow down its process.
(D) Large areas of land undergo the serious process of desertification, which can be hardly reduced unless the population in these areas is controlled in a proper way.

해설 정답 (A)

① In addition to the difficulty of slowing down the process, the huge numbers of people and the extensive areas of land influenced results in ② the formidable seriousness of desertification
→ ② Desertification is in extreme decline since ① not only is it difficult to slow its speed, but it influences massive numbers of people and vast areas of land

문장의 원인과 결과 사이의 관계를 명확하게 이해하였는지를 평가하고자 하는 문제로 문장의 주어이자 내용상의 원인(①)이 되는 'In addition to ~, the huge ~ influenced'과 결과(②)인 'the formidable ~ desertification'의 관계는 '~을 초래하다' 또는 '그 결과 ~가 되다'라는 의미를 갖고 있는 result in 을 통해 명확히 알 수 있다. 이러한 문장의 경우 원인과 결과를 규명하기 위해 문장을 크게 바라보는 능력을 키우는 것과 주어의 경우 크게 두 가지 포인트가 나오고 이 두 가지 포인트가 'in addition to'로 연결되어 있음을 감지하는 것이 매우 중요하다. 이렇게 주요 아이디

91

어를 잘 파악하고 나면 보기에서 원인과 결과의 관계가 명확하지 않은 오답을 가려내기 쉬워지며 그 다음에 남은 보기들 중 세부적인 내용을 비교해 보고 답을 고르면 훨씬 정답을 고르기 수월해진다. Paraphrase 할 때에는 원문의 하나의 절로 이루어진 문장을 두 개의 절로 이루어진 문장으로 재구성할 수 있다. 즉, 원문의 주부이자 원인인 ①은 '~이므로', '~때문에'라는 의미를 갖고 있는 접속사 'since'가 이끄는 종속절의 형태로 덧붙여 질 수 있으며 이 때에 원문의 구의 형태로 나열된 크게 두 가지의 핵심 내용들은 'A뿐만 아니라 B도'라는 의미를 갖고 있는 'not only A, but also B'라는 관용 구문을 활용하여 두 개의 절의 형태로 나열 될 수 있다. 또한, 원문에서 내용상 결과를 나타내며 구의 형태로 언급된 ②는 재진술 문장의 주절의 형태로 'Desertification is in extreme decline'와 같이 재구성될 수 있다.

오답의 근거

(b) The difficulty of delaying the speed of desertification as well as the huge areas of land and the enormous numbers of people affected result from the excessive expansion in desert areas.
→ 원인과 결과의 위치가 원문과 반대로 나열된 경우로 오답이다. 왜냐하면 result from은 '~이 원인이다'라는 의미로 "(원인) result in (결과)."의 문장 구조를 갖게 되는 result in과 달리 result from은 "(결과) result from (원인)."의 문장 구조를 갖게 되기 때문이다.

(c) Desertification becomes serious unless it is affected by the great numbers of people and large areas of land, which make it hard to slow down its process.
→ 접속사 'unless' 이하의 내용은 그 앞의 내용의 원인이 되어야 한다. 하지만 원인이 되는 두 가지 포인트가 원인 'it is affected ~ of land'와 결과 'which make ~ its process'의 관계로 나열되었을 뿐만 아니라 사막화와 그것의 원인 사이의 관계가 명확하지 않으므로 오답이다.

(d) Large areas of land undergo the serious process of desertification, which can be hardly reduced unless the population in these areas is controlled in a proper way.
→ 원문에 언급된 내용들의 단순한 나열일 뿐 원인과 결과의 관계가 명확하지 않으며, 밑줄 친 부분의 정보는 언급된 내용이 아니므로 오답이다.

다른 방식으로 paraphrase 하기

In addition to the difficulty of slowing down the process, the huge numbers of people and the extensive areas of land influenced results in the formidable seriousness of desertification.

→ The excessive expansion in desert areas results from the influence on vast areas and many people as well as the difficulty of reducing desertification.

REVIEW TEST [DAY 01-05]

원인과 결과를 나타내기 위해 '~을 초래하다' 또는 '그 결과 ~가 되다'라는 의미의 'result in'은 "(원인) result in (결과)."의 문장 구조를 갖게 되며 이는 '~이 원인이다'라는 의미의 'result from'을 활용하여 "(결과) result from (원인)."의 문장 구조로 재진술 될 수 있다.

→ The undue severity of desertification is caused not only by the difficulty of reducing desertification but also by the influence on vast areas and many people.
→ The influence on vast areas and many people as well as the difficulty of reducing desertification cause the undue severity of desertification.

문장을 paraphrase하는 효과적인 방법 중 하나는 능동태를 수동태로 또는 수동태를 능동태로 전환하는 것이다. 또한 두 가지 아이디어를 동등하게 나열할 때에는 단순히 'A 그리고 B'의 의미로 접속사 'and'를 활용할 수 있지만, 'A뿐만 아니라 B도'라는 의미의 'not only A but (also) B' 또는 'B as well as A'라는 표현을 활용할 수 있다. 이 경우의 두 가지 아이디어는 문장에서 동등한 중요도를 가지므로 둘 중 하나만 언급하는 것은 중요한 내용의 누락이 될 수 있으므로 둘 다 반드시 언급하도록 한다.

16. Unlike the insistence presented by some that Polynesians who lost direction and went adrift settled in many parts of the pacific islands by accident, it is more persuasive to believe that their settlement was intentional journey for colonization in that the expeditions were carefully prepared by stocking up with provisions as well as **domestic** animals and plants.

    (A) Some believe that the pacific islands were settled by Polynesians who got lost and went adrift by chance, while others think that they were deliberately colonized.
    (B) Considering the fact that the journey was perfectly planned for colonization, Polynesians seem to settle in the pacific islands not accidentally but intentionally.
    (C) As many have presented, the settlement of the Pacific islands appears to be accidental rather than intentional since Polynesians found the islands while wandering off course.
    (D) It might be reasonable to say that Polynesian expeditions colonized the pacific islands in a deliberate way, but this argument has been adversely commented upon by much evidence.

> 해설   정답 (B)

Unlike the insistence presented by some that ① Polynesians who lost direction and went adrift settled in many parts of the pacific islands by accident, **it is more persuasive to believe** that ② their settlement was intentional journey for colonization in that ③ the expeditions were carefully prepared by stocking up with provisions as well as **domestic** animals and plants.
→ Considering the fact that ③ the journey was perfectly planned for colonization, Polynesians seem to settle in the pacific islands **not** ① accidentally **but** ② intentionally.

문장을 명확하게 이해하려면 원문의 핵심을 정확하게 파악하는 것이 중요하다. 제시된 문장의 경우 폴리네시아인들이 태평양의 섬들을 우연히 발견하고 정착하게 되었는지 계획적으로 그 섬들을 식민지로 만들었는지를 명확히 이해하는데 있다. 따라서 문장을 paraphrase 할 때는 원문의 주요 아이디어에 집중하여 세부적인 내용만을 열거한다거나 주요 내용을 누락하는 실수를 범하지 않도록 한다. 이러한 점을 고려하여 원문의 문장을 재진술 할 때에 원문의 전치사 'unlike' 이하의 '폴리네시아인들은 우연히 태평양의 섬들을 발견하여 정착했음'을 언급하는 주장 ①은 재진술 문장에서는 '우연히'라는 의미의 부사 'accidentally'로 간략하게 언급될 수 있으며 원문의 또 다른 주장인 '폴리네시아인들은 태평양의 섬들을 계획적으로 식민지로 만들었음'을 언급하는 ②는 재진술 문장에서는 '의도적으로'라는 의미의 부사 'intentionally'로 간략하게 언급될 수 있고, 이 두 의견 사이의 관계는 원문에서 ②가 더 설득력이 있다고 말하고 있으므로 'A가 아니라 B이다'라는 의미의 'not A but B' 구문을 활용하여 간략하게 'not ① (accidentally) but ② (intentionally)'라고 재진술 할 수 있다. 원문의 ③의 내용은 ②의 주장의 근거가 되는 부분으로 재진술 시에는 '~라는 사실을 고려할 때'라는 의미의 'considering the fact that~'이라는 구문을 활용하여 덧붙여질 수 있다.

> 오답의 근거

(A) Some believe that ① the pacific islands were settled by Polynesians who got lost and went adrift by chance, while others think that ② they were deliberately colonized.
→ 원문의 두 가지 주장(폴리네시아인들의 태평양의 섬들에의 정착이 우연인지(①) 계획적인지(②))이 언급되기는 하였으나 어느 쪽의 주장이 더 설득력이 있는지에 대한 언급이 누락되어 있다. 따라서 주요 내용의 누락으로 오답이다.

(C) As many have presented, the settlement of the Pacific islands appears to be accidental rather than intentional since Polynesians found the islands while wandering off course.
→ 원문의 주요 내용과 완벽하게 대치되는 내용으로 잘못된 정보를 제공하고 있으므로 오답이다.

(D) It might be reasonable to say that Polynesian expeditions colonized the pacific islands in a deliberate way, but this argument has been adversely commented upon by much evidence.
→ 보기의 밑줄 친 부분에 제시된 내용은 원문에 언급되어 있지 않은 내용으로 오답이다.

REVIEW TEST [DAY 01-05]

다른 방식으로 paraphrase 하기

Unlike the insistence presented by some that ① Polynesians who lost direction and went adrift settled in many parts of the pacific islands by accident, it is more persuasive to believe that ② their settlement was intentional journey for colonization in that ③ the expeditions were carefully prepared by stocking up with provisions as well as domestic animals and plants.

→ Considering the fact that ③ the journey was perfectly planned for colonization, Polynesians seem to settle in the pacific islands not ① accidentally but ② intentionally.
→ The evidence that ③ the journey was perfectly planned for colonization makes it more plausible to say that the pacific islands seem to be settled by Polynesians ② intentionally, not ① accidentally

두 가지 아이디어들 중 하나를 선택해야 할 때 'A가 아니라 B이다'라는 의미의 'not A but B' 또는 'B, (but) not A'라는 표현을 활용할 수 있다.

→ As many have presented, the settlement of Polynesians in the Pacific islands appears to be ② intentional rather than accidental since ③ there exists reasonable evidence that their exploration was perfectly prepared.
→ The argument that ② Polynesians settled in many parts of the pacific islands deliberately is more convincing than the one that ① their settlement was accidental because ③ their journey were carefully prepared.

두 가지 아이디어 중 하나가 더 ~함을 언급하고자 할 때 '~는 B라기 보다는 A하다'라는 의미의 '~ is A rather than B' 또는 'A가 B보다 더 ~하다'라는 의미의 'A is more ~ than B'라는 표현을 활용할 수 있다.

051 precarious

Day 06
Agriculture

SYNONYMS adj. unstable, insecure, uncertain, dangerous, risky, unsure, hazardous, shaky, perilous, unsettled, chancy

불안정한, 위태로운, 위험한

precarious
[prikέəriəs]

One of the disadvantages of monoculture plantations is that the farmlands are so **precarious** that the entire crop can be highly vulnerable to continuous bad weather or the intrusion of a single pest.

단일 재배 농장의 단점들 중 하나는 농장이 너무 불안정해서 작물 전체가 지속적인 기상 악화 또는 단일 해충의 침입에 상당히 취약해질 수 있다는 것이다.

PARAPHRASE 1

Agricultural lands occupied by one type of crop are so **unstable** that deteriorating weather conditions or the encroachment of one type of pest can decimate the whole crop.

PARAPHRASE 2

Single-crop farmlands are too **insecure** to buffer the entire crop against worsening weather conditions or the invasion of one type of pest.

052 integrate

Political Science

SYNONYMS v. unite, merge, blend, combine, incorporate, amalgamate, mingle, assimilate, mix, compound, alloy, coalesce, federate, consolidate, converge, synthesize, fuse

결합하다, 연합하다, 통합하다

integrate
[íntəgrèit]

The Democrats governed semisubsistence agricultural areas secluded and abandoned in terms of economy. On the other hand, the Whigs controlled towns and rural regions fully integrated into the market economy.

민주당은 경제적으로 격리되고 버려진 반자급 농업 지역들을 지배했다. 반면에, 휘그당은 시장 경제에 완전하게 통합된 도시와 시골 지역들을 지배했다.

PARAPHRASE 1 The Whigs were powerful in those areas that were completely united into the market economy, whereas the Democrats' authority was mighty in areas of poverty.

PARAPHRASE 2 The Democrats had enormous power in depressed areas, while the Whigs dominated regions totally merged into the market economy.

053　spectrum

Day 06
Visual Arts

| SYNONYMS | n. | range, extent, scope, stretch, space, compass, area, reach, expanse | 범위, 정도 |

spectrum
[spéktrəm]

From western civilization, the Chinese brought in a lot of peculiar forms of containers, such as long-necked bottles (←minor idea), and created a **spectrum** of ornament patterns, particularly for the European market.

중국인들은 서양 문명으로부터 주둥이가 긴 병과 같은 특이한 형태의 많은 용기들을 들여왔고, 특히 유럽 시장을 겨냥한 다양한 장식 문양을 고안해냈다.

PARAPHRASE 1

The Chinese adopted a great deal of unique vessel forms from western countries and a **range** of decorative patterns were fabricated by them, especially for the European market.

PARAPHRASE 2

The Chinese introduced various types of vessels from the West and devised an **extent** of adornment, notably for the European market.

054 clue

Linguistics — Day 06

SYNONYMS *n.* indication, hint, lead, implication, suggestion, evidence, mark, sign, symptom, manifestation

단서, 암시, 징후

clue
[kluː]

The comparison between infants' status prior to the introduction of a stimulus and their status during or right after the stimulus furnishes the researchers with a **clue** to the level and duration of the reaction to the stimulus.

자극을 주기 이전의 유아의 상태와 자극을 주는 동안 또는 직후의 유아의 상태에 대한 비교는 연구자들에게 자극에 대한 반응의 정도와 기간에 대한 실마리를 제공해 준다.

PARAPHRASE 1

An **indication** for the degree of the reaction to a stimulus is provided for the researchers through the analysis of the distinction between infants' status before the stimulus and their status after the stimulus.

PARAPHRASE 2

The researchers get a **hint** from infants' reactions to a stimulus by comparing infants' status prior to the stimulus with their status after the stimulus.

055 intentional

Day 06
Biology

SYNONYMS **adj.** deliberate, calculated, willful, conscious, designed, planned, purposeful, voluntary

고의적인, 계획된

intentional
[inténʃənəl]

The fungus Neurospora sustained normal diurnal periodicities of biological activity for a long time even in the case of intentional isolation from external cues generated from the Earth.

균류 뉴로스포라(붉은빵곰팡이)는 지구에서 발생하는 외부적인 신호로부터 의도적으로 격리된 경우에도 오랜 시간 동안 생물학적 활동의 정상적인 일주기성을 유지했다.

PARAPHRASE 1

Even under **deliberate** isolation from geophysical timing cues, normal daily periodicities were retained for long periods of time by the fungus Neurospora.

PARAPHRASE 2

In spite of **calculated** isolation from external cues, the fungus Neurospora continued to maintain normal circadian rhythms.

056 contemplate

Environmental Science

SYNONYMS v. consider, ponder, reflect, meditate, muse, brood, dwell on, think deeply

깊이 생각하다, 심사숙고하다

contemplate
[kɑ́ntəmplèit]

It is only recently that investigators have **contemplate**d an environmentally friendly approach known as bioremediation, which uses hyper accumulators in order to clean up soil and waste disposal sites polluted by poisonous heavy metals.

최근에서야 연구원들은 유해한 중금속에 오염된 토양과 쓰레기 처리장을 정화하고자 식물환경복원이라 알려진, 중금속 고축적 식물종을 사용하는 환경 친화적 방법을 심사 숙고해 왔다.

PARAPHRASE 1

Only currently have researchers **consider**ed the use of hyper accumulators to purify soil and landfills contaminated by pernicious heavy metals, which is an eco-friendly method known as phytoremediation.

PARAPHRASE 2

Researchers have only lately **ponder**ed an eco-friendly way of using hyper accumulators for the purification of soil degraded by toxic heavy metals, called phytoremediation.

057 ensuing

Earth Science

SYNONYMS adj. subsequent, consecutive, later, successive, sequential, serial, following

연속적인, 그 다음의

ensuing
[ensúːiŋ]

There are two primary factors that accelerate desertification: the destabilization of natural vegetation and the **ensuing** erosion of soil aggravated by wind and water.

자연 식생의 불안정화와 바람과 물에 의해 악화되는 토양의 뒤이은 침식은 사막화를 가속화하는 두 가지 주요한 원인들이다.

PARAPHRASE 1 The loss of balanced natural vegetation and the **subsequent** soil erosion that wind and water cause are the chief causes of desertification.

PARAPHRASE 2 Desertification is achieved largely through the loss of stable natural vegetation and the **consecutive** soil erosion by wind and water.

058 stringent

SYNONYMS **adj.** strict, rigid, rigorous, harsh, severe, austere, tight, inclement, ruthless, demanding

엄격한, 혹독한

stringent
[stríndʒənt]

The refining and burning of petroleum and its products which give rise to adverse environmental effects are controlled with the help of advanced technologies and stringent laws.

환경에 해로운 영향을 미치는 석유의 정제와 연소, 그리고 석유 생산물은 첨단 기술과 엄한 법률의 도움으로 통제된다.

PARAPHRASE 1

The advent of advanced technologies and strict laws help the regulation of the refining and burning of petroleum and its products which have adverse effects on the environment.

PARAPHRASE 2

Advanced technologies and rigid laws strengthen the control over the refining and burning of oil and its products which adversely affect the environment.

059 tremendous

Day 06
Astronomy

SYNONYMS *adj.* enormous, immense, massive, colossal, vast, huge, sizable, bulky, mammoth, gigantic, monstrous, large, grand, overwhelming

거대한, 막대한

tremendous
[triméndəs]

As the outflow channels on Mars are extremely wide and deep, the flow rates must have been **tremendous**, perhaps as much as a hundred times greater than the 100 tons per second the Amazon river carries.

화성의 방류 수로는 극도로 넓고 깊어서 흐르는 물의 양이 엄청났음에 틀림없다. 아마도 아마존 강이 운반하는 물의 양보다 백배는 많을 것이다.

PARAPHRASE 1

The water flow rates of outflow channels on Mars must have been **enormous** in consideration of their width and depth and in comparison to the volume of water provided from the Amazon river per second.

PARAPHRASE 2

Based on the width and depth of the outflow channels on Mars, the flow rates must have been **immense**: they were probably a hundred times more than the water volume per second discharged from the Amazon river.

104

060 haphazard

Day 06 — Space Science

| SYNONYMS adj. | random, chance, unplanned, casual, unpredictable, unsystematic, arbitrary | 임의적인, 우연의 |

haphazard
[hǽphǽzərd]

Although a few decades ago it was believed that Earth, living in a cosmic shooting gallery was vulnerable to **haphazard** violent events, the detailed analysis of current research shows that the threat posed by meteorite impacts is fairly uncommon.

수십 년 전에는 우주 사격장 안에 존재하는 지구가 예상치 못한 충돌 상황에 취약한 것으로 여겨졌지만, 최근 연구의 철저한 분석은 운석 충돌이 야기하는 위협은 꽤 드물다고 말한다.

PARAPHRASE 1

Earth, in a cosmic shooting range, was thought to be susceptible to unexpected **random** impacts several decades ago. However, the thorough analysis of research indicates that the hazard from massive collisions is quite rare.

PARAPHRASE 2

Earth, in a cosmic shooting gallery, was considered at risk to **chance** violent events decades ago, but recent study reveals that damage from collisions rarely occurs.

DAILY CHECK-UP

A. Find the answer that is closest in meaning to the highlighted word or phrase in the sentence.

01. Runoff channels are widely interconnected and intertwined systems that are **incorporated** into lager channels.

    (A) integrated   (B) encapsulated

02. The change has encouraged people to **muse** about how artificial interference can serve the degradation of ecological diversity.

    (A) meditate   (B) countervail

03. A fame of **rigorous** ethicality and ethnocentricity was enhanced by the unity of the village in New England.

    (A) extravagant   (B) severe

04. Even though East African herbivores inhabit the same environment, they have a **scope** of feeding preferences.

    (A) range   (B) antecedent

05. A **colossal** amount of energy was emitted by collisions with meteorite.

    (A) gigantic   (B) vigorous

06. Other methods help discover the **implications** of right-handedness.

    (A) crests   (B) effects

07. An increase in global warming caused by air pollution may accelerate aridity in the **consecutive** decades.

    (A) subsequent   (B) patchy

08. The ability of a species to survive **haphazard** ecological disasters is a criterion for survival.

    (A) random   (B) coherent

09. Nowadays the financial market seems to be a lot more **unsettled** than it was five years ago.

(A) exaggerated   (B) insecure

10. Conscious efforts and **purposeful** cooperation among regions are crucial to regulate and suppress piracy and lawless behavior on the sea.
    (A) focused   (B) affluent

B. Complete each sentence using one of the words or phrases given.

11. Computer models are utilized as a way to calculate how all the causes of climate variations will be _____ .
    (A) amalgamated   (B) domesticated

12. In the city of Teotihuacan, there are more than 2,000 apartment complexes, _____ religious buildings and financial centers.
    (A) massive   (B) spirited

13. The protostar can be observed in the _____ visible to the naked eyes only after it releases copious radiation of its own.
    (A) breakthrough   (B) spectrum

14. Appropriate management and investment are encouraged by the _____ guild system.
    (A) strict   (B) grotesque

15. The Ediacara formation provides few _____ about the origins of modern animals.
    (A) conversion   (B) hints

16. Genes associated with aggressive behavior have a higher chance to be passed down to _____ generations.
    (A) compulsory   (B) successive

---

01. (A) 02. (A) 03. (B) 04. (A) 05. (A) 06. (B) 07. (A) 08. (A) 09. (B) 10. (A)
11. (A) 12. (A) 13. (B) 14. (A) 15. (B) 16. (B)

107

061 far-reaching

Day 07 — Anthropology

SYNONYMS *adj.* comprehensive, extensive, entire, total, complete, overall, whole, broad, wide, commodious, general

포괄적인, 전체의

far-reaching
The dissemination of iron working had **far-reaching impacts on** a variety of organizations in economic, social, and political areas in Africa.

철제품 제작법의 보급은 아프리카의 경제, 사회, 정치 분야의 다양한 조직에 광범위한 영향을 미쳤다.

PARAPHRASE 1
Economic, social, and political organizations were influenced by iron working diffused throughout Africa in a **comprehensive** way.

PARAPHRASE 2
Iron working was spread throughout Africa, which led to **extensive** changes in various organizations of society.

062 abhor

World History

SYNONYMS v. loathe, detest, hate, abominate, strongly dislike

혐오하다, 싫어하다

abhor
[æbhɔ́ːr]

Those who admire power are liable to idolize whatever is mighty and are fascinated by the power of Rome rather than by the ingenuity of Greece, but there are still unshakable opinions that **abhor** Rome.

권력을 숭배하는 사람들은 무엇이든 강한 것을 우상화하는 경향이 있어서 그리스의 독창성 보다는 로마의 권력에 오히려 더 매료된다. 하지만 로마를 혐오하는 확고한 의견들은 여전히 존재한다.

PARAPHRASE 1

Unlike the power worshippers who are more captivated by the Roman power than by the Greek subtlety, other views that **loathe** Rome still exist.

PARAPHRASE 2

Some people admire the strong power of Rome, while others **detest** it.

063 devise

Day 07
Anthropology

SYNONYMS v. create, produce, contrive, invent, fabricate, compose, constitute, form, craft, fashion, shape, forge, configure, frame, mold, manufacture, make

고안하다, 만들어 내다

devise
[diváiz]

When outsiders were confronted with Pacific islanders at the very first, they hoped to learn about the origin of the islanders, but a lot of vagarious and separate hypotheses were devised because of a severe shortage of concrete evidence.

외부인들이 태평양 섬 주민들과 처음으로 대면했을 때, 그들은 섬 주민들의 기원에 대해 알아내고자 했으나 신뢰할 만한 증거의 심각한 부족으로 별개의 기발한 가설들이 수없이 만들어졌다.

PARAPHRASE 1

Outsiders who encountered Pacific islanders first began to make assumptions about their origins but the absence of reliable data created many fanciful and mutually exclusive theories.

PARAPHRASE 2

Since Pacific islanders were witnessed by outsiders, many whimsical and critical theories were produced due to insufficient data on their origin.

064 brilliance

Biology

SYNONYMS n. radiance, luminosity, brightness, luster, sheen

빛, 광채

brilliance
[bríljəns]

There seems to be no crucial distinction between the **brilliance** of plants and of animals, and it is thought by some that the ability to emit it is found in all creatures, even though observable in only a few, mostly inhabiting the ocean.

식물과 동물의 발광 사이에는 큰 차이가 없는 것 같다. 일부는 빛을 발하는 능력은 비록 일부의 생물에게서만 눈에 띄지만, 모든 생물, 특히 해양에 서식하는 생물들에게서 발견된다.

PARAPHRASE 1

Significant differences between the **radiance** of flora and of fauna is hardly found and some believe that all creatures, predominantly in the sea, have the power to release it, although only a few visibly produce it.

PARAPHRASE 2

The **luminosity** of flora and of fauna rarely has disparities and although conspicuous in only a few, such power belongs to all organisms, notably marine life.

Day 07

065 segregate

glaciology

> **SYNONYMS** v. divide, separate, detach, sever, disconnect, seclude, disunite, dissociate, isolate, set apart, disengage
>
> 분리하다, 떼어놓다

segregate
[ségrigèit]

Generally seen in the areas of the Amery Ice Shelf in East Antarctica, a green iceberg consists of two discrete parts: bubbly white ice and comparatively bubble-free ice segregated by a layer that reaches the thickness of a meter including elastic sediments.

일반적으로 남극대륙 동쪽의 에이머리 빙붕 지역에서 발견되는 녹색 빙산은, 탄성 퇴적암을 포함하는 1미터 두께에 달하는 층에 의해 거품이 있는 흰색 얼음과 상대적으로 거품이 없는 얼음으로 분리되는 별개의 두 부분으로 구성되어 있다.

PARAPHRASE 1

Bubbly white ice and clear bubble-free ice are two portions of a green iceberg commonly found in the regions of the Amery Ice Shelf in East Antarctica and are divided by an ice layer which is a meter in thickness and involves sediments.

PARAPHRASE 2

Green icebergs formed in the Amery Ice Shelf, East Antarctica, are separated into white and blue bands on the basis of an ice layer containing sediments.

066 fragile

Ecology

SYNONYMS *adj.* brittle, breakable, frail, delicate, feeble, weak, infirm, slender, flimsy, easily broken

약한, 부서지기 쉬운

fragile
[frǽdʒail]

Since hundreds of years are required to go back to the climax state, climax communities are regarded as the most unstable and fragile in the light of stability viewed as the restoration speed of an ecosystem after an environmental change.

환경 변화 이후 생태계의 회복 속도로 파악되는 안정성의 측면에서, 극상 상태로 돌아가는데에 수백 년이 요구되는 극상 군락은 가장 불안정하고 연약하다고 여겨진다.

PARAPHRASE 1

Considering stability, which means ecological resilience after a major destruction, climax communities would be the most precarious and brittle in that it takes them hundreds of years to go back to the state of climax.

PARAPHRASE 2

In terms of the ecological stability based on the recovery rate following a disturbance, climax communities which need hundreds of years for the return to the climax stage are considered the most insecure and breakable.

113

Day 07

067 emergence

Media and Communication

SYNONYMS n. introduction, advent, arrival, rise, appearance, influx, inflow, inrush

출현, 도래, 유입

emergence
[imə́ːrdʒəns]

Electronics and telecommunications companies compete and collaborate with each other and thus formulated the broadcasting industry in the United States, starting with the **emergence** of commercial radio programming in the early 1920s.

1920년대 초반 민방 라디오 프로그래밍의 도래와 함께 시작된 전기 전자 회사들과 원격 통신 회사들 간의 경쟁과 협력은 미국의 방송 산업을 만들어 냈다.

PARAPHRASE 1

The American broadcasting industry was established through rivalry and alliances among firms in the electronics and telecommunications industries initiated with the **introduction** of commercial radio programming in the early 20th century.

PARAPHRASE 2

With the **advent** of commercial radio programming in the early 1920s competitive-cooperative relations among electronics and telecommunications firms produced the American broadcasting industry.

114

068 confined

Day 07

Media and Communication

SYNONYMS adj. limited, restricted, narrow, finite, cramped   제한된, 한정된

confined
[kənfáind]

The authority of early theater owners to embody originality of the product was **confined** as ever, although they produced film programs through the combination of films and other entertainments in the way that caught the public fancy.

초기 극장주들은 청중들이 선호하는 방식으로 영화와 다른 오락물을 혼합한 필름 프로그램들을 제작하였지만, 작품의 창의성을 구현하기 위한 그들의 재량에는 여전히 한계가 있었다.

PARAPHRASE 1

Even though early theater operators made film programs by combining films with other entertainments in the way that attracted audiences most, their control over creativity was still **limited**.

PARAPHRASE 2

By mixing films with other entertainments in the manner that audiences preferred, early exhibitors created film programs, but their artistic control remained **restricted**.

069 perpetual

Day 07
Geology

| SYNONYMS | adj. | limitless, incessant, endless, ceaseless, permanent, lasting, constant, everlasting, enduring, continuous, persistent, continual, uninterrupted, unceasing, infinite, boundless, unlimited | 영구적인, 끊임없는, 무한한 |

perpetual
[pərpétʃuəl]

Any scenery is just a transitory phase in the **perpetual** struggle between rises and falls of the Earth's crust because dynamic weather phenomena break exposed rocks down into particles, which are carried away and eventually accumulated over time.

활발한 날씨 현상은 노출된 바위를 입자들로 분해하고 이는 운반의 과정을 거쳐 결국 오랜 시간동안 축적되기 때문에, 풍경은 지구 지각의 융기와 침강 사이의 지속적인 분투의 일시적인 단계일 뿐이다.

PARAPHRASE 1

Since rocks exposed on the surface are fragmented, carried away and subsequently deposited over a long period of time, any of Earth's landscapes are only a passing stage of the **limitless** surface deformations caused by tectonic forces.

PARAPHRASE 2

Any landscape is only a step in the **incessant** tectonic activities in which exposed rocks are smashed, carried away and subsequently deposited over billions of years.

070 involve

Archaeology

SYNONYMS v. include, contain, encompass, entail, embrace, hold, accommodate, lodge, make room for, comprise, embody, cover

포함하다, 수용하다

involve
[invάlv]

Even though crucial discoveries made in Egypt in 1989 were mostly incomplete frameworks of bones, the skeletons in an archaeocyte exceptionally involved a complete hind leg.

1989년 이집트에서의 주요한 발견들은 대개 불완전한 뼈대들이었지만, 원시세포에서 발견된 뼈대들은 예외적으로 완전한 뒷다리를 포함하고 있었다.

PARAPHRASE 1

Most skeletons found in Egypt in the late twentieth century were usually incomplete, but those of an archaeocyte were exceptional as a complete hind leg was included.

PARAPHRASE 2

Unlike the frameworks of bones discovered in Egypt in the late 20th century, a complete hind leg was contained in an archaeocyte.

117

DAILY CHECK-UP

A. Find the answer that is closest in meaning to the highlighted word or phrase in the sentence.

01. The architects have **shaped** constructions in consideration of locally available materials.

    (A) devised   (B) contemplated

02. Democrats believed that state and church should be strictly **segregated** and desperately objected to humanitarian law.

    (A) federated   (B) separated

03. **Comprehensive** irrigation in the area with poor drainage instigates the soil salinization.

    (A) Austere   (B) Extensive

04. **Radiance** is increased by the cooling of the outer layers of gas, which allows celestial bodies to become red and large.

    (A) Luminosity   (B) Acme

05. Technologically inadequate earlier efforts such as **weak** sound recordings would always happen again.

    (A) abysmal   (B) delicate

06. Films became the supreme form of mass consumption with the **influx** of projection.

    (A) mainstay   (B) advent

07. Fine-art objects barely have a functional purpose, so they are solely **restricted** in the light of the available materials.

    (A) limited   (B) contracted

08. Although waterpower in Lancashire and Scotland was abundant, it was barely suitable for **enduring** operation of machines.

    (A) infirm   (B) persistent

09. The myths **encompass** spiritual beings that are praised and hope to be affected by the rituals.

(A) disengage (B) comprise

10. Mill workers **abominated** the use of the factory clock that made them obey the sound of a bell and thus become living machines.

(A) forged (B) loathed

B. Complete each sentence using one of the words or phrases given.

11. As a white dwarf cools, its _____ will fall away until it stops to release visible rays.

(A) brightness (B) deviation

12. The semiarid areas bounding the deserts are ecologically _____ and thus have a hard time keeping balance.

(A) resilient (B) frail

13. Valuable information on cetacean origins was offered by the Pakicetus fossil even though _____ to a skull.

(A) immersed (B) limited

14. The _____ of the sense of beauty has fairly contributed to the growth of theaters in autonomous regions.

(A) impetus (B) appearance

15. Electric wiring, a cooling apparatus and plumbing are _____ in the equipment.

(A) contained (B) intrigued

16. Architects should _____ structures that provide inspiration and enjoyment.

(A) dismantle (B) fabricate

---

01. (A) 02. (B) 03. (B) 04. (A) 05. (B) 06. (B) 07. (A) 08. (B) 09. (B) 10. (B)
11. (A) 12. (B) 13. (B) 14. (B) 15. (A) 16. (B)

071 thrive

Day 08
Paleontology

SYNONYMS v. flourish, prosper, blossom, boom, succeed, bloom

번성하다, 번영하다

thrive
[θraiv]

Mass extinctions have occurred several times, but paleontologists have always been fascinated by the Cretaceous mass extinction since it marks the demise of the dinosaurs that once **thrived** but abruptly slipped away.

대량 멸종은 여러 차례 있어왔지만, 백악기 대량 멸종이 언제나 고생물학자들을 매료시켰던 것은 한때 번영했다가 갑자기 사라져버린 공룡들의 멸종을 다루고 있기 때문이다.

PARAPHRASE 1

Although there have been several mass extinctions, the Cretaceous mass extinction has captivated paleontologists at all times as it represented the end of the era of dinosaurs that had **flourish**ed but suddenly vanished.

PARAPHRASE 2

Despite several mass extinctions, paleontologists have always been enchanted by the Cretaceous mass extinction of the dinosaurs that had **prosper**ed but abruptly disappeared.

072 comparatively

Geology

SYNONYMS adv. relatively, by comparison   비교적, 꽤

comparatively
[kəmpǽrətivli]

Mountains and hills that withstand the devastating natural forces with success are frequently considered as the embodiment of perpetuity, but they are apt to be comparatively short-lived in terms of geological time.

파괴적인 자연력을 성공적으로 견뎌낸 산과 언덕은 종종 영속성의 전형으로 여겨지지만 지질 연대의 측면에서는 비교적 수명이 짧은 편이다.

PARAPHRASE 1

Mountains and hills exist for a relatively short period of geological time even though they appear to be a symbol of permanence, considering their resistance to the destructive power of nature.

PARAPHRASE 2

Although mountains and hills seem to exist eternally, they tend to be geologically ephemeral by comparison.

073 afford

Day 08
Marine Biology

SYNONYMS v. provide, furnish, supply, give, impart, render, restore, replenish, renew, refill, endow

공급하다, 보충하다

afford
[əfɔ́ːrd]

Some species of tuna that have large, high tails with back-tilted tips are the envy of engineers on account of their stunning adaptations that **afford** them a maximum of propulsion at a minimum of effort.

끝이 뒤로 젖혀진 크고 높은 꼬리를 갖고 있는 일부 참치 종들은, 최소의 노력으로 최대의 추진력을 제공해 주는 놀라운 적응력으로 엔지니어들의 부러움을 산다.

PARAPHRASE 1

Some tuna that have large, high tails with reflexed tips are the object of engineers' envy due to their perfect adaptations **provid**ing the maximum propulsion with the minimum effort.

PARAPHRASE 2

Engineers envy some species of tuna with specialized tails that **furnish** them with the maximum propulsion for the least effort.

074 simultaneously

Day 08

Anthropology

SYNONYMS adv. concurrently, at the same time 　　동시에

simultaneously
[sàiməltéiniəsli]

Simultaneously, workers were asked to get rid of old habits by reason that industrialism necessitated those who were bright, credible, and self-controlled.

동시에, 산업주의는 영리하고 신뢰할 만 하며 자제력 있는 일꾼을 필요로 했기 때문에, 노동자들은 옛 습관을 버려야 했다.

PARAPHRASE 1

Concurrently, industrialism, which needed those who were sharp, reliable, and self-disciplined, required workers to discard old habits.

PARAPHRASE 2

At the same time, as industrialism expected workers to be alert, trusty, and abstemious, they had to drop old habits.

075 outstanding

World History

SYNONYMS **adj.** preeminent, supreme, paramount, magnificent, great, superb, foremost, utmost, premier, optimum, crowning, ultimate, prime, brilliant, hellacious, sparkling

최고의, 최상의, 뛰어난

outstanding
[àutstǽndiŋ]

The main factor that enabled the Byzantine Empire to become the most powerful economy in the Mediterranean area for several centuries stemmed from the outstanding geographical location of its capital, Constantinople.

비잔틴 제국을 수세기 동안 지중해 지역의 가장 강력한 경제 대국으로 만든 주요한 원인은 제국의 수도인 콘스탄티노플의 최상의 지리적 위치에서 기인한다.

PARAPHRASE 1

The robust economy of the Byzantine Empire was established on the basis of the preeminent geographic position of the imperial capital, Constantinople.

PARAPHRASE 2

The supreme location of Constantinople, the capital city of the Byzantine Empire, contributed greatly to the imperial economic growth.

076 barren — Botany

SYNONYMS *adj.* sterile, infertile, unproductive, fruitless, unprolific, lifeless

불모의, 불임의

barren
[bǽrən]

Most spores of ferns and mosses are carried farther away by wind or water and eventually settle down on barren ground. On the other hand, only a few are deposited on land suitable for plant growth and begin new life.

대부분의 양치 식물과 이끼류의 포자는 바람과 물에 의해 멀리 운반되어 결국 불모의 땅에 떨어진다. 반면, 일부만이 식물 성장에 적합한 땅에 도달해 새 생명을 싹 틔운다.

PARAPHRASE 1

Only a few spores of ferns and mosses fall on hospitable locations and begin germinating, while the vast majority of them carried further afield by wind or water settle down on sterile ground.

PARAPHRASE 2

Whereas most spores of ferns and mosses spread out further are deposited on infertile land, a few of them fall on favorable ground.

077 barrier
Geography

Day 08

SYNONYMS n. obstacle, obstruction, barricade, blockade, block, hindrance, deterrent, impediment, difficulty, limitation, confinement, restriction, constraint, bar

장애물, 장벽, 제약

barrier
[bǽriər]

The Wilmington Field in Long Beach, California, has sunken approximately ten meters over nearly five decades, so there has been an urgent need to build protective **barriers** to prohibit salt water from inundating the region.

캘리포니아 롱비치에 위치한 윌밍턴 필드의 거의 50년에 걸친 대략 10미터의 지반 침하는, 해수 범람을 막아 줄 보호 장벽의 건설을 시급하게 요구했다.

PARAPHRASE 1

The demand for protective **obstacles** to prevent the area from being deluged with seawater has increased since the Wilmington Field has undergone substantial subsidence over several decades.

PARAPHRASE 2

Obstructions are urgently needed to be installed to protect the Wilmington Field, which has significantly subsided, against the overflow of seawater.

078 profound

Day 08
Forestry

SYNONYMS **adj.** weighty, deep, abysmal   심오한

profound
[prəfáund]

Trees and other plants have grown, undergoing a **profound** transformation regardless of whether the timberline is upper or lower.

수목한계선이 위쪽이든 아래쪽이든 상관없이, 나무들과 그밖의 식물들은 심오한 변화를 겪으면서 성장해왔다.

PARAPHRASE 1

At the tree line, whether upper or lower, trees and other plants have gone through an **weighty** transition in their growth.

PARAPHRASE 2

Whether the tree line is upper or lower, a **deep** alteration has occurred in tree growth.

079 inhospitable

Day 08 — Ecology

SYNONYMS *adj.* hostile, antagonistic, offensive, militant, inimical, aggressive, furious, vicious, fierce, ferocious, intimidating, unfavorable, threatening, unfriendly, opposed, menacing, adverse, negative

공격적인, 위협적인, 적대적인, 비우호적인

inhospitable
[inhάspitəbəl]

Spartina forces tidelands to be converted into high marshes **inhospitable** to a large number of indigenous species such as fish and birds that rely on the mudflats, which can bring up severe problems.

스파르티나는 개펄을 그것에 의존하는 어류와 조류와 같은 많은 토착종들에게 위협적인 높은 습지대로 바꾸어 놓았고, 이는 심각한 문제를 불러일으킬 수 있다.

PARAPHRASE 1

Serious problems can arise from Spartina, which transforms mudflats into high marshes **hostile** to a lot of native species.

PARAPHRASE 2

Spartina, which alters mudflats into high marshes **antagonistic** to many native species, can cause serious problems.

080 adaptable

Ornithology

Day 08

SYNONYMS **adj.** flexible, versatile, adjustable, pliable, malleable, all-around, plastic, resilient

융통성 있는, 적응성 있는, 유연한

adaptable
[ədǽptəbəl]

Many bird species have physical characteristics that have occurred as a result of adaptations to cope with their environment that allow them to be the most **adaptable** among wild creatures on the planet.

대부분의 조류 종들은 그들의 환경을 극복하기 위한 적응의 결과로 발생한 신체적 특징들을 갖고 있으며, 이는 그들을 지구상에서 가장 적응력 있는 생물들로 만들었다.

PARAPHRASE 1

Most birds that have adapted to their environmental changes have unique physical attributes that make them the most **flexible** wild animal on Earth.

PARAPHRASE 2

Physical features that most birds have evolved through adaptations to their environment enable them to be the most **versatile** wildlife on Earth.

DAILY CHECK-UP

A. Find the answer that is closest in meaning to the highlighted word or phrase in the sentence.

01. Eating food at restaurants **provides** people with chances to taste diverse foods.
    (A) percolates　　　　　　　(B) supplies

02. **Great** paintings in the Lascaux Cave reveal that ancient people were not unskillful, unintelligent, or insensible.
    (A) commodious　　　　　　(B) magnificent

03. Two of the most ancient kinds of terrestrial plants, ferns and mosses, **thrive** even in clefts in the rocks.
    (A) flourish　　　　　　　　(B) abate

04. **Simultaneously**, the first printing press operated by steam allowed for the mass production of books.
    (A) as a rule of thumb　　　　(B) at the same time

05. Drenching rains gradually soften the harsh, **lifeless** surfaces of the black rocks.
    (A) crowning　　　　　　　(B) sterile

06. A sediment-laden river flows from a mountain valley to **comparatively** even ground.
    (A) relatively　　　　　　　(B) inadvertently

07. With the use of the camel, the desert as a **hindrance** was turned into a still challenging but more passable path of trade.
    (A) deterrent　　　　　　　(B) navigation

08. It was not until the discovery of the remains of large land animals that scientists viewed the area as **unfriendly** to humans.
    (A) unceasing　　　　　　　(B) intimidating

09. James Watt devised a swift, **malleable**, fuel-efficient engine in the mid eighteenth century.

   (A) ludicrous   (B) pliable

10. The technological shift gives rise to **deep** changes in complex African societies.

   (A) ferocious   (B) profound

B. Complete each sentence using one of the words or phrases given.

11. Egyptians crossed the Pacific and constructed the _____ civilizations of the New World.

   (A) despondent   (B) crowning

12. Although volcanoes almost always erupt, it is a novelty that the eruption of four adjoining volcanoes happened _____ .

   (A) concurrently   (B) tentatively

13. The _____ of ice forced people to move in a southward direction.

   (A) manifestation   (B) barrier

14. The camel, capable of _____ in the harsh desert environment, was an effective means of transportation.

   (A) endowing   (B) thriving

15. Increasing populations have suppressed the land's ability to _____ food and fuel for them.

   (A) grasp   (B) furnish

16. Compared with the screen images, the images viewers saw in the earlier peepshows were tiny in size _____ .

   (A) by comparison x   (B) reciprocally

---

01. (B) 02. (B) 03. (A) 04. (B) 05. (B) 06. (A) 07. (A) 08. (B) 09. (B) 10. (B)
11. (B) 12. (A) 13. (B) 14. (B) 15. (B) 16. (A)

081 propagate

Day 09

Botany

SYNONYMS v. reproduce, breed, multiply, spawn   번식하다

propagate
[prάpəgèit]

Short-lived plants such as dandelions have a tendency to **propagate** prolifically in the way that a persistent rain of seeds on the periphery of parent plants is supplied.

민들레와 같은 단명하는 식물들은 모체 식물 주변에 지속적으로 씨를 뿌리는 방식으로 다량 번식하는 경향이 있다.

PARAPHRASE 1

Plants such as dandelions that do not last very long tend to **reproduce** prolifically by scattering a steady rain of seeds in the vicinity of parent plants.

PARAPHRASE 2

Ephemeral dandelions are more likely to **breed** prolifically by distributing as many seeds as possible around parent plants.

082 precious

Agriculture

SYNONYMS adj. valuable, priceless, invaluable, dear, valued

귀중한

precious
[préʃəs]

In the respect that dried animal refuse, regarded as a **precious** natural fertilizer and a source of vegetative nourishment, is no longer going back to the soil, the land has been unfavorably affected by an increase in its use as an alternative energy source.

귀중한 천연 비료이자 식물 양분의 원천인 말린 동물 분뇨가 더 이상 토양으로 돌아가지 않게 된다는 점에서, 대체 에너지로서 말린 동물 분뇨의 사용 증가는 토양에 해를 입힌다.

PARAPHRASE 1

The land has been harmed by the increased use of dried animal excrement as an alternative fuel in that this **valuable** natural manure and source of vegetative nourishment is not turned back to the soil anymore.

PARAPHRASE 2

An increase in the use of dried animal feces as a substitute energy source has led to soil degradation, as this **priceless** manure and basis of plant development is no longer utilized for the land.

083 relevant

Day 09
Psychology

SYNONYMS *adj.* applicable, pertinent, germane, cognate   관련된

relevant
[rélǝvǝnt]

One of the plausible explanations as to why people hardly recollect experiences before the age of three has a lot to do with physiological alterations relevant to the ability to remember.

사람들이 세 살 이전의 경험을 거의 기억하지 못하는 이유에 대한 그럴듯한 설명들 중 하나는 기억력에 관한 생리학적 변화와 관련이 깊다.

PARAPHRASE 1 People have a dim memory of events that happened to them in their early years and this stems from physiological fluctuations applicable to recollection.

PARAPHRASE 2 Physiological changes pertinent to recall are one of the major causes of infantile amnesia.

084 routinely

World History

SYNONYMS adv. generally, commonly, usually, largely, mostly, mainly, chiefly, primarily, predominantly, typically, regularly, habitually, normally, ordinarily, in general, on the whole, as a rule of thumb

일반적으로, 대개, 주로

routinely
[ruːtíːnli]

It was not until the middle of the sixteenth century that bills of exchange in substitute for gold or silver to exchange for purchasing other commodities were **routinely** received by financial capitalists and merchants.

16세기 중반이 되어서야 환어음이 금이나 은을 대신하여 상품 구매의 일반적인 교환 수단으로 금융업자들과 상인들에게 받아들여졌다.

PARAPHRASE 1

Not until the middle of the sixteenth century did moneylenders and dealers **generally** adopt drafts on behalf of gold or silver as a means of buying products.

PARAPHRASE 2

Money brokers and tradespeople **commonly** used drafts in lieu of gold or silver in order to purchase other goods by the mid-1500s.

085 intact

Day 09
Ecology

| SYNONYMS adj. | undamaged, unaffected, complete, uninjured, unimpaired, unbroken, sound, whole, entire, perfect, consummate | 손상되지 않은, 온전한 |

intact
[intǽkt]

The niche unoccupied by the extinct species can be nearly filled by the new population, which is different from the previous one, but can make the food web intact.

멸종된 종에 의해 비워진 틈은 새로운 종으로 채워지며, 이는 이전의 종과는 다름에도 불구하고 먹이 사슬을 손상되지 않은 채로 유지될 수 있게 한다.

PARAPHRASE 1

Even though the new species is of a distinct species, it can approximately fill the gap vacated by the extinct species and can keep the food chain undamaged.

PARAPHRASE 2

The new population, though dissimilar to the earlier one, can almost fill the vacancy of the extinct species, letting the food chain remain unaffected.

086 deluxe

World History — Day 09

SYNONYMS adj. luxurious, lavish, extravagant, opulent, rich, splendid, sumptuous

호화로운, 사치스러운

deluxe
[dəlʌ́ks]

It is well-known that while Rome was in flames, the Roman Emperor Nero took no concrete action and used the devastated land for building his deluxe palace, putting the blame for the large scale fire on the Christians he oppressed.

로마의 황제 네로는 로마가 불타는 동안 아무것도 하지 않았고 그 황폐해진 땅에 그의 호화로운 궁전을 지었으며, 화재의 탓을 그가 박해했던 기독교인들에게로 돌린 것으로 유명하다.

PARAPHRASE 1

The Emperor Nero is famous for watching Rome burn, constructing his luxurious palace in the devastated region, and ascribing the conflagration to the Christians.

PARAPHRASE 2

Nero is noted for building his lavish palace in the ruined area, attributing the big fire to the Christians, without taking proper measures against the conflagration.

087 boundary

Day 09 | Energy

SYNONYMS n. edge, margin, border, bound, limit, verge, precinct, periphery, rim, fringe

경계, 가장자리

boundary
[báundəri]

With the introduction of offshore drilling platforms, petroleum exploration was extended to the continental shelves which are gradually sloping areas below the surface of the sea at the **boundari**es of the continents.

연안 시추대의 도입으로, 석유 탐사는 대륙 가장자리의 경사가 완만한 지역인 대륙붕으로 확장되었다.

PARAPHRASE 1

Platforms used for offshore drilling made it possible to enlarge oil-search operations to the continental shelves, gently sloping submarine regions at the **edge**s of the continents.

PARAPHRASE 2

Drilling platforms off the coast expanded oil exploration to the continental shelves, rolling submarine regions around the continental **margin**s.

088 estimate

Pedagogy

| SYNONYMS | v. | calculate, speculate, gauge, measure, assume, suppose, presume, extrapolate, believe, determine, figure, project |

추산하다, 추정하다, 측정하다, 여기다

estimate
[éstəmèit]

The researchers **estimate** that for the basic training, the same teachers required almost 30 hours to look at situations objectively and the same amount of time was needed to practice the reflection skills.

연구자들이 추정하기를, 기본적인 훈련 과정에서 같은 교사들의 상황을 객관적으로 파악하는 데에는 거의 30시간이 필요하며, 생활 기술을 연마하는 데에도 동일한 양의 시간이 필요하다.

PARAPHRASE 1

The researchers **calculate** that the same teachers needed the same amount of time not only to receive the initial training to take an objective view of events but also to master the skills of reflection.

PARAPHRASE 2

The researchers **speculate** that training the same teachers to view matters objectively and to practice the skills of reflection required the same number of hours.

089 enhance

Oceanography

SYNONYMS v. improve, intensify, upgrade, enrich, better, ameliorate, refine, reform

개선하다, 향상시키다

enhance
[enhǽns]

The swimming machines such as tunas, mackerels and billfish (←minor idea) change almost all aspects of the shape and function of their body in order to enhance the ability to swim.

참치, 고등어, 주둥이가 긴 물고기 등의 수영 기계들은, 수영 능력을 향상시키기 위해 그들의 신체 형태와 기능의 거의 모든 측면을 바꾼다.

PARAPHRASE 1

Various aspects of the body shape and function of the swimming machines are adapted to improve swimming ability.

PARAPHRASE 2

In order to intensify swimming capacity, the swimming machines adjust their body form and function.

090 encroachment

Environmental Science

SYNONYMS n. intrusion, invasion, incursion, raid, violation, foray

침범, 침입

encroachment
[enkróutʃmənt]

Human populations expanded urban and suburban areas, which has brought about the **encroachment** on animals' habitats and sharp reductions in accessible sources of food.

인간은 도시와 교외 지역을 확장했고 이는 동물 서식지 침범과 접근 가능한 식량 원의 현저한 감소를 불러 일으켰다.

PARAPHRASE 1

Human **intrusion** into wildlife habitats and remarkable decreases in available sources of food have resulted from enlargement of urban and suburban regions.

PARAPHRASE 2

Expansion of urban areas and suburbs has increased human **invasion** of wildlife habitats and considerably shrunk available sources of food.

DAILY CHECK-UP

A. Find the answer that is closest in meaning to the highlighted word or phrase in the sentence.

01. A type of natural region **largely** called alpine tundra exists above the timberline.
    (A) concurrently (B) mainly

02. The plants that have a lesser chance of survival of an individual spore tend to produce a lot of spores to **multiply**.
    (A) embody (B) breed

03. Humans prefer constructions that will protect them and **enrich** their way of life by instinct.
    (A) improve (B) seclude

04. The major threats to wildlife habitat are agricultural **intrusion** and deforestation.
    (A) encroachment (B) prominence

05. Oilfields are composed of one or more oil pools that are **invaluable** subsurface accumulations of petroleum.
    (A) precious (B) brittle

06. During the dry season, the **border** areas have a hard time adapting to strains caused by settlement.
    (A) obstruction (B) boundary

07. It has been **assumed** that this process poses a threat to an extra one-fourth of the surface of the Earth.
    (A) supposed (B) limited

08. Since the transportation of goods imported over the Silk Road was difficult, the commodities were limited to **extravagant** items.
    (A) perilous (B) luxurious

09. A huge amount of information **relevant** to how volcanos are formed and what caused them has been produced in the field of modern geophysics.

(A) inimical (B) germane

10. **Unimpaired** habitats are more likely to prohibit the proliferation of contagious agents.

    (A) Undamaged (B) Resilient

B. Complete each sentence using one of the words or phrases given.

11. In order to _____ , ferns and lichens produce spores including all the directions essential for new life.

    (A) reproduce (B) demise

12. To _____ audiences' pleasure, storytellers continue to make stories more entertaining and memorable.

    (A) intensify (B) contrive

13. Over the centuries, Teotihuacan obsidian in the Maya region has certainly been acknowledged as a _____ product.

    (A) sumptuous (B) priceless

14. It is _____ that orangutan populations native to the Indian Ocean islands of Sumatra dwindled by 50%.

    (A) estimated (B) contemplated

15. Psychologists contend that emotional status is _____ reflected by facial expressions.

    (A) predominantly (B) tentatively

16. In spite of intermittent foreign _____ and reigns, China is one of the oldest surviving civilizations.

    (A) impediments (B) invasions

01. (B) 02. (B) 03. (A) 04. (A) 05. (A) 06. (B) 07. (A) 08. (B) 09. (B) 10. (A)
11. (A) 12. (A) 13. (B) 14. (A) 15. (A) 16. (B)

091 set

Day 10
Sociology

SYNONYMS **adj.** fixed, settled, agreed, planned, arranged, resolved, established, decided

합의된, 고정된

set
[set]

A group which becomes aware that particular actions conducted by the group are explicitly related to its intended consequences repeats, polishes and publicizes those actions into **set** ceremonies.

자신들이 행하는 특정 행동과 의도하는 결과 사이에 명백한 연관성이 있음을 인식했을 때, 한 집단은 그 행동들을 반복하고 개선함으로써 합의된 의식으로 공식화 한다.

PARAPHRASE 1

Acknowledging an evident relation between specific deeds a group does and the outcome it intends, the group reiterates, improves and formalizes those deeds into **fixed** rituals.

PARAPHRASE 2

In a group that recognizes a definite connection between certain of its acts and ensuing results, those acts are formalized as **settled** rites through repetition and refinement.

092 attribute

Hydrology — Day 10

SYNONYMS v. ascribe, impute, refer, credit, assign, put down

~의 탓(덕분)으로 돌리다

attribute
[ətríbjuːt]

The color of green icebergs is **attribute**d to an optical illusion when a near-horizon red Sun illuminates blue ice, while green icebergs stick out among white and blue icebergs under considerably diverse light conditions.

녹색 빙산의 빛깔은 지평선 근처의 붉은 태양이 비추는 푸른색 빙산으로 인한 환영 때문이지만, 상당히 다양한 빛 아래에서도 녹색 빙산은 다른 색의 빙산보다 더 눈에 띈다.

PARAPHRASE 1

Under a wide variety of light conditions, green icebergs stand out more than other colored icebergs although their color is **ascribe**d to a visual illusion arising from blue ice lit up by a near-horizon red Sun.

PARAPHRASE 2

Green icebergs seem different from others under various light conditions, but their color is **impute**d to be an optical illusion under particular light conditions.

145

093 barely

Anthropology

SYNONYMS adv. rarely, scarcely, hardly, seldom, infrequently

거의 ~않다

barely
[béərli]

Most Upper Paleolithic people seemed to think that painting human forms could result in injury or death, and if they really believed that, it might account for why images portrayed in cave art **barely** include human figures.

대부분의 후기 구석기 시대 사람들은 사람을 그리는 것이 부상 또는 사망을 초래할 수 있다고 믿었던 것 같다. 만일 정말로 그렇게 믿었다면, 이는 왜 동굴 벽화에 그려진 이미지가 인간의 형상을 거의 포함하고 있지 않은지를 설명해 줄 수 있다.

PARAPHRASE 1

The assumption that Upper Paleolithic people believed that injury or death could be caused by drawing human figures might help us to get a better understanding of why human images were **rarely** portrayed in cave art.

PARAPHRASE 2

If Upper Paleolithic people thought that the portrayal of human figures could have inauspicious consequences, why their cave art **scarcely** contains human images might be explained.

094 assort

SYNONYMS v. categorize, classify, sort, group, class, label, separate, arrange

분류하다

assort
[əsɔ́ːrt]

Dandelions are **assort**ed into opportunistic species of plants since they depend on their seeds being scattered in spaces where natural processes have eliminated rival plants within the environment.

민들레는 같은 환경 내의 경쟁 식물들이 자연적인 과정에 의해 제거된 공간에 씨앗을 뿌리기 때문에, 기회종으로 분류된다.

PARAPHRASE 1

Dandelions, whose seeds grow in places where competing plants have been eradicated by natural phenomena, are **categorize**d as an opportunistic species of plants.

PARAPHRASE 2

Dandelions are **classifi**ed as opportunistic plants in that their seeds develop in areas where rival plants no longer exist.

095 collide

SYNONYMS v. bump, smash, clash, crash, hit

충돌하다, 부딪히다

collide
[kəláid]

The Earth's crust is separated into large, movable plates which drift on a weak, malleable layer of rock and collide into each other and thrust up the rock around the plate boundaries, causing the formation of some mountains.

지구의 지각은 움직이는 거대한 판들로 이루어져 있으며, 이들은 연약하고 모양이 쉽게 변하는 암석층 위를 표류하다 서로 충돌하고 판 경계에서 암석을 밀어 올린다. 이는 결과적으로 일부 산맥의 형성을 야기한다.

PARAPHRASE 1

Floating upon a soft and pliable rock layer, huge movable plates of the Earth's crust bump into each other and force up the rock at the plate borders, shaping some mountains.

PARAPHRASE 2

Some mountains are shaped as a result of plates of the Earth surface which roam on a plastic rock layer and smash into each other and push up the rock at the plate margins.

096 collaboration

Pedagogy

| SYNONYMS | n. | cooperation, teamwork, alliance, association, coalition, confederation, confederacy, ally, affiliation, union, combination | 협력, 협동, 연합 |

collaboration
[kəlǽbərèiʃən]

Wildman and Niles reached a conclusion that reflective practices require instructors to make arduous efforts to obtain abundant resources, not to mention to step up the encouragement and collaboration of others.

윌드만과 나일즈는 반성적 실천을 위해 교사들간 격려와 협력 강화는 말할 것도 없고 풍부한 자원을 얻기 위한 끈질긴 노력이 요구된다는 결론에 도달했다.

PARAPHRASE 1

Wildman and Niles came to a conclusion that copious resources as well as stimulation and cooperation among instructors are required for reflective practices.

PARAPHRASE 2

Wildman and Niles found that not only motivation and teamwork among teachers but also ample resources are crucial for reflective practices.

149

097 important

Day 10
Ecology

SYNONYMS *adj.* significant, crucial, key, critical, essential, indispensable, central, imperative

중요한

important
[impɔ́ːrtənt]

As the short growth phase and low temperature make it hard for tree shoots to attain full maturity to withstand the harsh season, temperature is considered the most **important** component in the environment.

짧은 성장기와 낮은 기온은 나무의 새싹들이 혹독한 계절을 견뎌낼 만큼 충분히 성장하는 것을 어렵게 만들기 때문에, 기온은 환경에서 가장 중요한 구성 요소로 여겨진다.

PARAPHRASE 1

One of the most **significant** environmental factors is temperature since the growing period is too short and temperatures are too low for tree buds to develop enough to survive the harsh season.

PARAPHRASE 2

Temperature is the most **crucial** environmental element, for tree buds can grow fully under favorable conditions: ample growth period and adequate temperatures.

098 mundane

Day 10
Geology

SYNONYMS **adj.** ordinary, common, routine, commonplace, unexceptional, normal, mediocre, average, moderate

보통의, 평범한

mundane
[mʌndéin]

In a small village in England, a boy with the **mundane** name of William Smith who was born in 1769 as the son of a poor blacksmith became a world-renowned geologist.

1976년 영국의 작은 마을에서 가난한 대장장이의 아들로 태어난 윌리엄 스미스라는 평범한 이름의 소년은 세계적으로 유명한 지질학자가 되었다.

PARAPHRASE 1

Born to a poor blacksmith's family in England in 1769, a child with the **ordinary** name of William Smith grew into a world-famous geologist.

PARAPHRASE 2

A world-famed geologist with the **common** name of William Smith was born in 1769 to a poor blacksmith's family who lived in England.

099 phenomenon

Day 10
Biology

SYNONYMS **n.** occurrence, appearance, episode, event, incident, happening, occasion, affair

사건, 현상

phenomenon
[finɔ́mənən]

The genesis of the first living organisms on the Hawaiian Islands is intertwined with symbiosis, a **phenomenon** that relies on a collaborative relationship between two or more life forms.

하와이 제도의 최초의 생명체의 기원은 둘 또는 그 이상의 생명체들 간 협력 관계에 의존하는 현상인 공생과 밀접하게 관련되어 있다.

PARAPHRASE 1

On the Hawaiian Islands, the first organisms are closely connected with symbiosis, an **occurrence** that is dependent on a close collaboration among unlike organisms.

PARAPHRASE 2

The earliest creatures on the Hawaiian Islands are tightly linked to symbiosis, an **appearance** that depends on a close interaction of different species.

100 intermittently

Day 10 — Geography

SYNONYMS **adj.** occasionally, sporadically, periodically, infrequently, irregularly, at times, at intervals, now and then, once in a while, from time to time

때때로, 간헐적으로

intermittently
[intərmítəntli]

Even though most streambeds in deserts are dehydrated most of the time, they intermittently obtain large-scale streams of water and sediment deposits.

사막의 대부분의 강바닥 대부분은 일반적으로 바짝 말라있지만, 간헐적으로 대규모의 물과 침전물유입되기도 한다.

PARAPHRASE 1

Although most desert riverbeds are generally parched, occasionally they gain massive flows of water and deposition.

PARAPHRASE 2

Huge streams of water and deposits are sporadically brought into desert streambeds which are mostly dry.

DAILY CHECK-UP

A. Find the answer that is closest in meaning to the highlighted word or phrase in the sentence.

01. The causes for the recovery of high population numbers are **attributed** to other human activities.

    (A) credited (B) established

02. A massive object **collided** with Earth and quickly ended the dinosaurs' reign.

    (A) crashed (B) ameliorated

03. The Sitka black-tailed deer is **labeled** as a subspecies of the mule deer of the American West.

    (A) extrapolated (B) classed

04. Other kinds of evidence to validate this **occurrence** are provided by cave paintings.

    (A) phenomenon (B) affiliation

05. **Fixed** schedules travel agencies provide make people visit too many spots in a day.

    (A) planned (B) sustained

06. Events recurring **sporadically** in the environment generally blend in with the activity of animals.

    (A) predominantly (B) periodically

07. People hardly recall **routine** events they underwent during their infancy and toddler periods either.

    (A) ordinary (B) applicable

08. A further **important** consideration is that the maker of applied-art objects should be sensitive to physical laws.

    (A) significant (B) opulent

09. A sense of security is accomplished through **association** with those who are important to us.

(A) precinct (B) cooperation

10. Teachers **hardly** have time to observe their own lessons objectively.
    (A) seldom (B) exclusively

B. Complete each sentence using one of the words or phrases given.

11. Wind turbines are _____ according to the amount of power they can produce as well as their size.
    (A) presumed (B) assorted

12. A pot with huge holes in its sides without a bottom could _____ be regarded as a container.
    (A) perpetually (B) scarcely

13. Volcanic eruptions are predicted on the basis of the investigation of natural _____.
    (A) phenomena (B) metamorphosis

14. Huge meteorites are universally known to have _____ into Earth twice as often as they did in the twentieth century.
    (A) smashed (B) consolidated

15. Most of the contemporary structures designed in a _____ manner are attributed to both architects and clients.
    (A) feeble (B) mediocre

16. Some _____ data associated with the extinction of the dinosaurs cannot be elucidated by a single alteration in climate.
    (A) commonplace (B) indispensable

---

01. (A) 02. (A) 03. (B) 04. (A) 05. (A) 06. (B) 07. (A) 08. (A) 09. (B) 10. (A)
11. (B) 12. (B) 13. (A) 14. (A) 15. (B) 16. (B)

REVIEW TEST (DAY 06-10)

A. The word ▢▢▢ in the passage is closest in meaning to

01. A competitor, which is the antithesis of an opportunist, is the collective term for organisms that have a tendency to be long-lived, have **massive** bodies and pour less energy into propagation. As a typical example of a competitor, a **sizable** oak tree not only outcompetes all other tree species which form the canopy as it soaks up the water from the soil and throws a dense shadow but also occupies its land for more than 200 years.

(a) patchy
(b) hellacious
(c) ferocious
(d) immense

02. Compared with products manufactured in factories, those created by the hands of the craftsmen were more likely to be exquisite and high quality, but their pride in craftsmanship was broken due to increasing pressure on productivity improvement. As a new trend in a business emphasized a **more stringent** sense of time, the work of the artisans was superseded by factories.

(a) more tedious
(b) keener
(c) more ardent
(d) stricter

03. James Watt's separate condenser, developed to improve on the design of the engine invented by Thomas Newcomen, was completed in the 1760s and then he **contrived** a method to spin a wheel by the piston. As a result, he could transform alternating motion into rotational motion, by which an inefficient pump used restrictively could be converted into a steam engine that is widely employed.

(a) obscured
(b) devoured
(c) devised
(d) eschewed

REVIEW TEST (DAY 06-10)

04. Wind power is the most cost-effective in places where the winds blow steadily, but it needs backup power in areas with inconsistent winds. For this reason, standby power is generally provided by an energy storage system or an electric utility company and sometimes by the connection between wind farms and a solar cell or pumping-up waterpower. In addition to this, there are some weaknesses related to wind farms **involving** noise and visual pollution.

(a) encompassing
(b) ingesting
(c) provoking
(d) scouring

05. What enables the deer to survive under the brutal weather conditions is by migrating from highland areas in summer to the low-lying grounds in winter in search of an adequate diet. All through the winter, the movement of deer increases accessibility and availability of food sources. Even during periods of extreme snow, these forests **furnish** deer with greater variety of tree canopies and levels of understory plant growth.

(a) subdue
(b) ramble
(c) quarry
(d) provide

06. In locations formerly unsuitable for plant cultivation, some hardy GMOs can make soil fertile and thus suddenly thrive. Besides, people can cultivate crops in previously **inhospitable** areas by creating plants that can endure high salinity in soil and water or prolonged periods of dry weather.

(a) vigilant
(b) unfavorable
(c) astute
(d) convincing

07. Cloning of human beings can be the most advantageous way to solve many kinds of issues related to infertility. For example, human cloning offers the great opportunity to produce a child to **infertile** couples. According to the Human Cloning Foundation, the parents who lost their baby right after birth due to unavoidable circumstances such as a fire or a car accident can have their perfect baby back through human cloning.

(a) impending
(b) resolute
(c) sterile
(d) inert

08. As an integral part in public health, for several decades, fluoride has been added to water in efforts to control tooth decay. In many regions, this is accepted as fact, and not to fluoridate water would be considered an **obstruction** to public health. However, many are now raising questions about the safety and success of such measures.

(a) wreckage
(b) manifestation
(c) dissemination
(d) hindrance

09. Additive sculptors utilize diverse soft and **flexible** materials, but clay is most commonly used. Unlike the subtractive process, artists can fix mistakes easily by adding or removing materials. This pliability gives sculptors great freedom in terms of artistic creativity. Moreover, the finished work serves as the model encased in hard materials such as plaster, so it can produce multiple copies of the sculpture with the same mold.

(a) staggering
(b) pliable
(c) eccentric
(d) outrageous

REVIEW TEST [DAY 06-10]

10. Two species of deer, the Columbian white-tailed deer and the Sitka black-tailed deer, have become widespread in the United States, particularly in the Puget Sound Washington region in the Pacific Northwest. The Former once was widely distributed in this area but is now only found in deciduous river bottomlands and densely forested swamps along the lower Columbia River. It has been mostly replaced by the latter, which is the most prevalent today and **primarily** inhabits temperate coniferous forests along the Pacific Coast.

    (a) exclusively
    (b) concurrently
    (c) utterly
    (d) predominantly

11. Prescribed fires boost the production of seeds, flowers and fruits, increasing fruits and nuts available for wildlife consumption. After fires, insects also **propagate** quickly. Irregular prescribed burns in different regions and in different seasons foster high levels of biodiversity with a diverse and large wildlife population.

    (a) pulverize
    (b) dismantle
    (c) multiply
    (d) explicate

12. Ever since people had started to analyze the rock layers in certain outcrops of rock, they had hoped to be able to utilize them for the purpose of measuring geological age. However, as the data about rock strata from various locales were collated more and more, it became evident that the patterns of rocks **sporadically** vary in different localities and that the type of rock was never going to be considered a trustworthy indicator of determining geological age all over the world.

    (a) progressively
    (b) prohibitively
    (c) intermittently
    (d) assiduously

13. In several states where prairie dogs inhabit, they have been **classified** as pests for a long time. Western farmers and ranchers have never had affection for prairie dogs because rodents such as prairie dogs do a large amount of damage to grassland and livestock there. Livestock owners feel that prairie dogs compete with domestic animals for prey, as they are both plant eaters.

(a) labeled
(b) subdued
(c) inaugurated
(d) bombarded

14. A society, which is at the incipient stage of development, become conscious of powers that seem to affect or regulate its well-being and food supply. However, unless the society has a proper understanding of natural factors, whether the matters are advantageous and disadvantageous, they may be **ascribed** to paranormal or magical powers, and it will attempt to look for means to get on good side of these powers

(a) overseen
(b) incriminated
(c) squeezed
(d) attributed

답안

| 01. (D) | 02. (D) | 03. (C) | 04. (A) | 05. (D) | 06. (B) | 07. (C) |
| 08. (D) | 09. (B) | 10. (D) | 11. (C) | 12. (C) | 13. (A) | 14. (D) |

REVIEW TEST [DAY 06-10]

B. Which of the sentences below best expresses the essential information in the highlighted sentence in the passage? Incorrect choices change the meaning in important ways or leave out essential information.

15. With the emergence of projection, the relationship between the viewer and the image was not private any more, compared with the viewer's relationship with earlier peepshow devices such as the Kinetoscope and the Mutoscope, which were machines that provided moving pictures that only one person at a time could look at through a small hole.

    (A) With the advent of projection, the relationship between the viewer and the image became similar to the one between the viewer and peepshow devices, providing moving pictures for only a person at a time.
    (B) The viewer's relationship with the image was no longer public with the advent of projection, as it had been with earlier peepshow devices.
    (C) Earlier peepshow devices such as the Kinetoscope and the Mutoscope showed moving pictures to only one person at a time, and if it were not for the advent of projection, the viewer's relationship with the image might be more public.
    (D) Unlike the viewer's relationship with earlier peepshow devices, providing moving pictures that only a person at a time could watch, the one with the image became public with the advent of projection.

해설 정답 (D)

① With the emergence of projection, the relationship between the viewer and the image was not private any more, compared with ② the viewer's relationship with earlier peepshow devices such as the Kinetoscope and the Mutoscope, which were machines that provided moving pictures that only one person at a time could look at through a small hole.
→ Unlike ② the viewer's relationship with earlier peepshow devices, providing moving pictures that only a person at a time could watch, ① the one with the

image became public with the advent of projection.

특정 시점을 기준으로 과거와 현재에 어떠한 변화가 발생했는가를 명확히 이해하였는지를 평가하는 문제로 원문의 ①과 ②의 두 개의 부분 사이의 관계는 '~와 비교해 볼 때'라는 의미를 갖고 있는 'compared with'을 통해 명확하게 알 수 있다. 이 두 개의 의미상의 부분은 서로 비교의 대상으로 'not private any more'라는 언급을 통해 프로젝션의 등장 이전과 이후의 상황이 달라졌음을 더 명확하게 알 수 있다. 따라서 paraphrase할 때에는 'compared with'가 이끄는 구문을 문두로 옮겨 ①과 ②의 두 부분이 의미상 반대의 아이디어를 포함하고 있음을 노골적으로 전달하기 위해 '~와 달리'라는 의미의 전치사 'unlike'를 활용하여 과거와 현재에 정반대의 변화가 발생했음을 언급할 수 있다.

> **오답의 근거**

(A) With the advent of projection, the relationship between the viewer and the image <u>became similar</u> to the one between the viewer and peepshow devices, providing moving pictures for only a person at a time.
→ 프로젝션의 등장을 기준으로 관객과 영상 사이의 관계에 발생한 변화를 언급하는 주요 내용을 잘못 언급한 오답이다. (became similar to → became less private than / became more public than)

(B) The viewer's relationship with the image <u>was no longer public</u> with the advent of projection, as it had been with earlier peepshow devices.
→ 프로젝션의 등장을 기준으로 관객과 영상 사이의 관계에 발생한 변화를 언급하는 주요 내용을 정반대로 언급한 오답이다. (was no longer public → was no longer private)

(C) Earlier peepshow devices such as the Kinetoscope and the Mutoscope showed moving pictures to only one person at a time, and <u>if it were not for the advent of projection, the viewer's relationship with the image might be more public</u>.
→ 보기의 밑줄 친 부분의 정보는 원문의 내용을 통해 유추할 수 없는 언급되지 않은 내용으로 오답이다.

> **다른 방식으로 paraphrase 하기**

① With the emergence of projection, the relationship between the viewer and the image was not private any more, compared with ② the viewer's relationship with earlier peepshow devices such as the Kinetoscope and the Mutoscope, which were machines that provided moving pictures that only one person at a time could look at through a small hole.

→ ① The introduction of projection allowed the viewer's relationship with the image to become more public, which was completely different from ②

REVIEW TEST [DAY 06-10]

the viewer's relationship with earlier peepshow devices, containing moving pictures showed to only one person at a time.
→ ② The viewer's relationship with earlier peepshow devices, which showed moving pictures to only one person at a time, was private, but ① the advent of projection made the viewer's relationship with the image more public.
→ ① The viewer's relationship with the image was no longer private with the advent of projection, as ② it had been with earlier peepshow devices, provided to only a person at a time.

원문 문장의 의미상 중심 내용을 주어로 사용하여 문장의 구조를 바꿀 수 있다. 원문에서 내용상 중심이 되는 'the introduction of projection'을 주어의 자리에 놓음으로써 문장 구조도 바뀌고 문장의 의미도 더욱 정확하게 할 수 있다. 주어의 자리에 무엇을 두느냐에 따라서 같은 의미의 문장을 다양하게 Paraphrase 할 수 있다. 이러한 과정은 'sentence variety'를 강조하는 영어의 특성상 말하기와 쓰기 실력의 향상에 있어 매우 유용한 방법이라고 볼 수 있다.

16. The fact that many neighboring farmers gained a fair margin of profit by cultivating crops that consumed a large amount of water caused some farmers who desired to save water to lose their enthusiasm, and in the process the entire region suffered from a sharp drop in water supplies.

    (A) Although some farmers wished to save water, many of their neighbors used a great deal of water for crop cultivation, resulting in severe water shortages in the region.
    (B) Despite the fact that many neighboring farmers made a huge profit by growing crops that consumed much water, some farmers tried to conserve water, and water supplies of the entire region progressively increased in the process.
    (C) Many neighbors profited greatly from cultivation of crops that needed a lot of water, which discouraged some farmers from saving water, causing a steep decline in the entire region's water supplies.
    (D) The enthusiasm of the farmers who tried to conserve water was encouraged by many farmers who made a profit by growing crops using much water, and water supplies in the entire region decreased in the process.

> 해설   정답 (C)

① The fact that many neighboring farmers gained a fair margin of profit by cultivating crops that consumed a large amount of water ② caused some farmers who desired to save water to lose their enthusiasm, and ③ in the process the entire region suffered from a sharp drop in water supplies.
→ ① Many neighbors profited greatly from cultivation of crops that needed a lot of water, which ② discouraged some farmers from saving water, ③ causing a steep decline in the entire region's water supplies.

하나의 사건이 다른 사건에 어떻게 영향을 주었는가를 명확히 이해하였는지를 평가하는 문제로 원문의 주부(①)와 술부(②)의 두 부분 사이의 관계는 '~을 야기하다'라는 의미의 동사 'cause'를 통해 서로 원인과 결과의 관계임을 명확히 알 수 있다. 또한 이 두 부분은 'in the process'라는 표현을 통해 더 나아가 ③의 결과를 초래하였음을 알 수 있다. 따라서 paraphrase할 때에는 원문의 주부였던 ①을 하나의 절로 바꾸고 그 절 전체를 받는 관계대명사 which를 사용하여 which 이하에 앞 절에 대한 결과를 언급하고, 원문의 and 이하의 ③의 내용은 앞 부분의 내용에 대한 결과를 나타낼 때 쓰는 현재 분사 구문의 형태로 바꾸어 문장을 재구성할 수 있다. 또한 이 과정에서 원문은 문장의 구조를 바꾸는 것뿐만 아니라 동의어나 동의어구를 활용하여 각각의 단어나 어구들을 표현한다거나 (ex. gained a fair margin of profit → profited, a sharp drop → a steep decline) 품사를 전환하는 방법 (ex. cultivating crops → cultivation of crops) 등을 통해 문장을 좀 더 다양하게 재진술 할 수 있다.

> 오답의 근거

(A) <u>Although</u> some farmers wished to save water, many of their neighbors used a great deal of water for crop cultivation, resulting in severe water shortages in the region.
→ '많은 이웃 농부들이 물을 많이 소비하는 작물을 재배하여 수익을 얻었고 이러한 사실은 물을 절약하고자 하는 일부 농부들의 의욕을 꺾었다'는 원문의 내용과는 달리 원인과 그것이 미친 결과에 대한 명확한 규명이 없으므로 틀린 내용으로 오답이다.

(B) <u>Despite</u> the fact that many neighboring farmers made a huge profit by growing crops that consumed much water, some farmers tried to conserve water, and water supplies of the entire region progressively increased in the process.
→ '많은 이웃 농부들이 많은 물을 소비하는 작물을 재배함으로써 엄청난 수익을 얻었다는 사실에도 불구하고 일부 농부들이 물을 보호하려 애쓴 것'이 아니라 '많은 이웃 농부들이 물을 많이 소비하여 수익을 얻었기 때문에 일부 농부들의 물을 절약하려는 의욕이 꺾였음'을 원문은 언급하고 있으므로 틀린 내용으로 오답이다. 원인과 결과가 명확하게 규명되지 않은 대표적인 예라고 볼 수 있다.

(D) The enthusiasm of the farmers who tried to conserve water <u>was encouraged by</u> many farmers who made a profit by growing crops using much water, and water supplies in the entire region decreased in the

164

REVIEW TEST [DAY 06-10]

process.
→ 원문과 정반대의 정보를 제공하고 있으므로 오답이다. (was encouraged by → was discouraged by)

다른 방식으로 paraphrase 하기

① The fact that many neighboring farmers gained a fair margin of profit by cultivating crops that consumed a large amount of water ② caused some farmers who desired to save water to lose their enthusiasm, and ③ in the process the entire region suffered from a sharp drop in water supplies.

→ Since ① many neighboring farmers made a huge profit by growing crops that consumed much water, ② some farmers lost their desire to conserve water, and ③ therefore water supplies of the entire region rapidly decreased in the process.

원문 문장은 주부 ①과 술부 ②로 이루어진 하나의 절과 등위접속사 'and' 이하의 또 하나의 절, 즉 두 개의 절로 이루어진 문장 구조를 갖고 있으며 ①과 ②는 문제의 원인과 결과가 각각 언급하고 있다. 이는 의미상 적절한 접속사를 이용하여 앞 절의 원인과 결과를 두 개의 절로 나누어 설명할 수 있다. 예를 들어, '어떠한 이유로 어떠한 결과가 초래되었다.'라고 할 때에 이유를 나타내는 접속사 'because', 'since', 또는 'as' 등을 활용할 수 있다. 또한, '따라서'의 의미를 갖고 있는 'and therefore'를 활용하여 원문의 앞의 절에 대한 결과를 부가적으로 덧붙일 수 있다. 따라서 위의 재진술 문장은 세 개의 절로 이루어진 문장 구조를 갖게 되었다. 이렇게 paraphrase를 할 때는 하나의 절로 이루어진 문장을 접속사를 이용하여 두 개 또는 세 개의 절로 바꾸어 문장을 재구성 할 수 있다.

→ ② The enthusiasm of the farmers who tried to conserve water was discouraged by ① many farmers who made a profit by growing crops using much water, ③ which resulted in water shortages in the entire region.

의미상 중심 내용을 주어로 사용하고 원인과 결과의 위치를 바꾸어 주어 문장을 능동태에서 수동태로 전환할 수 있다. 원문에서 내용상 중심이 되는 'The enthusiasm of the farmers'를 주어의 자리에 놓음으로써 문장 구조도 바꾸고 문장의 의미도 더욱 정확하게 할 수 있으며, 이 앞 절의 전체 아이디어(①+②)는 관계대명사 which로 받아 앞 절에 대한 그 이상의 결과 ③의 형태로 언급할 수 있다.

101 outcome

SYNONYMS n. result, effect, aftermath, conclusion, consequence, ramification, end, product

결과, 영향, 여파

outcome
[άʊtkʌm]

The **outcome** of the Mexican-American War contained the annexation of new territory in the United States and conflicts between the Northern and the Southern part of America concerning slavery.

멕시코-미국 전쟁은 미국 내부의 새로운 영토 합병과 노예제도에 대한 미국 북부와 남부 지역 간 갈등을 초래했다.

PARAPHRASE 1

The Mexican-American War brought about some **result**s such as territorial expansion of the United States and internal struggles over slavery in the U.S.

PARAPHRASE 2

The Mexican-American War had huge **effect**s on the U.S.: vast territories acquired from Mexico and internal disputes over slavery.

102 arrangement

Nutritional Science

SYNONYMS *n.* configuration, structure, conformation, placement, disposition, grouping, ordering, organization, distribution

배치, 배열

arrangement
[əréindʒmənt]

Zebra and wildebeest consume distinctive diets on account of the differences in the **arrangement** of their digestive systems, which makes it possible for them to exist together in the same place.

얼룩말과 영양은 소화 기관 배열의 차이 때문에 서로 다른 음식을 섭취하며, 이는 그들이 같은 장소에서 공존하는 것을 가능하게 해준다.

PARAPHRASE 1

The intake of different diets between zebra and wildebeest emerges from the divergent **configuration** of their digestive organs and this enables them to coexist without competition.

PARAPHRASE 2

Zebra and wildebeest are not in competition in that their dissimilar **structure** of digestive apparatus makes them ingest different foods.

103 emerge

Day 11
Entomology

SYNONYMS v. arise, appear, loom, spring up, come out, crop up, take shape

발생하다, 나타나다

emerge
[imə́ːrdʒ]

Periodical cicadas begin to burrow holes to the surface of the earth in order to get ready to crawl out of the ground from several weeks before the nymphs emerge.

주기 매미의 유충은 땅 밖으로 나타나기 몇 주 전부터 이에 대한 준비를 하기 위해 지표면을 향해 굴을 파기 시작한다.

PARAPHRASE 1

Before the nymphs arise, periodical cicadas dig burrows to the ground surface for several weeks and make preparations to get out of the soil.

PARAPHRASE 2

By digging tunnels to the surface, periodical cicadas make ready to come out of the ground for weeks before the nymphs appear.

104 competitor

Anthropology

SYNONYMS n. antagonist, opponent, rival, adversary, enemy, foe, contestant

경쟁자, 적수, 상대방

competitor
[kəmpétətər]

With the use of the iron weapons, the Bantu Peoples could make a conquest of their **competitors** who depended on hunting and gathering, using stone wares.

반투족이 철제 무기를 사용하게 되면서, 아직 석기를 사용하고 수렵과 채집에 의존했던 경쟁자들을 정복할 수 있었다.

PARAPHRASE 1

Employing the iron weapons, it became possible for the Bantu Peoples to overpower their **antagonists** who lived by hunting and gathering with stone implements.

PARAPHRASE 2

The iron weapons of the Bantu Peoples helped them to conquer their hunting-gathering **opponents** using stone tools.

105 trigger

Day 11 — Agriculture

| SYNONYMS | v. | generate, cause, spark, create, induce, spawn, activate, provoke, evoke, spur, elicit, produce, arouse, incite, draw, stir, agitate, stimulate, instigate, engender, bring about, give rise to, lead to, result in | 자극하다, 야기하다 |

trigger
[trígər]

The decrease in the capability of taking up water **trigger**s the steady desiccation of the soil, which **gives rise to** the loss of vegetation and **create**s a cycle of increased soil deterioration.

수분 흡수 능력의 감소에 의해 야기된 토양의 점진적인 건조는 식물 손실을 불러 일으키고 늘어난 토양 악화 주기를 확립시킨다.

PARAPHRASE 1

The gradual desiccation of the soil **generate**d by insufficient ability to absorb water **brings about** the vegetation loss and growing soil degradation.

PARAPHRASE 2

The soil drying **cause**d by the decline in water absorption power **instigate**s vegetation loss and soil deterioration.

106 drawback

Business Administration

| SYNONYMS | n. | disadvantage, weakness, flaw, defect, demerit, handicap, shortcoming, blemish, fault, failing | 결점, 단점 |

drawback
[drɔ́ːbæ̀k]

The primary **drawback** of becoming a franchise owner is that most franchise contracts with definite standards prohibit franchisees from making alterations or additions to the brand and suppress any attempt to create new items or ideas.

가맹점주가 되는것에 대한 주요 단점은, 대부분 정확한 기준을 갖고 있는 가맹점 계약이 가맹주들로 하여금 브랜드에 변화를 주는것을 금하며 새로운 아이템이나 아이디어 시도를 억압한다는 것이다.

PARAPHRASE 1

The major **disadvantage** to being a franchise owner is that franchisers prevent franchisees from improving the brand and creating new items or ideas on the basis of franchise contracts.

PARAPHRASE 2

The restriction in terms of creativity as well as flexibility is the main **weakness** associated with becoming a franchise owner.

107 follow

World History

SYNONYMS v. ensue, result, succeed   뒤따라 일어나다

follow
[fɑ́lou]

The death of Charlemagne's son, Louis the Pious, was followed by civil war and resulted in the disintegration of European areas into feudal duchies.

샤를마뉴 대제의 아들인 루도비쿠스 경건왕의 죽음에 뒤따라 내전이 일어났고, 유럽 지역들을 봉건 영지들로 분할되었다.

PARAPHRASE 1

Civil war ensued and Europe was again segmented into feudal dominions after the son of Charlemagne, Louis the Pious, was dead.

PARAPHRASE 2

After Louis the Pious, Charlemagne's son, died, civil war and the fragmentation of European regions resulted.

108 consensus

Day 11
Cognitive Psychology

SYNONYMS n. agreement, conformity, accord, correspondence, accordance, unanimity, harmony, coincidence, concurrence

일치, 동의

consensus
[kənsénsəs]

Until researchers come to a **consensus** about the presence and the extent of the infant's feedback, the behavior of the infants can be observed by them through the repetition.

연구자들이 유아반응의 존재와 정도에 대한 의견의 일치에 도달할 때까지, 유아행동은 반복을 통해서 연구자들에 의해 관찰될 수 있다.

PARAPHRASE 1

Through the repetition, investigators can observe the infant's action until they arrive at an **agreement** about the existence and the degree of the infant's feedback.

PARAPHRASE 2

The repetition permits investigators to measure the infant's activity until they reach **conformity** about the infant's response.

109 conventional

SYNONYMS **adj.** orthodox, traditional, customary

전통적인, 통상적인

conventional
[kənvénʃənəl]

On the basis of the newly emerging economic structure, craft workers organized labor unions for the purpose of safeguarding their rights and maintaining **conventional** ways of life.

새롭게 등장한 경제 체제의 기반 위에서 목수, 인쇄업자, 재단사와 같은 장인들은 그들의 권리를 보호하고 전통적인 생활 방식을 유지할 목적으로 노동 조합을 조직했다.

PARAPHRASE 1

Under the newly rising economic system, labor unions were formed by craftsmen in order to guarantee their rights and **orthodox** ways of life.

PARAPHRASE 2

The new economic regime forced artisans to unionize for the protection of their rights and **traditional** lifestyle.

110 inundate

SYNONYMS v. overflow, flood, deluge, swamp, submerge, plunge, immerse, submerse

범람하다, 물에 잠기게 하다

inundate
[ínəndèit]

On condition that the volume of water flowing into the river goes beyond the river's capacity to accommodate water, the Nile River will **inundate** its embankments and floods will result.

강으로 흘러 들어오는 물의 양이 강의 수용 능력을 초과한다면, 나일강이 제방을 넘어서게 되면서 홍수가 일어날 것이다.

PARAPHRASE 1

The Nile River will **overflow** its levees and deluges will be caused, provided that it is not capable of holding the large volume of water running into the river.

PARAPHRASE 2

The Nile, not capable of holding the excessive amount of water entering the river, will **flood** its banks and generate floods.

DAILY CHECK-UP

A. Find the answer that is closest in meaning to the highlighted word or phrase in the sentence.

01. The continental shelf is the flat, **inundated** portion of a continent that stretches far out to the sea.

    (A) submerged (B) polished

02. Another **drawback** associated with biopolymers is that bio-plastics have adverse impacts on the environment.

    (A) deviation (B) demerit

03. As prairie dog populations can grow rapidly, they **provoke** these deadly pathogens to diffuse or move to new regions.

    (A) endow (B) create

04. **Opponents** of fluoridation are concerned that vulnerable people consume more water with excessive fluoride and consequently, their health can become worse.

    (A) predecessors (B) antagonists

05. The plates which go towards hotspots force volcanoes to **spring up** and disappear quickly, creating chains of islands.

    (A) crop up (B) give off

06. The development of the modern periodic table resulted from diverse conceptual **configurations** of elements.

    (A) arrangements (B) ramification

07. The final **result** of the combination of two galaxies is some galaxies with manifold nuclei.

    (A) raid (B) outcome

08. Discontent with **traditional** explanations of dinosaur extinctions elicited a startling observation presenting a new hypothesis.

    (A) consecutive (B) orthodox

09. As Fuller's dances were in **harmony** with the artistic merits already existent in Paris, her work was accepted well.

    (A) accord (B) inrush

10. In the Little Ice Age, decreased temperature and increased rainfall harmed harvests, and the Black Death **ensued**.

    (A) followed (B) speculated

B. Complete each sentence using one of the words or phrases given.

11. As a _____ of the severe drought, crop yields were markedly reduced.

    (A) blemish (B) consequence

12. If the part of the hypothalamus is sparked with electricity, typical aggressive behaviors are _____ in many animals.

    (A) plunged (B) induced

13. Conglomerates could sell a high-quality product at a good price, while they could set prices and damage _____ .

    (A) rivals (B) antecedents

14. As the Nile _____ every summer, the area around it became fertile.

    (A) loomed (B) flooded

15. Neap tides occur on condition that the Sun, Moon, and Earth are positioned at the corners of a triangular _____ .

    (A) orientation (B) disposition

16. The complication _____ in other technical problems such as the containment of drastic melting in warmer conditions.

    (A) arises (B) partakes

---

01. (A) 02. (B) 03. (B) 04. (B) 05. (A) 06. (A) 07. (B) 08. (B) 09. (A) 10. (A)
11. (B) 12. (B) 13. (A) 14. (B) 15. (B) 16. (A)

111 expand

Day 12

Anthropology

SYNONYMS v. amplify, escalate, intensify, magnify, rise, mount, augment, swell, surge, grow, extend, enlarge, prolong, lengthen, bloat, stretch, protract, broaden, widen, increase

확장하다,
연장하다,
확대하다,
증가하다

expand
[ikspǽnd]

An increase in pressures from **expand**ing populations has resulted in the elimination of woody vegetation in order that many urban regions are encompassed by extensive areas lacking in trees and shrubs.

증가하는 인구의 압력 증가는 많은 도시들이 나무와 관목이 부족한 광범위한 지역에 둘러싸일 수 있도록 하기 위한 목적으로 목본성 식물을 제거하는 결과를 초래했다.

PARAPHRASE 1

The disappearance of woody plants has resulted from the **amplify**ing populations so that many cities and towns are surrounded by vast regions totally destitute of trees and shrubs.

PARAPHRASE 2

The **escalat**ing populations have caused the devastation of woody plants so as to construct cities and towns encircled by areas devoid of vegetation.

112 distribution

Day 12
Geology

| SYNONYMS | n. | dissemination, dispersal, diffusion, circulation | 전파, 분배, 분포 |

distribution
[dìstrəbjúːʃən]

Even though the Ediacara formation was named after an Australian site, its distribution is universal and it dates back to the Precambrian time period.

에디아카라층은 한 호주 지역의 이름을 따서 명명되었지만, 사실 세계적으로 널리 사용하고 있으며 그 기원은 선캄프리아기로 거슬러 올라간다.

PARAPHRASE 1

Known to be formed during the Precambrian Time Period, the Ediacara formation named after an Australian site is virtually transglobal in dissemination.

PARAPHRASE 2

Dating back to the Precambrian Era, the Ediacara formation is named after a site in Australia, but it has a worldwide dispersal.

113 portion

Philosophy — Day 12

SYNONYMS *n.* part, segment, fragment, section, proportion, division, piece, shard, scrap, particle, fracture, slab, component, element, ingredient, constituent

조각, 부분, 요소

portion
[pɔ́ːrʃən]

Without a doubt, Albertus Magnus deserves credit for giving up all material benefits to dedicate a large **portion** of his entire life to the research regarding alchemical philosophy.

알베르투스 마그누스는 연금술에 관한 연구에 생애의 상당 부분을 헌신하기 위해 모든 물질적 이익을 포기한 것에 대해 의심의 여지없이 칭찬을 받아 마땅하다.

PARAPHRASE 1

In that Albertus Magnus devoted a huge **part** of his life to the study of alchemy without taking material gains, he is entirely worthy of praise.

PARAPHRASE 2

Albertus Magnus, who committed a big **segment** of his life to the study of alchemy instead of seeking material gains, is certainly respectable.

114 explain

Day 12 — Archeology

SYNONYMS v. elucidate, explicate, justify, illuminate, enlighten, clarify, construe, interpret, clear, account for, give a reason, shed light on

설명하다, 명백하게 하다

explain
[ikspléin]

In order to **explain** why the tremendous advancement took place in the Teotihuacan valley, there are some aspects to be considered: abundant natural resources, geographical conditions, and an intellectual elite.

놀라운 진보가 테우티우아칸 계곡에서 발생한 이유를 설명하기 위해 풍부한 천연 자원, 입지 조건, 그리고 지적 엘리트 집단과 같은 몇 가지 측면들이 고려되어야 한다.

PARAPHRASE 1

Teotihuacan's exceptional development may be **elucidate**d by several elements such as copious natural resources, geographical advantages, and an intelligent elite.

PARAPHRASE 2

Several factors to **explicate** Teotihuacan's extraordinary growth encompass rich natural resources, location requirements, and brainy elite.

115　be made up of

World History

SYNONYMS　**phr.**　be composed of, consist of, comprise　　~로 구성되다, 이루어지다

be made up of

The House of Commons of the United Kingdom that **is made up of** 650 members called Members of Parliament (MPs) is elected when the British public votes in a general election and holds more power than the House of Lords.

국회의원(MPs)이라고 불리는 650명의 구성원으로 이루어진 영국의 하원은 영국 시민이 총선거에서 투표할 때 선출되며, 상원보다 더 많은 권한을 갖고 있다.

PARAPHRASE 1

The House of Commons of Great Britain **is composed of** 650 members called MPs elected by the UK public and is predominant over the House of Lords.

PARAPHRASE 2

The House of Commons is a popularly elected body, **consisting of** 650 members, and has the greater political power of two Houses in British Parliament.

116 crude

Engineering

SYNONYMS adj. raw, natural, unrefined, unprocessed, rude, uncooked, rough

천연 그대로의, 가공하지 않은

crude
[kru:d]

Tremendous **crude** materials in the United States that could be employed for the sake of the manufacture of transportation facilities, machinery of all sorts, and consumers' goods contributed greatly to the growth of heavy industry.

미국에는 교통 시설, 각종 기계, 소비재의 제조에 사용 가능한 엄청난 양의 천연 재료들이 존재하며, 이는 중공업의 발달에 크게 기여했다.

PARAPHRASE 1

Thanks to the enormous **raw** materials that could be utilized to manufacture traffic facilities, all kinds of machinery, and consumer goods, the United States was able to attain development in heavy industry.

PARAPHRASE 2

The United States, with its immense **natural** resources, could build up its heavy industry by using them to produce traffic equipment, various machinery, and consumer items.

117 fascinate

Day 12 | Art

SYNONYMS v. intrigue, attract, interest, enthrall, captivate, enchant, mesmerize, allure, appeal, invite, lure, seduce, decoy, tempt, induce, entice, inveigle, coax, draw, charm

매혹하다, (마음을) 끌다

fascinate
[fǽsənèit]

Modigliani who was completely fascinated with the simplicity of African art, particularly masks and sculptures, engraved it deeply upon his mind, which had a considerable impact on his portraits.

아프리카의 예술, 특히 마스크와 조각의 단순성에 완전히 매료된 모딜리아니는 그의 마음 속 깊이 이를 새겼고 이는 그의 초상화에 상당한 영향을 미쳤다.

PARAPHRASE 1

The simplicity of African art, especially masks and sculptures, which entirely intrigued Modigliani was borne in his mind and as a result substantially influenced pictures by him.

PARAPHRASE 2

As the African art patterns, notably found in masks and sculptures, totally attracted Modigliani, they were laid up in his heart and reflected in his portraits.

118 abandon

Religion — Day 12

SYNONYMS v. desert, forsake, resign, surrender, relinquish, discard, quit, cede, yield, call off, give up, dispose of, cast aside, throw away

버리다, 포기하다

abandon
[əbǽndən]

Some early societies **abandon**ed religious ceremonies which were once considered vital for health and happiness. Nonetheless, others maintained and praised them for their artistic aspects.

일부 초기 사회들은 한 때 건강과 행복에 있어서 필수적인 것으로 간주되었던 종교 의식을 포기했다. 반면에, 다른 사회들은 예술적인 차원에서 그것들을 유지하고 칭송했다.

PARAPHRASE 1

In some early societies, religious rituals once considered integral to well-being were **desert**ed, whereas in other societies, they were retained and admired for their artistic value.

PARAPHRASE 2

Religious rites deemed necessary to well-being were **forsake**n in some early societies, while their artistic features allowed them to be kept and appreciated in others.

119 chief

Meteorology

SYNONYMS adj. major, principal, predominant, cardinal, central, essential, primary, main, leading, prime, primal, staple

주된, 주요한

chief
[tʃiːf]

Fog, a **chief** cause of fatal accidents on highways in some regions, leads thousands of people to lose their lives every year as it can decrease visibility.

일부 지역의 고속도로에서 발생하는 치명적인 사고의 주요 원인인 안개는 가시도를 저하시키기 때문에 매년 수 천명의 생명을 앗아간다.

PARAPHRASE 1

Fog is regarded as a **major** culprit behind traffic accidents since it decreases visibility and thus ruins thousands of lives every year.

PARAPHRASE 2

A **principal** cause of traffic accidents is fog, which blurs vision, resulting in high death rates every year.

120 consciousness

Day 12
Ecology

SYNONYMS n. awareness, recognition, appreciation, perception, understanding, realization, cognition, identification

인식, 인지

consciousness
[kάnʃəsnis]

The **consciousness** of the significance of biological diversity being deeply related to the health of the Earth and human well-being has increased along with concerns for the acceleration in the disappearance of species and habitats.

지구의 건강과 인류의 안녕에 깊이 관련되어 있는 생물 다양성의 중요성에 대한 인식과 함께, 생물 종과 서식지의 손실 증가에 대한 우려 역시 증가해왔다.

PARAPHRASE 1

Concerns for the acceleration in loss of species and habitats have come on the back of a growing **awareness** about the importance of biodiversity necessary to keep the Earth and humans healthy.

PARAPHRASE 2

As **recognition** of the significance of biological diversity has increased, concerns over loss of species and habitats has been growing.

DAILY CHECK-UP

A. Find the answer that is closest in meaning to the highlighted word or phrase in the sentence.

01. The **leading** reason for the restoration of the deer population has been closely linked with the forests.
    (A) unprolific   (B) predominant

02. If the drawings were created in hopes of a successful hunt, why only a few chips are found in cave art would be barely **illuminated**.
    (A) propagated   (B) clarified

03. Petroleum, which appears to stem from organic substances in marine deposition, is composed of natural gas and **crude** oil.
    (A) raw   (B) sterile

04. Generally, **abandoned** traditional plastics do not decay naturally and remain in the same area for several decades.
    (A) discarded   (B) epitomized

05. Fossils **consist of** the organic remains of prehistoric creatures that have been trapped in the rocks for a long time.
    (A) condense   (B) comprise

06. Paleontologists have been **captivated** by the Cretaceous mass extinction meaning the end of the dinosaur era.
    (A) enthralled   (B) contemplated

07. The conflict between animals and humans has been caused by **broadening** the use of urban and suburban land.
    (A) fabricating   (B) widening

08. The small **portion** of the Cascade Range in British Columbia is generally dubbed the Cascade Mountains.
    (A) inrush   (B) section

09. Substantial disparities in fossil **distribution** among the sedimentary strata were found in the samples.

(A) affiliation (B) dispersal

10. Humans in the Upper Paleolithic were capable of conscious **recognition** of their environment as well as complicated thought.

(A) appreciation (B) encroachment

B. Complete each sentence using one of the words or phrases given.

11. There is a _____ distinction between Democrats and Whigs involving the importance of the market in society.

(A) mundane (B) main

12. Each continental land mass in the Paleozoic era _____ distinctive parts of the modern continents.

(A) was made up of (B) put up with

13. The laws are _____ by the judiciary which ascertains whether new laws are in accordance with the Constitution.

(A) construed (B) prolonged

14. People who engage in trade transmitted religious beliefs and social conventions as well as _____ materials.

(A) unprocessed (B) disseminated

15. Three distinct _____ essential to form modern structures are equal to components of the human body.

(A) adversaries (B) constituents

16. Oil exploration _____ into more inhospitable environments as it became progressively exhausted.

(A) stretched (B) ensued

---

01. (B) 02. (B) 03. (A) 04. (A) 05. (B) 06. (A) 07. (B) 08. (B) 09. (B) 10. (A)
11. (B) 12. (A) 13. (A) 14. (A) 15. (B) 16. (A)

121 artisan

Sociology

SYNONYMS n. craftsman, craftsperson, manufacturer 장인, 기능 보유자

artisan
[ɑ́ːrtəzən]

A guild, an organization that paid heed to protecting its members and that insisted upon the highest degree of professionalism among its members, consisted of a group of artisans.

구성원들의 보호에 주력하며, 구성원들 간 고도의 전문성을 고수하는 조직인 길드는 장인들로 구성된 집단이다.

PARAPHRASE 1 A craftsman was affiliated with a guild, a society giving attention to being a shelter of its members and seeking a high level of specialty among its members.

PARAPHRASE 2 A craftsperson was a member of a guild, an association sticking to advanced professionalism as well as protecting its members.

122 exceptionally

Ecology

SYNONYMS adv. abnormally, unusually, eminently, extraordinarily

특별히, 유난히

exceptionally
[iksépʃənəli]

Theories which mainly deal with the variety of terrestrial organisms have been suggested and most of them placed emphasis on the exceptionally abundant living things related with tropical rainforests.

지금 생물들의 다양성을 주로 다루는 많은 이론들이 제시되어 왔으며, 그 중 대부분이 열대 우림 지역의 유난히 풍부한 생명체들에 역점을 두었다.

PARAPHRASE 1

Theories have predominantly handled the diversity of terrestrial organisms, particularly the abnormally copious creatures in tropical rainforests.

PARAPHRASE 2

Theories about the variety of terrestrial organisms, notably the unusually abundant life in tropical rainforests, have been proposed.

123 proponent

Day 13
Genetics

SYNONYMS n. advocate, supporter, partisan, adherent, disciple, upholder, patron

지지자

proponent
[prəpóunənt]

The **proponents** of cloning appear to disregard the fact that a lot of embryos have been sacrificed in order to create a cloned baby.

복제 기술의 지지자들은 복제된 새끼를 만들어내기 위해 많은 태아들이 희생되어왔다는 사실을 간과하고 있는 것 같다.

PARAPHRASE 1

At the expense of a host of embryos, a cloned baby has been produced, which appears to be overlooked by the **advocates** of cloning.

PARAPHRASE 2

The **supporters** of cloning seem to ignore the fact that a cloned baby has been created at the cost of many embryos.

124 accessible

Paleontology

SYNONYMS adj. reachable, available, obtainable, attainable, handy, at hand

이용 가능한, 접근하기 쉬운

accessible
[æksésəbəl]

Nobody knows why the Cambrian explosion characterized by the drastic evolution occurred. However, many zoologists argue that there were many ecological niches accessible without having to compete with surviving species.

급속한 진화를 특징으로 하는 캄브리아 폭발의 발생 원인이 무엇인지는 아무도 모른다. 하지만 여러 동물학자들의 주장에 따르면, 이는 현존하는 종들과 경쟁하지 않고도 접근이 가능했던 많은 생태학적 지위들이 있었기 때문이라고 한다.

PARAPHRASE 1

Why the evolution that rapidly occurred in the Cambrian explosion has not been identified, but zoologists think that it was because of the richness of ecological niches reachable with no competition.

PARAPHRASE 2

The main causes of the Cambrian explosion are still yet to be proven, but some contend that it was due to the abundance of available econiches and the absence of rivalry with existent species.

125 exaggerate

Day 13
Archeology

| SYNONYMS | v. | overstate, hyperbolize, enlarge, embroider, play up | 과장하다 |

exaggerate
[igzǽdʒərèit]

Not only other works of art, but figurines have been spotted at the archeological sites of the Upper Paleolithic period and the latter depicted the human female in an **exaggerate**d form and expressed a hope for fecundity.

다른 예술 작품들뿐만 아니라 작은 조각상들이 후기 구석기 시대의 유적지에서 발견되었고, 이 조각상들은 과장된 형태로 인간 여성을 묘사했으며 다산에 대한 희망을 표현하였다.

PARAPHRASE 1

From the Upper Paleolithic historic scenes, archeologists found human figurines portraying the woman in an **overstate**d way and representing a wish for fertility, not to mention other works of art.

PARAPHRASE 2

Female figurines showing the **hyperbolize**d portrayal as a symbol of fertility as well as other artworks were discovered at Upper Paleolithic sites.

126 consume

Energy

| SYNONYMS | v. | expend, exhaust, spend, squander, waste, deplete, lavish, use up, run out of | 소모하다, 소비하다 |

consume
[kənsúːm]

It was difficult to anticipate how societies would deal with this problem when fossil fuels began to be **consume**d at a brisk pace because people excessively depended on fossil fuels and this forced them into a trap.

화석 연료에의 지나친 의존은 사람들을 함정에 빠뜨렸기 때문에, 화석 연료가 빠르게 고갈되기 시작했을 때 각각의 사회들이 이 문제를 어떻게 해결할지를 예측하기란 어려웠다.

PARAPHRASE 1

Fossil fuels started to be **expend**ed at high speed, which made it hard to predict how societies would cope with this predicament since excessive reliance on fossil fuels had caused people to be caught in a trap.

PARAPHRASE 2

Rapidly **exhaust**ed fossil fuels made it hard for people to forecast how societies would handle this problem due to their extreme dependence on them.

127 show

Physics

| SYNONYMS | v. | exhibit, reveal, indicate, display, disclose, showcase, present, demonstrate, express, represent, unveil, uncover, expose, signify, imply, mean, denote, divulge, set forth, point out | 드러내다, 보여주다, 나타내다 |

show
[ʃou]

Isotopes perform an important function in the field of modern medicine because they **show** biochemical and metabolic processes with accuracy in the way that they are swallowed and traced in the human body.

동위원소가 신체 내에 섭취되고 축적되는 방식이 생화학적 과정과 대사 과정을 정확하게 보여준다는 점에서, 이는 현대 의학에서 중요한 역할을 한다.

PARAPHRASE 1

In view of the fact that isotopes swallowed and tracked through the body precisely **exhibit** biochemical and metabolic processes, they contribute significantly to modern medicine.

PARAPHRASE 2

Isotopes are very useful in modern medicine in that they accurately **reveal** biochemical and metabolic processes when tracked after being ingested within the body.

128 abrupt

Hydrogeology

SYNONYMS adj. rapid, sudden, hasty, sharp, quick, hurried, precipitous

급한, 갑작스러운

abrupt
[əbrʌpt]

During the dry years of the early 1930s, the first wells were excavated in the Ogallala, and the subsequent abrupt enlargement of irrigation agriculture altered the local economy for the 1950s.

1930년대 초 가뭄이 지속된 몇 년 동안 오갈라라에 최초의 유물들이 생겨났고, 뒤이은 관개 농업의 갑작스러운 확장은 1950년대 지역 경제를 바꾸어 놓았다.

PARAPHRASE 1

The wells initially sunken in the arid areas of Ogallala in the early 1930s sparked the rapid expansion of irrigation agriculture and the transformation of the local economy in the 1950s.

PARAPHRASE 2

Irrigation agriculture expanded at a sudden pace, which followed the first wells sunken in the Ogallala in the early 1930s, changing the local economy in the 1950s.

129 inborn

Day 13
Psychology

SYNONYMS **adj.** innate, natural, intrinsic, inherent, congenital, connate, unstudied, unlearned, gifted, ingrained

타고난, 선천적인

inborn
[ínbɔ́ːrn]

Piaget demonstrated that their cognitive structures are modified, shifting from some inborn reflex actions such as sucking (←minor idea) to fairly complicated actions of the mind as children develop.

피아제는 아이들이 성장함에 따라 그들의 인지 구조 역시 선천적인 반사 작용 몇몇에서 상당히 복잡한 정신 활동으로 발전한다는 사실을 입증해 보였다.

PARAPHRASE 1

Piaget testified that their cognitive structures improve from innate reactions to intricate mental activities as the children grow.

PARAPHRASE 2

Piaget argued that the children's cognitive structures develop from natural motor activities to mental activities with age.

130 locale

Geology

SYNONYMS n. place, location, site, venue, position, locality, spot, point

장소, 위치

locale
[loukǽl]

As the data about rock strata from various **locale**s were collated, it became evident that the patterns of rocks vary in different localities and that the type of rock could never be considered a trustworthy indicator of geological age.

다양한 지역의 암석 지층에 관한 자료를 분석해 보았을 때, 암석의 모양은 지역마다 다르며, 암석의 종류가 결코 지질학적 연대를 결정하는 신뢰할 수 있는 지수가 될 수 없다는 것이 명백해졌다.

PARAPHRASE 1

The investigation of rock strata from different **place**s unveiled that the geological time period could never be established on the basis of the rock type due to the different rock patterns in discrete sites.

PARAPHRASE 2

The examination of rock strata from different **location**s revealed that the geologic time period cannot be decided by rocks as the rock sequences differ regionally.

DAILY CHECK-UP

A. Find the answer that is closest in meaning to the highlighted word or phrase in the sentence.

01. The desert was transformed into a more **handiet** trade route with the help of the camel.
    (A) more accessible (B) more equivocal

02. Organisms are required to **spend** energy in order to grow, reproduce and undergo metabolic change.
    (A) expend (B) amplify

03. A **sudden** extinction of many organisms transpired at the end of the Mesozoic period.
    (A) ingrain (B) abrupt

04. The existence of great arts **indicates** that ancient humankinds were surely intelligent, skillful, and sensitive.
    (A) demonstrates (B) converges

05. **Supporters** of euthanasia have the American traditions of liberty and independence on their side.
    (A) Antecedents (B) Proponents

06. Art works created by the **artisans** of ancient Egypt are still outstanding today compared to when they were first.
    (A) forerunners (B) craftsmen

07. Modigliani's **inherent** ability was recognized by his mother who encouraged him to study further to develop his incredible talent.
    (A) innate (B) precipitous

08. The massive plates of the surface of the earth are diverging at a slow rate in various **locations**.
    (A) shortcoming (B) points

09. The Cambrian explosion is marked by the **abnormally** swift evolution of a wide variety of new plants and animals.

   (A) unusually (B) exclusively

10. Those with histrionic personality disorder show dramatics and **overstated** emotional expressions.

   (A) exaggerated (B) protracted

B. Complete each sentence using one of the words or phrases given.

11. The _____ floods provided the sterile land with a substantial amount of water, though they were considerably devastating.

   (A) commonplace (B) abrupt

12. Samples excavated from the expedition _____ striking disparities in the composition of chemistry and fossil dispersion in sedimentary strata.

   (A) prolonged (B) disclosed

13. Water soaking the land and filling up the _____ empty space is called groundwater.

   (A) available (B) utmost

14. Kramer conjectured that caged starlings could determine their location depending on the _____ of the Sun.

   (A) position (B) identification

15. For the sake of the rural distractions, urban residents occasionally spend their time in the open country _____.

   (A) at intervals (B) at hand

16. For thousands of years, stern artistic regulations restricted the originality of the _____ in ancient Egypt.

   (A) craftspeople (B) adversaries

---

01. (A) 02. (A) 03. (B) 04. (A) 05. (B) 06. (B) 07. (A) 08. (B) 09. (A) 10. (A)
11. (B) 12. (B) 13. (A) 14. (A) 15. (B) 16. (A)

131 mimic

Day 14
Biology

| SYNONYMS | v. | imitate, copy, emulate, follow, mock, simulate, reproduce, duplicate | 모방하다, 복제하다 |

mimic
[mímik]

An example of mimicry, a self-defense mechanism that some animals use to deceive either prey or predators, is to mimic a bright-colored beautiful monarch butterfly that has an unpleasant taste.

먹이나 포식자를 속이기 위해 일부 동물들이 사용하는 자기 방어 기제인 의태에 대한 하나의 예시로는, 불쾌한 맛이 나는 밝은 색의 아름다운 제왕 나비를 모방하는 것이 있다.

PARAPHRASE 1

Mimicry is a method some animals utilize to cheat prey or predators and one example is to **imitate** a foul-tasting monarch butterfly with a bright and beautiful color.

PARAPHRASE 2

Copying a monarch butterfly with a gorgeous color but a bad taste is one way of mimicry, employed by some animals for their survival.

132 lacking in

Ecology

SYNONYMS *phr.* destitute of, devoid of, deficient in, low in, poorly for

~이 결여된, ~이 부족한

lacking in

As serpentine soils are **lacking in** micro nutrients such as calcium, only plants that are able to endure a low degree of this mineral can remain alive in these types of soils.

사문암토양은 칼슘과 같은 미량 영양소가 부족하기 때문에 이 낮은 수준의 미네랄을 견딜 수 있는 식물들만이 이러한 종류의 토양에서 살아남을 수 있다.

PARAPHRASE 1

In serpentine soils **destitute of** micro nutrients such as calcium, only plants that can tolerate a low level of this mineral can be left alive.

PARAPHRASE 2

Serpentine soils are **devoid of** calcium, and therefore only plants requiring this low-level mineral can survive there.

133 utterly

Marine Biology

SYNONYMS *adv.* completely, totally, absolutely, perfectly, entirely, wholly, thoroughly, fully, in every respect

전적으로, 철저히, 완전히

utterly
[ʌ́tərli]

Most tunas' swim bladder, the sac full of gas playing a key role in the buoyancy of most other fish, has mostly or utterly deteriorated, which has forced them to continue to swim to keep them afloat.

대부분의 다른 어류에서 부유에 중요한 역할을 하는 기체 주머니인 부레가 대부분의 참치에게는 상당 부분 완전히 퇴화되었고, 이 때문에 참치들은 가라앉지 않도록 끊임없이 헤엄쳐야 한다.

PARAPHRASE 1 Tunas must constantly swim to avoid sinking, as most have largely or completely undergone the degeneration of the air bladder essential for most other fish to be buoyant.

PARAPHRASE 2 Tunas which have nearly or totally lost the gas-filled bladder can never stop swimming to maintain the status of floating.

134 shatter

Earth Science

SYNONYMS v. destroy, consume, break, batter, pulverize, smash, crash, wreck, devastate, ruin, demolish, maim, spoil, disassemble, disintegrate, dismantle, take apart

부수다,
분해하다
파괴하다

shatter
[ʃǽtər]

It is estimated that meteorite impacts have generated massive amounts of nitric acid and molten rock that spewed out from many parts of the Earth, bringing about far-reaching fires that shattered most of the environment.

운석 충돌은 지구의 여러 지역에서 다량의 질산과 용융 암석이 방출되도록 했고, 이는 환경의 대부분을 파괴하였던 거대 화재를 야기했던 것으로 추정된다.

PARAPHRASE 1

Collisions of meteorites are presumed to have created large quantities of nitric acid and melted rock emitted from various parts of the planet, sparking extensive fires that destroyed most environments.

PARAPHRASE 2

Released throughout the world, nitric acid and melted rock were produced by meteorite impacts, triggering huge fires that consumed most environments.

135 indigenous

Sociology

SYNONYMS *adj.* aboriginal, native, inherited   토착의

indigenous
[indídʒənəs]

Rights to conserve their culture and language and rights to enjoy autonomy over their own aboriginal affairs belong to human rights associated with their identity exercised by **indigenous** inhabitants.

원주민이 행사하는 정체성과 관련된 인권에는 그들의 문화와 언어를 보존할 권리와 그들의 토착지에 대한 자치권을 누릴 권리가 포함된다.

PARAPHRASE 1

There are human rights enjoyed by **aboriginal** peoples involved in their identity: rights to maintain their culture and language and rights to have autonomy over indigenous affairs.

PARAPHRASE 2

Human rights linked to the identity of **native** peoples contain rights for their culture and language maintenance and rights for autonomy on indigenous affairs.

136 participate in

Technology

SYNONYMS v. partake in, share, join, take part in

함께하다, ~에 참여하다

participate in

The introduction of satellite and cable TV made it possible for almost everyone to be able to **participate in** the enlargement of a wide range of new entertainment choices without reference to location.

인공 위성과 케이블 TV의 도입은 거의 모든 사람들로 하여금 지역에 상관없이 새로운 오락거리 선택 범위의 광범위한 확장에 참여할 수 있도록 하였다.

PARAPHRASE 1

Wherever they are, most people are enabled to **partake in** the expansion of enormous new entertainment choices with the emergence of satellite and cable TV.

PARAPHRASE 2

With the advent of satellite and cable TV, the growth of vast new entertainment choices could be **share**d by most people regardless of location.

137 divert

Agricultural Engineering

SYNONYMS v. switch, change, redirect, deviate, deflect, shift, avert, reroute

전환하다, 바꾸다

divert
[divə́ːrt]

The Ogallala aquifer has inevitably been depleted and many farmers have made an attempt for the conservation of water by supplying land with water less frequently or by **divert**ing to crops that consume less water.

오갈라라 대수층은 피할 수 없는 고갈에 직면했고, 많은 농부들은 땅에 물을 덜 자주 공급하거나 물을 덜 소비하는 작물로 전환하는 등의 방법으로 물 보존을 위해 노력해왔다.

PARAPHRASE 1

In reaction to the unavoidable exhaustion of the Ogallala aquifer, many farmers have attempted water conservation by irrigating land intermittently or by **switch**ing to water efficient crops.

PARAPHRASE 2

Many farmers have reduced the frequency of irrigation or have **change**d to water-saving crops in order to preserve water due to the depletion of the Ogallala aquifer.

138 readily

SYNONYMS adv. easily, effortlessly, unhesitatingly, promptly, quickly, smoothly — 쉽게

readily
[rédəli]

The fact that cave paintings in France and Spain were found particularly in areas which people could hardly reach indicates that those who created them preferred not to be **readily** found.

프랑스와 스페인의 동굴 벽화는 특히 사람들이 도달하기 어려운 지역에서 발견되었으며 이는 벽화가 쉽게 발견되기를 원하지 않았을 제작자들의 의도를 알게 해 준다.

PARAPHRASE 1

Cave paintings in France and Spain were found in restricted areas of the caves that could barely get natural light, which means that whoever drew them did not want to be **easily** known.

PARAPHRASE 2

Artists who painted in caves in France and Spain worked in confined dark spaces and this indicates that they did not want to be **effortlessly** discovered.

139 motivation

World History

SYNONYMS n. impetus, stimulus, incentive, spur, incitement, impulse, catalyst

자극, 격려, 동기

motivation
[móutəvèiʃən]

In the Sumerian city-state, the **motivation** for rulers who exercised control over the exchange of surplus crops with other states to generate local wealth was provided by a plentiful supply of food.

풍부한 식량 자원에 의해 동기 부여를 받은 수메르 도시 국가의 지도자들은 부를 창출하고자 다른 국가들과의 잉여 농산물 교역에 통제권을 행사하였다.

PARAPHRASE 1

Rulers of the Sumerian city-state who regulated the interexchange of surplus products abroad to produce local wealth gained **impetus** from the abundant food supply.

PARAPHRASE 2

A fat supply of food gave **stimulus** to the rulers of the Sumerian city-state to control the trade of surplus goods abroad to create local wealth.

140 extinct

Paleontology

SYNONYMS **adj.** vanished, defunct, lost, dead, gone   사라진, 멸종된

extinct
[ikstíŋkt]

Animals present in the Tommotian fossil formations were primarily classified as modern animal groups, but now they are labeled as groups that appeared and became **extinct** during the Cambrian period.

토모티안 화석층에 존재하는 동물들은 처음에는 현대 동물 집단으로 분류되었지만, 지금은 캄브리안 시대에 발생했다가 사라진 동물들의 집단에 속한다.

PARAPHRASE 1

Animal fossils from the Tommotian strata which were originally classed as modern animal groups are now assigned to the groups that appeared and **vanished** during the Cambrian period.

PARAPHRASE 2

Animals in the Tommotian formation, which now belong to the emerged and **defunct** groups in the Cambrian epoch, were misclassified as modern animal groups at first.

DAILY CHECK-UP

A. Find the answer that is closest in meaning to the highlighted word or phrase in the sentence.

01. Zebra mussels are notorious for overwhelming **indigenous** species and upsetting the ecological balance of the area.
    (A) lurid (B) native

02. Children sometimes release their suppressed aggressive impulses to parents in indirect ways such as **smashing** furniture.
    (A) nebulous (B) breaking

03. Sometimes, the wind blew loose topsoil away **entirely** and left a sterile surface.
    (A) wholly (B) scrupulously

04. States **took part in** the construction of a variety of domestic infrastructure facilities including freeways, railways and canals.
    (A) predisposed to (B) participated in

05. Birds can **change** their direction according to the position of the sun and the stars.
    (A) abate (B) reroute

06. A labor force that got used to working at factories was not **easily** created.
    (A) readily (B) exclusively

07. Some animals have one body part that **emulates** another part of other animals for survival.
    (A) nutshells (B) duplicates

08. Collisions of meteorites were beneficial for some species that flourished, while it was hazardous to other **extinct** species.
    (A) defunct (B) bustling

09. Vast tracts of land vulnerable to the erosion by wind and water and **deficient in** vegetal cover resulted from the failure of crops.

(A) susceptible to   (B) devoid of

10. The presence of extensive ice provided a strong **impetus** for people to migrate south.

    (A) stimulus   (B) accord

B. Complete each sentence using one of the words or phrases given.

11. The rays of the sun have been prevented _____ from reaching the earth's surface by a tremendous amount of dust.

    (A) thoroughly   (B) remarkably

12. In the economy, government plays an important role in encouraging competition by _____ monopolies and giving choice to consumers.

    (A) demolishing   (B) contemplating

13. The first generation that goes through the rapid developments is less likely to adapt to them _____ .

    (A) habitually   (B) promptly

14. Some female butterflies _____ physical traits of other species that have an unpleasant taste.

    (A) imitate   (B) ameliorate

15. The Anasazi is the early _____ American tribe that inhabited the southwestern portion of the United States.

    (A) aboriginal   (B) incessant

16. Doctors _____ experience have difficulty solving the problems in an emergency.

    (A) partaking in   (B) lacking in

---

01. (B) 02. (B) 03. (A) 04. (B) 05. (B) 06. (A) 07. (B) 08. (A) 09. (B) 10. (A)
11. (A) 12. (A) 13. (B) 14. (A) 15. (A) 16. (B)

141 scorching

Meteorology

SYNONYMS **adj.** burning, boiling, baking, broiling, exceedingly hot

몹시 뜨거운, 타는 듯한

scorching
[skɔːrtʃiŋ]

The unsettled air around the surface of the earth arising from the **scorching** temperatures in the Sahara increases the probability of particles of dust being blown up into the atmosphere by even light winds.

사하라 사막의 몹시 뜨거운 날씨가 만들어지기 때문에, 지표면 주변의 공기를 불안정하게 만들어 약한 바람에도 먼지 입자가 대기 중으로 날아 오르게 될 가능성이 높아진다.

PARAPHRASE 1

In the Sahara, **burning** temperatures lead the air near the ground to be insecure, which means a greater chance that even moderate winds will blow dust particles away into the atmosphere.

PARAPHRASE 2

The Sahara's **boiling** temperatures lead to unstable air conditions near the surface, making even gentle breezes stir up dust particles into the atmosphere.

142 preoccupied

Day 15 — Art

SYNONYMS *adj.* obsessed, absorbed, engrossed, occupied 몰두한, 사로잡힌

preoccupied
[priɑ́kjəpaid]

Classical sculptors were **preoccupied** with carving physically perfect and proportioned figures, while Hellenistic sculptors concentrated on stark and incomplete aspects of life such as age and emotion (← minor idea).

고전기 조각가들은 신체적으로 완벽하고 균형 잡힌 형상을 조각하는 데에 몰두했던 반면, 헬레니즘 시대의 조각가들은 나이, 감정과 같은 삶의 냉엄하고 불완전한 측면에 초점을 맞추었다.

PARAPHRASE 1

Hellenistic sculptors attempted to represent incomplete factors of the stark reality of life contrary to Classical sculptors **obsessed** with externally balanced figures.

PARAPHRASE 2

Unlike Classical sculptors **absorbed** with making physically idealized forms, Hellenistic counterparts focused on more realistic sides of life.

143 various

Day 15 — Meteorology

SYNONYMS adj. diverse, multiple, varied, a variety of, a range of, many kinds of,

다양한

various
[véəriəs]

Using computer models of the global climate is one method to take into account all the various elements which cause climatic fluctuation.

세계 기후에 대한 컴퓨터 모델을 사용하는 것은 기후 변화를 야기하는 다양한 요소들을 모두 고려할 수 있는 하나의 방법이다.

PARAPHRASE 1

One way to calculate how all the diverse components contribute to climatic variation is by using computer models of the global climate.

PARAPHRASE 2

Computer models of the global climate are employed to put all the multiple reasons of climate change together.

144 assess

Archaeology

SYNONYMS v. appraise, evaluate, estimate, judge, value, size up

평가하다, 판단하다

assess
[əsés]

Modern scientists can **assess** when stone tools were used and determine whether those who used them were right-handed or left-handed through the close and sharp observation of the tools.

도구들에 대한 면밀하고 날카로운 관찰을 통해 현대의 과학자들은 돌로 만든 도구들이 언제 사용되었는지를 판단하고 이를 사용했던 사람들이 오른손잡이였는지 왼손잡이였는지를 알아낸다.

PARAPHRASE 1

Observing the instruments thoroughly allows modern researchers to **appraise** the age of implements made of stone and get to know whether they were utilized in the right hand or the left.

PARAPHRASE 2

By scanning the tools, modern scientists can **evaluate** the era of the stone tools and decide whether they belonged to right handers or left handers.

145 despite

Literature

| SYNONYMS | prep. notwithstanding, regardless of, in spite of | ~에도 불구하고 |

despite
[dispáit]

Books had to be arduously duplicated by hand and this interrupted the development of literature **despite** the fact that aboriginal languages were progressively used and oral folk tales were incorporated.

구전설화의 통합과 토착 언어의 점진적인 사용에도 불구하고, 책들은 수작업으로 힘들게 복사되어야 했고 이는 문학의 발전을 저해했다.

PARAPHRASE 1

Notwithstanding the increasing use of the vernacular and the integration of oral folk stories, the growth of literature was hampered as books had to be laboriously copied out by hand.

PARAPHRASE 2

Regardless of the combination of dialect and folk tales, labor-intensive duplication of books by hand discouraged the growth of literature.

146 allocate

Botany

SYNONYMS v. assign, allot, apportion, designate, distribute, divide, administer, deal out, parcel out

분배하다, 할당하다

allocate
[ǽləkèit]

Reproduction requires the consumption of almost all of the energy in an organism and very little energy is allocated to strengthening the body.

하나의 유기체가 번식을 하는 데에는 거의 모든 에너지의 소비를 필요로 하며, 에너지의 매우 적은 양만이 신체를 강화하는데에 할당된다

PARAPHRASE 1
An organism uses almost all of its energy for the sake of reproduction and assigns very little to reinforcing the body.

PARAPHRASE 2
Most energy in an organism is spent on reproduction, with very little allotted to physical development.

147 adroit

SYNONYMS **adj.** skilled, skillful, professional, specialized, proficient, dexterous, adept, expert, deft, accomplished, consummate

능숙한, 숙련된

adroit
[ədrɔ́it]

The factory workers in the new market producing wealth for the few were designated into smaller positions that barely required them to be **adroit**, which resulted in decreases in their wages.

소수를 위해 부를 창출하는 새로운 시장에서 공장 노동자들은 숙련된 능력이 요구되지 않는 하찮은 역할을 배정받았고, 이는 그들의 임금 저하를 초래했다.

PARAPHRASE 1

As the new market created fortunes for the few and tasks in the factory system were segmented into trivial and less **skilled** parts, the payment of workers became lower.

PARAPHRASE 2

In the new market exclusively for the few, the factory system reduced the laborers' wages by assigning them into unimportant and less **skillful** parts.

148 evade

Botany

SYNONYMS v. elude, avoid, eschew, flee — 피하다

evade
[ivéid]

The plants in the alpine region are characterized by their low growth form and this makes it easier for them to **evade** the harshness of strong winds and to make use of the higher temperatures near the surface of the earth.

고산 지대의 식물들은 낮은 성장 형태를 특징으로 하며, 이는 혹독한 강풍을 피하고 지표면 근처의 더 높은 온도를 이용하는 것을 용이하게 한다.

PARAPHRASE 1

Low growth form is the most conspicuous attribute of the alpine plants, which enables them to **elude** the severity of high winds and to benefit from warmth near the ground.

PARAPHRASE 2

The most remarkable trait of the alpine plants, low growth form, allows them to **avoid** gales and to employ the warmth close to the surface.

149 trivial

Day 15
Astronomy

> **SYNONYMS** **adj.** frivolous, slight, trifling, petty, minor, negligible, unimportant, insignificant, secondary, incidental, inconsequential
>
> 사소한, 하찮은, 중요하지 않은

trivial
[tríviəl]

The leading cause of the colorful cloud bands that determine the appearance of Jupiter is trivial chemical and temperature distinctions between the bands.

목성의 외관을 결정하는 구름 띠들이 형형색색을 띠는 주요한 원인은 띠들 사이의 미세한 화학적 차이와 온도 차이 때문이다.

PARAPHRASE 1

Frivolous chemical and temperature disparities between the bands on the surface of Jupiter are responsible for their different colors.

PARAPHRASE 2

The shades of Jupiter's cloud bands are different due to slight chemical and temperature differences between the bands.

150　accumulate

Day 15
Environmental Science

| SYNONYMS | v. | amass, build up, aggregate, collect, assemble, cluster, group, gather, pile up, pack together | 모으다, 축적하다 |

accumulate
[əkjúːmjəlèit]

Some plants can be a solution to clean up contaminated soils containing particular minerals full of high levels of toxicity because they can **accumulate** high levels of these minerals.

일부 식물들은 특정 무기물을 상당히 많이 축적할 수 있기 때문에, 독성으로 가득 찬 이러한 무기물로 오염된 토양을 정화하기 위한 하나의 해결책이 될 수 있다.

PARAPHRASE 1

Since some plants can **amass** high levels of certain minerals, they can be used for the purification of the soils filled with these toxic minerals.

PARAPHRASE 2

Some plants which can significantly **build up** specific minerals can be utilized to purify polluted soils with these pernicious minerals.

DAILY CHECK-UP

A. Find the answer that is closest in meaning to the highlighted word or phrase in the sentence.

01. Only Egyptians were believed to be so **specialized** that they could go across and colonize the Pacific Ocean.
    (A) fierce   (B) adept

02. Considering teachers' morale, teachers should not be **assessed** by their students.
    (A) evaluated   (B) speculated

03. As high temperatures make it harder for planes to take off, the **exceedingly hot** weather became a major problem for airlines.
    (A) opulent   (B) baking

04. Eating food at restaurants allows people to sample **a variety of** foods.
    (A) diverse   (B) hostile

05. Merchants could **shun** the identification and assessment of the value of diverse coins issued in a lot of different regions.
    (A) elude   (B) entice

06. The Pueblo Indians **engrossed** with protecting against nomadic attacks took an unfriendly attitude toward Christianity.
    (A) aggregated   (B) absorbed

07. All functional objects show differences in **insignificant** details that do not hinder their cardinal function.
    (A) principal   (B) incidental

08. All the Jovian planets spin much faster than terrestrial planets **in spite of** their larger size.
    (A) although   (B) despite

09. Microorganisms which settle to the bottom of the seafloor **amass** in sea mud.
    (A) pile up   (B) accomplish

10. Energy within all organic bodies is **parceled out** into development, maintenance, propagation, and storage.

    (A) distributed   (B) hyperbolized

B. Complete each sentence using one of the words or phrases given.

11. Members in small groups are more likely to form intimate relationships with each other, allowing them to _____ others.

    (A) judge   (B) squander

12. People can make use of human cloning technology in _____ areas.

    (A) the number of   (B) a wide range of

13. A desert is often pictured as a _____ area lacking in vegetation where sand is blown by the wind

    (A) scorching   (B) freezing

14. In order to _____ the desiccation of the Sahara, tribes who dwelled in the area may have decided to leave there.

    (A) evade   (B) apportion

15. Johnson was extremely _____ with the Vietnam War while he was in public office for six years.

    (A) clustered   (B) obsessed

16. Socrates barely wrote _____ the fact that he occupied a prominent position in the history of ideas.

    (A) notwithstanding   (B) even though

---

01. (B) 02. (A) 03. (B) 04. (A) 05. (A) 06. (B) 07. (B) 08. (B) 09. (A) 10. (A)
11. (A) 12. (B) 13. (A) 14. (A) 15. (B) 16. (A)

REVIEW TEST (DAY 11-15)

A. The word _____ in the passage is closest in meaning to

01. Observed in the clouds of Jupiter, the vivid colors seem to the **product** of delicate chemical reactions of the microelements existing in the Jovian atmosphere, which include sulfur whose combinations partake of a great diversity of colors. Nevertheless, the detailed information related with the colors is largely unknown.

(a) appreciation
(b) consequence
(c) venue
(d) competence

02. Prescribed burning is a method that is designed and widely used to achieve the goals for specific forestry management. Despite the fact that it **generates** a lot of controversy, many experts still think that it has definite benefits such as reactivating vegetation communities, and facilitating the improvements of habitats for wildlife and livestock, which promotes biodiversity.

(a) hyperbolizes
(b) squanders
(c) pulverizes
(d) arouses

03. Experts claim that cloning will be the answer to curing life-threatening diseases and creating human organs to save human life. However, we shouldn't overlook the fact that this cannot be accomplished without experimentation on embryos. **Opponents** of cloning point out that under the current condition of cloning techniques, scientists need to victimize a number of embryos in order to create a cloned organism.

(a) Disciples
(b) Antagonists
(c) Predecessor
(d) Upholders

REVIEW TEST (DAY 11-15)

04. According to the archaeologists, including Peter Ucko and Andree Rosenfeld, the **cardinal** geological locations of paintings in the caves of western Europe are largely found in three parts: in cave mouths and rock shelters; in places just off the populated areas of caves; and in deeper and inaccessible parts of the caves, in which it has been assumed that some of the cave dwellers performed magical and religious rituals.

(a) unsurpassed
(b) luminous
(c) voracious
(d) prime

05. Biodegradable plastics should not be recycled with other plastics because non-biodegradable plastics can be polluted if they are blended with biodegradable plastics. Another reason is that unless biodegradable plastics are appropriately **thrown away**, they will increase landfill waste. This inappropriate disposal results in an inefficient decomposition of the plastics, emitting poisonous substances into the environment.

(a) played up
(b) partaken in
(c) aggregated
(d) discarded

06. The conclusive evidence was that the corpses of a massive number of animals were discovered in the grave, but domestic animals were not there. This implies that it was prior to the arrival of humans who brought livestock to the island. Besides, the bones in the grave were believed to be at least 500 years old, explaining that the animals could be isolated by repeated cyclones, flooding or an **abrupt** rise in seawater levels.

(a) frivolous
(b) sudden
(c) dexterous
(d) menacing

07. Utility of place means that since a good or service sells better in a certain **locale**, it should be available in the ideal place where people are more likely to purchase it. To illustrate, people living in tropical regions don't have to wear the winter coat and thus no one buys it. On the other hand, in Alaska, people would be willing to purchase it because the warm winter coat is one of the necessities to people in cold areas.

(a) spot
(b) agitation
(c) turmoil
(d) eminence

08. Agriculture is one of the most significant elements which influence soil productivity. Due to their higher potential for food production, the finest quality lands can move up production. However, the average quality of land drops as more and more land is cleared for the purpose of agricultural production and thus decreases latent productivity per hectare. Crops which **use up** nutrients reduce soil fertility, which ultimately causes a decline in crop yields.

(a) further
(b) cede
(c) exhaust
(d) forsake

09. Even the strongest **adherents** of bird migration based on geography are skeptical to include birds migrating long-distances in this category. This is because unlike the belief that like humans, birds migrate according to major geographical features, radar evidence reveals that flocks of migrating birds detected by radar generally ignore noticeable landmarks such as major rivers, valleys and hills.

(a) craftsmen
(b) foes
(c) antecedents
(d) proponents

REVIEW TEST (DAY 11-15)

10. Once found in abundance, the dodo, a flightless bird native to the Indian Ocean Island of Mauritius, has become **defunct** since the mid-to-late 17th century. Although there have been many assumptions about the species' extinction, many people still think that it was due to human activity.

    (a) fastidious
    (b) daunting
    (c) extinct
    (d) cumbersome

11. Cloning has been studied and can be applied to a wide variety of fields. First, human cloning might obviate the human aging process. The anti-aging business is often a prime target because doing so has already been a multibillion business. Second, cloning can be utilized for scientific research purposes such as **duplicating** laboratory rats.

    (a) prospering
    (b) reproducing
    (c) extrapolating
    (d) ameliorating

12. The job of surveying canal courses allowed Smith to observe and study the large areas of rock exposed by the newly excavated canal. Later travelling every nook and cranny of the land and working on similar jobs, he **piled up** mineral samples and fossils and examined the newly revealed strata, which led him to make rudimentary discoveries about the nature of the Earth's past.

    (a) assembled
    (b) fabricated
    (c) contemplated
    (d) mingled

13. Many experts think that the carnivores such as coyotes, eagles, and hawks which are mostly at the very top of the food chain can be a solution to keep the prairie dog population down. Also, scientists claim that since there are many kinds of herbivores in that area, these predators still have a variety of prey if it were not for enough prairie dogs and thus prairie dogs play a **trifling** role in ecosystem.

(a) inauspicious
(b) pertinent
(c) petty
(d) formidable

14. In the stage of conscious competence, a person knows how to do a task without supervision and assistance, but conscious thought and concentration are required in order to perform it reliably. As it becomes **deft**, the person reaches the next stage of competence, unconscious competence. In this phase, it becomes possible to perform the task while doing something else, and as it becomes instinctual, it might be even harder to explain how the person does.

(a) commonplace
(b) engrossed
(c) secluded
(d) adept

답안

01. (B) 02. (D) 03. (B) 04. (D) 05. (D) 06. (B) 07. (A)
08. (C) 09. (D) 10. (C) 11. (B) 12. (A) 13. (C) 14. (D)

REVIEW TEST [DAY 11-15]

B. Which of the sentences below best expresses the essential information in the highlighted sentence in the passage? Incorrect choices change the meaning in important ways or leave out essential information.

15. Although orally transmitted sources were progressively incorporated, medieval culture was predominantly based on the contents of the manuscripts written by the previous writers, but not spontaneous responses of the authors to observations on their society and environment.

(A) Orally transmitted materials were gradually included, but medieval culture depended more upon the influences from the society and environment than the contents of existing documents.

(B) Despite the sources handed down by tradition, medieval culture was heavily dependent both on the contents of remaining manuscripts and the writers' responses to observation of the environment.

(C) In spite of the gradual addition of orally transmitted documents, medieval culture was not responses of the authors who observed their society and environment, but relied chiefly on the contents of extant manuscripts.

(D) Medieval culture which was passed down from mouth to mouth relied largely on the writers' responses to observation on the society and environment as well as the contents of remaining manuscripts.

해설 정답 (C)

Although ① orally transmitted sources were progressively incorporated, medieval culture was predominantly based on ② the contents of the manuscripts written by the previous writers, **but not** ③ spontaneous responses of the authors to observations on their society and environment.
→ **In spite of** ① the gradual addition of orally transmitted documents, medieval culture was **not** ③ responses of the authors who observed their society and environment, **but** relied chiefly on ② the contents of extant manuscripts.

문장을 크게 접속사 'although'를 기준으로 두 부분의 절로 나누었을 때 그 두 부분 사이의 관계와 주절에서 말하고자 하는 핵심 내용을 명확하게 이해하였는지를 평가하고자 하는 문제이다. 원문의 두 절은 '~에도 불구하고' 또는 '~이긴 하지만'이라는 의미의 접속사 'although'로 연결되어 두 절 사이의 관계가 역접 관계임을 알 수 있다. 또한 주절에서는 'A가 아니라 B이다'라는 의미의 'B, (but) not A' 구문이 사용되어 '중세 문화'는 A, 즉 ③의 내용이 아니라, B, 즉 ②의 내용에 의존하였음 파악하는 것이 매우 중요하다. Paraphrase 할 때에는, 접속사 'although'가 이끄는 종속절을 같은 의미를 갖고 있는 'In spite of'가 이끄는 전치사구로 바꾸어 표현할 수 있다. 이는 문장의 재구성을 위한 효율적인 방법으로 접속사 다음에는 반드시 절을, 전치사 다음에는 반드시 명사 또는 명사 상당어구를 두어야 한다. 또한 문장을 재구성하기 위해 'A가 아니라 B이다'라는 의미의 'B, (but) not A' 구문을 같은 의미를 갖고 있는 구문 'not A, but B'를 활용하여 재구성할 수 있다. 이 때 주절의 핵심 내용인 B와 비교 대상이 되는 A를 혼동하지 않도록 한다.

오답의 근거

(A) Orally transmitted materials were gradually included, but medieval culture depended more upon ③ the influences from the society and environment than ② the contents of existing documents.
→ 중세 문화는 현존하는 문서의 내용들(②)에 주로 의존하였으므로, 원문의 주절의 핵심 내용을 반대로 이해한 경우로 오답이다.

(B) Despite the sources handed down by tradition, medieval culture was heavily dependent both on ② the contents of remaining manuscripts and ③ the writers' responses to observation of the environment.
→ 중세 문화는 현존하는 문서의 내용들(②)에 주로 의존하였으므로, 원문의 주절의 핵심 내용을 잘못 이해한 경우로 오답이다.

(D) Medieval culture which was passed down from mouth to mouth relied largely on ③ the writers' responses to observation on the society and environment as well as ② the contents of remaining manuscripts.
→ 중세 문화는 현존하는 문서의 내용들(②)에 주로 의존하였으므로, 원문의 주절의 핵심 내용을 잘못 이해하였고, 또한 '입에서 입으로 전해진 자료들이 추가되었음에도 불구하고' 라는 원문의 종속절의 전제가 중세 문화를 설명하는 내용으로 잘못 언급되었으므로 오답이다.

다른 방식으로 paraphrase 하기

Although ① orally transmitted sources were progressively incorporated, medieval culture was predominantly based on ② the contents of the manuscripts written by the previous writers, **(but) not** ③ spontaneous responses of the authors to observations on their society and environment.

→ ① Orally transmitted materials were gradually included, but medieval culture depended largely on ② the contents of existing documents **rather than** ③ the influences from the society and environment.

REVIEW TEST [DAY 11-15]

원문의 두 절은 '~에도 불구하고' 또는 '~이긴 하지만'이라는 의미의 접속사 'although'로 연결되어 두 절 사이의 관계가 역접 관계임을 알 수 있으므로, 같은 의미를 갖고 있는 등위접속사 'but'을 활용하여 문장을 재구성할 수 있으며 이는 paraphrase과정에서 가장 빈번하게 발견되는 문장 재구성 방법으로 토플에서도 빈번하게 원문과 보기의 정답 문으로 나오므로 반드시 기억해 두도록 한다.

→ **Despite** ① the sources handed down by tradition, ② the contents of remaining manuscripts provided a solid foundation for medieval culture, but ③ the influences from the society and environment had little effect on it.

Paraphrase 할 때에는, 접속사 'although'가 이끄는 종속절을 같은 의미를 갖고 있는 'despite'가 이끄는 전치사구로 바꾸어 표현할 수 있다. 또한 원문 문장의 의미상 중심 내용을 주어로 사용하여 문장의 구조를 바꿀 수 있다.

16. There seem to be a number of aspects associated with reflective practice that have never been studied, such as the benefits of reflection that might be practiced by educators motivated externally in contrast with those of reflection by educators who might reflect habitually.

    (A) There has not been enough research done to clearly substantiate the assertion that it might be difficult for teachers to practice habitual reflection if it were not for external motivation.
    (B) A lot of matters of reflective practice have been unexplored, and one example is the relative value of externally motivated reflection compared to that of habitual refection practiced by educators.
    (C) It is believed that most teachers become a reflective practitioner more easily when there is no external motivation than when they are externally motivated.
    (D) Educators no longer need to study a great deal of matters on reflective motivation, including how external motivation affects their behavior in class compared to when it does not exist.

해설 정답 (B)
① There seem to be a number of aspects associated with reflective practice

that have never been studied, such as ② **the benefits of reflection that might be practiced by educators motivated externally in contrast with** those of reflection by educators who might reflect habitually.
→ ① A lot of matters of reflective practice have been unexplored, and one example is ② the relative value of externally motivated reflection **compared to** that of habitual refection practiced by educators.

원문 문장이 'reflective practice'의 일반적 특징과 그것의 하나의 예를 언급하는 두 부분으로 나누어져 있음을 파악하고, 이 두 부분의 내용이 올바르게 재진술 된 보기를 선택하는 문제이다. 원문은 '~인 것 같다'라는 의미의 관용적인 표현 'there seem to be ~'를 활용하여 'reflective practice'와 관련된 많은 양상들의 일반적 특징을 언급하고, 뒤이어 '예를 들어'의 의미의 'such as'를 활용하여 이러한 것들 중에 하나의 예를 들고 있다. Paraphrase 할 때에는, 원문 문장의 의미상 중심 내용, 'a number of aspects associated with reflective practice'을 문두에 두어 문장의 구조를 바꿀 수 있다. 또한, 같은 의미를 갖고 있는 표현들 'a lot of matters of reflective practice'을 활용하여 좀 더 주어를 간략하게 할 수 있다. 원문의 'reflective practice'의 특징을 설명하는 관계대명사절 'that have never been studied'는 재진술 문장의 주부가 된 원문의 중심 내용의 술부, 'have been unexplored'로 언급되어 하나의 절을 완성할 수 있다. 원문의 두 번째 부분, 즉 원문의 하나의 예는 등위접속사 'and'로 연결하여 하나의 절의 형태로 올 수 있고 이 때에는 'such as' 대신에 같은 의미를 갖고 있으며 절의 주어와 동사의 역할을 해 줄 수 있는 'one example is'로 바꾸고 나머지 부분을 덧붙여 줄 수 있다.

오답의 근거

(A) There has not been enough research done to clearly substantiate the assertion that <u>it might be difficult for teachers to practice habitual reflection if it were not for external motivation</u>.
→ '습관적으로 반성할 수 있는 교육자들의 가치와 외부적으로 동기 부여되었을 때 반성할 수 있는 교육자의 가치'를 비교하고 있는 원문 ②의 예시는 위의 밑줄 친 부분이 담고 있는 외부적 동기부여와 습관적 반성 사이의 관계와는 다르므로 오답이다.

(C) It is believed that most teachers become a reflective practitioner more easily when there is no external motivation than when they are externally motivated.
→ 프로젝션의 등장을 기준으로 관객과 영상 사이의 관계에 발생한 변화를 언급하는 주요 내용을 정반대로 언급한 오답이다. (was no longer public → was no longer private)

(D) Educators no longer need to study a great deal of matters on reflective motivation, including how external motivation affects their behavior in class compared to when it does not exist.
→ 원문 ①은 '연구된 적이 없는 반성적 실습과 관련된 많은 양상들이 존재하는 것 같음'을 언급할 뿐 '교육자들이 더 이상 연구할 필요가 없음'을 언급하지 않았을 뿐만 아니라 예시의 내용도 잘못 진술 되었으므로 틀린 내용으로 오답이다.

REVIEW TEST [DAY 11-15]

다른 방식으로 paraphrase 하기

① There seem to be a number of aspects associated with reflective practice that have never been studied, such as ② the benefits of reflection that might be practiced by educators motivated externally in contrast with those of reflection by educators who might reflect habitually.

→ ① Many aspects of reflective practice, which have been unexplored, contain ② the comparative value of externally motivated reflection and that of habitual refection practiced by educators as an example.

원문은 상위 범주(①)와 하위 범주(②)를 '예를 들어'의 의미를 갖고 있는 'such as'로 연결한 반면, paraphrase할 때에는 원문의 중심 내용을 주부의 자리에 두고 관용적 표현 'there seem to be ~'를 생략함으로써 문장을 더욱 간략히 할 수 있고, 뒤이어 '~을 포함하다'라는 의미의 동사 'contain' 또는 'include'를 놓아 예를 나열할 수 있다. 이 때에 하나의 예만을 제시하고 있음을 강조하기 위해 문장의 마지막에 '하나의 예로써'라는 의미의 'as an example'을 덧붙일 수 있다.

→ One of ① many unexplored matters about reflective practice is ② the contrast between benefits of externally motivated reflection **and** those of habitual reflection among educators.

원문을 간략하게 재진술 하기 위해 원문의 관계대명사절 'that have never been studied'을 '탐험되지 않은'의 의미를 갖는 형용사 'unexplored'를 활용하여 진술할 수 있다. 또한, 하나의 예를 제시하기 위해 'one of 복수명사'라는 표현을 활용하여 예시를 위의 재진술 문장의 ②와 같이 덧붙일 수 있다.

151 depict

Day 16
Fine Art

| SYNONYMS | v. | portray, picture, render, illustrate, represent, describe | 묘사하다 |

depict
[dipíkt]

Sculptures created by ancient Egyptian craftsmen include three-dimensional statuary that **depict**s non-elite members as well as formal statuary that represents gods, emperors, and celebrated elite members.

고대 이집트 장인들이 만든 조각들에는 신이나 왕, 또는 유명한 지식인을 묘사하는 형식적인 조각상뿐만 아니라 지식인 계층이 아닌 일반인들을 묘사하는 입체적인 조각상 역시 있다

PARAPHRASE 1

In addition to those of deities, kings, and a named elite population, the sculptures of Ancient Egyptians encompass three-dimensional forms **portray**ing general figures.

PARAPHRASE 2

Ancient Egyptian sculptors produced not only sculptures illustrating deities, rulers, and elite members but also three-dimensional ones **pictur**ing common people.

236

152 drastically

Geohydrology

SYNONYMS adv. severely, strikingly, extremely, radically, desperately, exceedingly, surpassingly, excessively, overly, prohibitively

지나치게, 극단적으로 엄청나게

drastically
[drǽstikəli]

The thoughtless consumption of a limited groundwater resource destitute of a natural water source that can replenish the water supply has caused the levels of groundwater in the area to lower **drastically**.

상수도를 다시 채워주는 자연수원이 부족한 상태에서 한정된 지하수원의 무분별한 소비는 이 지역의 지하수면을 극심하게 낮아지게 했다.

PARAPHRASE 1

The main reason why water tables of the region have dropped **severely** is because of a groundwater resource that was rarely recharged but indiscriminately used.

PARAPHRASE 2

The reckless use of a finite groundwater resource has led water tables in the area to fall **strikingly**.

153 solitary

Energy

SYNONYMS adj. isolated, secluded, lonely, remote   외딴, 고독한

solitary
[sάlitèri]

The extraction of hydrogen gas from water might be enabled through the use of electricity from large wind plants in **solitary** areas during all but periods when electricity is demanded most.

물로부터의 수소 가스 추출은 전력이 가장 많이 요구되는 기간을 제외한 나머지 기간 동안에 외딴 지역의 거대 풍력 발전소의 전력을 사용함으로써 가능해졌다.

PARAPHRASE 1

Hydrogen gas might be made from water by using electricity from large wind farms in **isolated** regions excluding at times of peak demand for electricity.

PARAPHRASE 2

Except when it is required most, electricity from huge wind plants in **secluded** areas might be utilized to split hydrogen gas from water.

154 vagarious

Anthropology

| SYNONYMS | adj. | unpredictable, capricious, whimsical, arbitrary, changeable, inconstant, fickle | 변덕스러운, 엉뚱한, 기발한 |

vagarious
[vəgéəriəs]

The Upper Paleolithic cave art largely included animals that the artists may have been most afraid of on account of their size, speed, **vagarious** behavior and natural weapons such as horns and tusks.

후기 구석기 동굴 벽화의 주요한 주제는 그 크기와 속도, 변덕스러운 행동, 그리고 뿔이나 엄니같은 천연 무기들 때문에 예술가들이 가장 두려워했을 동물들이었다.

PARAPHRASE 1

The main theme portrayed in the Upper Paleolithic cave art was animals that the painters may have dreaded most because of their size, speed, **unpredictable** behavior and natural weapons.

PARAPHRASE 2

Found in the Upper Paleolithic cave art as a main theme, large, nimble or **capricious** animals with natural weapons may have been feared by the artists.

155 equilibrium

Hydrology

SYNONYMS n. evenness, balance, symmetry, stability   평형

equilibrium
[kwəlíbriəm]

The rate of water movement is so slow that the flow of saline ground waters in the Indus plain has not reached equilibrium yet even after 70 years of being utilized.

물의 움직임이 너무 느린 탓에 인더스 평야의 염분 지하수의 흐름은 사용된 지 70년이 지났음에도 불구하고 아직 평형 상태에 도달하지 못했다.

PARAPHRASE 1

Although salty ground water in the Indus plain has been used for 70 years, its movement has still not reached evenness due to the slow movement of water.

PARAPHRASE 2

The slow water flow has made it difficult for saline ground waters in the Indus plain, tapped for 70 years, to reach balance.

156 mixed

Psychology

SYNONYMS adj. ambivalent, unsure, undecided

불확실한, 반대 감정이 병존하는

mixed
[mikst]

There are **mixed** viewpoints that research results on catharsis suggest. Some represent that it discourages future aggression by offering an outlet for tension, while others show that making people vent out anger instigates more aggression.

카타르시스에 관한 연구 결과는 상반된 의견들을 낳았다. 일부 연구에서는 카타르시스가 긴장의 발산 수단을 제공함으로써 미래의 공격성을 줄인다고 보는 반면 다른 연구에서는 사람들의 분노 표출은 더 많은 공격성을 조장한다고 본다.

PARAPHRASE 1

Research findings indicate **ambivalent** opinions on catharsis. Some suggest that it results in decreases in tension and further aggression, but others indicate that it promotes more aggression.

PARAPHRASE 2

Studies on catharsis reveal **unsure** viewpoints such as those that it lowers tension and aggression and those that it encourages more aggression.

157 comprehend

Day 16
Psychology

SYNONYMS v. understand, grasp, apprehend, catch, perceive, realize, conceive, be aware of

이해하다, 파악하다

comprehend
[kὰmprihénd]

As infants and toddlers encode and improve information that they have heard, they may be better able to **comprehend** and remember stories, which encourages them to recollect future affairs.

영유아들은 들은 정보를 암호화하고 개선해감에 따라 이야기를 더 잘 이해하고 기억할 수 있게 되며 이는 그들로 하여금 미래의 일까지 기억해내도록 촉진한다.

PARAPHRASE 1

Progressive decipherment of information that preschoolers gain may allow them to better **understand** and recollect stories. Thus, the stories lead them to recall coming events.

PARAPHRASE 2

Advanced encryption of what preschoolers hear may enable them to better **grasp** and recall stories, making the stories more helpful for recalling things to come.

158 advantageous

Day 16 — Pedagogy

SYNONYMS *adj.* profitable, beneficial, gainful, helpful, lucrative, useful, serviceable, fruitful

유익한, 도움이 되는

advantageous
[dvəntéidʒəs]

There are a variety of opinions concerning what leads teachers to be willing to become reflective, but the most noticeable reason why teachers work toward reflective practice is that they firmly believe that it is **advantageous**.

무엇 때문에 교사들이 기꺼이 신중히 행동하는 지에 대해서는 다양한 의견들이 있지만, 교사들의 신중한 행위의 가장 명백한 이유는 그 행위가 이롭다는 그들의 믿음 때문이다.

PARAPHRASE 1

There is disagreement about what makes teachers become reflective. However, the most apparent reason is because of their belief that it is **profitable**.

PARAPHRASE 2

Although opinions differ as to why teachers work toward reflective practice, the most apparent reason is due to their belief that it is **beneficial**.

159 with regard to

Day 16
Art

SYNONYMS phr. with respect to, in terms of, in relation to   ~에 대하여, ~라는 점에서

with regard to

It was once general to think of crafts **with regard to** function, leading them to be classified as the applied arts, but we now have a tendency to mention the varied crafts on the basis of the materials used.

한 때는 기능의 측면에서 공예품을 떠올리는 것이 일반적이었고 이때문에 공예품은 응용 예술로써 분류되었지만, 이제 우리는 사용된 재료를 바탕으로 다양한 공예품들에 대해 이야기하는 경향이 있다.

PARAPHRASE 1

While crafts were once commonly thought of **with respect to** function and this caused them to be known as the applied arts, we are now apt to refer to the diverse crafts according to the materials used.

PARAPHRASE 2

Unlike in the past when crafts were mentioned **in terms of** function, which became known as the applied arts, the various crafts are now referred to depending on the materials used.

244

160 elegant

Day 16
Sociology

| SYNONYMS | adj. | sophisticated, delicate, refined, exquisite, fine, stylish, polished, graceful |

우아한, 멋진, 정교한

elegant
[éləgənt]

Goods manufactured in factories were not as complete or **elegant** as those produced by hand, and artisan spirit gave way under the pressure from productivity improvement.

공장에서 생산된 제품들은 수공품들만큼 완벽하거나 정교하지 않았고 장인정신은 생산성 향상에 대한 압박아래 무너져내렸다.

PARAPHRASE 1 Products created by factories were less finished or **sophisticated** than artisans' handcrafts, and the pressure from the growth of production replaced workmanship.

PARAPHRASE 2 Factory goods were less perfect or **delicate** than handcrafts, and the pressure to improve productivity substituted for craftsmanship.

245

DAILY CHECK-UP

A. Find the answer that is closest in meaning to the highlighted word or phrase in the sentence.

01. In the beginning, the natural forces were regarded as **whimsical**.
    (A) unpredictable (B) frivolous

02. Paul Ekman asked people to express what kinds of emotions were **portrayed** in photographs.
    (A) accumulated (B) depicted

03. People who do not conceal feelings barely think that they can have **ambivalent** emotions of love and hatred for the same person.
    (A) fragile (B) mixed

04. By locating wind farms in **secluded** regions and upgrading their design, the problems of visual and noise pollution can be solved.
    (A) isolated (B) sophisticated

05. Birds oriented based on solar position, so when the Sun was blocked and mirrors were used, they oriented **with regard to** the new Sun.
    (A) with respect to (B) by means of

06. When surface radiation is equal to or lesser than the energy released at the core, stars are in a state of **balance**.
    (A) asymmetry (B) equilibrium

07. In order to **comprehend** human behavior, particularly aggression, inner conflicts should be explored.
    (A) understand (B) misidentify

08. Native mussels and clams can be **strikingly** affected by zebra mussels which hinder their development and reproduction.
    (A) severely (B) utterly

09. By begging loudly, fledglings can obtain more food and this allows them to grow rapidly or to become larger, either of which is **beneficial**.

(A) adverse (B) advantageous

10. Skillful and **graceful** performers were admired and this stimulated them to develop activities into keenly fulfilled theatrical performances.
    (A) elegant (B) revolting

B. Complete each sentence using one of the words or phrases given.

11. It is hard to say that they are _____ in that animals hardly have love-hate relationships with humans or with each other,
    (A) conscientious (B) ambivalent

12. The theater is one way for people to define and _____ their world or get away from displeasing realities.
    (A) perceive (B) neglect

13. Modern ecologists agree that the rate of disturbances is often so great that ecosystems have difficulty remaining in _____ endlessly.
    (A) equilibrium (B) appreciation

14. Plants are diffused to large areas of land, even to _____ islands, with the help of the seeds of grasses and flowers.
    (A) capricious (B) remote

15. The universal form of applied-art objects have been determined by the laws of physics, not some _____ decision.
    (A) vagarious (B) dexterous

16. Magma is formed when the lower crust mantle is melted and liquefied by _____ high temperature and pressure.
    (A) rudimentary (B) extremely

---

01. (A) 02. (B) 03. (B) 04. (A) 05. (A) 06. (B) 07. (A) 08. (A) 09. (B) 10. (A)
11. (B) 12. (A) 13. (A) 14. (B) 15. (A) 16. (B)

161 reflection

Topography

SYNONYMS n. indication, manifestation, expression   반영

reflection
[rifékʃən]

As a general rule, it is believed that high mountains were formed relatively more recently than low mountains. In other words, the height of a mountain is a **reflection** of the length of its existence.

일반적으로, 높은 산들은 낮은 산들보다 비교적 더 최근에 형성된 것으로 여겨진다. 즉, 산의 높이는 그 산이 얼마나 오래 존재해왔는지를 반영한다.

PARAPHRASE 1

Generally, the higher a mountain is, the more currently it was shaped, which suggests that the height of a mountain is an **indication** of how long it has existed.

PARAPHRASE 2

Commonly, the lower a mountain is, the older it is, which means that the current height of a mountain is a **manifestation** of its age.

162 discover

Architecture

| SYNONYMS v. | determine, find, detect, ascertain, recognize, perceive, discern, sense, spot, locate, pinpoint, identify, find out | 확인하다, 찾아내다, 인지하다 |

discover
[diskʌvər]

As methods of support are based on physical laws, they are utilized in architecture and have not changed over time since they were discovered first even when construction materials have undergone dramatic changes.

건물의 하중을 지탱해주는 방법들은 물리학 법칙에 기반하기 때문에, 건축자재들이 극적인 변화를 겪을 때에조차 최초로 발견된 형태 그대로 건축에 사용되고 있다.

PARAPHRASE 1

Even while building materials have radically developed, methods of support with little alternation since people first determined them are employed in architecture because they are based on the laws of physics.

PARAPHRASE 2

Regardless of the change in building materials, methods of support based on the laws of physics are used in architecture without change since they were first found.

163 original

Day 17

Anthropology

SYNONYMS **adj.** creative, ingenious, inventive, innovative, clever, imaginative, unique

독창적인

original
[ərídʒənəl]

As Africans developed **original** furnaces which make it possible to generate intense heat and regulate the volume of air, iron was available in the African continent from an earlier date than in the Americas.

높은 열의 발생과 공기의 양 조절을 용이하게 하는 독창적인 용광로를 개발한 덕분에, 아프리카인들은 아메리카 대륙에서 보다 더 이른 시기부터 아프리카 대륙에서 철을 이용할 수 있었다.

PARAPHRASE 1

Unlike in the Americas, Africans could use iron from relatively early days, by inventing **creative** heating systems that gave off high heat and regulated the volume of air.

PARAPHRASE 2

Africans could make iron a lot earlier than Americans, developing **ingenious** furnaces to emit high heat and to control the amount of air.

250

164 implant

Marine biology

SYNONYMS v. embed, insert, fix, lodge in   꽂아 넣다, 박다

implant
[implǽnt]

Whenever the oyster shells open up in order to respire and feed, small marine particles or organisms get into the oyster and these foreign substances become **implant**ed between the shell and the mantle.

호흡을 하고 먹이를 먹기 위해 조개 껍질이 열릴 때마다, 작은 해양 입자들이나 유기체들이 조개 안으로 유입되며 이러한 이물질들은 조개 껍질과 외투막 사이에 박히게 된다.

PARAPHRASE 1

Tiny marine particles flow into the oyster when the shell valves are open for breathing and feeding and these alien substances become **embed**ded between the shell and the mantle.

PARAPHRASE 2

Foreign matter entering while the oyster keeps its shell valves open to breath and feed are **insert**ed between the shell and the mantle.

165 misleading

Law

> **SYNONYMS** **adj.** deceitful, deceptive, dishonest, deluding, confusing
>
> 속이는, 현혹시키는

misleading
[mislíːdiŋ]

An extensive prohibition against **misleading** conduct in commercial transactions has been a rudimentary part of Australian law since 1974, and this remains unaffected under the Australian Consumer Law.

상거래 기망 행위에 대한 포괄적인 금지는 1974년 이래 호주 법률의 기초적인 부분이 되었고, 이는 호주 소비자법 아래에 변하지 않은 채로 남아있다.

PARAPHRASE 1

A far-reaching ban on **deceitful** conduct in commercial deals, which has been the basis for Australian law since 1974, remains unchanged under the Australian Consumer Law.

PARAPHRASE 2

Since 1974, Australian law has been based on a veto on **deceptive** conduct in business deals, which has not changed under the Australian Consumer Law.

166 melt

Glaciology

SYNONYMS v. dissolve, thaw, fuse, defrost, unfreeze, liquefy

녹다, 용해되다

melt
[melt]

During the last glacial period, the gigantic continental glaciers that covered North America **melt**ed away, and copious amounts of water flowed out from them.

마지막 빙하기 동안, 북미 대륙을 덮고 있는 거대 대륙 빙하가 녹아내렸고, 그로부터 엄청난 양의 물이 흘러나왔다.

PARAPHRASE 1

As the colossal ice sheets, covering North America during the last ice age, **dissolve**d away, huge volumes of water flowed from them.

PARAPHRASE 2

Large amounts of water flowed out when the great ice sheets in North America during the last ice age **thaw**ed.

167　suitable

Day 17
Botany

| SYNONYMS | adj. | appropriate, proper, applicable, adapted, adequate, well-suited, fit, correct, right | 적절한, 적당한 |

suitable
[súːtəbəl]

Wherever seeds are dropped into a **suitable** surface of the earth, new plants will make an abrupt appearance, but since they have small bodies, they cannot compete against other plants for natural resources such as space and water.

씨앗이 적절한 지표면에 떨어질 때마다, 새로운 식물이 발생한다. 하지만 새로 발생한 식물의 작은 크기는 공간이나 물과 같은 자연 자원을 두고 다른 식물들과 경쟁하는 것을 어렵게 한다.

PARAPHRASE 1

New plants will spring up when seeds fall on an **appropriate** soil surface, but they cannot compete with other plants for natural resources as they do not have big bodies.

PARAPHRASE 2

Seeds that fall on a **proper** soil surface emerge as new plants. However, their tiny size makes it hard for them to vie with other plants for natural resources.

168 surmise

Anthropology

SYNONYMS v. assume, speculate, hypothesize, suppose, presume, conjecture, suspect, guess, fancy

가정하다, 추측하다

surmise
[sərmáiz]

European settlers who initially arrived at the greater Pacific region named Oceania **surmise**d that the island's indigenous people must have wandered into Oceania, probably from Egypt or the Americas.

오세아니아라 불리는 더 거대한 태평양 지역 최초로 도달했던 유럽 정착자들은 그 섬의 토착민들이 아마 이집트나 미대륙으로부터 오세아니아까지 표류해 왔을 것으로 추정했다.

PARAPHRASE 1

That Oceania's original inhabitants must have gotten lost and strayed to the greater Pacific region, from Egypt or the Americas, was **assume**d by the first Europeans to arrive at the island.

PARAPHRASE 2

The first Europeans who reached Oceania **speculate**d that the island's native people must have drifted to Oceania from other areas.

169 withstand

Day 17
Forestry

| SYNONYMS | v. | endure, bear, sustain, tolerate, stand, resist, persevere, survive, support, uphold, hold, put up with |

지탱하다, 견디다

withstand
[wiðstǽnd]

A population of oaks shows relative stability through time, and it is reliant more on its ability to **withstand** the pressures of predation or competition than on its ability to make use of accidental events for survival.

오크 나무 개체는 시간이 흘러도 상대적인 안정성을 보이며 생존을 위해 우연적인 사건을 이용하는 능력보다는 포식자의 강탈과 경쟁의 압박을 견디는 능력에 더 많이 의존한다.

PARAPHRASE 1

A population of oaks is relatively settled through time, and it tends to survive by **endur**ing the pressures of predation or competition rather than by utilizing chance events.

PARAPHRASE 2

A population of oaks is stable through time, and its survival depends heavily on **bear**ing the stress of predation or competition.

170 procure

Agriculture

SYNONYMS v. gain, obtain, derive, earn, acquire, secure, get, achieve, attain, draw, reap

얻다, 획득하다

procure
[proukjúər]

Substantial increases in pumping costs resulted from the cost of water **procure**d through grand plans, which reduced the competitiveness of irrigated agricultural products from the area in the domestic and foreign markets.

펌핑 비용이 상당히 증가한 것은 거창한 계획을 통해 물을 얻어내려는 데에서 발생한 비용 때문이고, 이는 그 지역의 관개 농산물의 국내외 시장에서의 경쟁력을 감소시켰다.

PARAPHRASE 1

The cost of water **gain**ed through grand schemes increased pumping costs considerably, and thus the cost of irrigated agricultural goods produced in the region became uncompetitive in the internal and external markets.

PARAPHRASE 2

Obtained through grand plans, the cost of water escalated pumping costs, weakening price competitiveness of irrigated crops from the region in the world markets.

257

DAILY CHECK-UP

A. Find the answer that is closest in meaning to the highlighted word or phrase in the sentence.

01. It is not easy to make a **manifestation** on a complicated task like teaching.
    (A) reflection   (B) dissemination

02. The fossil called Pakicetus was **implanted** in rocks which were shaped from river sediments.
    (A) embedded   (B) eschewed

03. Small snowdrifts **thawed** by means of rocks heated by the sun at roughly 6,100 meters on Makalu in the Himalayas.
    (A) aggregated   (B) melted

04. Wells start to be drilled for the production of oil whenever an oil pool or field is **located**.
    (A) averted   (B) discovered

05. Although the paintings were drawn by spraying water by mouth, people could **guess** which hand was used in the operation.
    (A) presume   (B) elucidate

06. Some fossils **survived** over long periods of time, indicated by the fact that they are discovered in a number of strata.
    (A) prolonged   (B) endured

07. Ekman **acquired** research results in various cultures by allowing participants to report that facial expressions show multiple emotions.
    (A) discarded   (B) obtained

08. Loie Fuller who was a **creative** dancer enlarged her concerns to newly rising artistic media.
    (A) ingenious   (B) ambivalent

09. Spartina forms natural communities when its seeds drop into an **adequate** ground and begin to bud.

(A) exquisite (B) appropriate

10. Some species make good use of **deceptive** strategies in order to get away from their predators.

    (A) furious (B) confusing

B. Complete each sentence using one of the words or phrases given.

11. If rainwater, _____ snow or rivers no longer replenishes the Ogallala Aquifer, the aquifer could be depleted.

    (A) burning (B) melting

12. In the 1940's, Lascaux Grotto was _____ by children who were living in Southwest France.

    (A) discovered (B) triggered

13. Aggressive people who tend to distort others' intentions _____ that others deliberately try to harm them.

    (A) suspect (B) instigate

14. An increase in sucking behavior and heart rate are _____ of an infant's interest in a new stimulus.

    (A) affiliations (B) expressions

15. The control of political power was _____ by those who knew the secret methods of producing iron.

    (A) procured (B) buffered

16. Populations that are able to _____ environmental alterations are produced by competitive organisms.

    (A) tolerate (B) percolate

---

01. (A) 02. (A) 03. (B) 04. (B) 05. (A) 06. (B) 07. (B) 08. (A) 09. (B) 10. (B)
11. (B) 12. (A) 13. (A) 14. (B) 15. (A) 16. (A)

171 foundation

Day 18
Psychology

SYNONYMS **n.** basis, base, underpinning, ground, groundwork, infrastructure

기초, 기반

foundation
[faundéiʃən]

People determine whether they will commit an act of aggression or not on the **foundation** of elements including aggressive situations that they have undergone and their interpretation of others' incentives.

사람들이 공격적인 행동의 실행 여부를 결정할 때에는, 그들이 겪어 온 다른 공격적인 상황들이나 다른 사람들의 동기에 대한 해석 등의 요소들을 기반으로 한다.

PARAPHRASE 1

Whether people will show aggression or not is decided on the **basis** of various elements: their experiences with aggression and their analysis of others' motives.

PARAPHRASE 2

People judge if they will act in aggressive ways or not on the **base** of several factors.

172 protrude

Oceanography

| SYNONYMS | v. | project, extend, bulge, stick out, stretch out | 돌출하다, 튀어나오다 |

protrude
[proutrúːd]

Most tuna species do not have **protrud**ing eyes at all as well as lack scales all over the body, which allows their skin to be smooth and glassy.

대부분의 참치 종은 온몸에 비늘이 부족하기 때문에 그들의 피부는 부드럽고 매끈할 뿐만 아니라 그들의 눈 역시 돌출되어 있지 않다.

PARAPHRASE 1

Most tuna species are void of scales throughout the body, which enables their skin to be slippery, and their eyes do not **project out** at all.

PARAPHRASE 2

Most tunas have smooth skin with few scales and do not have **extend**ing eyes.

173 task

Day 18
Environmental Science

| SYNONYMS | n. | plan, project, scheme, job, assignment, enterprise, undertaking | 계획, 사업, 과제 |

task
[tæsk]

The introduction of artificial water points, along with the construction of veterinary fences in vast areas of the Kalahari, had resulted in the prompt desertification and analogous **task**s have had the identical impact in the Southern Kalahari.

칼라하리의 방대한 지역에 가축 울타리를 설치하고 인공 급수장을 도입함에 따라 급속한 사막화를 초래되었고, 유사한 계획들 역시 칼라하리 남부지역에 동일한 영향을 미쳤다.

PARAPHRASE 1

The swift desertification in the Kalahari had resulted from the broad erection of veterinary fences and artificial reservoirs, and similar **plans** have comparably influenced the Southern Kalahari.

PARAPHRASE 2

Large areas of the Kalahari had rapidly desertified after building stockyards and artificial reservoirs, and the Southern Kalahari has been equally affected by similar **projects**.

174 utilization

Film History

Day 18

SYNONYMS n. employment, application, use, appliance, exploitation

이용

utilization
[júːtəlàizéiʃən]

For **utilization** in Kinetoscope parlors, consisting of a few private machines and allowing one spectator to watch a short film, Thomas Edison created the peepshow device named the kinetoscope.

토마스 에디슨은 몇 개의 개인용 기계들로 구성되어 있어서 한 명의 관객이 짧은 영화를 볼 수 있도록 하는, 키네토스코프라는 이름의 활동 사진 영사소용 관람 기구를 만들었다.

PARAPHRASE 1

Thomas Edison's kinetoscope was devised for **employment** in kinetoscope parlors, containing some personal machines permitting one person to see a short film.

PARAPHRASE 2

Thomas Edison invented the kinetoscope for **application** in kinetoscope parlors, which included a few individual machines that played a short film for one viewer.

175 antiseptic

Day 18 · Chemistry

SYNONYMS adj. sanitary, hygienic, pure, pristine, clear, clean, sterile, unspoiled, unstained, immaculate, sterilizing

깨끗한, 청결한, 위생적인

antiseptic
[æntəséptik]

Portland inhabitants took a ballot in order to decide whether to support or protest the inclusion of dangerous fluorine additives to their extremely **antiseptic** water supply.

포트랜드 주민들은 그들의 매우 청결한 상수도에 위험한 불소 첨가물을 포함 시킬지 말지를 결정하기 위해 투표를 했다.

PARAPHRASE 1

Portland residents cast a vote for or against adding hazardous fluoride to their water supply that is so **sanitary** and pure.

PARAPHRASE 2

Portland dwellers took a vote on an issue of whether or not to fluoridate their greatly **hygienic** water supply.

176 arduous

Day 18
Architecture

| SYNONYMS | adj. | difficult, taxing, laborious, demanding, exacting, severe, effortful, tough, tricky, problematic, troublesome, annoying, burdensome, irritating, cumbersome, clumsy, awkward, fastidious, picky, choosy, grueling | 힘든, 어려운, 까다로운 |

arduous
[ά:rdʒuəs]

Ancient cities entirely developed from the **arduous** work of dealing with stone and this is proved by the fact that the world's most outstanding stone construction is found in the remains of the ancient Inca city of Machu Picchu.

고대의 도시들은 석재를 다루는 힘든 일을 통해 전체적인 발전을 이루었고, 이는 세계에서 가장 훌륭한 석재 구조물이 마추픽추의 고대 잉카 도시 유적에서 발견되었다는 사실에 의해 입증된다.

PARAPHRASE 1

The fact that ancient cities grew as a result of the **difficult** process of handling stone is testified to by the most brilliant stone architecture excavated in the ruins of the ancient Inca city of Machu Picchu.

PARAPHRASE 2

The world's finest stone structures found in the ancient Inca city of Machu Picchu testify to the fact that ancient cities grew from the **taxing** task of using stone.

265

177 arise from

Day 18
Biology

SYNONYMS *phr.* originate from, emerge from, derive from, stem from, be rooted in, be based on

~에서 기인하다, 유래하다 ~에 근거를 두다

arise from

Microglia **arise from** the bone marrow and are constantly replenished during life. On the other hand, other cells develop from the neural tube, the identical structures that produce the rest of the nervous system.

소교세포는 골수에서 생성되어 평생 동안 지속적으로 채워지는 반면 다른 세포들은 이와 동일한 구조를 가지고 있으며 신경계의 나머지를 생산하는 신경관에서 성장한다.

PARAPHRASE 1

Microglia continually renewed for life **originate from** the bone marrow, whereas other cells grow from the neural crest, identical with the structures generating the rest of the nervous system.

PARAPHRASE 2

Microglia **emerge from** the bone marrow and continue to be renewed for life, while other cells develop from the neural tube that originates the rest of the nervous system.

178 fame

Day 18
Folk Art

SYNONYMS **n.** reputation, celebrity, honor, renown, eminence, distinction, repute, mark, notice, note, prestige

명성, 명망

fame
[feim]

In order to earn money on the side, local craftspeople drew portraits. However, some talented men or women who depicted family members frequently won local fame and had a rush of orders for portraits.

지방의 장인들은 부업으로 돈을 벌기 위해 초상화를 그렸다. 하지만 자기 가족들을 그리던 일부 재능 있는 사람들이 종종 지역에서 명성을 얻어 그들에게 초상화 주문이 쇄도하기도 했다.

PARAPHRASE 1

Local craftsmen painted portraits as a lucrative side job, but sometimes some gifted people who sketched family members earned a local reputation, being swamped with orders for portraits.

PARAPHRASE 2

Although local artists took portraits as a profitable sideline, an able individual often gained celebrity, with orders for portraits pouring in.

179 dreadful

Day 18
Biology

SYNONYMS adj. threatening, horrendous, formidable, daunting, terrifying, intimidating, dreadful, fearful, frightful, menacing, dismaying, terrible, awful, horrific, dire.

겁나는, 무서운

dreadful
[drédfəl]

The microbes which resulted in the most **dreadful** tragedies through centuries had been hunted down one after another by the microbe investigators who dominated the first two decades of this century.

수세기에 걸쳐 가장 무시무시한 재앙의 원인이 되었던 미생물들은 금세기 첫 20년동안 지배적인 활동을 펼쳤던 탐구자들에 의해 차례로 추적되었다

PARAPHRASE 1

The microbe researchers who governed early in this century had tracked down, one by one of the microbes, the main causes of the most **threatening** scourges of centuries.

PARAPHRASE 2

It was the dominant microbe hunters early in this century that had searched out the microbes bringing on the most **horrendous** calamities for centuries.

180 chaos

US History

Day 18

SYNONYMS **n.** turbulence, agitation, tumult, disturbance, turmoil, commotion, disorder, confusion, disruption

동요, 혼란, 소란

chaos
[kéias]

It was not until the 1850s that a 10 hour workday became a reality in most industries, thanks to more than a decade of chaos, and the need of a strike by workers was realized by the courts, but these attainments had little prompt effect.

10년 이상 지속된 혼란의 결과로 1850년대가 되어서야 10시간 근무제가 대부분의 산업에서 실현되었고 노동자들에 의한 파업의 필요성이 법정에서 인정되었지만 이러한 성과가 즉각적인 영향을 미치지는 못했다.

PARAPHRASE 1

Although more than a decade of turbulence reduced a workday to 10 hours in various industries by the 1850s and the courts recognized that a strike is unavoidable, these gains hardly had instant influence.

PARAPHRASE 2

The actualization of a 10 hour workday through more than a decade of agitation, and the courts' recognitions of workers' strikes did not come into effect immediately.

DAILY CHECK-UP

A. Find the answer that is closest in meaning to the highlighted word or phrase in the sentence.

01. The Glomar Challenger's explorers had another **assignment**: that is to learn about where the domelike masses buried deep under the Mediterranean seabed originated.

    (A) perception   (B) task

02. The bronze alloy which was more durable and less fragile than iron was notably effective for **burdensome** tasks.

    (A) taxing   (B) crowning

03. The story goes that his **distinction** finally reached John Cremer, the head of Westminster Abbey at the time.

    (A) reputation   (B) indication

04. Tunas tuck their fins into special hollows or dents when their **use** is not acquired.

    (A) breakthrough   (B) utilization

05. Stability means how fast an ecosystem gets back to a specific form after a main **tumult** such as fire.

    (A) dissonance   (B) disturbance

06. The assassination of John F.Kennedy was an **awful** shock to the American people.

    (A) horrendous   (B) exquisite

07. Phenol is utilized as a **pristine** baby product in the form of a powder.

    (A) sublime   (B) pure

08. The culture of the Pacific islands had the **foundation** essential to adapt to the marine environment effectively.

    (A) underpinning   (B) obstruction

09. The evolutionary success of coelacanths partially **stems from** their ability to cease their metabolisms at will.

   (A) derives from (B) distracts from

10. Teotihuacan's green jade mask is characterized by parted lips and **projecting** mouth with a wide upper lip.

   (A) procuring (B) protruding

B. Complete each sentence using one of the words or phrases given.

11. Edison's kinetoscope business took the biggest hit with the extensive _____ of projection technology.

   (A) use (B) placement

12. Ancient Egyptian figures represent a wide variety of actions in proper poses as they perform their _____ .

   (A) fractures (B) undertakings

13. In the south of England, many tall, old yew trees were blown down by an _____ storm.

   (A) explicating (B) intimidating

14. The layering which occurs on a yearly _____ allows the observed alterations in the records to be easily dated.

   (A) basis (B) venue

15. By handling eggs in a careful and _____ way, salmonella poisoning can be decreased.

   (A) hygienic (B) intrinsic

16. President Theodore Roosevelt achieved _____ as a result of his domestic policies for economic and social reform.

   (A) eminence (B) affiliation

---

01. (B) 02. (A) 03. (A) 04. (B) 05. (B) 06. (A) 07. (B) 08. (A) 09. (A) 10. (B)
11. (A) 12. (B) 13. (B) 14. (A) 15. (A) 16. (A)

181 consume

Zoology

SYNONYMS v. eat, ingest, take, have, devour, take in 먹다, 섭취하다

consume
[kənsúːm]

For the survival of approximately 40 people, there was no choice but to **consume** a great number of deer and elk, which were abundant enough to provide food, particularly in that area.

약 40명의 생존을 위해서는 특히 그 지역에서 식량을 제공할만큼 충분히 풍부한 수가 존재했던 사슴들을 먹는 것 이외에는 선택의 여지가 없었다.

PARAPHRASE 1

Almost 40 people had no choice but to **eat** a lot of deer and elk, abundant in that area, for food in order to keep them alive.

PARAPHRASE 2

About 40 people could survive by **ingest**ing deer and elk, dominant in that region.

182 terminal

Hydrology

SYNONYMS adj. conclusive, final, ultimate, decisive, definite, definitive

결정적인, 궁극적인, 마지막의, 최종의

terminal
[tə́ːrmənl]

Regardless of the **terminal** alternative to the water crisis, it is obvious that irrigation water within the High Plains will never again be a copious and cost-effective resource in comparison to during the agricultural boom years.

수자원 위기에 대한 궁극적 대안이 무엇이든간에, 고원지대 내의 관개 용수는 농업 전성기 때와 비교했을 때 다시는 풍부하고 비용 효율적인 자원이 되지 못할 것임이 명백하다.

PARAPHRASE 1

Within the High Plains, irrigation water will not provide the plentiful and reasonable resource anymore compared to during the heyday of agriculture with no regard to the **conclusive** answer to the water crisis.

PARAPHRASE 2

Irrigation water of the High Plains will no longer be the ample and cheap source without reference to the **final** answer to the water crisis.

183 progressively

Day 19
Agriculture

SYNONYMS **adv.** gradually, steadily, slowly, increasingly, little by little

점차적으로

progressively
[prəgrésivli]

As the congestion of the population has increased, the cultivation of crops has stretched out into **progressively** more arid regions, which are liable to have intense dry periods and thus undergo crop failures.

인구 밀도가 증가함에 따라 작물 재배는 심각한 건기로 흉작을 겪을 가능성이 높은 더 건조한 지역까지도 점차적으로 확장되어 나갔다.

PARAPHRASE 1

The cultivation of crops has expanded into **gradually** drier regions, inclined to have serious dry seasons resulting in a failure of crops, due to the population increase.

PARAPHRASE 2

The population growth has led to the enlargement of crop cultivation into **steadily** drier areas, which seem to have periods of severe dryness, causing crop failures.

184 similar to

Day 19
Architecture

| SYNONYMS | phr. | comparable to, analogous to, akin to, similar to, parallel to, corresponding to | ~와 유사한, ~에 가까운 |

similar to

The forms of contemporary architecture consist of three elements **similar to** those of the human body, including an inner skeleton, an outer skin enclosing the internal spaces, and equipment, **comparable to** major organs in the body.

현대 건축의 형태는 인간의 신체 요소들과 유사한 세가지 요소, 즉 내부 뼈대, 내부 공간을 덮고 있는 외피, 그리고 신체의 주요 기관들과 유사한 장치들로 구성되어 있다.

PARAPHRASE 1

There are three components in modern architectural forms **analogous to** those of the human body: an inside skeleton, an outside skin covering the inner spaces, and devices, reminiscent of the body's vital organs.

PARAPHRASE 2

Modern architectural forms have three parts **akin to** those of the human body such as an internal skeleton, an external skin, and devices.

185 deny

Film History

SYNONYMS v. reject, refuse, negate, contradict, gainsay, decline, renounce, dismiss

부인하다, 거절하다

deny
[dinái]

Thomas Edison **deni**ed the development of projection technology, believing that if a projector was made and sold by him, film exhibitors would buy the one created from him in lieu of several machines.

토마스 에디슨은 그가 영사기를 만들어 판매한다면 영화관 사장들이 여러 기계들 대신에 그가 만든 영사기 살 것이라 믿었기 때문에 영사기 개발을 거절했다.

PARAPHRASE 1

Since Edison wanted film exhibitors to purchase one of various machines instead of a single projector he made, Edison **reject**ed the development of projection technology.

PARAPHRASE 2

Edison **refuse**d to create projection technology as he believed that the projector he made could restrict the range of machines film exhibitors could buy.

186 ancient

SYNONYMS *adj.* archaic, primitive, primeval, pristine, prehistoric, antique, old, aged

고대의, 원시의, 옛날의

ancient
[éinʃənt]

Now universally known as the Tower of the Winds, the most well-known weather vane in **ancient** history is the ancient Greek Triton, which has disappeared for centuries, but the building it rotated above can still be found.

현재 바람의 탑이라 알려져 있는, 고대사에서 가장 유명한 풍향계인 고대 그리스의 트리톤은 수세기 전에 사라졌지만, 그것이 존재했던 건물은 여전히 남아 있다.

PARAPHRASE 1

The ancient Greek Triton, which is the most famous weather vane in **archaic** history, has vanished for centuries, but the structure it stood above still remains and is now generally known as the Tower of the Winds.

PARAPHRASE 2

Although the ancient Greek Triton, the most noted weather vane in **primitive** history, has not survived, the structure it existed above is still preserved and is now known as the Tower of the Winds.

187 stimulate

Sociology

| SYNONYMS | v. | encourage, activate, motivate, prompt, spur, provoke, fuel, inspire, promote, further, advance, hearten, foster, cheer up | 격려하다, 촉진하다, 자극하다 |

stimulate
[stímjəlèit]

The three factors that contributed to **stimulate** the revolution in factory production were the lower priced transportation networks, the availability of capital and credit, and the growth of cities.

공장 생산의 변혁을 촉진하는데에 기여했던 세가지 요소는 저가 수송망, 자본과 신용의 이용 가능성, 그리고 도시의 성장이었다.

PARAPHRASE 1

Reasonable transport networks, the availability of capital and credit, and the rise of cities all **encouraged** the innovation in factory production.

PARAPHRASE 2

Cheap transport networks, the availability of capital and credit, and the urban growth all **activated** the change to factory production.

188 product

Economy

| SYNONYMS | n. | commodity, goods, merchandise, wares, staple, produce | 상품 |

product
[prάdəkt]

The production of products, preservation, and commerce was funded by capital that emerged primarily from gold and silver Spanish vessels brought from the Americas.

상품의 생산과 보존, 거래는 스페인 선박이 미국 대륙으로부터 가져온 금과 은을 통해 주로 마련된 자본에 의해 조달되었다.

PARAPHRASE 1

Originated chiefly from gold and silver from the Americas, the capital supported the production of commodities, storage, and trade.

PARAPHRASE 2

Spanish ships brought gold and silver from the Americas and this capital was spent on producing, storing, and trading goods.

189 controversy

SYNONYMS n. debate, argument, dispute, discussion, disagreement

논의, 논쟁

controversy
[kάntrəvə̀ːrsi]

The earliest man-made craftworks with artistic purposes are still the subject of intense **controversy**, but contrary to the general expectation that early artistic works would be coarse, the existence of workmanship traces back to the Upper Paleolithic era.

인간의 예술적인 목적으로 만든 최초의 공예품들은 여전히 강한 논란의 대상이지만, 초기 예술 작품이 조잡할 것이라는 일반적인 예상과 달리 예술적 기교의 존재는 후기 구석기 시대까지 거슬러 올라간다.

PARAPHRASE 1

The earliest handcrafts created with artistic goals are still the subject of **debate**, but unlike the belief that early artistic works would be crude, the existence of workmanship dates back to the Upper Paleolithic era.

PARAPHRASE 2

Although there has been an **argument** regarding what the earliest artifacts with artistic aims are, craftsmanship evidently existed in the Upper Paleolithic era.

190 inauspicious

| SYNONYMS | adj. | ominous, unfavorable, foreboding, threatening, doomful, inclement |

불길한

inauspicious
[inɔːspíʃəs]

Indians regarded an owl as an **inauspicious** animal due to their belief that one of the family members living in a house will face inevitable death if an owl sits on a tree near their house or on their roof.

만일 집 근처의 나무나 지붕 위에 올빼미가 앉아 있다면 그 집에 살고 있는 가족 중 한 명이 죽게 될 것이라는 믿음 때문에 인도인들은 올빼미를 불길한 동물로 간주했다.

PARAPHRASE 1

An owl is considered **ominous** by Indians in that they believed that a family member living in that house will meet his or her death if an owl is found on a tree near their house or on their roof.

PARAPHRASE 2

Indians believed that when an owl roosts in a tree near your house or on your roof, someone in that house will die, so they consider an owl **unfavorable**.

DAILY CHECK-UP

A. Find the answer that is closest in meaning to the highlighted word or phrase in the sentence.

01. When the pressure of gas **increasingly** fades away, oil is drawn from a well.
    (A) intermittently   (B) progressively

02. The lights emitted from color television are considerably **analogous to** the bright lights of the aurora.
    (A) akin to   (B) inclined to

03. Humans excessively deprived soil of water, promoting soil salinization, which became the **decisive** cause of desertification.
    (A) ultimate   (B) mediocre

04. Pakicetus has been found in the adjacent river, not from deposits of the **ancient** ocean called the Tethys Sea.
    (A) aboriginal   (B) archaic

05. The **foreboding** warning signs of landmines immediately attracted public attention.
    (A) ominous   (B) hospitable

06. Deer that inhabit Puget Sound **take in** a wide range of foods, migrating according to the season.
    (A) furnish   (B) consume

07. Factory production was dependent on the movement of **goods** to remote areas and the centralized workforce.
    (A) scrapes   (B) products

08. The **controversy** has arisen over whether water once existed on Mars.
    (A) disagreement   (B) consensus

09. Nowadays, satires are frequently used to **stimulate** critical thinking in political science courses.

(A) prompt (B) deter

10. Abraham Lincoln, the 16th United States President, was once designated as the governor of Oregon, but he **declined** the offer.
    (A) assented (B) refused

B. Complete each sentence using one of the words or phrases given.

11. In order to predict upcoming weather phenomena, _____ Egyptians measured the condition of their environment.
    (A) ancient (B) indigenous

12. The _____ indication of brainstem dysfunction is periodic or irregular breathing.
    (A) inauspicious (B) lucrative

13. As a weathervane on church steeples, people _____ started to use the shape of a rooster.
    (A) overly (B) gradually

14. A climax community, the _____ stage of ecological succession, remains stationary until destroyed by an external stimulus.
    (A) final (B) precarious

15. The quantity and variety of food an herbivore needs to _____ is determined by its size and metabolic rate.
    (A) ingest (B) percolate

16. Instead of gold or silver for other _____ , bills of exchange were generally accepted by capitalists and merchants.
    (A) infrastructure (B) merchandise

```
01. (B)  02. (A)  03. (A)  04. (B)  05. (A)  06. (B)  07. (B)  08. (A)  09. (A)  10. (B)
11. (A)  12. (A)  13. (B)  14. (A)  15. (A)  16. (B)
```

191 empty

Botany

SYNONYMS adj. hollow, vacant, void, blank, unoccupied, bare

텅 빈

empty
[émpti]

The seed heads of dandelions develop high enough above the ground so that they can be blown off by the wind and although their stems are empty, their water content allows them to stand straight.

민들레의 관모구(민들레의 솜털이 붙은 열매)는 바람에 날릴 수 있도록 지표면에서 충분히 높이 올라간 곳에서 성장한다. 그리고 그들의 줄기는 텅비어 있지만, 그들의 수분함량은 똑바로 서있는 것을 가능하게 해준다.

PARAPHRASE 1

The blowballs of dandelions raise high enough so as to let them be blown away by the wind and though they have hollow stems, they stand upright due to their water content.

PARAPHRASE 2

The clocks of dandelions grow high enough to catch the wind and despite their vacant stems, their water content enables them to stand erect.

192 depend on

Day 20 — Film

SYNONYMS phr. rely (up)on, be reliant (up)on, be dependent (up)on, turn to, count on

~에 의존하다, 의지하다

depend on

Motion pictures were significantly distinguished from other kinds of entertainment, which **depend**ed **on** either live performances or the active participation of a master of ceremonies.

영화는 라이브 공연, 또는 사회자의 적극적인 참여에 의존하는 다른 종류의 오락물들과 상당히 구별되었다.

PARAPHRASE 1

Relying **on** either live performance or the energetic involvement of a presenter, other forms of entertainment were widely different from motion pictures.

PARAPHRASE 2

Other types of entertainment **being reliant on** either live performance or the active involvement of a host differed considerably from movies.

285

193 govern

Day 20
Political Science

| SYNONYMS | v. | control, dominate, rule, master, manage, prevail, reign, regulate | 통치하다, 지배하다 |

govern
[gʌ́vərn]

The Whig Party **govern**ed cities, towns, and rural regions completely integrated into the market economy. On the other hand, the Democratic Party gained control over agricultural areas that were economically isolated and deprived.

휘그당은 시장 경제에 완전히 통합된 시, 읍 그리고 도시 근교 지역을 지배했던 반면, 민주당은 경제적으로 격리되고 궁핍한 농업 지역의 통치권을 얻었다.

PARAPHRASE 1

The Whigs **control**led urban and rural areas fully united into the market economy, whereas the Democrats' power was stronger in economically depressed farming regions.

PARAPHRASE 2

The Whigs **dominate**d economically powerful areas, while the Democrats had more power in poorer areas.

194 subsidize

Economy

SYNONYMS v. finance, support, fund, back, assist, pay for

후원하다, 자금을 조달하다

subsidize
[sʌ́bsidàiz]

Groups of investors who took part in short-term financial collaboration, joint-stock partnerships, and wealthy tradespeople were sources of funds used to **subsidize** European economic expansion.

단기 금융 협력에 참여했던 투자 그룹들, 합자 회사들, 그리고 부유한 상인들은 유럽의 경제 팽창을 지원하는데에 활용된 자금 주체들이었다.

PARAPHRASE 1

Funds from investors who achieved financial cooperation in the short term, joint-stock companies, and wealthy merchants were used to **finance** European economic growth.

PARAPHRASE 2

The growth in the European economy was **support**ed by funds from investors involved in short-term financial cooperation, joint-stock companies, and rich dealers.

287

195 capability

Sociobiology

SYNONYMS n. capacity, ability, proficiency, flair, talent, competence, faculty, aptitude, expertise, mastery, skill

재능, 능력, 능숙함

capability
[kéipəbiləti]

The sociobiological view has been adversely commented upon for numerous reasons, and one is that human capability to be superior to other species, with the exception of their aggressiveness, seems to be the decisive factor in human survival.

사회 생물학적 견해는 여러 가지 근거로 공격 받아왔고, 공격성을 제외하고는 다른 종들보다 우월한 인간 능력이 인간 생존의 결정적 요인이라는 것이 그 중 하나이다.

PARAPHRASE 1

The sociobiological point of view has been disputed on several grounds, one of which is that the dominant factor in human survival is people's capacity to outweigh other species, except for their aggression.

PARAPHRASE 2

The sociobiology view has been attacked for various reasons, and one is that human survival seems to be possible due to the human ability to outwit other species, not their aggression.

196 tend

Entomology

SYNONYMS v. look after, care for, attend, foster, take care of

돌보다, 보살피다

tend
[tend]

Worker termites are classified into three groups: nest workers, who construct the nest and tend the eggs; foragers, who search for food and share it with nest mates; and soldiers, who safeguard the colony from external enemies.

일꾼 흰개미는 집을 만들고 새끼를 돌보는 일개미, 먹이를 찾아 다른 개미들과 공유하는 사냥개미, 외부의 적으로부터 자신들의 영역을 보호하는 병정개미 이렇게 세 개의 집단으로 분류된다.

PARAPHRASE 1

Worker termites fall into three groups including nest workers building the nest and looking after the eggs, foragers feeding the nest, and soldiers protecting the colony against attack.

PARAPHRASE 2

Worker termites are divided into nest workers, who care for the nest and eggs, foragers, who provide food, and soldiers, who keep the colony safe from attackers.

289

197 symbolize

Psychology

SYNONYMS v. typify, incarnate, represent, exemplify, embody

대표하다, 상징하다, 구현하다

symbolize
[símbəlàiz]

The flapping wings of a butterfly **symbolize** a small fluctuation in the initial condition of the system, which gives rise to a series of events resulting in large-scale phenomena such as a tornado.

펄럭이는 나비 날개는, 토네이도와 같은 대규모 현상을 야기하는 일련의 사건들의 시발점인 시스템 초기 조건의 작은 변화를 상징한다.

PARAPHRASE 1

The flaps of butterfly wings **typify** a slight alteration in the early stage of the system, which brings about a chain of events leading to staggering phenomena.

PARAPHRASE 2

A tiny change in the initial phase of the system, eventually causing huge phenomena is **incarnate**d by the wingbeats of a butterfly.

198 retain

Cultural Anthropology

SYNONYMS v. maintain, sustain, keep, reserve, preserve, continue

유지하다, 보유하다, 지속하다

retain
[ritéin]

Although some early societies abandoned certain rites vital for their well-being, they retained the myths as parts of oral tradition and praised them not for their religious usefulness but for their artistic qualities.

일부 초기 사회들이 삶에 필수적인 특정 의식들을 포기하기는 했지만, 구전의 일부로서 신화는 유지했으며 이를 유용성이 아닌 예술적 가치의 측면에서 찬양했다.

PARAPHRASE 1

In some early societies, particular rituals essential to their well-being were abandoned, but as parts of oral tradition, the myths were maintained and admired due to their artistic qualities, not their religious usefulness.

PARAPHRASE 2

In some societies' tradition, myths, unlike rites, were sustained and valued due to their artistic values even when they were no longer religiously useful.

199 contaminate

Environmental Science

SYNONYMS v. pollute, taint, stain, corrupt, foul

더럽히다, 오염시키다

contaminate
[kəntǽmənèit]

It is only recently that investigators have taken into account using hyper accumulators to clean up soil that have been **contaminate**d by harmful amounts of heavy metals, which is an environmentally friendly approach named phytoremediation.

중금속에 오염된 토양을 정화하기 위해 연구자들은 하이퍼 어큐뮬레이터를 사용하는, 식물환경복원이라 불리는 환경 친화적인 접근법을 최근에서야 고려하고 있다.

PARAPHRASE 1

Only recently have researchers taken account of phytoremediation, an eco-friendly method using hyper accumulators for the clean-up of land **pollute**d by toxic heavy metals.

PARAPHRASE 2

The use of hyper accumulators to clean up **taint**ed soil has only recently been considered, which is an eco-sound technique called phytoremediation.

200 implement — Art

SYNONYMS n. instrument, tool, device, appliance, apparatus, mechanism, utensil

도구, 기구, 장비

implement
[ímpləmənt]

As right-handed artists prefer to flash a light upon the left in order that the end of the engraving **implement** does not stand in the shadow of their hand, light beams down on most engravings from the left.

손 그림자가 새기는 판화 도구의 끝자락과 겹치게 하지 않기 위해 오른손잡이 예술가들은 왼쪽에서 빛이 비추기를 선호하고, 따라서 대부분의 판화는 왼쪽에서 빛이 비춘다.

PARAPHRASE 1

Right-handed artists want to give light on the left so that the edge of the engraving **instrument** is not covered by the shadow of their hand and thus most engravings are best lit from the left.

PARAPHRASE 2

Not to cast a dark shadow of their hand over the tip of the carving **tool**, most engravings of right-handers are best lit from the left.

DAILY CHECK-UP

A. Find the answer that is closest in meaning to the highlighted word or phrase in the sentence.

01. Birds have a mapping **ability**, which helps them to decide the right direction.
    (A) immensity   (B) capacity

02. The blacksmiths made cooking **utensils** in the western part of Africa where iron was available.
    (A) tools   (B) dregs

03. Dandelions **are dependent on** their seeds which grow in places where competing species are absent.
    (A) take advantage of (B) rely on

04. Pueblos who constructed a stone town **exemplify** one of the Anasazis' crowning accomplishments.
    (A) decimate   (B) represent

05. **Vacant** bones which have been found nearby are presumed to be used to make tubes.
    (A) Empty   (B) Rugged

06. Most scales of mackerels have been lost, but a patch of coarse scales around the head has been **kept**.
    (A) furnished   (B) maintained

07. Leaf mustard has been used in order to decrease levels of selenium salts in **tainted** soils.
    (A) contaminated   (B) unsettled

08. Attempts to examine the subterranean water in dry regions have been **subsidized** by the World Bank.
    (A) backed   (B) contemplated

09. Walt Whitman decided to move to Washington, D.C. to **take care of** his brother wounded in the war.

(A) cheer up (B) look after

10. There is a considerable divergence of opinion among people about whether aggressive urges **dominate** them.

    (A) conceive (B) rule

B. Complete each sentence using one of the words or phrases given.

11. Costumes and masks were employed to _____ the mythological characters and supernatural power in the rites.

    (A) persevere (B) incarnate

12. Offshore platforms may cause oil spills, create oil slicks which _____ the beaches and destroy surrounding environment.

    (A) configure (B) foul

13. The large ones cut the leaves, while the smaller ants _____ the fungus.

    (A) care for (B) set forth

14. The _____ to express one's self in another language aids students in their career development.

    (A) ability (B) disposition

15. _____ thorns provide optimum nesting sites for some ant species that eat the nectar.

    (A) Hollow (B) Delicate

16. The decrease in plants even in the regions that _____ a soil cover deteriorates the water absorption capacity of the soil.

    (A) conjecture (B) sustain

---

01. (B) 02. (A) 03. (B) 04. (B) 05. (A) 06. (B) 07. (A) 08. (A) 09. (B) 10. (B)
11. (B) 12. (B) 13. (A) 14. (A) 15. (A) 16. (B)

295

REVIEW TEST (DAY 16-20)

A. The word _____ in the passage is closest in meaning to

01. The nestlings of ground-nesting warblers create higher-frequency begging cheeps compared to tree-nesting birds. These sounds of higher frequencies do not reach that far, and thus the individuals producing them may be effectively hidden, which is very **beneficial** considering the fact that these ground nesters are especially vulnerable to predators.

(a) useful
(b) tremendous
(c) noteworthy
(d) substantial

02. The results of a study done by researchers, Patricia Rice and Ann Paterson, suggest that the cave paintings discovered in southwestern France has certain symbolic significance. The data presented reveal that the overwhelming majority of animal images **portrayed** in the cave walls were the animals with meat and materials cave dwellers preferred.

(a) illustrated
(b) typified
(c) deteriorated
(d) implemented

03. Psychoanalysts who adopt a psychodynamic approach regard the behavior that vents aggressive urges as catharsis, which plays a role as a safety valve. However, there have existed **ambivalent** research results on the utility of catharsis. Some findings present that catharsis instigates more aggression, while others suggest that it reduces stress and the potential for future aggression.

(a) affable
(b) tenacious
(c) mixed
(d) cryptic

REVIEW TEST [DAY 16-20]

04. Many studies indicate that as a keystone species in the American prairie, prairie dogs play a crucial role in promoting biodiversity. If it were not for them, many aspects of life on the grasslands would change or disappear. Prairie dog colonies also provide other animals with **appropriate** habitats. Their abandoned burrows become homes for rabbits, salamanders, and snakes.

(a) commencing
(b) heedful
(c) incompatible
(d) suitable

05. Genetically modified plants are more resistant to harsh weather conditions. This advantage can protect crops from the threat of burning heat, drought or severe frost. For example, some sensitive plants such as tobacco and potato can be damaged under the unexpected frost. However, plants with an antifreeze gene from cold water fish can **bear** the cold weather in which unmodified ones would be generally destroyed.

(a) exude
(b) stand
(c) procrastinate
(d) reproach

06. According to the anthropologist Alexander Marshack, a system of notation carved on stone, bone and ivory may have been utilized by hunters to mark lunar phases as early as 30,000 B.C. If true, it would imply that humans in the Upper Paleolithic were capable of complicated thought and conscious awareness of their environment. Not only other works of art, but figurines depicting the human female in exaggerated form have been **spotted** at Upper Paleolithic sites.

(a) denounced
(b) indicted
(c) deposed
(d) located

07. Without the **application** of water fluoridation, most nations in Europe have experienced significant decreases in cavities. For instance, in Germany and Finland, the rates of dental caries were steady or kept reducing after water fluoridation stopped. Fluoridation may help to improve oral health in the U.S. because unlike most European countries, fluoridated water is the major source of exposure to fluoride for many U.S. children.

(a) employment
(b) credo
(c) dearth
(d) underpinning

08. Euthanasia is the act of killing someone who is extremely sick and will never recover to terminate their pain, generally done at their request or with their agreement. The issue of euthanasia has led to ongoing heated **debates**, but many people still disagree to euthanasia with good reasons.

(a) solicitudes
(b) wares
(c) disruptions
(d) controversies

09. Prescribed burning is frequently used in order to make people revitalize vegetation communities. Many landowners and public agencies carry out prescribed fire to help natural forests to restore and improve their conditions. In particular, burning in the natural forests **stimulates** germination or growth of native plants. It is also possible to alter the structure and composition of existing vegetation.

(a) encourages
(b) conjectures
(c) relinquishes
(d) deviated

REVIEW TEST (DAY 16-20)

10. In subtractive sculpting, one of the methods to form a sculpture, sculptors start with a solid mass of material larger than the **ultimate** work and carve unnecessary parts out of the mass until the sculpture achieves its completed form. The main materials are stone, wood, plaster and so on. The greatest downside of subtractive process is that it is very difficult for sculptors to modify their sculptures once something is removed.

    (a) scorching
    (b) sanitary
    (c) final
    (d) adroit

11. Many researches show that both a sun compass for diurnal migration and a star compass for nocturnal migration play an essential role in aiding birds in migrating in the proper direction. Diurnal animals decipher directions in space according to the position of the sun. Also, scientists have currently discovered that when most nocturnal birds are quite young, **capability** for star compass starts to be developed.

    (a) impetus
    (b) luster
    (c) shift
    (d) aptitude

12. In Pakistan, ecotourism provides direct financial support for local areas where tourism activities are generated and enjoyed. Money earned from tourism might be used to improve local facilities and develop innovative technology. For many countries such as Costa Rica, Ecuador, Nepal, Kenya, Madagascar and Antarctica, ecotourism is a major industry of the national economy, not simply a marginal activity to **finance** protection of the environment.

    (a) impute
    (b) support
    (c) clash
    (d) embroider

13. Since bioplastic industries **are** highly **reliant on** food crops such as corn, bioplastics compete with food production, causing the increased demand for food crops, rising food prices, negative impacts on agriculture. This mass production can also seriously influence food prices and opportunity cost of land usage.

(a) count on
(b) take part in
(c) put up with
(d) set apart

14. Even when the price of a product increases, its demand can increase due to the fact that people think that quality products **symbolize** wealth and status. Although this point counters the argument that the increase in a product price results in the decrease in demand for its product. Companies selling these items bring up the price of their products and thus sell more and make more money.

(a) smash
(b) incarnate
(c) plunge
(d) protract

답안
01. (A) 02. (A) 03. (C) 04. (D) 05. (B) 06. (D) 07. (A)
08. (D) 09. (A) 10. (C) 11. (D) 12. (B) 13. (A) 14. (B)

REVIEW TEST [DAY 16-20]

B. Which of the sentences below best expresses the essential information in the highlighted sentence in the passage? Incorrect choices change the meaning in important ways or leave out essential information.

15. People who believe that aggressive behavior is unacceptable and cannot be justified no matter what the reason are less likely to commit an act of aggression, while those who think that aggression can be justified and it is even indispensable in certain situations such as war are more likely to behave in an aggressive way.

   (A) Some people contend that in particular situations aggression is acceptable, whereas others argue that aggressive behavior should not be justified regardless of what the reason may be.
   (B) Even those who think that an act of unprovoked aggression is unjust and should not be justified acknowledge the necessity of defensive violence in such situations as during wartime.
   (C) Even though most people generally think that aggression is sometimes needed and can be justified, they barely behave aggressively because they think through the consequences of their actions.
   (D) People who believe that aggression can never be justified by any reason are less likely to show aggression than those who do not think like that.

해설 정답 **(D)**

① People who believe that aggressive behavior is unacceptable and cannot be justified no matter what the reason are less likely to commit an act of aggression, while ② those who think that aggression can be justified and it is even indispensable in certain situations such as war are more likely to behave in an aggressive way.
→ ① People who believe that aggression can never be justified by any reason are less likely to show aggression than ② those who do not think like that.

문장을 크게 접속사 'while'을 기준으로 두 부분의 절로 나누었을 때 그 두 부분 사이의 관계와 각각의 절의 주부와 술부 사이의 의미 관계를 명확하게 이해하였는지를 평가하고자 하는 문제이다. 원문의 두 절은 '반면에' 또는 '~인데 반하여'라는 의미의 접속사 'while'로 연결되어 두 절 사이의 관계가 역접 관계임을 알 수 있다. 또한 주절(①)과 종속절(②) 사이의 의미 관계를 살펴보면 공격성을 받아들이는 정도에 따라 공격성을 드러내는 정도 또한 달라짐을 알 수 있다. 따라서 Paraphrase 할 때에는, 이 두 가지 종류의 생각을 갖고 있는 사람들과 그 생각에 따른 결과를 비교급 구문을 활용하여 올바르게 비교할 수 있다. 이 과정을 통해 두 개의 절로 이루어진 원문을 하나의 절로 이루어진 문장으로 재구성 할 수 있다.

오답의 근거

(A) Some people contend that in particular situations aggression is acceptable, whereas others argue that aggressive behavior should not be justified regardless of what the reason may be.
→ 위의 보기의 문장은 원문의 비교의 대상인 '공격성은 정당화 될 수 있다고 생각하는 사람들'과 '공격성은 정당화 될 수 없다고 생각하는 사람들'에 대해 단순히 언급할 뿐 이들의 생각이 공격성을 드러내는 정도에 어떠한 영향을 미치는가와 같은 원문의 주요 정보를 언급하고 있지 않으므로 오답이다.

(B) Even those who think that an act of unprovoked aggression is unjust and should not be justified acknowledge the necessity of defensive violence in such situations as during wartime.
→ 원문은 단순히 '공격성을 받아들이는 정도에 따라 공격성을 드러내는 정도 또한 달라짐'을 언급하고 있을 뿐 '공격성은 정당화되어서는 안 된다고 생각하는 사람들이 특정한 경우에는 폭력의 필요성을 인정한다'는 언급은 없으므로 오답이다.

(C) Even though most people generally think that aggression is sometimes needed and can be justified, they barely behave aggressively because they think through the consequences of their actions.
→ 원문은 '공격성에 대한 두 가지의 다른 생각을 가진 사람들이 공격성을 다르게 드러냄'을 언급하고 있으며, '공격성은 정당화될 수 있다고 생각하는 사람들은 공격성을 더 드러내는 경향이 있다'고 언급하고 있으므로 보기의 밑줄 친 부분의 내용은 원문에 언급되지 않았을 뿐만 아니라 원문의 정보를 통해 추론할 수 없는 내용이므로 오답이다.

다른 방식으로 paraphrase 하기

① **People** who believe that aggressive behavior is unacceptable and cannot be justified no matter what the reason are less likely to commit an act of aggression, while ② **those** who think that aggression can be justified and it is even indispensable in certain situations such as war are more likely to behave in an aggressive way.

→ Whereas ② **people** who think that aggression can be justified and it is even indispensable in certain situations are more likely to behave aggressively, ① those who believe that aggressive behavior cannot be

REVIEW TEST [DAY 16-20]

justified no matter what the reason are less likely to commit an act of aggression.
→ ① People who believe that aggressive behavior is unacceptable and cannot be justified no matter what the reason are less likely to commit an act of aggression. On the other hand, ② those who think that aggression can be justified and it is even indispensable in certain situations such as war are more likely to behave in an aggressive way.

원문의 두 절은 '반면에' 또는 '~인데 반하여'라는 의미의 접속사 'while'로 연결되어 두 절 사이의 관계가 역접 관계임을 알 수 있으므로, 같은 의미를 갖고 있는 접속사 'whereas'를 활용하여 문장을 재구성할 수 있다. 이때에 'whereas'가 이끄는 종속절을 주절의 앞에 놓고 지시대명사 'those'는 지시어 'people'로, 주절의 지시어 'people'은 지시대명사 'those'로 바꾸어 줄 수 있다. 문장을 재진술 하는 다른 방법으로는 두 개의 절로 이루어진 원문의 두 개의 문장으로의 분할을 들 수 있는데, 이때에는 앞서 언급한 절과 절을 연결해주는 접속사 'whereas'' 대신에 이와 같은 의미를 갖고 있지만 문장과 문장을 연결해주는 'on the other hand'나 같은 맥락의 '반대로'의 의미를 갖고 있는 'on the contrary', 'in contrast', 'conversely'와 같은 표현들을 활용할 수 있다.

→ ② People who think that aggression can be justified and ① those who don't act in a different way.
→ People tend to react differently **depending on** the level of their awareness of aggression.
→ How people recognize aggression determines their behavior.

일반적으로 재진술 된 보기의 문장들은 원문보다 좀 더 단순화되어 있는 것이 특징이며 이를 위해 원문의 중심 내용을 포함하고 있지만 단순히 일부 또는 전체의 내용을 동의어를 사용한다거나 문장의 구조를 재배치하는 것과 같은 재진술 방법을 사용하는 것 이외에도 이러한 주요 내용을 구체적으로 명시하는 대신에 주요 내용을 포함하는 일반화된 문장으로 요약하여 재진술 될 수도 있음을 기억해두도록 한다.

16. Even when the environment surrounding the organism undergoes substantial transformations in external factors, including light and temperature, which would be expected to have a strong influence on biological activity, one of the primary characteristics of the biological clock is that its cycle duration remains stable with great precision.

   (A) In spite of sizable changes in external factors, which might affect biological activity, the biological clock's period maintains stability, which is considered to be one of its main features.

(B) A cardinal feature of the biological clock's period, stability is expected to be highly influenced by a variety of external causes such as light and temperature.
(C) When considering the various changes in environmental factors, the characteristic cycle length of each organism can be measured with considerable accuracy.
(D) One of the main characteristics of the biological clock is that the organism's biological activity can vary significantly depending on external causes, such as light and temperature.

해설   정답 (A)

Even when ① the environment surrounding the organism undergoes substantial transformations in external factors, including light and temperature, which would be expected to have a strong influence on biological activity, ② one of the primary characteristics of the biological clock is that its cycle duration remains stable with great precision.
→ In spite of ① sizable changes in external factors, which might affect biological activity, ② the biological clock's period maintains stability, which is considered to be one of its main features.

원문의 문장을 크게 접속사 'even when'을 기준으로 두 부분의 절로 나누어 그 두 부분 사이의 의미 관계를 명확히 이해하였는지를 평가하고자 하는 문제이다. 원문의 두 절은 '심지어 ~일 때에도'라는 의미의 'even when'으로 연결되어 종속절(①)에서 언급하고 있는 '외부적인 요인들'이 주절(②)에서 언급하고 있는 '생체 시계의 순환 주기의 안정성'에 영향을 주지 못함을 알 수 있다. Paraphrase 할 때에는, 이 두 절 사이의 관계를 명확히 할 수 있도록 '~에도 불구하고'라는 의미의 'in spite of'를 활용하여 두 부분을 연결할 수 있으며 이때에 'in spite of' 뒤에는 명사 또는 명사 상당 어구를 두어야 하므로 자연스럽게 원문의 절을 구로 전환할 수 있다. 종속절(①)에 언급되고 있는 내용 중 'including light and temperature'는 'external factors'의 예로 언급되었으며 상위 범주인 'external factors'의 언급만으로도 문장의 주요 내용에 영향을 주지 않으므로 세부적인 내용으로 생략 가능하다. 또한, 주절(②)의 보어의 역할을 하는 'that its cycle duration ~ great precision' 부분을 명사절이 아닌 문장의 주절로 바꾸어 쓸 수 있고, 원문 주절(②)의 주부의 내용 'one of the ~ biological clock'은 관계 대명사 계속적 용법을 활용하여 그 뒤에 덧붙일 수 있다.

오답의 근거

(B) A cardinal feature of the biological clock's period, stability <u>is expected to be highly influenced by a variety of external causes such as light and temperature</u>.

REVIEW TEST [DAY 16-20]

→ 보기의 밑줄 친 부분의 내용은 원문에 따르면 생물학적 활동에 대한 서술이라고 볼 수 있으며, 따라서 안정성에 대한 설명과는 거리가 있으므로 틀린 내용일 뿐만 아니라 원문의 주요 내용이 언급되어 있지 않으므로 오답이다.

(C) When considering the various changes in environmental factors, <u>the characteristic cycle length of each organism can be measured with considerable accuracy</u>.
→ 원문은 '환경적 요인들에 있어서의 다양한 변화를 고려할 때'가 아니라 그것과 관계 없이 생체 시계 주기의 안정성은 유지된다고 언급하고 있으며, 원문의 정보로부터 보기의 밑줄 친 부분의 내용을 유추할 수 없으므로 언급되지 않는 내용으로 오답이다.

(D) One of the main characteristics of the biological clock is <u>that the organism's biological activity can vary significantly depending on external causes, such as light and temperature</u>.
→ 원문에 따르면 밑줄 친 부분의 내용은 사실이지만, 그것이 생체 주기의 주요 특징 중 하나는 아니므로 틀린 내용으로 오답이다.

다른 방식으로 paraphrase 하기

Even when ① the environment surrounding the organism undergoes substantial transformations in external factors, including light and temperature, which would be expected to have a strong influence on biological activity, ② one of the primary characteristics of the biological clock is that its cycle duration remains stable with great precision.

→ **Notwithstanding** ① sizable changes in external factors, which might affect biological activity, ② the biological clock's period maintains stability, which is considered to be one of its main features.

→ ② A main feature of biological clock is that its period stays stable **despite** ① sizable changes in external causes.

원문은 문장을 크게 접속사 'even when'을 기준으로 두 부분의 절로 나누었다면, Paraphrase 할 때에는 그 두 부분 사이의 의미 관계를 고려하여, '~에도 불구하고'라는 의미의 'in spite of' 또는 같은 의미를 갖고 같은 기능을 하는 'notwithstanding' 또는 'despite'를 활용하여 두 부분을 연결할 수 있다. 재진술 된 문장의 ①의 부분의 밑줄 친 부분은 문장의 주요 내용에 큰 영향을 주지 않는 정보이므로 생략 가능하며 이를 통해 재진술 된 문장은 좀 더 간결하고 명확하게 원문의 주요 내용을 담을 수 있다. 또한, 전치사 'notwithstanding'과 'despite'가 이끄는 구는 위의 재진술 된 문장들에서와 같이 문두에 또는 문미에 적절하게 위치할 수 있음을 기억하도록 한다.

201 monotonous

Social Studies — Day 21

SYNONYMS *adj.* unvaried, tedious, irksome, boring, dull, tiresome, wearisome, prosaic, uninteresting, tiring

단조로운, 지루한

monotonous
[mənάtənəs]

All members of the family who played a role in conventional family-centered agricultural lifestyles were torn apart by the long hours of **monotonous** factory work which were required of all of them if they were to make money to survive.

전통적인 가족 중심 농업 생활방식에서 일익을 담당했던 모든 가족 구성원들은 생존에 필요한 돈을 벌기 위해 그들 모두에게 요구되었던 장시간의 단조로운 공장 노동에 의해 뿔뿔이 흩어졌다.

PARAPHRASE 1

Many hours of **unvaried** factory work required of all family members in order to earn enough to survive split apart the family playing a role in traditional family-centered agrarian lifestyles.

PARAPHRASE 2

As all family members who played a role in family-centered agrarian ways of life had to do **tedious** work in factories for a long time to earn a living, they were scattered.

202 actually

SYNONYMS adv. genuinely, truly, really, precisely, surely, literally, indeed, in fact, in truth, as a matter of fact

사실상, 실제로, 정말로

actually
[ǽktʃuəli]

Since ecologists can hardly determine population size by **actually** calculating all populations within geographical boundaries, they generally use diverse sampling techniques to estimate total population sizes and densities.

생태학자들이 개체군 크기를 파악하기 위해 지리적인 경계 내의 모든 개체들의 수를 실제로 셀 수는 없기 때문에, 대개는 전체 개체의 크기와 밀도를 추산하기 위한 다양한 견본 기법들을 사용한다.

PARAPHRASE 1

Ecologists utilize various sampling techniques to evaluate total population sizes and densities because population size cannot be decided by **genuinely** computing all individuals within geographical boundaries.

PARAPHRASE 2

Varied sampling techniques are employed to gauge total population sizes and densities as it is impossible to **truly** count all individuals within geographical borders.

307

203 apprehension

Day 21
Agriculture

SYNONYMS **n.** concern, worry, care, anxiety, fear, distress, unease, dread, solicitude

우려, 근심, 염려, 불안

apprehension
[prihénʃən]

Mineral depletion of soils has been considered to be a major **apprehension** of modern agriculture, since **harvesting crops** makes it hard for nutrients to be recycled back into the soil.

작물 수확 때문에 영양분이 토양으로 재순환되는 것이 어려워진 이래로, 토양에서의 광물 고갈은 현대 농업의 주된 우려로 간주되어왔다.

PARAPHRASE 1

Crop harvesting that prevents nutrients from being recycled back into the soil has made soil mineral depletion a prime **concern** in modern agriculture.

PARAPHRASE 2

As crop harvesting interrupts the recycling of nutrients back to the soil, mineral depleted soils become a main **worry** in modern agriculture.

204 aggravate

Day 21
Economics

SYNONYMS v. exacerbate, worsen, deteriorate, deepen, compound

악화시키다

aggravate
[ǽgrəvèit]

As the stock market collapsed, the troublesome economic trends were **aggravate**d, degrading both consumer and investor confidence resulting from the sharp drop in average share prices.

주식 시장이 붕괴함에 따라 경제 흐름의 고질적인 문제들은 악화되었고, 평균 주가의 급격한 하락은 소비자들과 투자자들의 신뢰를 저하시켰다.

PARAPHRASE 1

The economy's annoying trends were **exacerbate**d by the stock market crash, with the slip in both consumer and investor confidence caused by the depreciation of average stock prices.

PARAPHRASE 2

The stock market crash **worsen**ed the irritating economic trends and the steep fall in average stock values dampened both consumer and investor confidence.

205 commence

Day 21
Geology

SYNONYMS v. initiate, start, begin, originate, create, innovate, install, inaugurate, launch, pioneer, embark on

시작하다, 착수하다

commence
[kəméns]

The islands of Hawaii were far removed from other continents five million years ago when they commenced emerging above the surface of the ocean as volcanoes.

하와이의 섬들이 화산의 형태로 해양 표면 위에 나타나기 시작했을 때인 5백만년 전, 그 섬들은 다른 대륙들과 크게 동떨어져 있었다.

PARAPHRASE 1

Five million years ago, the volcanic Hawaiian islands initiated their formation above the ocean's surface and they were very remote from other landmasses.

PARAPHRASE 2

The volcanic Hawaiian islands which started forming on the sea five million years ago were isolated from other landmasses.

206 enthusiastic

Politics

SYNONYMS adj. eager, avid, ardent, passionate, fervent, intense, zealous

열정적인, 열성적인

enthusiastic
[enθùːziǽstik]

The Whig party made an appeal to workers who wished to improve themselves, to farmers who were enthusiastic about selling farm produce, and planters who called for credit to support their trade of cotton and rice in the world market.

휘그당은 스스로를 개선하고자 하는 노동자들과 농산품 판매를 열망하는 농부들, 그리고 세계 시장에서 면과 쌀의 무역에 자금을 대기 위해 융자를 필요로 하는 농장 경영주들에게 호소했다.

PARAPHRASE 1

The Whigs addressed an appeal to workers hoping for an improvement, to farmers eager to sell produce, and to planters requiring credit to finance cotton and rice trade in the world market.

PARAPHRASE 2

Whigs appealed to workers anxious to improve themselves, to farmers avid for the sale of crops, and to planters in need of financial support for trade.

207 emphasize

Social Studies
Day 21

SYNONYMS v. highlight, stress, underline, underscore, accentuate, reinforce, make much of

강조하다

emphasize
[émfəsàiz]

The fire at the Triangle Shirtwaist Company factory in New York City **emphasize**d that a lot of industrial workers were confronted with inhumane working conditions, such as low wages, long working hours and a dangerous work environment.

뉴욕에서의 트라이앵글 셔츠웨이스트 공장 화재는 많은 산업 노동자들이 저임금, 장시간 근무, 불안전한 근무 환경과 같은 비인도적인 근무 조건에 직면했음을 강조했다.

PARAPHRASE 1

The terrible working conditions faced by many workers, including low pay, long hours and an insecure work environment were **highlight**ed by the Triangle Shirtwaist Factory fire in New York City.

PARAPHRASE 2

The Triangle Shirtwaist Factory fire **stress**ed the poor working conditions of workers who worked excessive hours for low pay in an unsafe work environment.

208 sparse

Biology

| SYNONYMS | adj. | scarce, rare, meager, scanty, limited, short, deficient, insufficient | 빈약한, 부족한, 드문 |

sparse
[spɑːrs]

Most species, with a combination of some competitive and some opportunistic characteristics, exist somewhere between the two extremes of a continuum. Thus, the pure competitor or pure opportunist is **sparse** in nature.

대부분의 종들은 기회주의적 특성과 경쟁적 특성을 골고루 가지고 있으며, 이러한 특성의 조합에 따라 연속체의 양 극단 사이 어딘가에 위치한다. 따라서 자연 생태에서는 순수 경쟁주의자나 순수 기회주의자를 찾아보기 어렵다.

PARAPHRASE 1

The pure competitor or pure opportunist is **scarce** in nature. This is because most species fall between both extremes of a continuum, displaying a blend of some competitive and some opportunistic features.

PARAPHRASE 2

The pure competitor or pure opportunist is **rare** in nature because most species, which show a blend of some traits of each, lie between extreme ends of a continuum.

209 conceal

Ornithology

SYNONYMS v. disguise, mask, hide, camouflage, obscure, bury, cloak, pretend

감추다, 숨기다, 위장하다

conceal
[kənsíːl]

The high frequency begging calls ground-nesting warblers produce do not travel far, and this allows the individuals, particularly susceptible to predators, to better conceal themselves.

땅에 둥지를 트는 울새들이 내는 먹이를 달라고 조르는 고주파의 소리는 멀리 이동하는 경우가 드물며, 이는 포식자들에게 특히 취약한 개체들을 더 잘 숨겨준다.

PARAPHRASE 1

Ground-nesting warblers produce high-frequency begging calls which do not travel far, and thus better disguise the individuals, especially vulnerable to predators.

PARAPHRASE 2

High-frequency sounds from ground-nesting warblers, which rarely move far, better mask the individuals, notably weak to predators.

210 even though

Day 21 — Energy

SYNONYMS conj. although, though, albeit

비록 ~일지라도, ~이지만

even though

Even though there are some downsides to wind farms such as noise and visual pollution, modifying their design and positioning them in isolated spots make it possible for them to be overcome.

소음 공해나 시각 공해와 같은 풍력발전의 단점들이 있지만, 디자인의 개선과 서로 동떨어진 장소로의 배치는 이러한 단점들을 개선할 수 있게 해준다.

PARAPHRASE 1

These can be remedied by placing them in remote areas as well as enhancing their design although shortcomings to wind farms include noise and visual pollution.

PARAPHRASE 2

Though noise and visual pollution are two of the disadvantages of wind energy, these can be solved through design improvements and placement in isolated regions.

DAILY CHECK-UP

A. Find the answer that is closest in meaning to the highlighted word or phrase in the sentence.

01. Factory work was hard and **boring**, but a lot of women appreciated the economic freedom from working there.

    (A) vagarious (B) monotonous

02. According to other studies, more aggressiveness can **actually** be promoted later on by letting some anger escape.

    (A) surely (B) eminently

03. Many economists such as those as famous as Anna Schwartz argue that the Great Depression was **aggravated** by the Fed.

    (A) exacerbated (B) mesmerized

04. Drivers who had a restless night may go through higher levels of **anxiety**, stress, and depression.

    (A) blemish (B) unease

05. Master craftsmen work in bursts of **passionate** labor which alternates with more leisure time.

    (A) intense (B) daunting

06. Kramer **launched** significant new sorts of research on how birds orient and navigate.

    (A) initiated (B) aggregated

07. Members of poor tenant farmer's families supplemented **scanty** family income by spinning or weaving cloth at home.

    (A) fervent (B) meager

08. The trendy Art Nouveau style **accentuated** flowing, sinuous lines and nature images.

    (A) underlined (B) divulged

09. **Although** Ambulocetus didn't have a fluke, it swam like modern whales, which

was demonstrated by its backbone structure.

(A) Even though (B) Despite

10. The trickster is commonly male, but sometimes **camouflages** himself in the form of a female.

    (A) disguises (B) eludes

B. Complete each sentence using one of the words or phrases given.

11. In order to devise more effective propulsion systems for ships, engineers _____ the study of the ability of fish.

    (A) embarked on (B) partook in

12. The American economy based on arduous farm labor was replaced by _____ factory work with while-collar jobs.

    (A) mundane (B) wearisome

13. _____, volcanoes and solar activity have contributed to slow down the pace of global warming.

    (A) Willingly (B) Indeed

14. A lot of tribal hunters wear animal heads and hides to _____ themselves.

    (A) camouflage (B) relinquish

15. Eye shadow and mascara have changed as a way of _____ the eyes for everyday occasions.

    (A) scorching (B) accentuating

16. Tunas and mackerels retain an area of rough scales around their heads _____ they have been lost most of their scales

    (A) in spite of (B) although

---

01. (B) 02. (A) 03. (A) 04. (B) 05. (A) 06. (A) 07. (B) 08. (A) 09. (A) 10. (A)
11. (A) 12. (B) 13. (B) 14. (A) 15. (B) 16. (B)

211 bombard — Geology

SYNONYMS v. attack, assault, aggress, assail, strike — 공격하다

bombard
[bambάːrd]

The wind, which is the primary catalyst of erosion in arid regions, carries minute particles of sand, which bombard exposed surfaces of rock.
건조 지역의 침식의 주요 촉매인 바람은 미세한 모래 입자를 운반하며, 이는 노출되어 있는 암석 표면을 공격한다.

PARAPHRASE 1

The wind, which accelerates erosion in dry regions, transfers microscopic particles of sand that attack exposed rock surfaces.

PARAPHRASE 2

Tiny sand particles carried by the wind, the major agent of erosion in dry areas, assault naked rock surfaces.

212 feasible

Botany

| SYNONYMS | adj. | viable, practicable, workable, possible, achievable, reasonable, attainable |

실행 가능한

feasible
[fíːzəbəl]

Self-pollination, though known to be advantageous, may prevent a plant from developing adaptability and block mutations. Consequently, there is no possibility for the next generation to display more **feasible** combinations of genes.

자가 수분이 이로운 것으로 알려져 있기는 하지만, 이는 식물의 적응력 발달을 막고 돌연변이를 차단할 수도 있다. 따라서, 그 식물의 자손이 실현 가능한 유전자 조합을 추가로 보여줄 가능성은 없다.

PARAPHRASE 1

While self-pollination can be beneficial, it may hamper a plant's adaptability and hinder mutations. Thus, there is no chance of its offspring revealing more **viable** gene combinations.

PARAPHRASE 2

Self-pollination can be useful, but it may lower the adaptability of a plant and bar mutations, so its offspring have no chance to show more **practicable** gene combinations.

213 investigate

Day 22
Geology

SYNONYMS v. examine, probe, scrutinize, explore, inspect, search, research, study, scan, survey, view, check, monitor, comb, scour, seek

조사하다, 탐색하다

investigate
[invéstəgèit]

William Smith collected mineral samples and fossils and **investigate**d the strata that were newly discovered, while he engaged in similar jobs, travelling over the length and breadth of the land.

방방곡곡을 여행하며 유사한 직종에 종사하는 동안, 윌리엄 스미스는 광물 견본들과 화석들을 수집했고, 새롭게 드러난 지층을 조사했다.

PARAPHRASE 1

Travelling every nook and cranny of the land and working in similar professions, William Smith gathered mineral samples and fossils and **examine**d the newly revealed strata.

PARAPHRASE 2

William Smith, who crisscrossed the entire country and pursued similar jobs, collected mineral samples and fossils and **probe**d the newly revealed strata.

214 position

SYNONYMS adj. place, deploy, arrange, dispose, order, distribute, exhibit, display, array, set up

놓다, 배치하다, 배열하다

position
[pəzíʃən]

The ability to use gestures, signs, pictures and words to symbolize real-life objects is developed, and the skill to position diverse systems such as language or drawing is achieved by the time children are five years old.

아이들은 5세가 되면 실제 사물을 나타내기 위해 몸짓이나 신호, 그림, 단어를 사용하는 능력을 발달시키며 언어 그림과 같은 다양한 체계를 배열할 수 있게 된다.

PARAPHRASE 1

Not only do children of five years of age develop the ability to utilize gestures, signs, pictures and words to represent real life objects, but they are proficient in placing multiple systems.

PARAPHRASE 2

Five-year-old children develop the skill to deploy various systems as well as the ability to use gestures, signs, images and words, to embody ordinary objects.

215 compact

Geology

SYNONYMS v. compress, condense, squeeze, contract, concentrate

압축하다, 응축하다

compact
[kəmpǽkt]

The rapid speed of a rock avalanche takes place as a result of air captured and **compact**ed beneath the dropping mass of detritus, which enables it to slide down the slope.

암석 사태는 파편 덩어리들 아래 갇혀 압축된 공기 때문에 일어나는데, 이는 그것이 경사면을 따라 미끄러져 내려가게 만든다.

PARAPHRASE 1

The fast pace of a rock avalanche results from air that becomes trapped and **compress**ed below the falling bulk of debris, enabling it to go down the slope.

PARAPHRASE 2

Air caught and **condense**d under the falling mass of debris brings about the high speed of a rock avalanche, allowing it to descend the slope.

216 placid

Art

SYNONYMS adj. tranquil, calm, serene, peaceful, undisturbed, quiet, untroubled, restful

평온한, 차분한

placid
[plǽsid]

The realization that the First Nations culture might not be there one day stimulated Emily Carr to make a record of the **placid** and beautiful moments of her earlier days with her aboriginal people.

캐나다 원주민 문화가 언젠가 사라질 수 있다는 깨달음은 에밀리 카로 하여금 원주민 친구들과 함께 했던 그녀의 어린 시절의 평온하고 아름다운 순간들을 기록하도록 했다.

PARAPHRASE 1

Since Emily Carr became aware that the First Nations culture might one day disappear, she set out to visually record **tranquil** and beautiful parts of her earlier years among aboriginal people.

PARAPHRASE 2

Emily Carr, who thought that the First Nations culture might one day be gone, started recording stories about her **calm** and pleasant times spent with indigenous people.

217 predict

Film

SYNONYMS v. forecast, anticipate, expect, foresee, foretell, prophesy, await, reckon on

예상하다, 예측하다, 기대하다

predict
[pridíkt]

Although it may be hard to imagine from a later point of view, some unfavorable opinions in the 1920s predicted that sound pictures would soon drop out of sight, just as had many attempts which date back before the First World War.

이후의 관점으로는 상상하기 어려운 일이지만, 1920년대의 일부 비판적인 견해들은 유성 영화가 제1차 세계 대전 이전의 많은 시도들이 그랬던 것처럼 시야에서 곧 사라질 것이라고 예측했다.

PARAPHRASE 1

From a later perspective, it may be barely conceivable, yet some critical views in the 1920s forecast that sound film would vanish from sight as quickly as many attempts had before the First World War.

PARAPHRASE 2

It seems unconceivable today, but, in the 1920s, some critics anticipated that the new attempts at sound films would disappear as fast as the attempts made before the War.

218 excavate

Geology

SYNONYMS v. unearth, unbury, dig up, exhume, disinter, quarry

발굴하다, 파내다

excavate
[ékskəvèit]

Smith was able to make observations of and conduct a study on the large areas of rock unsheltered by the newly **excavate**d canal when he worked as a surveyor of canal courses.

스미스는 운하의 경로를 측량하는 일을 하면서 새롭게 파낸 운하로부터 노출된 거대 암석 지역을 관찰하고 연구할 수 있었다.

PARAPHRASE 1

The job of measuring canal routes gave Smith a chance to observe and research the large areas of rock that were exposed by the newly **unearth**ed canal.

PARAPHRASE 3

Smith could observe and study the huge regions of rock found in the newly **unburi**ed canal while surveying canal courses.

219 motionless — Ornithology

SYNONYMS *adj.* stationary, inactive, inert, sedentary, unmoving, still, static, stagnant

정지한, 움직이지 않는

motionless
[móubəl]

Kramer performed his experiment with artificial suns and found that, provided that the location of the artificial Sun remained **motionless**, the birds' migration route would be altered with regard to it at a rate of approximately 15 degrees per hour.

인공 태양을 가지고 한 크레이머의 실험에서, 그는 만일 인공 태양이 정지해 있다면 태양을 향한 새의 이동 경로는 시간당 대략 15도 정도로 바뀔 것임을 알아냈다.

PARAPHRASE 1

In an experiment with artificial suns, Kramer discovered that in case of the **immobile** artificial Sun, the birds would change their direction with respect to it at a constant 15 degrees per hour.

PARAPHRASE 2

According to Kramer's research, when the position of the artificial Sun was **stationary**, the birds would modify their course toward it at a steady degree.

220 luminous

Botany

SYNONYMS *adj.* brilliant, bright, glowing, vivid, radiant, beaming, shining, gleaming

빛나는, 반짝이는

luminous
[lúːmənəs]

The wildflower named black-eyed Susan is characterized by a dark center encompassed by **luminous** yellow petals, which is a target that is easy to spot by many species among prairie grasses.

노랑 데이지라 불리는 야생화는 밝은 노랑색 꽃잎으로 둘러싸인 꽃의 가운데 부분이 어두운 색을 띠는 특징이 있으며, 이는 많은 생물들이 대초원의 목초들 틈에서 노랑 데이지를 찾기 쉽도록 하는 하나의 표적이 된다.

PARAPHRASE 1

A dark center surrounded by **brilliant** yellow petals features prominently in the wildflower called a black-eyed Susan, and this allows many species to easily identify it among prairie grasses.

PARAPHRASE 2

The black-eyed Susan has a dark center encircled by **bright** yellow petals, a distinct feature that makes many species able to locate it among prairie grasses with ease.

DAILY CHECK-UP

A. Find the answer that is closest in meaning to the highlighted word or phrase in the sentence.

01. **Unearthed** in southern Africa, the naturalistic paintings on slabs of stone also show similar evidence.
    (A) disinterred (B) buried

02. As the weight of the upper rocks **compresses** the lower rocks, deeper bedrock layers become progressively dense.
    (A) compacts (B) incarnates

03. Water oozes through springs or flows into other aquifers, not staying **still** in an aquifer.
    (A) mobile (B) stationary

04. Even today, Earth continues to be **assailed** by fine meteorites which fall on both land and sea.
    (A) attacked (B) vanished

05. Icebergs appear **shining** pink or gold in the morning due to the angle of the Sun.
    (A) congenital (B) glowing

06. When buildings are economically **reasonable**, providing shelter and improving space efficiency, they can enhance people's lives.
    (A) irrational (B) feasible

07. Life satisfaction can be **predicted** more by income among middle-aged and older adults than among young adults.
    (A) foreseen (B) divulged

08. NASA was asked to **scrutinize** the danger caused today by meteorite impacts on Earth in 1991
    (A) investigate (B) agitate

09. The eggs in a **quiet** nest are more likely to survive compared with those in a noisy nest.

(A) perpetual   (B) serene

10. The identical feed boxes, containing food in only one of them, are **placed** at various locations on a compass.

(A) arranged   (B) ameliorated

B. Complete each sentence using one of the words or phrases given.

11. When the butterfly or moth caterpillar is in the pupal stage, it is _____ inside the cocoon.

(A) fervent   (B) motionless

12. The reflective plates on other _____ sea creature are different from those of the bobtail squid found in Hawaii.

(A) prosaic   (B) luminous

13. Some uncommon geologic features as well as shifts in invertebrate fauna were _____ by the Glomar Challenger expedition.

(A) explored   (B) stained

14. The most unequivocal example of aggressive action is when one animal _____ another.

(A) apportions   (B) attacks

15. The element of meteorites that is diluted by the terrestrial material _____ from the crater is distinguished with ease.

(A) dug up   (B) forsaken

16. GM seeds which are genetically modified make the crops unable to create _____ seeds by themselves.

(A) viable   (B) frivolous

---

01. (A) 02. (A) 03. (B) 04. (A) 05. (B) 06. (B) 07. (A) 08. (A) 09. (B) 10. (A)
11. (B) 12. (B) 13. (A) 14. (B) 15. (A) 16. (A)

221 contradictory

Day 23
Social Science

SYNONYMS *adj.* opposite, contrary, inconsistent, paradoxical, incompatible, conflicting, clashing, opposing, reverse, converse

모순되는, 상충되는, 상반되는

contradictory
[kὰntrədíktəri]

Workers were indignant at the industrial structure and their loss of status and got together to resist them. However, they were separated by gender, **contradictory** religious points of view, distinctions in occupation, and ethnic and racial animosities.

노동자들은 산업 체제와 그들의 지위 상실에 분개했으며 이에 저항하기 위해 함께 힘을 모았지만, 성별, 상반되는 종교적 견해, 직업적 차이, 민족이나 인종간 적개심에 의해 분리되었다.

PARAPHRASE 1

The industrial system and their loss of status infuriated workers and made them act together, but gender, **opposite** religious viewpoints, professional gaps, and hostility between races split them.

PARAPHRASE 2

Workers acted together to resist the industrial system and their loss of status. Nevertheless, they held **contrary** views on manifold points.

222 impending

Day 23
Hydrology

| SYNONYMS | adj. approaching, upcoming, looming, coming, imminent | 임박한, 곧 닥칠 |

impending
[impéndiŋ]

Copious amounts of water have been conveyed by canal from neighboring rivers through several alternatives proposed in the face of the **impending** water supply crisis, but the cost of the water gained would cause dramatic increases in irrigation costs.

임박한 수자원 위기에 직면하여 제안된 몇몇 대안들에 따라 엄청난 양의 물이 인접한 강으로부터 운하를 통해 운반되었지만, 이렇게 얻어진 물의 비용은 관개 수로 비용을 상당히 증가시켰다.

PARAPHRASE 1

Faced with the **approaching** water supply crisis, many solutions have been suggested to carry vast amounts of water by canal from adjacent rivers. However, the irrigation costs would be greatly increased by the obtained water.

PARAPHRASE 2

Several schemes to solve the **upcoming** water supply crisis have been offered. Unfortunately, none of them would keep the costs of irrigation down.

223 approximately

Day 23
Art

| SYNONYMS adv. | roughly, nearly, virtually, almost, about, more or less | 대략, 거의 |

approximately
[əprάksəmèitli]

Some naturalistic paintings on slabs of stone found in southern Africa appear to have been colored as much as **approximately** 28,000 years ago, which indicates that these types of paintings in Africa may have existed much longer than those in Europe.

아프리카 남부 지역의 석판 위에 그려진 일부 자연주의적 그림들은 대략 28,000년 전에 채색된 것으로 보이며, 이는 아프리카 벽화들이 유럽의 벽화들보다 훨씬 더 오래 존재해 왔을지도 모른다는 점을 암시한다.

PARAPHRASE 1

Unearthed in southern Africa, some naturalistic paintings on slabs of stone seem to have been daubed **roughly** 28,000 years ago, which suggests that these African paintings may precede European paintings.

PARAPHRASE 2

Some colored paintings on stone slabs in southern Africa made **nearly** 28,000 years ago imply that African paintings may be much older than European ones.

224 effect

Meteorology

SYNONYMS n. influence, impact, repercussion, impression, clout, pull, power, consequence

효과, 영향(력), 권력

effect
[ifékt]

When determining whether current climatic phenomena result from the **effect** of human activities, the most difficult aspect is that it is hard to measure what comprises the natural variability of the climate.

인간 활동이 최근의 기후 현상에 대한 원인이 되었는지 아닌지를 판달 할 때, 가장 어려운 부분은 기후의 자연적인 변동성을 구성하는 것이 무엇인지를 측정하기 어렵다는 점이다.

PARAPHRASE 1

The hardest side of judging if human activities have an **influence** on current climatic events is that it is barely possible to gauge what composes natural climate variability.

PARAPHRASE 2

Whether human activities have an **impact** on recent climatic changes is hard to decide due to the difficulty of assessing what constitutes natural climate variability.

225 compressed

Day 23
Social Science

SYNONYMS adj. compact, dense, thick, heavy   빽빽한, 조밀한, 짙은

compressed
[kəmprést]

The domestication of wild animals had a direct impact on human populations which became more **compressed** as livestock yielded more food compared with that provided by a hunter-gatherer lifestyle.

수렵–채집 생활과 비교했을 때 가축을 통해 더 많은 식량을 생산할 수 있었다는 점에서, 야생 동물의 사육은 더욱 조밀해지는 인구에 직접적인 영향을 미쳤다.

PARAPHRASE 1

The direct reason that human populations became more **compact** was stockbreeding, which provided more food than the hunter-gatherer lifestyle could produce.

PARAPHRASE 2

Compared to the hunter-gatherer lifestyle, the livestock breeding, which created more food, gave direct rise to **dense**r human populations.

226 raise

SYNONYMS v. nurture, rear, foster, breed, feed, nourish, nurse, bring up

기르다, 양육하다, 영양분을 공급하다

raise
[reiz]

The most well-known parasites among vertebrates are birds such as cowbirds and cuckoos, whose females lays eggs in nests belonging to other birds and make the host **raise** them.

척추동물 중 가장 잘 알려진 기생 동물들에는 찌르레기와 뻐꾸기등의 조류가 있으며, 그 암컷은 다른 새들의 둥지들 중 하나에 알을 낳고 숙주 동물들에 의해 길러지도록 한다.

PARAPHRASE 1

Among vertebrates, the best-known parasites are birds like cowbirds and cuckoos and the female spawns in the nest of another species and lets the bird **nurture** them.

PARAPHRASE 2

Cowbirds and cuckoos are the best-known parasites among vertebrates and their females parasitize by leaving their eggs to be **rear**ed by other species in their nests.

227 bond

world History

SYNONYMS **n.** tie, connection, link, cohesion, union, association, alliance, relation, relationship, adhesion

유대, 결속, 관계

bond
[band]

Stone-built roads connected each province with Rome and military establishments were situated in each province, and these military and road networks were included in the physical bonds.

돌로 만든 도로들이 각각의 지방 도시들을 로마와 연결하는 한편 지방 도시마다 군사 기지가 주둔했고, 이러한 도로들과 군사망들은 물리적인 결속에 포함되어 있었다.

PARAPHRASE 1

The physical ties encompassed the network of roads, constructed with stone linking the provinces with Rome and the network of military garrisons, stationed in each province.

PARAPHRASE 2

The physical connections contained the network of stone-built roads, linking each province with Rome and the network of military bases, located in every province.

228 banish

Art

SYNONYMS v. expel, exile, oust, deport, depose, eject, evict

추방하다, 쫓아내다

banish
[bǽniʃ]

Since most surrealist artists in the 1930s had pronounced views on politics, apolitical Salvador Dali who did not mix anywhere was banished from the group through a trial among the surrealists in 1934.

1930년대 대부분의 초현실주의 예술가들은 확고한 정치적 견해를 갖고 있었고, 정치에 관심이 없던 살바도르 달리는 어디에도 어울리지 않았기 때문에 1934년 초현실주의자들 가운데서 이루어진 재판의 결과 그 집단에서 추방되었다.

PARAPHRASE 1

Most surrealist artists in the 1930s had strong political views, and apolitical Salvador Dali did not fit in anywhere, so the surrealist group expelled him in 1934.

PARAPHRASE 2

In 1934, Salvador Dali, who was not interested in politics at all, was exiled from the surrealist group who had firm political viewpoints.

229 staunch

U.S.History

| SYNONYMS | adj. | strong, firm, faithful, steadfast, resolute, unshakable, unwavering, resolved, decided, determined, stalwart, loyal, fixed, indisputable | 확고한, 단호한 |

staunch
[stɔːntʃ]

Even though Lincoln had a **staunch** belief in domestic development from the beginning of his political career in Illinois, national economic difficulties in 1837 led his efforts to a failure in the long run.

링컨은 일리노이에서 시작한 정치 생활의 초창기부터 국내 발전에 대한 믿음을 가지고 있었지만, 1837년에 국가가 직면한 경제적 어려움은 결국 그의 노력을 실패로 이끌었다.

PARAPHRASE 1

Lincoln had a **strong** belief in internal development from the start of his political life in Illinois. However, national economic hardship in 1837 caused his efforts to be unsuccessful.

PARAPHRASE 2

Since he started his political life in Illinois, Lincoln had a **firm** belief in domestic improvements, but his endeavors eventually failed due to national economic troubles in 1837.

230 supervise

Environmental Science

Day 23

| SYNONYMS | v. | administer, manage, oversee, conduct, control, direct |

감독하다, 관리하다

supervise
[súːpərvàiz]

As animals tend to be crowded around pools of water and overgraze the region, the supply of drinking water which was planned and **supervise**d in an incorrect way has played a part in rapidly expanding desert areas in recent years.

동물들은 샘 주변에 군집하고 그 지역에서 과도하게 방목하는 경향이 있기 때문에, 부적절하게 계획되고 관리된 식수의 공급은 최근 몇 년사이 빠르게 이루어진 사막 지역의 확장에 일조해왔다.

PARAPHRASE 1

The enormous expansion of deserts in recent years resulted from provision of drinking water planned and **administer**ed incorrectly, leading to a giant gathering of animals around waterholes and their overgrazing in those areas.

PARAPHRASE 2

Improperly supplied and **manage**d drinking water has accelerated desertification in recent years as animals group around waterholes and overgraze these areas.

DAILY CHECK-UP

A. Find the answer that is closest in meaning to the highlighted word or phrase in the sentence.

01. Games have negative **repercussions** on humans because they make people more violent.
    (A) exploitations   (B) effects

02. Water is **more compact** than oil and gas that commonly shoot up through waterlogged rock and sediment.
    (A) denser   (B) severer

03. War seemed **impending** once again as soon as the League commissioner poorly handled German claims on Danzig.
    (A) imminent   (B) sedentary

04. **Incompatible** views exist as to the influence of silver on humankind and the environment
    (A) foreboding   (B) clashing

05. There are two kinds of **ties** in order for people to be bound within relationships: expressive bonds and instrumental bonds.
    (A) agitations   (B) bonds

06. He was **deported** by outraged Whigs because, as president, Tyler objected to the entire Whig economic program.
    (A) exiled   (B) conjectured

07. The Roman Empire became too immense to **oversee** and protect, which resulted in the Dark Ages.
    (A) elude   (B) administer

08. The deserts take up **almost** a fourth of the Earth's total surface area.
    (A) virtually   (B) eminently

09. Moisture and mineral salts absorbed by the fungi are transferred into waste matter essential to **nurture** algae.

(A) assemble (B) nourish

10. Although some incomprehensible biological elements appear to be at work, there are no **unwavering** theories to prove them.

   (A) tranquil (B) unshakable

B. Complete each sentence using one of the words or phrases given.

11. _____ 3 billion years ago, the outflow channels were shaped by flooding.

   (A) About (B) Utterly

12. When people collaborate with other people to accomplish their objectives, social _____ are formed.

   (A) links (B) blemishes

13. The research on eruptive processes largely concentrates on the indicators that signify an _____ eruption.

   (A) dexterous (B) upcoming

14. While diplomatic policies are determined by the State Department, the nations' money is _____ by the Treasury Department.

   (A) managed (B) hyperbolized

15. The American Constitution has been developed through the need to adjust balance between diverse _____ interests.

   (A) broiling (B) conflicting

16. Meteorite impacts have had substantial _____ on Earth, notably in the area of biological evolution.

   (A) impetuses (B) influences

01. (B) 02. (A) 03. (A) 04. (B) 05. (B) 06. (A) 07. (B) 08. (A) 09. (B) 10. (B)
11. (A) 12. (A) 13. (B) 14. (A) 15. (B) 16. (B)

231 characteristic

Day 24
Art

SYNONYMS **n.** character, feature, attribute, nature, quality, property, trait, tendency, peculiarity, hallmark, flavor

특징, 특성

characteristic
[kæ̀riktərístik]

As containers or shelters, works of applied art perform functions, and objects with the identical function show analogous characteristics because they are confined in terms of their purpose.

응용 미술품들은 무언가를 담거나 보호하는 역할을 수행하며, 동일한 기능을 가진 작품들 역시 기능적인 목적의 제한 때문에 이와 유사한 특성을 보인다.

PARAPHRASE 1

Applied-art objects fulfill functions, containing or sheltering, and objects with the same function hold similar characters in that their purpose restricts them.

PARAPHRASE 2

As their goal limits them, similar features are shown in applied-art objects which function in a common way.

232 unintentionally

Anthropology

SYNONYMS *adv.* inadvertently, accidentally, casually, unconsciously

우연히, 뜻하지 않게

unintentionally
[ʌnintén ʃənəli]

The evil eye, a factor common in many cultures, is universally believed to result in injury or bad luck to others and many legends indicate that an envious person can **unintentionally** damage another when staring at him or her maliciously.

여러 문화에 공통적으로 찾아볼 수 있는 요소인 악마의 눈은 일반적으로 다른 사람들에게 피해나 불운을 야기한다고 여겨지며, 많은 전설에 따르면 질투심을 품은 사람이 악의적으로 다른 사람을 쳐다볼 때 그사람에게 본의 아니게 피해를 줄 수 있다고 한다.

PARAPHRASE 1

In various cultures, the evil eye is thought to induce injury or misfortune to others and many myths state that someone can be **inadvertently** harmed when he or she is gazed at by a person with covetous eyes.

PARAPHRASE 2

The concept of the evil eye in diverse cultures encompasses the belief that a covetous person can **accidentally** affect another in an unfavorable way through a vicious glance.

233 alternative

Public Health

SYNONYMS n. choice, option, substitute, selection 대안, 선택권

alternative
[ɔːltə́ːrnətiv]

There are other **alternative**s to decrease dental caries, which can be utilized by people in the U.S. to be exposed to fluoride: fluoride toothpaste, mouthwash, and fluoridation of salt and milk.

충치를 줄이려는 목적으로 불소에 노출되려 하는 미국인들은 불소 치약, 구강 청결제, 소금이나 우유의 불소화 등 다른 대안들을 활용할 수 있다.

PARAPHRASE 1

Americans can reduce tooth decay by using other **choice**s of exposure to fluoride such as fluoride toothpaste, mouthwash, and fluoridation of salt and milk.

PARAPHRASE 2

In order to reduce cavities, Americans can employ other **option**s for fluoride usage including fluoride toothpaste, mouthwash, and fluoridation of salt and milk.

234 roam

Day 24 — Geology

SYNONYMS v. wander, prowl, ramble, rove, stroll — 배회하다

roam
[roum]

Orphaned at the age of eight, William Smith grew up with his uncle and he obtained a rudimentary education, and from an early age, **roam**ing his uncle's farm, he collected and investigated the fossils abundant in the limestone of the Cotswold Hills.

8살의 나이에 고아가 된 윌리엄 스미스는 삼촌과 함께 살며 기초 교육을 받았고, 어린 시절부터 삼촌의 농장을 돌아다니며 카츠월드 구릉지대의 석회암 속에서 풍부한 화석들을 수집하고 조사했다.

PARAPHRASE 1

William Smith, left an orphan at the age of eight, lived with his uncle, receiving a basic education. He collected and examined the ample fossils found while **wander**ing his uncle's farm, from his early years.

PARAPHRASE 2

From the age of eight, William Smith lived with his uncle and got basic schooling. Also, he **prowl**ed his uncle's farm, exploring and gathering fossils.

345

235 unparalleled

U.S.History

SYNONYMS **adj.** incomparable, unsurpassed, peerless, unequaled, superlative, superior, matchless, unique, unrivaled

최고의, 최상의, 비길 데 없는

unparalleled
[ʌnpǽrəlèld]

The Union had **unparalleled** manpower and available resources, which allowed it to win against the Confederate Army which had some brilliant strategists and got the upper hand in early war years.

북부연합은 최상의 인력과 가용 자원을 가지고 있었고, 이 덕분에 몇몇 뛰어난 전략가들을 보유한 데다가 전쟁 초반에 우세를 보였던 남부 연합군에 대항하여 승리할 수 있었다.

PARAPHRASE 1

While the Confederate Army had some remarkable commanders and did well in the early part of the war, the Union had **incomparable** manpower and available resources, which steered it to victory.

PARAPHRASE 2

The Confederate Army, with some excellent tacticians, did well at the onset of the war, but the **unsurpassed** manpower and resources of the Union contributed to its victory.

346

236 perspective

U.S.History

SYNONYMS **n.** prospect, outlook, vista, view, possibility, chance

가망성, 전망

perspective
[pə:rspéktiv]

Since high-quality tobacco was first cultivated in Virginia and settlers realized the possibility of the tobacco being cured and sold in the British market, the economic perspective became brighter.

고품질의 담배가 버지니아에서 최초로 재배되었고, 정착민들이 이를 보존 처리하여 영국 시장에서 판매하는것에 대한 가능성을 깨닫게 되면서 경제적 전망은 밝아졌다.

PARAPHRASE 1

The first superlative tobacco produced in Virginia lightened the economic prospect because settlers perceived that cured Virginian tobacco could be sold in England.

PARAPHRASE 2

The economic outlook brightened through the first prime tobacco yielded in Virginia as settlers recognized that stored tobacco could go to the British market.

237 struggle

World History — Day 24

SYNONYMS v. attempt, strive, endeavor, try, seek   노력하다, 애쓰다

struggle
[strʌ́gəl]

While the church struggled to keep up literacy and literature during the Dark Ages, the domination of literacy and literature by the church and dependence upon earlier literary authorities increased.

암흑 시대 동안 교회가 읽고 쓰는 능력과 문학을 유지하기 위해 애쓰는 동안, 교회의 읽고 쓰는 능력과 문학에 대한 지배와 이전의 문학적 권위에 대한 의존성은 증가했다.

PARAPHRASE 1

The church attempted to sustain literacy and literature during the Dark Ages but the control of the church over them and dependency on former literary authorities developed.

PARAPHRASE 2

The church which strived to retain literacy and literature during the Dark Ages got more dominance over them, and more reliance on prior literary authorities grew.

238 favorable

Geography

Day 24

| SYNONYMS | adj. | congenial, pleasant, agreeable, friendly, affable | 호의적인, 쾌적한 |

favorable
[féivərəbəl]

The valleys in the tropical regions appear to have more **favorable** conditions in terms of environment due to the fact that they are less likely to become very dry, and have deeper soils with less frost.

열대 지방의 계곡은 매우 건조해질 가능성이 낮고 서리가 적게 내리는 깊은 토양을 가지기 때문에 환경적인 측면에서 보다 쾌적한 조건을 가지는 것으로 보인다.

PARAPHRASE 1

As the valleys in the tropics are less liable to dry out, and have less frost and deeper soils, their environmental conditions seem to be more **congenial**.

PARAPHRASE 2

The tropical valleys are more **pleasant** because they tend to become less desiccated, and have less frost and deeper soils.

349

239 prudent

Day 24
Social Science

| SYNONYMS | adj. | cautious, alert, wary, vigilant, careful, distrustful, heedful, discreet, deliberate, thoughtful, attentive, wakeful, watchful |

경계하는,
조심하는,
신중한

prudent
[prúːdənt]

As societies became industrialized, the very nature of work transformed in the manner that workers were forced to be prudent, trustworthy, and self-disciplined, not to mention to get rid of old habits.

사회가 산업화 됨에 따라, 일의 본질은 노동자들로 하여금 오래된 습관을 버리는 것은 물론이고 신중하고, 믿음직스럽고, 자기 관리를 잘 하는 사람들이 되도록 강요하는 방식으로 바뀌었다.

PARAPHRASE 1

Industrialization changed the essence of work in the way that it required workers not only to abandon old habits but also to be cautious, dependable, and self-disciplined.

PARAPHRASE 2

That workers had to be alert, reliable, and self-disciplined as well as drop old habits, was one way the nature of work changed in industrialized societies.

240 diligently

Day 24
Oceanography

SYNONYMS adv. industriously, earnestly, assiduously, carefully

열심히, 부지런히, 주의 깊게

diligently
[dílədʒəntli]

In many parts of the world including Britain, research on shipwreck had been **diligently** carried out for a long time before the 1939-45 war and as information was compiled, peculiar equipment was designed for use in lifeboats and on rafts.

영국을 포함한 세계 각지에서 조난 사고에 대한 열띤 연구가 제 2차 세계대전 이전에 오랫동안 이루어졌고, 관련 정보가 수집됨에 따라 인명 구조선과 구명보트에서의 사용을 위한 특수 장비가 고안되었다.

PARAPHRASE 1

Shipwreck had been **industriously** researched in many areas of the world for ages before World War II and special equipment based on collected data was prepared to use in lifeboats and on rafts.

PARAPHRASE 2

Compiled data on shipwreck conducted **earnestly** around the globe for long periods before World War II contributed to the devising of equipment for use in lifeboats and on rafts.

351

DAILY CHECK-UP

A. Find the answer that is closest in meaning to the highlighted word or phrase in the sentence.

01. Architects are exploring eco-friendly **alternatives** to replace environmentally-unfriendly traditional plastics.

    (A) boons (B) substitutes

02. Low growth form is the most conspicuous **hallmark** of the plants which inhabit the alpine zone.

    (A) eminence (B) characteristic

03. The invasion was soon suppressed by the **unparalleled** Greek forces under the command of Miltiades.

    (A) unrivaled (B) stipulated

04. Due to the development in microscopic technique, scientists could offer new **prospects** on the function of living things.

    (A) groundwork (B) vistas

05. Most of Walt Whitman's life was spent **struggling** to support himself and his parents, living on a small salary.

    (A) endeavoring (B) persevering

06. According to legend, Homer was a **roving** minstrel, travelling around and reciting stories about heroes or gods.

    (A) wandering (B) daunting

07. The Byzantine government exercised trade regulation, and this generated a **favorable** environment for lucrative speculative businesses.

    (A) congenial (B) inauspicious

08. Even the **wary** grower might have to put up with drought, heat, blight and other frustrations during the spring and summer.

    (A) solitary (B) heedful

09. Henri Becquerel, a French physicist, **accidentally** made a startling discovery on

phosphorescence and fluorescence in 1896.

(A) surpassingly (B) unconsciously

10. Impressionists **assiduously** tried to describe actual emotions by using just beautiful bright colors, not lines.

(A) earnestly (B) steadily

B. Complete each sentence using one of the words or phrases given.

11. The kinds of trees and their physical _____ of an upper timberline are affected by its geographical position.

(A) radiance (B) properties

12. The UN suggested an _____ to mediate the differences of opinion between developed countries and developing countries.

(A) option (B) inflow

13. Some companies, recognizing the wider _____ of the power industry, are contemplating large-scale wind-farm projects.

(A) manifestation (B) outlook

14. Some plants can inhabit even some of the _____ microenvironments above the snowline.

(A) ambivalent (B) favorable

15. It has been believed that natural vitamins are far too _____ to be compared with manmade synthetic ones, but it is still unsupported.

(A) superior (B) vagarious

16. Though the colonists _____ to avoid various diseases, malnutrition, and the elements, few people survived the bleak winter.

(A) sought (B) ameliorated

```
01. (B)  02. (B)  03. (A)  04. (B)  05. (A)  06. (A)  07. (A)  08. (B)  09. (B)  10. (A)
11. (B)  12. (A)  13. (B)  14. (B)  15. (A)  16. (A)
```

241 perplexing

Day 25 — Art History

SYNONYMS *adj.* puzzling, mysterious, cryptic, mystic, inscrutable

알기 어려운, 불가사의한

perplexing
[pərpléksiŋ]

One of the most **perplexing** factors of the cave paintings in France and Spain is that they are located in secluded spots far from cave entrances, which indicates that artists were forced to work in limited spaces without natural light.

프랑스와 스페인 동굴 벽화의 가장 불가사의한 측면들 중 하나는 벽화들이 동굴 입구에서 멀리 떨어져 있는 후미진 곳에 위치해 있으며, 이는 예술가들이 빛이 비치지 않는 한정된 공간에서 작업을 해야 했음을 의미한다는 점이다.

PARAPHRASE 1

The most **puzzling** aspect of the cave paintings in France and Spain is that they are situated in areas far away from inlets of caverns, implying that artists had to work in dark and narrow spaces.

PARAPHRASE 2

The French and Spanish cave paintings are most **mysterious** in that they are found in remote areas of caves, meaning that artists had to paint in dark cramped spaces.

242 acute

Zoology

SYNONYMS adj. incisive, keen, sharp, astute, shrewd, canny, pungent, pointed, poignant, biting, penetrating

예리한, 신랄한, 기민한

acute
[əkjúːt]

The development of **acute** senses helps white-tailed deer to prevent themselves from being attacked by their predators. In particular, they are heavily reliant on their sense of smell and their outstanding senses of sight and hearing also help them to avoid predation.

날카로운 감각의 발달은 흰꼬리 사슴이 포식자들의 공격을 스스로 피할 수 있도록 돕는다. 특히, 그들은 후각에 상당히 의존하며 그들의 뛰어난 시각과 청각 역시 그들이 포식자들을 피할 수 있도록 돕는다.

PARAPHRASE 1

In order to evade their enemies, white-tailed deer, who have developed **incisive** senses, rely heavily on their excellent senses of smell, sight and hearing.

PARAPHRASE 2

Whitetails have **keen** senses to avoid being eaten or killed by their predators in terms of olfactory, visual and auditory senses.

243 respect

Day 25
Performing Art

| SYNONYMS | n. | regard, reverence, veneration, homage, worship, admiration, affection, awe, adoration, appreciation, recognition, consideration | 존경, 감탄, 호감 |

respect
[rispékt]

Respect for breathtaking virtuosity, skill and grace of the performers is regarded as motivation for developing their activities into thoroughly completed theatrical performances.

공연자들이 보이는 기교, 기술, 그리고 우아함에 대한 존경은, 그들의 활동을 완전한 연극으로 실현시키는 데에 대한 동기 부여로 간주된다.

PARAPHRASE 1

The performers' stunning virtuosity, skill and grace won people's **regard**, and this motivated them to elaborate the activities into fully accomplished theatrical performances.

PARAPHRASE 2

Reverence for the performers' virtuosity, skill and grace stimulated them to make the activities completely realized plays.

244 extant

Literature

| SYNONYMS | adj. | existing, surviving, remaining, living, existent |

현존하는, 남아 있는

extant
[ekstǽnt]

Tristan and Iseult, which is a poem dealing with strong romantic and tragic themes and does not survive today in a complete form written in French, can be pieced together through extant German translations.

극도로 낭만적이고 비극적인 주제를 다루는 시작품인 트리스탄과 이졸데의 프랑스어본은 완벽한 형태로 남아 있지 않지만, 현존하는 독일어 번역본을 통해 끼워 맞춰질 수 있다.

PARAPHRASE 1

A complete copy of Tristan and Iseult written in French is not in existence. Fortunately, existing German versions enable us to put together the poem including stories about strong romance and tragedy.

PARAPHRASE 2

Whereas no French versions of Tristan and Iseult remain, surviving German translations allowed us to synthesize the poem containing strong romantic and tragic themes.

245 extol

Literature

Day 25

| SYNONYMS | v. | exalt, praise, hail, commend, acclaim, applaud, laud, admire | 칭찬하다, 칭송하다, 격찬하다 |

extol
[ikstóul]

Epics have a tendency to extol the ruthlessness of battle in the way that they emphasize the heroes who quarrel with unrivaled strength to get over difficult situations and extremely demonstrate fidelity between fellow soldiers.

서사시는 막강한 힘에 대항하여 어려움을 극복하는 영웅들을 강조하고 전우들 사이의 의리를 극단적인 방식으로 보여줌으로써 전쟁의 잔혹함을 칭송하는 경향이 있다.

PARAPHRASE 1

In Epics, the brutality of battle is apt to be exalted by highlighting the heroes who fight with extensive power to tide over difficulties and illustrating loyalty between comrades to the extreme.

PARAPHRASE 2

Epics stress the heroes fighting with great power to surmount difficulties and show comradeship extremely. In this way, they tend to praise the cruelty of battle.

246 obstinate

Art

Day 25

SYNONYMS adj. stubborn, unyielding, headstrong, determined, dogged, rigid, persistent, tenacious, adamant, unbending, inflexible

완고한, 완강한

obstinate
[ɔ́bstənit]

Statues sculpted in ancient Egypt can be readily accused of their **obstinate** attitudes that remained stationary for thousands of years on condition that they are separately seen without respect to their contextual and functional parts.

문맥적이고 기능적인 부분에 대한 고려없이 별개로 붙여졌을 때, 고대 이집트 조각상들의 수 천년 동안 변함 없는 완고한 태도는 쉽사리 비난받을 수도 있다.

PARAPHRASE 1

Seen in isolation with no regard to their function and original context, ancient Egyptian statues are subject to criticism for their **stubborn** attitudes that have been kept immutable for thousands of years.

PARAPHRASE 2

If ancient Egyptian statues remain isolated regardless of their original context and function, their **unyielding** attitudes staying the same for thousands of years can be easily criticized.

247 pragmatic

SYNONYMS *adj.* utilitarian, practical, practicable, useful, functional, effective

실용적인

pragmatic
[prægmǽtik]

In 1874, a shepherd first invented the **pragmatic** machine used to produce barbed wire, and until the end of the 19th century, approximately 400 kinds of barbed wire were devised. However, only a dozen were ever deployed on a commercial scale.

1874년, 한 농부가 실용적인 철조망 제조 기계를 최초로 발명한 이래로 19세기 말까지 대략 400 종류의 철조망이 고안되었다. 하지만 그 중 단지 십여 개 정도만이 상용화 되었다.

PARAPHRASE 1

There were hundreds of different kinds of barbed wire devised until the end of the century since the **utilitarian** device for making barbed wire was initially invented in 1874, but only a dozen were ever put to practical use.

PARAPHRASE 2

After the invention of the **practical** barbed wire-making machine in 1874, of many types of barbed wire created until the end of the century, only a dozen were ever commercialized.

248 overwhelm

World History

SYNONYMS v. overthrow, overpower, quell, subjugate, subdue, crush, dominate, master, triumph, overcome, prevail

압도하다, 이기다

overwhelm
[òuvərhwélm]

The government that had agreed to the Versailles Peace Treaty was overwhelmed by Adolf Hitler, thereby he acquired power and made it possible for Germany to break away from the treaty in 1933.

아돌프 히틀러는 베르사유 평화 조약에 가입하였던 이전 정부를 전복하면서 권력을 얻었고, 이로 인해 독일이 1933년에 조약으로부터 탈퇴하는 것이 가능해졌다.

PARAPHRASE 1

Adolf Hitler came into power through overthrowing the government that had agreed to the Versailles Peace Treaty, allowing Germany to disaffiliate from the treaty in 1933.

PARAPHRASE 2

As a result of overpowering the government that had signed the Versailles Treaty, Adolf Hitler obtained power, and enabled Germany to secede from the treaty in 1933.

249 initial

Day 25 — U.S.History

SYNONYMS **adj.** primary, original, first, inceptive, incipient, beginning, commencing, early, opening

초기의, 처음의

initial
[iníʃəl]

The **initial** American response following the outbreak of war in Europe in 1939 was neutral, but Japan bombarded the Pearl Harbor naval base in 1941, and this became the immediate cause of the war between the United States and Japan.

1939년 유럽에서 일어난 전쟁에 대한 미국의 초기 반응은 중립적이었지만, 일본이 1941년 진주만 해군 기지를 폭격했고, 이는 미국과 일본간 전쟁 발발의 즉각적인 원인이 되었다.

PARAPHRASE 1

Neutrality was the **primary** American reaction to the war that broke out in Europe in 1939, but in 1941, the bombardment of the Pearl Harbor naval base by Japan led up to the war first against Japan.

PARAPHRASE 2

Unlike the neutral **original** response to the war in Europe in 1939, the United States declared war first against Japan when the Pearl Harbor naval base was bombed by Japan in 1941.

250 disrupt

Environmental Science

SYNONYMS v. intervene, interfere, intrude, meddle, intercede, mediate, tamper

간섭하다, 방해하다

disrupt
[disrʌpt]

Birds of prey tend to hunt in the same realms, which are suited for wind turbines. Accordingly, in these particular regions, they have been killed frequently, and the flight patterns of migratory birds have been **disrupt**ed.

새들을 사냥하는 영역과 풍력 발전용 터빈에 적합한 영역이 대체로 겹치기 때문에, 이러한 지역에서 새들이 죽임을 당하거나 철새들의 비행패턴이 방해를 받아왔다.

PARAPHRASE 1

Some areas ideal for both wind turbines and birds of prey have caused an increase in the death rate of birds of prey and have **intervene**d in the flight patterns of migratory birds.

PARAPHRASE 2

Birds of prey have been killed and the flight patterns of migratory birds have been **interfere**d with in certain zones, preferred for hunting by birds of prey and perfect for wind turbines.

DAILY CHECK-UP

A. Find the answer that is closest in meaning to the highlighted word or phrase in the sentence.

01. Apprentices could have their own shops and gain **admiration** as master craftsmen if they acquired skills perfectly.
    (A) dissonance (B) respect

02. Athens was defeated in the second Peloponnesian War and its empire was entirely **overthrown**.
    (A) propagated (B) crushed

03. Architecture is the art and science of planning, designing, and building structures for symbolic and **utilitarian** purposes.
    (A) practical (B) outrageous

04. Three different but related views were suggested to **clarify** the cryptic origin and importance of the cave paintings.
    (A) sanitary (B) enigmatic

05. Heroic tales of battle were replaced by passionate love stories and women were **admired** as nearly goddess-like beings.
    (A) exalted (B) decimated

06. Absence and tardiness decreased overall productivity and **interfere with** the regular factory routine as work was specialized.
    (A) disrupted (B) spurred

07. The **first** alchemical document is known as the Emerald Tablet of Hermes Trismestigustus.
    (A) deluding (B) primary

08. The United States emerged as a leading industrial power, and **incisive** businessmen amassed fabulous wealth right after the Civil War.
    (A) cumbersome (B) shrewd

09. **Extant** diseases were rapidly spreading to humans in destroyed and

environmentally degraded areas.

(A) Existing (B) Lucrative

10. The government adhered to its **unyielding** stance on the issue of taxes.

    (A) defunct (B) adamant

B. Complete each sentence using one of the words or phrases given.

11. New York City had a big transportation problem, but unsurprisingly, there was no _____ solution.

    (A) headstrong (B) pragmatic

12. Henry Ford was _____ in that he instituted the assembly line in automobile manufacturing plants.

    (A) cramped (B) praised

13. Laissez faire is a predominating economic doctrine, meaning that the government should not _____ in commerce.

    (A) meddle (B) divest

14. Neptune lies in a region of space called the Kuiper Belt, which is a _____ ring, filled with frozen bodies.

    (A) deliberate (B) mysterious

15. Medieval culture relied mainly on the content of _____ documents, not responses of the writers.

    (A) remaining (B) malignant

16. The grips of _____ tools such as spears and similar objects were adorned with animal figures.

    (A) ludicrous (B) functional

---

01. (B) 02. (B) 03. (A) 04. (B) 05. (A) 06. (A) 07. (B) 08. (B) 09. (A) 10. (B)
11. (B) 12. (B) 13. (A) 14. (B) 15. (A) 16. (B)

REVIEW TEST (DAY 21-25)

A. The word _____ in the passage is closest in meaning to

01. In later times, the survival of the deer population should have been jeopardized as the numbers continue to decrease. As early explorers and settlers invaded the wilderness landscape by logging and farming as well as exploiting it for commercial and residential development, there was no doubt that the plight of deer populations was expected to **deteriorate** significantly and their numbers diminished still further.

    (A) dwindle
    (B) exacerbate
    (C) counter
    (D) puncture

02. The extinction of dodo was started, as the Portuguese sailors set their foot on the island first. As the European sailors appreciated the strategic location with the island, their ships plying on this route used to stop over in the island. Prior to their arrival, mammals had never existed on the island, which indicated that the dodo was no threat from predators and had no **dread** of humans.

    (A) acme
    (B) enigma
    (C) fear
    (D) luster

03. Animals' defensive adaptations developed to safeguard themselves against external threats are important because a matter of life and death for most animals can be determined by them. For example, turtles have a hard outer shell which provides them with protection. When

    (A) camouflage
    (B) explicate
    (C) furnish
    (D) ramble

REVIEW TEST (DAY 21-25)

threatened from other animals, they can **conceal** their body inside the bony shell. This makes it impossible for predators to open them.

---

04. The first advantage of being a franchise owner is that there is a lower risk of failure because someone else has already undergone trial and error and found out the most **feasible** goods and services in reality. As a result, franchise owners can offer these reliable items as well as duplicate tried-and-true formula regardless of location.

(A) precarious
(B) fervent
(C) workable
(D) discreet

---

05. Ancient Egyptian statues represent ordinary people, notably servants from the nonelite group, in addition to formal statues which depict deities, kings, and the elite. These servant statues carved to function as servants in the elite's tombs in the afterlife show dynamic poses depending on the tasks they perform, unlike formal figures confined to **stationary** postures.

(A) ambivalent
(B) static
(C) capricious
(D) tedious

---

06. At the same time, while researching the rocks in France, Georges Cuvier made the same discovery. Inspired by these finding, other geologists started to analyze the records of fossils and rocks scattered in various places on the earth. Shortly, it became realized that this law of faunal succession was widely applied in **nearly** every part of the world as well as in England or France.

(A) virtually
(B) progressively
(C) prohibitively
(D) ultimately

07. Prairie dogs as prolific herbivores, skilled diggers, and latent carriers of diseases transmitted by fleas have had a conspicuous **repercussion** on their environment. In this regard, many people now believe that their populations should be controlled in order to prohibit their negative effects.

(A) string
(B) attachment
(C) provision
(D) impact

08. In one experiment, researchers covered the birds' heads with little magnetic caps to **reverse** magnetic polarity. When released, the birds flew exactly in the reverse direction that they had been expected to fly. Through similar experiments conducted by molecular biologists, they have found a magnetic particle in cells of some birds' brains detecting the magnetic field.

(A) steadfast
(B) imminent
(C) inceptive
(D) opposite

09. Hippocratic physicians do not accept the viewpoint that the patient's **choice** for death can make taking his life right. The deepest ethical principle limiting the physician's power is not the autonomy or freedom of the patient but the dignity and mysterious power of human life itself.

(A) indication
(B) option
(C) fracture
(D) venue

REVIEW TEST (DAY 21-25)

10. Another predominant **trait** is that the metabolic rate of the lungfish is markedly fallen as the dry season starts. In water-deficient areas, the Australian lungfish undergo a drop at the rate of one-sixtieth in the standard rate of metabolism, necessary to maintain life. Thus, these amazing species cannot take in food. Instead, since they breathe air by lungs, not by gills, they just inhale oxygen through its mouth, which allows it to survive for years without water in unfavorable habitats.

(A) adornment
(B) pinnacle
(C) feature
(D) disposition

11. As the government debt had leaped from $65 million in 1861 when the war began to almost $3 billion in 1865 when the war was over, financial matters came to the fore greatly in both the South and the North. In those days, this sum was colossal, but it could be paid if the government were **attentive**. Simultaneously, war taxes needed to be cut back to be less burdensome.

(A) intrinsic
(B) lucrative
(C) prudent
(D) inclement

12. Porcupines are large rodents which have a coat of long, sharp quills loosely attached to their body. Although they do not throw the quills, the long stiff hairs with barbed ends can fall out of their body and stick into the enemy, often causing severe injury or death. Thus, predators try to avoid attacking them because of their **functional** weapons that help them to survive and thrive in their environments.

(A) pragmatic
(B) irksome
(C) discreet
(D) obstinate

13. Accuracy in capturing voters' intent has been highly **praised**, but shock and vibration that may occur during transport may cause the sensors in touch screen machines to be knocked out of alignment. If these sensors are not realigned properly at the polling station before the beginning of voting, a voter's intent can be misread by touch screen devices.

(A) meddled
(B) lauded
(C) evicted
(D) preponderated

14. Roughly 20 million years ago, a wide waterway that connected the Mediterranean with the Atlantic by two narrow straits was blocked by deformation of the earth's crust. The landlocked Mediterranean started to evaporate and then an increase in salinity wiped out many invertebrates and only a few survived. Also, constant evaporation increased the density of the **extant** salt water.

(A) despicable
(B) vigorous
(C) depraved
(D) remaining

답안
01. (B) 02. (C) 03. (A) 04. (C) 05. (B) 06. (A) 07. (D)
08. (D) 09. (B) 10. (C) 11. (C) 12. (A) 13. (B) 14. (D)

REVIEW TEST [DAY 21-25]

B. Which of the sentences below best expresses the essential information in the highlighted sentence in the passage? Incorrect choices change the meaning in important ways or leave out essential information.

15. The animal fossils excavated in strata of the Tommotian age which were once classified as various modern groups of animals are now considered not to be the ancestors of the modern animal groups since it turned out that they have unique forms of body that emerged and vanished during the first geological period of the Paleozoic Era.

    (A) It was believed that modern animal groups descended from the animals found in the Tommotian formation, but now the Tommotian fossils are labeled as the groups that existed only during certain period of the Paleozoic Era.
    (B) Body forms of the animals present in fossil beds of the Tommotian stage made scientists now believe that the modern animal groups originated from them.
    (C) In the past, the ancestors of modern animal groups were thought to be the animals in the Tommotian fossil beds due to their unique body forms, but this is now contradicted by several reasons.
    (D) The animal species found in the Tommotian fossil layers were not believed to belong to the modern animal groups at one time, but now it turned out that they are the origins of the groups due to their body forms.

해설 정답 (A)

① The animal fossils excavated in strata of the Tommotian age which were once classified as various modern groups of animals ② are now considered not to be the ancestors of the modern animal groups since ③ it turned out that they have unique forms of body that emerged and vanished during the first geological period of the Paleozoic Era.

→ ① It was believed that modern animal groups descended from the animals found in the Tommotian formation, but ② now the Tommotian fossils are labeled as the groups ③ that existed only during a certain period of the Paleozoic Era.

원문의 문장을 크게 주부(①)와 술부(②)로 나누고 그 두 부분 사이의 의미 관계가 접속사 'since'이하의 내용을 근거로 결정됨을 명확하게 이해하였는지를 평가하고자 하는 문제이다. 원문의 주부는 과거의 사실을 언급하고 있으며 술부는 현재의 사실을 언급하고 있고, 과거의 잘못된 인식이 '~한 이래로'의 의미의 접속사 'since'로 연결된 절의 내용을 계기로 달라졌음을 알 수 있다. Paraphrase 할 때에는, 원문의 주부와 술부 사이의 역접 관계를 등위접속사 'but'을 사용하여 더욱 명백하게 할 수 있고, 원문의 주부에서 관계대명사절의 형태로 언급되었던 과거의 사실을 절의 형태로 서술하고 술부에 언급되었던 현재의 사실도 'but' 이하에 절의 형태로 서술할 수 있다. 또한, 접속사 'since'로 연결되었던 절은 'the groups'를 수식하는 관계대명사절의 형태로 바꿀 수 있다.

오답의 근거

(B) Body forms of the animals present in fossil beds of the Tommotian stage made scientists now believe that <u>the modern animal groups originated from them</u>.
→ 원문에 따르면, '토모티안 시대의 화석층에 존재하는 동물의 신체 형태 때문에 현대의 동물군은 그들의 후손이 아니다'라고 언급하고 있으므로 보기의 밑줄 친 부분은 반대의 정보를 언급하고 있으므로 오답이다.

(C) In the past, the ancestors of modern animal groups were thought to be the animals in the Tommotian fossil beds <u>due to their unique body forms</u>, but this is now contradicted by several reasons.
→ 보기의 밑줄 친 부분의 이유로 '현대의 동물군의 조상이 토모티안 화석의 동물들이라고 여겨진 것'이 아니라, '토모티안 화석의 동물들이 현대의 동물군의 조상이 아님'의 근거가 되었으므로 틀린 내용으로 오답이며 접속사 'but'이하의 내용은 원문에 언급된 내용이 아니므로 또한 오답이다.

(D) The animal species found in the Tommotian fossil layers <u>were not believed to belong to the modern animal groups at one time</u>, but now it turned out that <u>they are the origins of the groups</u> due to their body forms.
→ 보기의 밑줄 친 부분의 정보는 원문의 내용과 완벽하게 반대되는 내용으로 오답이다.

다른 방식으로 paraphrase 하기

① The animal fossils excavated in strata of the Tommotian age which were once classified as various modern groups of animals ② are now considered **not** to be the ancestors of the modern animal groups since ③ it turned out that they have unique forms of body that emerged and vanished during the first geological period of the Paleozoic Era.

→ With ③ unique body forms that appeared and disappeared during the Cambrian Period, ② the animals present in fossil beds of the Tommotian

REVIEW TEST [DAY 21-25]

stage are now **no longer** thought to belong to the modern animal groups.

원문의 접속사 'since'가 이끄는 절 ③의 내용은 토모티안 시대의 화석층에 존재하는 동물의 특징이므로 전치사 'with'를 활용하여 구의 형태로 서술하고, '더 이상 ~이 아니다'라는 의미의 'no longer'를 사용함으로써 과거의 사실이 더 이상 현재에는 사실이 아님을 언급할 수 있고, 이는 원문의 주부(②)에서 과거의 사실을 언급하는 관계대명사절 'which were ~ animals'의 내용을 생략하여도 그 의미를 짐작할 수 있게 한다. 따라서 원문의 두 개의 절로 이루어진 문장은 하나의 절로 재구성 될 수 있다.

→ ① In the past, the animals in the Tommotian fossil beds were thought to be the origins of modern animal groups, but ② now it turned out that it is not true anymore because of ③ their forms of body that existed during the Cambrian Period.
→ ① The animal species found in the Tommotian fossil layers were believed to belong to the modern animal groups at one time, but ② now it turned out that they are not the origins of the groups due to ③ their body forms.

원문의 접속사 'since'가 이끄는 절 ③의 내용은 토모티안 시대의 화석층에 존재하는 동물의 특징으로 과거와 현재의 사실이 달라지는 결정적인 원인이므로 '~때문에'라는 의미의 'because of' 또는 'due to'를 활용하여 절을 구의 형태로 서술할 수 있다.

16. When researchers use observational assessment as a method in the study of perceptual abilities of infants, the best of care is required not to make the mistake of hasty generalization about the data or to depend too much on a few researches as decisive proof of a specific perceptual ability of the infant.

(A) In order to avoid overgeneralizations about the data or the heavy reliance on a few studies, researchers must use observational assessment in the study of perceptual abilities of infants

(B) Although observational assessment has limitations such as making hasty generalizations about the data and relying heavily on a few studies, researchers often use the method to study perceptual abilities of infants.

(C) The use of observational assessment, a technique for studying perceptual abilities of infants, must be discouraged in that it instigates overgeneralizations from the data or the dependence on a few research results.

(D) Researchers who use observational assessment for the study on perceptual abilities of infants must avoid overgeneralizations about the data or draw a conclusion from many studies.

해설 정답 (D)

When ① researchers use observational assessment as a method in the study of perceptual abilities of infants, ② the best of care is required not to make the mistake of hasty generalization about the data or (not) to depend too much on a few researches as decisive proof of a specific perceptual ability of the infant.
→ ① Researchers who use observational assessment for the study on perceptual abilities of infants ② must avoid overgeneralizations about the data or draw a conclusion from many studies.

원문의 문장을 접속사 'when'을 기준으로 크게 두 부분으로 나누었을 때, 그 두 부분 사이의 의미 관계를 명확하게 이해하였는지를 평가하고자 하는 문제이다. 원문의 '~할 때'라는 의미의 접속사 'when'이 이끄는 종속절(①)은 주절의 전제가 되며 주절(②)은 그 전제에 대한 유의 사항을 언급하고 있음을 알 수 있다. 따라서 Paraphrase 할 때에는, 원문의 종속절(①)을 문장의 주부로 원문의 주절(②)은 술부로 놓을 수 있고 이렇게 함으로써 원문의 두 개의 절은 하나의 절로 이루어진 문장으로 바꾸어 표현될 수 있다.

오답의 근거

(A) In order to avoid overgeneralizations about the data and the heavy reliance on a few studies, researchers must use observational assessment in the study of perceptual abilities of infants.
→ 원문에서는 밑줄 친 두 가지 문제점을 극복하기 위해 '관찰 평가를 사용하는 연구자들은 최대한의 주의를 기울여야 한다'라고 언급하고 있는 반면 보기에서는 이러한 문제점을 피하기 위해 '연구자들은 관찰 평가를 사용해야 한다'라고 언급하고 있으므로 틀린 내용으로 오답이다.

(B) Although observational assessment has limitations such as making hasty generalizations about the data and relying heavily on a few studies, researchers often use the method to study perceptual abilities of infants.
→ 보기에서 언급하고 있는 '관찰 평가는 한계가 있음에도 불구하고 연구자들이 이 방법을 자주 사용'하고 있는지는 원문의 정보를 통해 유추하기 어려우며, 원문에서는 '한계점에 있으므로 주의해서 사용해야 한다'라고 언급하고 있으므로 엄밀히 주요 내용이 포함되어 있지 않으므로 오답이다.

(C) The use of observational assessment, a technique for studying perceptual abilities of infants, must be discouraged in that it instigates overgeneralizations from the data or the dependence on a few research results.
→ 원문은 '관찰 평가는 문제점들이 있으므로 사용시 주의해서 사용해야 한다'라고 언급하고 있으므로 보기의 '관찰 평가는 문제점이 있으므로 사용해서는 안 된다'는 내용과는 전혀 다르므로 틀린 내용으로 오답이다.

REVIEW TEST [DAY 21-25]

다른 방식으로 paraphrase 하기

When ① researchers use observational assessment as a method in the study of perceptual abilities of infants, ② the best of care is required not to make the mistake of hasty generalization about the data or to depend too much on a few researches as decisive proof of a specific perceptual ability of the infant.

→ ② In order to overcome limitations of observational assessment (such as overgeneralizations about the data and the heavy reliance on a few studies), researchers must be careful when ① using the method in the study of perceptual abilities of infants.

원문의 접속사 'when'이 이끄는 종속절(①)은 주절(②)의 뒤에 놓일 수 있으며 이 때에 접속사 'when'이 이끄는 종속절의 주어와 재진술 된 문장의 주어 'researchers'가 일치하므로 종속절의 주어는 생략하고 동사에 ~ing를 붙여 축약형으로 쓸 수 있다. 또한 원문의 주절에서는 '최대한의 주의가 요구된다'라는 의미의 'the best of care is required'라는 표현을 사용하여 수동문의 형태를 취한 반면 재진술 시에는 주의를 기울여야 하는 주체인 'researchers'를 주어로 내세우고 'must be careful'과 같이 능동의 형태로 서술할 수 있다. 원문의 주절에서 언급하고 있는 '관찰 평가'의 문제점들은 재진술 시 강조를 위해 'in order to'를 사용하여 문두에 둘 수 있음도 기억하도록 한다.

→ ① The use of observational assessment, a research technique for the study on infants' perceptual abilities, ② requires the best of care in terms of the potential for overgeneralizations from the data or the dependence on a few studies.

문장을 paraphrase 할 때에는 무엇을 강조할 것인가에 따라 주어를 바꿀 수 있으며 이는 문장을 다양하게 재구성하는 하나의 효과적인 방법이 될 수 있다. 위의 재진술 문장에서는 '관찰 방법의 사용'을 주어로 두어 이 방법의 사용 자체가 주의를 요함을 언급하고 있다. 또한 이 관찰 방법의 두 가지 한계점을 언급할 때 품사 바꾸기를 통해 원문에서는 동사의 형태('make the mistake of hasty generalization about the data', 'depend too much on a few researches as decisive proof of a specific perceptual ability of the infant)를 사용하여 진술을 하였던 반면, 재진술 문장에서는 명사의 형태('overgeneralizations from the data', 'the dependence on a few studies')를 활용하여 문장을 좀 더 다양하게 표현할 수 있다.

251 surplus

Day 26
Agriculture

SYNONYMS **n.** excess, extra, redundance, excessive quantity

나머지, 여분, 잉여, 과잉

surplus
[sə́ːrplʌs]

For the support for investment and trade, as well as for the increasing population that resulted in the growth of rural industry, sufficient food to create surpluses was produced by bringing more land under cultivation.

농촌 지역의 산업 성장의 원인이 되었던 인구 증가 뿐만 아니라, 투자와 무역을 지원하기 위해, 잉여가 발생할 정도의 충분한 식량이 더 많은 토지의 개간을 통해 생산되었다.

PARAPHRASE 1

More land reclamation which produced enough food to acquire excess gave support not only to the larger population that led to industrial growth in rural areas, but also to investment and trade.

PARAPHRASE 2

Food production enough to obtain extra both for the growing population and for investment and trade was enabled by clearing more land.

252 release

SYNONYMS v. discharge, emit, exude, exhale, shed, radiate, give off

방출하다, 발산하다

release
[ríːs]

There are some advantages related to large wind farms such as producing a moderate and fairly high net energy and releasing no heat-trapping carbon dioxide or other sources of air contamination.

거대 풍력발전지역은 상당량의 고효율 에너지 생산 및 열을 가두는 이산화탄소나 공해의 원인이 되는 물질의 방출 억제 등의 장점을 갖고 있다.

PARAPHRASE 1

Huge wind farms do have the virtue of creating a moderate and high output of net energy and not discharging carbon dioxide that traps heat or other air contaminants.

PARAPHRASE 2

Large wind farms with a moderate and high net energy yield do not emit substances that pollute the air.

253 immediately

Pedagogy

SYNONYMS adv. instantly, directly, presently, shortly, soon, promptly, straight away, right away, on the spot, in the same breath

즉시, 당장

immediately
[pɪnɪtreɪt]

Children commonly have a tendency to give vent to aggressive impulses on other people, such as their parents, because it is impossible for even the most considerate parents to gratify all of their requirements immediately.

가장 사려 깊은 부모조차도 아이들의 모든 요구사항을 즉시 충족시켜줄 수 없기 때문에, 아이들에게는 보통 부모를 포함한 다른 사람들에게 공격적인 충동을 표출하는 경향이 있다.

PARAPHRASE 1

As even the most thoughtful parents have difficulty in meeting all of their children's demands instantly, children are generally apt to release aggressive impulses on other people, including parents.

PARAPHRASE 2

Even the most attentive parents are unable to satisfy all of their children's needs directly, so their aggressive impulses normally tend to be vented on others.

254 persuasive

SYNONYMS adj. convincing, compelling, influential, valid, credible, plausible, cogent, convictive, irrefutable, telling

설득력 있는, 강력한

persuasive
[pərswéisiv]

On the whole, known as special effects and techniques, another illusion of film is employed by filmmakers when it is hard to make a scene **persuasive**, although costumes, makeup, and stunts are used.

의상이나 분장, 스턴트가 사용되었음에도 불구하고 설득력 있는 장면을 연출하기 어려울 때, 영화 제작자들은 보통 특수 효과와 기법이라는 이름으로 알려진 영화 속 환영을 도입한다.

PARAPHRASE 1

When costumes, makeup, and stunts are still not enough to make a scene **convincing**, filmmakers utilize another illusion of film known largely as special effects and techniques.

PARAPHRASE 2

Filmmakers use special effects and techniques when a scene is not adequately **compelling** despite the use of costumes, makeup, and stunts.

255 above and beyond

Biology

SYNONYMS phr. in addition to, as well as, along with, together with, aside from, besides

~에 더하여, ~뿐만 아니라

above and beyond

Up-to-date evidence for the usefulness of disruptive colors, above and beyond that conferred by background matching, in experiments has been founded upon man-made prey with patterns destitute of a plane of symmetry.

(위장에 있어) 배경맞추기(background matching)뿐 아니라 최근의 분열 패턴(disruptive colors)의 유용성이, 비대칭 패턴을 가진 인공 먹이에 대한 실험에서 입증되었다.

PARAPHRASE 1

On the basis of artificial prey with patterns low in a plane of symmetry, recent experiments on the efficacy of disruptive colors, in addition to that given by background matching, has been conducted.

PARAPHRASE 2

Artificial prey with patterns lacking in a plane of symmetry have become the foundation of recent experimental proof for the utility of disruptive colors, as well as that of background matching.

256 place

SYNONYMS v. situate, locate, lay, deposit, set, put 두다, 놓다

place
[pleis]

In spite of the fact that only running water was cut out for the continuous operating of machines, it had one big weakness: water-driven factories had to be **place**d close by the water whether or not the place was ideal for other reasons.

오직 흐르는 물만이 기계의 지속적인 작동에 적합하기는 하지만, 수력으로 작동하는 공장들은 이러한 위치 선정이 다른 이유로도 이상적인가에 대해서는 전혀 고려하지 못한 채 물가에 위치해야만 하는 큰 단점을 가지고 있었다.

PARAPHRASE 1

Running water was the only energy source suitable for consistent operation of machines. However, to benefit from it, factories had to be **situate**d near the water, without regard to whether such spots made sense otherwise.

PARAPHRASE 2

When factories were **locate**d along the water, regardless of other conditions, running water, the only power source fit for the constant use of machines, could be optimized.

257 potential

SYNONYMS adj. latent, dormant, prospective, possible

잠재적인, 가능성 있는

potential
[pouténʃəl]

An information-analyzing method like that of a scientist is used to arrive at a causal attribution, in which people analyze their action in consideration of whether various potential factors are present or absent.

과학자가 사용하는 것과 같은 정보 분석 방법은 인과적 귀속에 도달하는 것을 목적으로 하며, 이때 사람들의 행동은 다양한 잠재 요소들의 존재와 부재의 측면에서 분석된다.

PARAPHRASE 1

People analyze information to make a causal attribution in the same way that a scientist would. In other words, their behavior is assessed in light of the presence or absence of diverse **latent** causes.

PARAPHRASE 2

A causal attribution is made by doing information analysis equal to that of a scientist. That is, people judge their action in view of whether or not varied **dormant** causes exist.

258 delay

SYNONYMS v. suspend, postpone, defer, procrastinate, adjourn, put off

연기하다, 미루다

delay
[diléi]

The main reason why transition to sound film was delayed was that in Europe, a lot of small producers had a hard time bearing the costs of sound, and that in different regions of the world, there were problems with rights or access to equipment.

유럽에서는 많은 소규모 제작자들이 음향 비용을 부담하는 데에 어려움을 겪었기 때문에, 그리고 그 밖의 세계 각지에서는 장비에 대한 권한이나 접근을 둘러싼 문제들 때문에 음성 영화로의 전환이 지연되었다.

PARAPHRASE 1

The conversion to sound cinema was suspended, chiefly due to many small producers for whom the costs of sound were prohibitive in Europe, and problems related with equipment in other areas of the world.

PARAPHRASE 2

Many small producers in Europe could not afford sound costs, and issues relevant to equipment existed in other parts of the world. These reasons postponed the shift to sound film.

259 doctrine

Politics

Day 26

SYNONYMS **n.** principle, dogma, tenet, belief, credo, creed, conviction, faith

원리, 주의, 교리, 신념, 신조

doctrine
[dɔ́ktrin]

On the basis of the **doctrine** that sovereignty resided in the people, democratic states were established and as citizenship was granted to women as well as to classes formerly excluded, this principle of democratic sovereignty became all-inclusive.

주권은 국민에게 있다는 원리의 기반 하에, 민주주의 국가들이 설립되었고, 이전에 시민권에서 배제되었던 계층들뿐만 아니라 여성들에게도 시민권이 주어짐에 따라 국민 주권의 원리는 모든 이들을 포함하게 되었다.

PARAPHRASE 1

The **principle** that all the people had sovereignty became the foundation of democracies and as classes formerly excluded and women obtained citizenship, all were included in this principle.

PARAPHRASE 2

Democracies rested on the **dogma** of popular sovereignty and citizenship given to formerly neglected classes of people included all in this belief.

260 substitute

Psychology

SYNONYMS v. replace, displace, supersede, supplant, exchange, swap, switch, change, transfer

대체하다, 대신하다

substitute
[sʌ́bstitjùːt]

Cognitive psychotherapies seek to encourage the emotionally chaotic person who considers unfortunate events as their own failures to face up to the absurdity of this recognition and to substitute it with more reasonable assessments of such events.

인지 정신치료는 불운한 사건들을 스스로의 실패로 간주하는 정서적 장애가 있는 사람으로 하여금 이러한 인식의 불합리성을 직시하도록 하며, 이를 같은 사건들에 대한 보다 합리적인 평가로 대체하도록 한다.

PARAPHRASE 1

For the treatment of the mentally unstable person who perceives negative incidents as personal failures, cognitive psychotherapies attempt to make them recognize the irrationality of this awareness and to replace it with critical evaluations.

PARAPHRASE 2

Cognitive psychotherapies try to displace the wrong perceptions of a mentally ill person of adverse effects with more objective appraisals by realizing their absurdity.

DAILY CHECK-UP

A. Find the answer that is closest in meaning to the highlighted word or phrase in the sentence.

01. Alternative energy is a source of energy that can **replace** traditional fuel sources.
    (A) divulge   (B) supersede

02. Rock paintings made by Bushmen in South America were **situated** near the open entrances of caves.
    (A) mocked   (B) located

03. American agricultural output had **excessive quantities** to supply to industrial hubs of Europe.
    (A) surpluses   (B) venues

04. Conservation efforts of unhelpful farmers only **postponed** the exhaustion of the aquifer.
    (A) disassembled   (B) delayed

05. Innovative **principles** were realized by the atmospheric engine created by Thomas Savery.
    (A) incitements   (B) tenets

06. When the initiating source of energy was eliminated, phosphorescence was **released** constantly.
    (A) radiated   (B) embodied

07. The teacher as a reflective practitioner will rarely occur for the simple reason that it is a brilliant or even **persuasive** idea.
    (A) compelling   (B) engrossed

08. Mimicry is when an organism imitates the appearance of another organism that is repulsive or detrimental to a **possible** enemy.
    (A) potential   (B) frivolous

09. In the early 1800s, the early settlers stated that deer were abundant, but **in the**

same breath lamented over their shortage.

(A) utterly   (B) immediately

10. Early explorers invaded the wilderness landscape by logging and farming, **in addition to** exploiting it for commercial and residential development.

(A) as well as   (B) with respect to

B. Complete each sentence using one of the words or phrases given.

11. It is commonly believed that human beings can never be _____ by machines.

(A) supplanted   (B) conferred

12. The Athenian democratic government was seen as a _____ threat to the Spartan aristocratic government.

(A) voracious   (B) potential

13. The principle of faunal succession was applicable almost everywhere _____ in France or England.

(A) above and beyond   (B) in the same breath

14. Until a white dwarf cools and then stops _____ visible light, its luminosity will shrink steadily.

(A) setting up   (B) giving off

15. Intense interest in sound film in the 1920s _____ the commercialization of other innovations in techniques.

(A) stretched out   (B) put off

16. Sediment on the ocean floor may be _____ inland at some date in the future when the land rises or the sea level falls.

(A) situated   (B) reigned

---

01. (B) 02. (B) 03. (A) 04. (B) 05. (B) 06. (A) 07. (A) 08. (A) 09. (B) 10. (A)
11. (A) 12. (B) 13. (A) 14. (B) 15. (B) 16. (A)

261 grant

Day 27
American Culture

SYNONYMS v. confer, award, accord, give, bestow   주다, 수여하다

grant
[grænt]

People attended the rural fairs in different ways: men exchanged domestic animals and obtained needed commodities; women displayed food prepared at home; and everyone would engage in diverse sports, which granted prizes to the victors.

사람들은 다양한 방식으로 지방 축제에 참여했다. 남자들은 가축을 교환하여 필요한 물품을 얻었고, 여자들은 집에서 준비한 음식을 진열했으며, 모든 사람들이 우승자에게 경품을 주는 다양한 스포츠에 참여할 수 있었다.

PARAPHRASE 1

In the rural fairs, men bartered farm animals, acquiring necessary goods, while women displayed home-cooked food. Meanwhile, multiple sports, with prizes conferred to the winners, were offered to everyone.

PARAPHRASE 2

While women exhibited home-made food, men traded livestock and got necessities in the rural fairs. Also, everyone could enjoy varied sports, awarding prizes.

262 difference

Biology

SYNONYMS **n.** distinction, divergence, disparity, inequality, gap, discrepancy, discrimination, dissidence

차이

difference
[dífərəns]

Two connected **differences** among the species, in their body sizes and digestive systems could be the answer to why herbivores which inhabit East Africa show dissimilar feeding preferences.

생물 종들 사이에 존재하는 서로 연관된 두 가지 차이점, 즉 신체 크기와 소화 체계의 차이는 동아시아에서 서식하는 초식동물들이 서로 다른 먹이를 선호하는 이유에 대한 답이 될 수 있다.

PARAPHRASE 1

The answer to the distinctive feeding preferences of herbivores in East African areas lies in two associated **distinctions** among the species, in their body sizes and digestive systems.

PARAPHRASE 2

The disparate feeding preferences of East African herbivores stems from two related **divergences** in their body sizes and digestive systems.

263 chaotic

Day 27
Economics

SYNONYMS *adj.* disordered, disorganized, anarchic, tumultuous, riotous, lawless, uncontrolled, jumbled, turbulent

무질서한, 무법상태의, 혼란 상태인

chaotic
[kéiɑtik]

The real value of the currency goes up and down every month and the inflation accelerates, so relationships between creditors and debtors, which form the foundation of capitalism, become so entirely chaotic that they become almost meaningless.

화폐의 실가가 매달 등락을 거듭하고 인플레이션이 가속화 될 때, 자본주의의 기초가 되는 채권자와 채무자 사이의 관계는 아주 혼란스러워서 거의 무의미한 상태가 된다.

PARAPHRASE 1

Monthly fluctuations in the real value of the currency and the ongoing inflation make connections between creditors and debtors, forming the basis of capitalism (←minor idea), so **disordered** as to become nonsensical.

PARAPHRASE 2

Relations between creditors and debtors become so **disorganized** as to be pointless as the real value of the currency varies monthly and inflation continues.

264 qualification

Day 27
Astronomy

SYNONYMS n. prerequisite, requirement, stipulation, provision, proviso, necessary condition

필요 조건, 자격 조건, 조항

qualification
[kwὰləfəkéiʃən]

All of the **qualifications** required for life to exist are satisfied through all the available evidence discovered on Mars although it is difficult to say that living things ever lived there for the simple reason that there was water on the planet.

화성에 물이 존재했다는 이유만으로 생명체가 그곳에 살았다고 말하기는 어렵지만, 화성에서 발견된 모든 유효한 증거들이 생명체가 존재하기 위한 요구 조건들을 전부 충족하고 있다.

PARAPHRASE 1

The fact that water existed on ancient Mars does not automatically mean that life ever emerged there. However, all the available evidence indicates that Mars fulfills all the **prerequisites** needed to support life.

PARAPHRASE 2

It can hardly be said that it ever supported living creatures simply because ancient Mars had water, but all the available proof found on Mars meets all the **requirements** essential for life.

265 weaken

Physiology — Day 27

| SYNONYMS | v. | undermine, attenuate, lessen, decrease, impair, diminish, abate, soften | 약화시키다 |

weaken
[wíːkən]

According to several studies, if a person gets less than six hours of sleep per night, his or her coordination, judgment, and reaction time are weakened, and, as a result, he or she becomes more likely to be exposed to a severe risk of accident or injury.

몇몇의 연구에 따르면, 하루에 6시간 이하의 수면을 취했을 때 조정력, 판단력, 반응력이 약화되며 결과적으로 사고나 부상의 심각한 위험에 노출될 가능성이 더 높아진다.

PARAPHRASE 1

Several studies indicate that when sleeping less than six hours a night, coordination, judgment, and reaction time are undermined and thus serious accident or injury can be caused.

PARAPHRASE 2

Several studies show that sleeping less than six hours a night attenuates coordination, judgment, and reactions, potentially causing fatal accidents or injury.

266 require

SYNONYMS v. demand, claim, require, postulate, request, declare, propose, necessitate, seek, desire, entail, enjoin, ask, invoke, call for, call upon

요구하다, 요청하다

require
[rikwáiər]

Climax communities which **require** hundreds of years to get to the steady state would be the least balanced and the most breakable providing that stability is defined as how fast an ecosystem goes back to a specific form after a major disturbance.

만약 안정성이 생태계가 커다란 대란을 겪은 후에 얼마나 빨리 특정한 상태로 되돌아가는가를 의미한다면, 안정 상태로 돌아가는데 수 백 년이 요구되는 극상 군락이야말로 가장 불안정하고 연약한 군락일 것이다.

PARAPHRASE 1

In the case that stability implies how quickly an ecosystem gets back to a certain form after a main disturbance, climax communities would be the least stable and the most brittle, as hundreds of years are **demand**ed to return to the climax state.

PARAPHRASE 2

If stability means the pace with which an ecosystem returns to normality after a disturbance, climax communities, **claim**ing hundreds of years to reach the climax state, would be the least stable and the most fragile.

267 covetous

Day 27
Chemistry

SYNONYMS **adj.** voracious, greedy, insatiable, gluttonous, avid, avaricious,

탐욕적인, 만족할 줄 모르는

covetous
[kʌ́vitəs]

In the hope of an increase in profits, **covetous** tradespeople entrusted their gold, silver, and precious stones to the self-styled alchemists. However, Pope John XXI prohibited them from practicing alchemy under pain of death.

수익의 증가를 원했던 탐욕스러운 상인들은 그들의 금, 은, 그리고 보석들을 스스로 연금술사라 칭하는 사람들에게 맡겼다. 하지만 교황 요하네스 21세는 이를 위반할 경우 사형에 처한다는 조건으로 연금술의 실행을 금지했다.

PARAPHRASE 1

Valuables of **voracious** merchants who longed for a rise in profits were assigned to the would-be alchemists, but the practice of alchemy was forbidden on pain of death by Pope John XXI.

PARAPHRASE 2

Greedy merchants hoping for earnings growth trusted the alleged alchemists with their gems, but Pope John XXI banned alchemy on pain of death.

268 potent

| SYNONYMS | adj. | powerful, strong, mighty, forceful, influential, robust, sturdy, vigorous, tough, overwhelming, overpowering |

강한, 강력한

potent
[póutənt]

Just as the **potent** Roman cement and the regular design held the stone in a Roman wall together, the various parts of the Roman Empire were integrated into a monolithic entity through physical, psychological, and organizational domination.

로마 건축에서 벽을 이루던 돌들이 강력한 로만 시멘트와 규칙적인 디자인에 의해 결합되었던 것처럼, 로마 제국의 다양한 부분들은 물리적, 정신적, 조직적 지배를 통해 하나의 단일 존재로 통합되었다.

PARAPHRASE 1

Physical, psychological, and organizational controls bonded the various parts of the Roman realm into a single entity, like the Roman stone walls were fused by the **powerful** Roman cement and their regular design.

PARAPHRASE 2

As Roman walls were banded together by the **strong** cement and their even design, the Roman realm was united by several kinds of controls.

269 repair

Environmental Science

SYNONYMS v. remedy, correct, amend, remodel, mend, rectify, fix, patch

고치다, 수선하다

repair
[ripéər]

There are many ways of decreasing deforestation and repairing forests that have been damaged: controlling the use of paper, coal and firewood, increasing the use of recycled paper-products, and promoting tree planting.
종이, 석탄, 장작의 사용을 규제하고, 재활용된 종이 제품의 사용을 늘리고, 식목을 장려하는 등 삼림벌채를 줄이고 파괴된 삼림을 회복시키는 데에는 많은 방법들이 있다.

PARAPHRASE 1

Including restrictions on the use of paper, coal and firewood, the reutilization of paper products, and tree planting, various methods have been offered to reduce deforestation and to remedy destroyed forests.

PARAPHRASE 2

Deforestation can be curtailed, and destroyed forests can be corrected by limiting the use of paper, coal and firewood, recycling paper products and planting more trees.

270 misconception

Astronomy — Day 27

| SYNONYMS | n. | misunderstanding, fallacy, illusion, false belief, false impression | 오해, 잘못된 생각 |

misconception
[mìskənsépʃən]

Two widespread **misconceptions** arising when asked why the Hubble Space Telescope is considered unique and different from ground telescopes are that it is bigger than any other telescope on Earth and that it is closer to the stars, making it possible to take amazing images.

왜 허블 망원경이 특별하고 지구상의 다른 망원경들과 차별화 되는지를 물었을 때 드는 두 가지 일반적인 오해는 허블 망원경이 다른 어떤 망원경들보다도 크기가 크며, 항성들과 가까이 위치하기 때문에 훌륭한 이미지를 취할 수 있다는 것이다.

PARAPHRASE 1

Common **misunderstandings** concerning what makes the Hubble Space Telescope vastly superior to telescopes on Earth include that it is the largest telescope and that it takes better images as it is closer to the stars.

PARAPHRASE 2

The size being larger than ground telescopes and the distance to the stars being short enough to take better pictures are two prevailing **fallacies** regarding what makes the Hubble Space Telescope special.

397

DAILY CHECK-UP

A. Find the answer that is closest in meaning to the highlighted word or phrase in the sentence.

01. Energy allocation displays conspicuous **discrepancies** between growth and reproduction.

    (A) gaps (B) illusions

02. The European monarchies were **abated** by a series of revolutions in the previous centuries.

    (A) weakened (B) postulated

03. In many societies in West Africa, iron weapons had symbolic meaning to make the warrior more **influential**.

    (A) jumbled (B) powerful

04. Land was **bestowed** to aristocrats by emperors in return for their fidelity when the Roman Empire began to disintegrate.

    (A) granted (B) interceded

05. Rehabilitation work is now underway to resurface the road and **repair** bridges.

    (A) tamper (B) fix

06. Termites decide the nature of the progressing construction depending on the **necessary conditions** of the colony.

    (A) creeds (B) requirements

07. There is a **false belief** that the survival of the fittest means that only the most aggressive can survive.

    (A) peculiarity (B) misconception

08. Freud states that suppressed impulses continuously exist and **call for** expression.

    (A) demand (B) rectify

09. The Democrats had a tendency to see society as a constant conflict between **gluttonous** aristocrats and the subjects.

(A) greedy   (B) convictive

10. According to the second law of thermodynamics, the universe we live in is becoming even more **chaotic**.

    (A) avaricious   (B) disordered

B. Complete each sentence using one of the words or phrases given.

11. Greater freedom of expression was _____ to architects thanks to the development in construction methods.

    (A) given   (B) obscured

12. The border security in Egypt is being threatened by the _____ situation in Libya.

    (A) lawless   (B) poignant

13. The space shuttle Atlantis launched the _____ and improved Hubble Space telescope into space.

    (A) subdued   (B) mended

14. The immune system is _____ by sleep deprivation and this makes a person more vulnerable to diseases.

    (A) impaired   (B) incarnated

15. The zebra and wildebeest consume separate parts of the identical plants which meet the _____ suitable for their digestive system.

    (A) underpinnings   (B) requirements

16. The applied arts and the fine arts show the consistent _____ in attitude of artists towards the materials.

    (A) agitation   (B) divergence

---

01. (A) 02. (A) 03. (B) 04. (A) 05. (B) 06. (B) 07. (B) 08. (A) 09. (A) 10. (B)
11. (A) 12. (A) 13. (B) 14. (A) 15. (B) 16. (B)

399

271 distinctive

Formative Arts

SYNONYMS **adj.** special, peculiar, characteristic, idiosyncratic, singular, unique, exceptional

독특한, 특유의

distinctive
[distíŋktiv]

People would fail to comprehend why ancient Egyptian art was developed or the notions that led it to assume its distinctive forms, if it were not for considering the world view of the elite Egyptians and the contexts and functions of the art produced for them.

만약 이집트 엘리트 계층의 세계관과 그들을 위해 고안된 예술의 문맥과 기능을 고려하지 않는다면, 고대 이집트 미술이 창조된 이유와 그 특유의 형태의 기반이 되는 개념들을 이해할 수 없을 것이다.

PARAPHRASE 1

But for the attention to the elite Egyptians' view of the world and the contexts and functions of the art devised for them, it would be hard to understand why ancient Egyptian art was produced or what caused its special forms to be adopted.

PARAPHRASE 2

Without regard for the elite Egyptians' world view and the contexts and functions of the art made for them, why ancient Egyptian art was created or what led it to take its peculiar forms could not be fully understood.

272 evidence

Art

SYNONYMS n. proof, testimony, witness, sign   증거, 징후

evidence
[évidəns]

The alternate belief that painting the images of animals guarantees the success of hunting is supported by the evidence of scratch marks in the animal depictions created by spears thrown at the paintings.

동물의 이미지가 사냥의 성공을 보장한다는 믿음에 기반한 또 다른 설명은, 동물 그림위로 던져진 창에 의해 긁힌 자국들이 남아 있다는 증거에 의해 뒷받침된다.

PARAPHRASE 1

Another explanation, based on the belief that successful hunting is ensured by painting animal images, is supported by the proof of scratch marks in the painted animals made by throwing spears at the drawings.

PARAPHRASE 2

The testimony of chips in the depicted animals by spears thrown backs up another assumption, based on the belief that drawing animal figures ensures successful hunting.

273 ultimately

Day 28
Geology

| SYNONYMS | adv. | eventually, finally, at last, after all, in the end, in the long run | 결국, 마침내, 궁극적으로 |

ultimately
[ʌ́ltəmitli]

Even though **Smith's contribution to the field of geology was overlooked at first**, he was **ultimately** appreciated by the Geological Society of London as the **"Father of English Geology"**, when he made the maps showing the geologic composition of the land.

초기에는 지질학의 분야에의 그의 기여가 간과되기도 했지만, 결국 스미스는 지역의 지질학적 구조를 잘 나타낸 그의 지도들 덕분에 런던 지질학회에 의해 "영국 지질학의 아버지"로서의 진가를 인정받았다.

PARAPHRASE 1

At first, the Geological Society of London ignored Smith who had contributed much to geology, but it **eventually** recognized him as the "Father of English Geology", in virtue of his maps, which show geological features of the region.

PARAPHRASE 2

Smith, disregarded despite his contribution to geology, **finally** received credit for his maps showing the geological makeup of the area by the Geological Society of London as the "Father of English Geology".

274 surprise

Day 28
Modern Art

| SYNONYMS | v. | startle, amaze, astonish, astound, alarm, upset, shock, frighten, stun, daze, stupefy | 놀라게 하다 |

surprise
[sərpráiz]

Marcel Duchamp, who was the forerunner of the Dadaists, surprised the art establishment with "readymades", commonplace manufactured objects that he selected and exhibited, including a comb and a bottle rack.

허무주의적 예술가(다다이스트)들의 선구자였던 마르셀 뒤샹은 레디메이드, 즉 그가 선택하고 전시한 빗과 병 받침대 등의 평범한 기성 제품들로 미술계의 기득권층을 놀라게 했다.

PARAPHRASE 1

The "readymades" of Marcel Duchamp, the pioneer of the Dadaists, were mundane manufactured goods that he chose and displayed, containing a comb and a bottle rack (←minor idea), which startled the art establishment.

PARAPHRASE 2

The art establishment was amazed by "readymades", ordinary manufactured items picked and showed by Marcel Duchamp, the pioneer of the Dadaists.

403

275 surpass

Day 28
Economics

SYNONYMS v. exceed, outdo, transcend, excel, outmatch, outstrip, outrun, beat, outweigh, preponderate, outbalance, override, prevail over, go beyond, be superior to

능가하다, 뛰어나다

surpass
[sərpǽs]

The steamship was able to **surpass** the sailing ship as the primary mode of transportation in international trade thanks to developments in technology as well as the completion of the Suez Canal in 1867.

1867년 수에즈 운하의 완성과 기술의 발달로 인해, 증기선은 국제 무역의 주요 운송 수단으로서 범선을 능가할 수 있었다.

PARAPHRASE 1

Technical innovation, together with the completion of the Suez Canal in 1867, made it possible for the steamship to **exceed** the sailing ship, becoming the principal means of international trade.

PARAPHRASE 2

Along with the Suez Canal's completion in 1867, technical advances allowed the steamship to **outdo** the sailing ship as the chief mode of international trade.

PARAPHRASE 3

The completed Suez Canal and technical advances made the steamship **trancend** the sailing ship as the main means of international trade.

276 authenticate

Nutritional Science

SYNONYMS v. prove, verify, substantiate, confirm, justify, attest, support, testify, provide evidence

증명하다, 입증하다

authenticate
[ɔːθéntikèit]

Countless reports argue that fertilized eggs are superior in nutrition to unfertilized ones, that natural vitamins are better than synthetic ones, and that untreated grains are superior to fumigated grains, but none of them have yet been authenticated.

수많은 보고서에서 수정란이 비수정란보다 영양적인 면에서 우수하고, 천연 비타민이 합성 비타민 보다 더 좋으며, 따로 가공되지 않은 곡물이 훈증 소독된 곡물보다 우수하다고 주장하고 있지만, 이들 모두 아직 입증된 바가 없다.

PARAPHRASE 1

There are numerous reports insisting on the excellence of fertilized eggs, natural vitamins, and untreated grains compared to unfertilized ones, synthetic ones, and fumigated ones. Unfortunately, none of them has yet been proved.

PARAPHRASE 2

None of many reports, stating that fertilized eggs, natural vitamins, and untreated grains have superiority over unfertilized eggs, synthetic vitamins, and fumigated grains, has yet been verified.

277 additional

Anthropology

SYNONYMS *adj.* auxiliary, extra, added, spare, supplementary, further, secondary, subordinate, subservient, second

추가적인, 부차적인

additional
[ədíʃənəl]

Native Americans along the West Coast of the United States use quite diverse languages, which indicates that people have settled the longest in this region. The fact provided **additional** support to Fladmark's hypothesis on the coastal migration route.

미국 서부 해안을 따라 거주하는 원주민들은 꽤 다양한 언어를 사용하며, 이는 인류가 이 지역에 오랫동안 정착해왔음을 암시한다. 위와 같은 사실은 해안 이주 경로에 관한 프레드마크의 가설에 부가적인 지지를 제공해 주었다.

PARAPHRASE 1

Fladmark's hypothesis on the coastal migration route gained **auxiliary** support from the fact that the West Coast of America shows great variety in Native American languages, meaning that people have populated the longest there.

PARAPHRASE 2

Native American languages which vary greatly along the American West Coast gave **extra** support to Fladmark's hypothesis on the coastal migration route as it implies that this area has been inhabited the longest.

278 accelerate

Environmental Science · Day 28

| SYNONYMS | v. | expedite, hasten, quicken, precipitate, bring on, speed up | 촉진시키다, 가속화하다 |

accelerate
[æksélərèit]

Desertification leads to the degeneration of the land's ability to sustain life, influencing people, wild species, domesticated animals, and agricultural products and the decrease in plant cover that occurs with it **accelerate**s soil erosion by wind and water.

사막화는 생명을 부양하는 토양의 능력 저하를 초래하여 사람들, 야생 생물들, 가축들, 그리고 농작물들에 영향을 미치고, 사막화와 함께 발생하는 식물 분포의 감소는 바람과 물에 의한 토양 침식을 가속화한다.

PARAPHRASE 1

Desertification deteriorates the capacity of land to keep life alive, affecting people, wild species and livestock, and farm crops (←minor idea) and the reduction in plant cover accompanying it **expedite**s land erosion by wind and water.

PARAPHRASE 2

The land's ability to support life is reduced by desertification, coming with the decrease in plant cover that **hasten**s soil erosion by wind and water.

407

279 ephemeral

Day 28
Geography

SYNONYMS **adj.** lasting for only a short period, short-lived

수명이 짧은, 단명하는

ephemeral
[ifémərəl]

Mountains and hills, which are frequently considered as the embodiment of permanence, successfully withstand the destructive power of nature. However, in reality they are inclined to be comparatively ephemeral in terms of geological time.

영속성의 전형으로 자주 여겨지는 산과 언덕이 자연의 파괴력을 성공적으로 견뎌내기는 하지만, 지리적 측면에서 볼 때에는 사실 수명이 비교적 짧은 편이다

PARAPHRASE 1

In terms of the successful resistance of mountains and hills to the destructive forces of nature, they are commonly regarded as the epitome of permanence, but in fact they are apt to be lasting for only a relatively short period in geological terms.

PARAPHRASE 2

Often remarked upon, as the archetype of perpetuity, mountains and hills effectively endure the devastating forces of nature, but virtually they tend to be rather short-lived geologically.

280 satisfy

Architecture

| SYNONYMS | v. | fulfill, meet, gratify, appease, content, indulge, pacify, please, delight, amuse, charm | 만족시키다, 충족시키다, 기쁘게 하다 |

satisfy
[sǽtisfài]

As they are based on physical laws, methods of support have been employed in architecture invariably since first discovered, even while construction materials have changed drastically, to accomplish the size and strength of the structure essential to **satisfy** its purpose.

목적을 충족시키는데에 필수적인 구조의 크기와 힘을 달성하기 위해, 물리학 법칙에 기반한 지지법들은 건축 자재가 극적으로 바뀔 때에도 최초로 발견된 형태 그대로 건축에 사용되어 왔다.

PARAPHRASE 1

Even when building materials underwent dramatic shifts, the architectural structure achieved the size and strength crucial to **fulfill** its purpose by using supporting methods continuously since first found, as they are based on physical laws.

PARAPHRASE 2

Unlike building materials, the methods of support used in architecture have not changed over time, attaining the size and strength of the structure vital to **meet** its purpose, as they are based on physical laws.

DAILY CHECK-UP

A. Find the answer that is closest in meaning to the highlighted word or phrase in the sentence.

01. Plant-eating dinosaurs starved to death, and carnivores **eventually** had no meat to eat.
    (A) in the end (B) at least

02. Advantages offered by old, historic structures far **outweigh** the ones provided by newly-built skyscrapers.
    (A) construe (B) exceed

03. The unique style of poetry that **amazed** Ralph Waldo Emerson afterwards was developed constantly by Walt Whitman.
    (A) embodied (B) astonished

04. Usually people tend to remember only a few events that are significant and **idiosyncratic**.
    (A) peculiar (B) bumpy

05. Fantasy or fiction allows people to exteriorize their fears and anxieties and have their wishes **fulfilled** in fiction even if not real.
    (A) amplified (B) gratified

06. The argument that Pacific islanders came from Southeast Asia was substantiated by the powerful **testimony** of archaeology.
    (A) demise (B) evidence

07. Drought, floods, or harsh winters negatively influence opportunist species since each individual is **ephemeral**.
    (A) precarious (B) short-lived

08. Erosion was **speeded up** as a result of the reduction in water absorption followed by the rise in runoff.
    (A) accelerated (B) contemplated

09. The **further** heat near the surface is very important in a region where life is

restricted by low temperatures.

(A) far-reaching (B) supplementary

10. Jupiter is encircled by 16 known satellites, consisting of the four large moons and 12 small ones, but others are not yet **attested**.

(A) denoted (B) confirmed

B. Complete each sentence using one of the words or phrases given.

11. Before the Peloponnesian War in 431, other states in Greece had been _____ by the increasing power of Athens.

(A) aggregated (B) startled

12. The refining and burning of oil and its by-products results in atmospheric pollution _____.

(A) in this regard (B) in the long run

13. Steel is lighter than bricks and _____ iron as well as bricks in terms of tension and compression strength.

(A) is superior to (B) above and beyond

14. The sediment layer rich in iridium in the Yucatan region of Mexico _____ that there was a huge meteorite impact on Earth about 65 million years ago.

(A) authenticates (B) procrastinates

15. _____ plants tend to scatter a large number of seeds near parent plants in a very short time.

(A) short-lived (B) tentative

16. Large-scale runoff and outflow channels on Mars have _____ features showing that great quantities of water once existed there.

(A) vigorous (B) special

01. (A) 02. (B) 03. (B) 04. (A) 05. (B) 06. (B) 07. (B) 08. (A) 09. (B) 10. (B)
11. (B) 12. (B) 13. (A) 14. (A) 15. (A) 16. (B)

281 absence

Ecology

SYNONYMS n. want, lack, deficiency, shortage, insufficiency, scarcity, omission, need, dearth, destitution, scantiness, defect, deficit, paucity

결핍, 부족, 결여

absence
[ǽbsəns]

Generally, random spaced distribution, taking place in the **absence** of strong attraction or repulsion among individuals in a population, is uncommon in nature, with most populations having a tendency toward either clumped or uniform dispersion patterns.

대부분의 군집들은 집중 또는 균일 분포형을 띠기 때문에, 하나의 군집 안에서 개체들 간 강력한 끌림이나 반발이 없을 때 발생하는 무작위 분포형을 자연 상태에서 찾아보기는 어려운 편이다.

PARAPHRASE 1

For **want** of strong attraction or repulsion among individuals in a population, random spaced distribution occurs, but mostly it is unusual in nature since most populations tend towards either clumped or uniform patterns of dispersion.

PARAPHRASE 2

The **lack** of strong attraction or repulsion among individuals in a population causes random spaced distribution, rare in nature as either clumped or uniform distribution is more common in most populations.

282 corrupt

U.S. History

SYNONYMS **adj.** dissolute, decayed, depraved, decadent, vicious, debased, degraded, degenerate, lapsed, immoral, improper, sinful, rotten

부패한, 타락한, 부도덕한

corrupt
[kərʌ́pt]

There were still opponents who denounced them by arguing that the **corrupt** governments infringed upon the whites' rights, although new Republican governments came to power on the basis of an alliance of Freedmen, composed of Northerners who moved to the South and native white Southerners.

새 공화 정부는 남부로 이주한 북부인들과 남부 토박이 백인들이 함께 포함되어 있는 자유민 연합에 기반하여 정권을 이루었지만, 부패한 정부가 백인들의 권리를 침해했다고 주장하며 비난을 가했던 반대 세력은 여전히 존재했다.

PARAPHRASE 1

New Republican governments who seized power aided by a coalition of Freedmen, including Northerners who moved to the South and native white Southerners (←minor idea), were still blamed by opponents stating that they were **dissolute** and violated the rights of whites.

PARAPHRASE 2

A coalition of Freedmen allowed new Republican governments to rise to power, but opponents still criticized them by saying that the **decayed** governments transgressed the whites' rights.

283 recollect

Day 29
Psychology

| SYNONYMS v. | recall, evoke, remember, reminisce, look back, call to mind | 회상하다, 기억해 내다 |

recollect
[rèkəlékt]

On condition that a person calls a certain phone number repeatedly, it becomes transferred from short-term memory to long-term memory and can be recollected several weeks after the person first looked it up.

특정한 전화 번호로 반복해서 전화를 걸었을 때, 이 번호가 단기 기억에서 장기 기억의 영역으로 전환되면서 처음 번호를 접한 이래로 몇 주가 지난 후에도 계속 기억에 남게 된다.

PARAPHRASE 1

The information, which becomes stored in long-term memory, can be recalled several weeks after a person initially looked it up, provided that a specific phone number is often called.

PARAPHRASE 2

The phone number moved to long-term memory by its frequent use can be evoked several weeks after it was looked up first.

284 indignation

U.S. History

SYNONYMS n. resentment, wrath, anger, fury 분노

indignation
[indignéiʃən]

As a result of the Mexican-American War, Mexico fell into self-doubt and political extremism, bringing about the **indignation** among the Mexicans against the United States, which has negatively influenced relations between the U.S. and Mexico.

멕시코–미국 전쟁의 결과 멕시코는 자기 회의와 정치적 과격주의에 빠졌고, 이는 미국에 대한 멕시코인들의 분노를 유발하며 두 국가 사이의 관계에 악영향을 미쳤다.

PARAPHRASE 1

The Mexican-American War threw Mexico into self-doubt and political extremism and stirred up **resentment** in Mexico against the United States, adversely affecting relations between the U.S. and Mexico.

PARAPHRASE 2

The Mexican-American War, which brought self-doubt and political extremism to Mexico, aroused the Mexicans' **wrath** against the U.S., harming U.S.-Mexico relations.

285 obsolete

Politics

SYNONYMS **adj.** outdated, old-fashioned, antiquated, outmoded, dated, old, out of date

시대에 뒤진, 구식의

obsolete
[ɔ́bsəliːt]

It was not until the 1960s that monarchy, in which the symbolic leader of a parliamentary nation was a king or queen, which had remained in Europe, became an **obsolete** form of government.

왕이나 여왕이 의회 국가의 상징적 지도자 역할을 하는 군주제는 유럽에서 계속 존속되어 오다가 1960년대가 되어서야 비로소 구식의 정부 형태가 되었다.

PARAPHRASE 1

In Europe, where a single person symbolized the head of a parliamentary state, monarchy had survived as a governmental form, but not until the 1960s did it become an **outdated** form.

PARAPHRASE 2

Monarchy, a governmental form in Europe where a monarch represented a parliamentary state, became **old-fashioned** by the 1960s.

286 exercise

Ornithology

SYNONYMS v. exert, apply, wield, employ, practice, use

(힘을) 발휘하다, 행사하다

exercise
[éksərsàiz]

As soon as a crossbill locates a cone, its crossed mandibles allow it to **exercise** a powerful biting force at the bill tips, which is very important to skillfully move them between two overlapping scales on the cone and strip the scales from the cone.

원뿔형 열매를 발견한 솔잣새는 교차된 부리를 통해 부리 끝에 먹이를 강하게 무는데, 이는 열매의 포개어진 두 껍질 층 사이에서 교묘하게 움직이며 껍질을 열매로부터 분리하는 데에 중요한 역할을 한다.

PARAPHRASE 1

A crossbill which finds a cone can **exert** a potent biting force at the bill tips by using its crossed mandibles, and this is vital for manipulating them between two overlapping scales on the cone and spreading the scales apart.

PARAPHRASE 2

When a crossbill spots a cone, its crossed mandibles, which enable it to **apply** a mighty biting force at the bill tips, are adjusted between two overlapping scales on the cone and separate the scales from the cone.

287 force

Environmental Science

| SYNONYMS | v. | compel, drive, propel, impel, oblige, coerce, constrain | 억지로 ~하게 하다, 강요하다 |

force
[fɔːrs]

An increase in poverty and population **force**d poor people to exploit their environment thoughtlessly in a brief time, without alternatives for the long-term influences of their actions, which contributed to desertification.

빈곤의 확산과 인구의 증가는 가난한 이들로 하여금 자신들의 행동이 장기적으로 미칠 수 있는 영향에 대한 대안을 고려하지 않은 채로 짧은 기간 동안 환경을 무분별하게 착취하도록 했고, 이는 사막화로 이어졌다.

PARAPHRASE 1
Desertification was accelerated as a result of poverty and population growth that **compel**led the poor to overuse their environment in a short period of time, without solutions to the long-term impacts of their actions.

PARAPHRASE 2
Not considering the long-term aftermath, poverty and population growth **drove** the poor to abuse the environment in the short term, leading to desertification.

288 unbiased

Psychology — Day 29

SYNONYMS *adj.* objective, detached, impartial, fair, open-minded, impersonal, disinterested, unprejudiced, even-handed, neutral, equitable, just, equal

편파적이지 않은, 선입견 없는, 공평한

unbiased
[ʌnbáiəst]

When it comes to life satisfaction, there are some factors everyone regards as reliable predictors, such as health, particularly self-consciousness for one's own health rather than a professional's **unbiased** evaluation for health.

생활적인 측면의 만족을 측정하는 데에 있어 모두가 신뢰할 수 있는 예측 변수들에는 건강, 특히 전문가의 객관적인 건강 평가보다는 스스로의 건강함에 대한 자각과 같은 요소들이 있다.

PARAPHRASE 1

Certain factors are credible predictors which ensure life satisfaction for everyone. One example is health, especially self-awareness of one's own health instead of **objective** medical examination by a doctor.

PARAPHRASE 2

Everyone agrees that one of the sound predictors of life satisfaction is health, notably perception of one's own health, not a doctor's **detached** health assessment (←minor idea).

419

289 tangible

Day 29 / Archeology

SYNONYMS *adj.* material, substantial, concrete, real, corporeal, physical, bodily, touchable, palpable

실질적인, 물질적인 육체의

tangible
[tǽndʒəbəl]

Organic materials are generally dated by the radiocarbon dating method, while the age of pyramids is primarily determined according to their location in the development of Egyptian architecture and **tangible** culture over 3,000 years.

유기물이 얼마나 오래 되었는지는 보통 방사성 탄소 연대 측정법에 의해 파악되지만, 피라미드의 연대는 3,000년에 걸쳐 이루어진 이집트 건축과 물질 문화의 발달사에서 해당 피라미드가 어디쯤 위치하는지에 따라 추정된다.

PARAPHRASE 1 Unlike organic materials, people largely measure the era of pyramids depending on their place in the development of Egyptian architecture and **material** culture over 3,000 years.

PARAPHRASE 2 Organic materials are radiocarbon dated, but the pyramids are dated by their position in the evolution of Egyptian architecture and **substantial** culture over 3,000 years.

290 transport

| SYNONYMS | v. | carry, convey, ferry, transfer, bear, shift, move, take | 운반하다, 운송하다 |

transport
[trænspɔːrt]

The construction of the canals for the purpose of **transport**ing coal necessitated the help of surveyors for the companies, not only to discover the coal deposits suitable for mining but also to determine the optimum routes for the canals.

석탄을 운반하기 위해 운하를 건설했던 회사들은 채광에 적합한 석탄 매장 층을 찾기 위해서뿐만 아니라 최상의 운하 경로를 결정하기 위해서도 측량사들의 도움을 필요로 했다.

PARAPHRASE 1

The companies constructing the canals in order to **carry** coal required surveyors, as they had to decide the optimal routes for the canals as well as locate the coal beds fit for mining.

PARAPHRASE 2

Building the canals to **convey** coal, the companies needed surveyors to find the coal mines and to decide the ideal paths for the canals.

DAILY CHECK-UP

A. Find the answer that is closest in meaning to the highlighted word or phrase in the sentence.

01. Learned motor skills can be carried out with ease without consciously **recollecting** each step needed to do them.

    (A) recalling   (B) indulging

02. About 1 atmosphere of gas pressure is **applied to** the human body for every 10 meters of depth in seawater.

    (A) extricated from   (B) exerted on

03. Modigliani was **obliged** to work as a merchant when his father ended his career as a banker.

    (A) overturned   (B) forced

04. One explanation concerning the **shortage** of fossils during this period is that early animals had soft bodies that were rarely fossilized.

    (A) absence   (B) fallacy

05. A reliable ability to comprehend classroom events in an **unbiased** way is required for systematic reflection on teaching.

    (A) jumbled   (B) objective

06. In 1894, through packing materials for oysters brought from the east coast, Spartina was **transferred** to Washington State.

    (A) accorded   (B) transported

07. Charles Darwin pointed out that baring the teeth in an antagonistic manner may be a common indication of **fury**.

    (A) credo   (B) anger

08. Despite the government's announcement to ban illegal logging, environmentalists still denounced **rotten** government officials.

    (A) corrupt   (B) riotous

09. The advent of state-of-the-art technologies has made a lot of previous

technologies **obsolete**.

(A) cutting-edge   (B) out of date

10. Several rounds of meetings led to results giving **substantial** benefits to both countries.

    (A) covetous   (B) tangible

B. Complete each sentence using one of the words or phrases given.

11. People who own a large stake in the country _____ great power in order to make it flourish.

    (A) protruded   (B) wielded

12. The limbic system in the brain performs a central function to manage emotions such as pleasure, _____ and sadness.

    (A) wrath   (B) flair

13. The words on the list given with scents are more likely to be _____ by children than the ones given without scents.

    (A) subjugated   (B) remembered

14. The _____ of carbonate rock layers supports that Mars has never had the prolonged mild period necessary for the formation of lakes and oceans.

    (A) agitation   (B) scarcity

15. President Woodrow Wilson adopted a _____ policy in response to the outbreak of World War I in Europe.

    (A) latent   (B) neutral

16. When the profitable trade route was blocked, European countries were _____ into finding a new path to the east.

    (A) coerced   (B) entailed

| 01. (A) | 02. (B) | 03. (B) | 04. (A) | 05. (B) | 06. (B) | 07. (B) | 08. (A) | 09. (B) | 10. (B) |
| 11. (B) | 12. (A) | 13. (B) | 14. (B) | 15. (B) | 16. (A) |

291 repulsion

Day 30
Psychology

SYNONYMS **n.** antipathy, hatred, disgust, distaste, aversion, loathing, revulsion, dislike, nausea, abhorrence, repugnance, detestation

혐오감, 증오심

repulsion
[ripʌ́ʃən]

Prejudice is defined as an unreasonable **repulsion** and skepticism of people who are distinct from you to a certain degree, conspicuously in terms of their sex, race, and religion.
편견이란 특히 인종이나 성별, 종교적인 측면에서 스스로와 다른 이들에 대해 느끼는 불합리한 반감과 불신으로 정의될 수 있다.

PARAPHRASE 1

Defined as an unfounded **antipathy** and suspicion of people who are somewhat different from you, prejudice occurs, in particular, owing to their race, gender and religion.

PARAPHRASE 2

Prejudice means an irrational **hatred** and mistrust of people dissimilar to you in some way, especially due to their race, gender and religion.

292 blame

Environmental Science

SYNONYMS v. criticize, denounce, reproach, censure, condemn, reprimand, impeach, accuse, incriminate, indict, charge, reprove, rebuke, scold

비난하다, 비판하다, 꾸짖다

blame
[bleim]

Since DDT had been **blame**d for the risk posed to endangered birds such as the bald eagle whose eggshells were thinned, as well as birth defects in humans, a treaty that forbids the use of it, together with other industrial chemicals, came into effect around the globe in 2004.

DDT가 인간에게 선천성 결손을 유발하고 흰머리 독수리의 알 껍질을 얇아지게 하는 등 야생 조류에게 위협을 가한다며 비난 받은 이래로, 다른 공업용 화학 약품들과 더불어 DDT의 사용을 금지하는 협정이 2004년 전 세계적으로 시행되었다.

PARAPHRASE 1 DDT had been **criticize**d for threats to humans and endangered birds such as the bald eagle. As a result, a convention on the prohibition of it, along with other industrial chemicals, took effect all over the world in 2004.

PARAPHRASE 2 Globally, a treaty became effective to ban the use of DDT and other chemicals in 2004, as it was **denounce**d for harming humans and endangered species.

293 inclination

Developmental Psychology

SYNONYMS **n.** preference, penchant, fondness, affection, attachment, liking, love

애정, 애호

inclination
[inklənéiʃən]

Of the fluctuations in the infant's sucking behavior recorded after stimuli were given, swells in the number of sucks were utilized to represent the infant's **inclination** for or attention to a presented visual display.

자극이 주어진 후에 기록된 유아의 흡입 작용의 변화들 가운데, 흡입 수의 증가는 주어진 시각적 자극에 대한 유아의 선호도와 관심도를 나타냈다.

PARAPHRASE 1

Alterations in the infant's sucking behavior were recorded after stimuli were applied, and an increasing number of sucks indicated the infant's **preference** for or interest in a given visual display.

PARAPHRASE 2

The infant's **penchant** or concern for a given visual display was reflected by rises in the number of sucks after stimulus presentation.

294 declare

U.S. History

SYNONYMS v. announce, proclaim, trumpet, reveal, disclose, release, report, publish, broadcast, advertise, make known

발표하다, 공표하다

declare
[dikléər]

The American Civil War began when 11 states which broke away from the Union declared themselves a self-existent nation after Abraham Lincoln, an uncompromising enemy of slavery, won the presidential election in 1860.

노예제를 단호하게 반대했던 아브라함 링컨이 1860년 대선에서 승리한 이후 연방을 탈퇴했던 11개의 주들이 스스로를 독립 국가로 선포한 순간, 미국 남북 전쟁이 시작되었다.

PARAPHRASE 1

Abraham Lincoln, a resolute enemy of slavery, was elected president in 1860, and 11 states seceded from the Union and announced themselves an independent nation, which led to the beginning of the American Civil War.

PARAPHRASE 2

After the victory of Abraham Lincoln in the presidential election in 1860, 11 states left the Union, proclaiming independence, causing the American Civil War.

295 grab

Geohydrology

SYNONYMS v. hold, grip, grasp, seize, clutch, snatch, take, catch, pluck, clasp, hang on, take hold of

붙들다, 붙잡다

grab
[græb]

The water in large pores exist as drops, too heavy for surface tension to **grab**, which makes the water drain away, whereas the water in small pores exist as thin films, too light to withstand surface tension, which makes the water firmly held.

큰 기공 안의 물은 표면 장력이 잡아두기에는 너무 무겁기 때문에 물이 빠져 나가는 물방울로 존재하는 반면, 작은 기공 안의 물은 표면 장력을 견디기에는 너무 가볍기 때문에 물이 완벽하게 남아 있는 얇은 막으로 존재한다.

PARAPHRASE 1

Droplets of water in large pores are too heavy for surface tension to **hold** them together, while thin films of water in small pores are light enough for surface tension to maintain them.

PARAPHRASE 2

Weak surface tension cannot **grip** drops of water in large pores, but strong surface tension can maintain thin films of water in small pores.

296 nourishment

U.S.History

SYNONYMS n. sustenance, food, fare, nutrient 양분, 음식

nourishment
[nə́ːriʃmənt]

Many of the colonists came from privileged backgrounds and were unaccustomed to working with their hands, so they asserted that they had a hard time engaging in agriculture for their own nourishment on account of merciless regulations of the company.

많은 식민지 주민들이 특권 계층 출신이었으며 육체 노동에 익숙하지 않았기 때문에, 그들은 자신들의 생계를 위한 농사를 짓는 데에 어려움을 겪었던 이유가 회사의 가혹한 규정 때문이었다고 주장했다.

PARAPHRASE 1

Many settlers who had privileged backgrounds and were unfamiliar with doing physical labor claimed that cruel rules of the company prohibited them from farming for their own sustenance.

PARAPHRASE 2

Many settlers who had come from privileged classes and were new to doing manual labor argued that the company's rules were too harsh for them to farm for their own food.

429

297 sequence

Day 30 — Entomology

SYNONYMS n. series, string, succession, chain — 일련, 연속

sequence
[nə́ːrifmənt]

Born with a very distinguishing appearance compared with that of their parents, a great number of insects must go through a **sequence** of transformations until there becomes the affinity between them and adults.

자신들의 부모와 매우 다른 외관을 갖고 태어난 곤충들 중 대다수는 성충의 모습과 비슷해질 때까지 일련의 변화를 겪어야 한다.

PARAPHRASE 1

When the majority of insects are born, they are very different in shape from their parents, but as they must experience a **series** of transformations, they end up being analogous to adults.

PARAPHRASE 2

Most insects born with a very dissimilar shape to that of their parents must undergo a **string** of transformations before they closely resemble the adults.

298 manipulate

Biology

SYNONYMS adj. control, manage, maneuver, operate, handle, treat, deal with

조종하다,
조절하다,
다루다

manipulate
[mənípjəlèit]

In temperature-dependent sex determination, the mother could determine whether her offspring develops as male or female by regulating the temperature of the nest in which her eggs are incubated, but so far, there exists no evidence that parental care **manipulate**s sex ratios.

온도에 따른 성별 결정에 있어서, 어미는 알이 부화되는 둥지의 온도를 조절함으로써 태어날 자손이 수컷 또는 암컷으로 성장할지를 결정할 수 있다. 하지만 어미의 양육을 통한 성비 조절의 증거는 아직 존재하지 않는다.

PARAPHRASE 1

Temperature-dependent sex determination enables the mother to decide the sex of her offspring by altering the temperature of the nest. However, it has never been clearly verified that the sex ratio is **control**led by parental care.

PARAPHRASE 2

It has not been proved that in temperature-dependent sex determination, parental care can **manage** the sex ratio of the offspring by varying the temperature in the nest.

299 brave

Literature — Day 30

SYNONYMS *adj.* daring, bold, courageous, heroic, adventurous, audacious, fearless, dauntless, gallant

대담한, 용감한

brave
[breiv]

Among fictional characters that show up frequently in works of American literature, a hero is described as someone who is admired a great deal because of brave deeds and commendable qualities, combating crime or saving people from fatal danger.

미국 문학 작품에 자주 등장하는 가상 인물들 가운데, 영웅들은 범죄와 맞서 싸우며 사람들을 치명적인 위험으로부터 구해내는 용감한 행동과 훌륭한 성품으로 존경 받는 이들로 묘사된다.

PARAPHRASE 1

Of fictional characters, heroes, appearing frequently in American literature, are defined as those who fight crime or defend people from mortal peril, and are greatly admired due to their daring deeds and good characters.

PARAPHRASE 2

Heroes, popular in American literature, are typical fictional characters who fight crime or danger, and thus are respected for their bold actions and noble qualities.

300 contemptible

Social Science — Day 30

SYNONYMS adj. despicable, mean, ignoble, shameful, shabby, dishonorable, vile, petty, cowardly, base, ungenerous, sinister

비열한

contemptible
[kəntémptəbəl]

Afraid of job losses, workers who had emigrated from Europe could not complain about their poor conditions in factories and excessive working hours for low wages to **contemptible** factory owners who cared about nothing but money.

유럽으로부터 이민해 온 노동자들은 일자리를 잃는 것을 두려워했기 때문에, 돈만 밝히는 비열한 공장주들에게 열악한 근무 조건과 낮은 임금에 비해 과도한 근무 시간에 대해 불평할 수 없었다

PARAPHRASE 1

Immigrant workers from Europe, who desperately needed jobs, were compelled to keep silent about poor working conditions and tolerate exploitation by **despicable** factory owners who knew nothing but money.

PARAPHRASE 2

Mean and greedy factory owners forced European immigrant workers to endure poor conditions and exploitation without complaint to keep their jobs.

433

DAILY CHECK-UP

A. Find the answer that is closest in meaning to the highlighted word or phrase in the sentence.

01. Although East African herbivores all inhabit the identical environment, they have a diversity of **preferences** for food.

    (A) peculiarity　　　　　　　　(B) inclination

02. Dada stemmed from **repulsion** for the conservative values in society and desperation over World War I.

    (A) redundance　　　　　　　　(B) disgust

03. A **chain** of finlets found around the tails of most billfishes and tunas helps decrease the body's resistance to the flow of water.

    (A) series　　　　　　　　　　(B) cohesion

04. Ancient humans are believed to have **held** meat between their teeth and cut it into pieces with knives made of stone.

    (A) deferred　　　　　　　　　(B) grabbed

05. Fruits, vegetables, and dairy products which were unavailable in the past were used to have more abundant **food**.

    (A) fare　　　　　　　　　　　(B) clout

06. Unlike humans, flies have to locate the best place to prosper because they cannot **control** the surrounding temperature.

    (A) supersede　　　　　　　　(B) manipulate

07. Modernism is a movement that represents **audacious** and noble experimental styles and forms in the art.

    (A) bold　　　　　　　　　　　(B) peerless

08. The indiscriminate use of pesticides that exterminate mosquitos was **blamed** for environmental destruction.

    (A) subdued　　　　　　　　　(B) criticized

09. A Columbia scientist **released** that an ancient crocodile that had existed for

millions of years prior to dinosaurs was accidentally discovered in Connecticut.

(A) scoured (B) announced

10. Aristocrats considered saving a **dishonorable** behavior, while conscious spending behavior was regarded as honorable.

(A) inscrutable (B) shameful

B. Complete each sentence using one of the words or phrases given.

11. Paul Ekman took pictures of those who show feelings such as _____, happiness, and sadness.

(A) competence (B) hatred

12. Former German Chancellor Gerhard Schroeder _____ the policy of the EU on the recent situation in Ukraine.

(A) persevered (B) condemned

13. The opposable thumbs of Australopithecus robustus enabled them to _____ objects such as tools.

(A) take hold of (B) incarnate

14. Lascaux Grotto, discovered by children, consists of a _____ of narrow cave chambers including large prehistoric paintings.
A film is actually a series of tiny still pictures, or frames.

(A) succession (B) disruption

15. Each animal species shows its own _____ for food and resources, which allows animals to coexist and not to compete.

(A) eminence (B) preference

16. There are no birds which are more directly correlated with their source of _____ than crossbills.

(A) demise (B) sustenance

01. (B) 02. (B) 03. (A) 04. (B) 05. (A) 06. (B) 07. (A) 08. (B) 09. (B) 10. (B)
11. (B) 12. (B) 13. (A) 14. (A) 15. (B) 16. (B)

REVIEW TEST (DAY 26-30)

A. The word _____ in the passage is closest in meaning to

01. The most tragic aspect of the dodo population was the **prospective** impacts humans could have on the environment, and the ease with which humankind could destroy the delicate balance of the island's ecosystem. One of the earliest examples of the deliberate destruction of the ecosystem by humans was that the Portuguese sailors on the island exterminated the dodo by damaging the forests where the bird inhabited and further exacerbated nature in unpredictable ways.

(a) stagnant
(b) placid
(c) inscrutable
(d) latent

02. **Aside from** threatening the areas where livestock grazes, prairie dogs have the potential to carry fleas and harbor infectious diseases. These harmful and fatal diseases are more likely to spread to humans and to their pets. As prairie dog populations can grow rapidly, they cause these deadly pathogens to diffuse or move to new regions. Nowadays, no one would want these animals near their homes nor put a child at risk around these animals.

(a) contrary to
(b) with respect to
(c) in terms of
(d) In addition to

03. Biodegradable plastics are sustainable and can be carbon neutral unlike petroleum-based plastics which **discharge** carbon dioxide, a major greenhouse gas that causes global warming. Bio-based plastics are made out of plant materials

(a) intercede
(b) exhale
(c) commend
(d) exhume

REVIEW TEST [DAY 26-30]

such as corn and soybeans, which continue to grow yearly and as a result, they are always renewable.

---

04. As the one and only time marker, rocks could not be used even without the problem of locational **distinctions**. Calcite is calcite – a common mineral which is composed of crystallized calcium carbonate – there's no choice between calcite of the Pleistocene era (two million years ago) and Cambrian calcite (500 million years ago).

(a) disparities
(b) adhesions
(c) hallmarks
(d) fallacies

---

05. In that primary groups act as **robust** tools of social control, they are basic. Members of the groups provide and receive a lot of compensations not only that are so essential to people but also that make their lives valuable. If the compensations should not take effect, members will refuse or intimidate to exclude those who depart from standard practice of the group, by which they can win with frequent.

(a) auxiliary
(b) ephemeral
(c) potent
(d) sedentary

---

06. Saying that the government has no right to **confer** power to kill one group of people to another, opponents of euthanasia argue that the federal government should play a legitimate role in patients' end of life decision-making. The government should focus more on prohibiting a flagrant misuse of euthanasia because euthanasia is not a private act but a matter of very public concern in that it can cause terrific exploitation and abuse of care for the most helpless people.

(a) tamper
(b) accord
(c) shed
(d) taint

07. Utility of form means that a good or service has specific features that **indulge** customers' needs, offering benefits or satisfaction to them. If a winter coat is made using the special materials that can make the coat waterproof as well as block out the cold winds, it can be more attractive to the customers. This is because the product is developed in a useful form which corresponds to the consumers' needs.

(a) embed
(b) protrude
(c) appease
(d) elude

08. Through highly interesting discoveries, scientists could reconstruct the most plausible origin of cetaceans **in the long run**. Particularly, found in northern Pakistan by a team that was searching for fossils in 1979, the fossil was demonstrated to be the oldest fossil whale. The fossil called Pakicetus in remembrance of the nation in which it was discovered was embedded in rocks which were made with river deposits that were 52 million years old.

(a) after all
(b) concurrently
(c) subsequently
(d) at intervals

09. Although franchises ensure a secure running of the business through continuous support, franchisees should not overlook that the difficulties a franchiser encounters can directly affect an individual franchisee, causing the high risk of failure. Also, cooperative relationships between parent companies and their suppliers **compel** franchisees to buy supplies only from an approved list of suppliers, possibly at a higher cost and a low quality.

(a) pluck
(b) forage
(c) clutch
(d) drive

REVIEW TEST [DAY 26-30]

10. Frequent droughts and poor harvests, immediate causes of a **deficiency** of water for drinking and agriculture purposes, have led to many problems such as conflicts between groups or regions. However, cloud seeding that provides increased rainfall is rapidly rising as an alternative to these problems as it enables clouds to deliver rain in the target areas and this rainfall can offer not only enough drinking water but also agricultural water.

   (a) devastation
   (b) strain
   (c) shortage
   (d) aversion

11. Video game advocates maintain that most research on violence in video games is fatally flawed and that there is no causal relationship between video games and social violence. They claim that violent video games decrease violence by acting as a safe outlet for negative feelings such as anxiety, frustration and **resentment**.

    (a) sustenance
    (b) indignation
    (c) scantiness
    (d) deviation

12. Nowadays, many researchers think that stem cells will change the face of medicine sooner or later. This is because the stem cells can be **manipulated** to act like other types of cells and consequently, this may provide new solutions to cure diseases such as cancer and Alzheimer's. Also, proponents of human cloning believe that when the body organs such as lung, kidney, heart or liver suddenly do not function properly, the most priceless solution would be a cloned body organ in time of emergency.

    (a) rectified
    (b) impeached
    (c) maneuvered
    (d) seized

13. Primary effect is a phenomenon that when people learn and hear a **succession** of items on a list, the first few items mentioned are a lot more quickly recalled and remembered than subsequent items in the middle of the list. For example, if a man gives a good first impression on others, people will still think that he is a good person although he makes several mistakes since then. On the other hand, a man who leaves a bad impression on others at the very first time will continue to be considered a bad person no matter how hard he tries to change his image.

(a) penchant
(b) stipulation
(c) dissidence
(d) string

14. At the age of twenty-six, Emily Carr who had been interested in the aboriginal culture of British Columbia from early in life made a sketching tour to Ucluelet Peninsular located on the west side of Vancouver Island for the first time. She sought to catch the spirit of scene, transcending physical reality, and a string of totem poles drawn in a daring style mirrored her **affection** for aboriginal culture.

(a) abhorrence
(b) fondness
(c) detestation
(d) clout

답안
01. (D) 02. (D) 03. (B) 04. (A) 05. (C) 06. (B) 07. (C)
08. (A) 09. (D) 10. (C) 11. (B) 12. (C) 13. (D) 14. (B)

REVIEW TEST [DAY 26-30]

B. Which of the sentences below best expresses the essential information in the highlighted sentence in the passage? Incorrect choices change the meaning in important ways or leave out essential information.

15. As primary groups not only give members a sense of their unity which is very important for social solidarity, but also serve as transmitter, interpreter and mediator of cultural patterns in a society, they are deemed as bridges which connect individuals with the larger social group.

   (A) Social solidarity and cultural patterns are crucial factors to form primary groups which link members with the larger social community.
   (B) Primary groups help social solidarity between individuals and the larger society, by heightening the sense of unity and preserving a society's cultural patterns.
   (C) In primary groups, a sense of their unity is vital to social solidarity and cultural patterns act as mediators between individuals and secondary groups.
   (D) Developing the sense of solidarity and maintaining cultural styles play an important role in enhancing the bond between the individual and the larger social community.

해설   정답 (B)

As ① primary groups not only give members a sense of their unity which is very important for social solidarity, but also serve as transmitter, interpreter and mediator of cultural patterns in a society, ② they are deemed as bridges which connect individuals with the larger social group.
→ ② Primary groups help social solidarity between individuals and the larger society, by ① heightening the sense of unity and preserving a society's cultural patterns.

원문의 문장을 접속사 'as'를 기준으로 크게 두 부분으로 나누고 그 두 절 사이의 의미 관계를 명확하게 이해하였는지를 평가하고자 하는 문제이다. 원문의 접속사 'as'가 이끄는 종속절(①)은 '~이기 때문에'의 의미를 갖고 있는 접속사 'as'를 통해 주절(②)의 내용의 근거 또는 방법이 됨을 알 수 있다.

따라서 Paraphrase 할 때에는, 원문의 종속절(①)은 'primary groups'의 기능을 언급하고 있으므로 같은 맥락의 방법 또는 수단을 나타내는 전치사 'by'를 사용하여 전치사구의 형태로 언급할 수 있고, 원문의 주절(②)의 내용은 결국 'primary groups'가 '개인과 보다 큰 사회 집단 사이의 가교역할을 함'을 언급하고 있으므로 의미 관계를 따져서 '이 두 집단 사이의 결속을 돕는다'라고 재진술할 수 있다. 이 과정에서 종속절의 구 전환으로 원문의 두 개로 이루어진 절은 재진술 문장과 같이 단문의 형태로 재구성 될 수 있다.

오답의 근거

(A) <u>Social solidarity and cultural patterns</u> are crucial factors to form primary groups which link members with the larger social community.
→ 원문에 따르면 보기의 밑줄 친 부분은 원문의 종속절에 언급된 'primary groups'가 구현하는 역할이므로 "primary groups' 형성의 중요한 요소라고 볼 수 없으므로 틀린 내용으로 오답이다.

(C) In primary groups, a sense of their unity is vital to social solidarity and <u>cultural patterns act as mediators between individuals and secondary groups</u>.
→ 위의 보기는 단순히 원문의 내용들을 어지럽게 나열하였을 뿐 원문의 내용과 전혀 일치하지 않으므로 오답이다. 특히 보기의 밑줄 친 부분을 보면 '개인들과 제2차집단 사이의 가교' 역할을 한 것은 '문화 양식'이 아니라 '제1차 집단'이었음을 원문을 통해 알 수 있으므로 명확히 틀린 답이다.

(D) Developing the sense of solidarity and maintaining cultural styles play an important role in enhancing the bond between the individual and the larger social community.
→ 원문의 주요 내용이 대부분 언급되었으나 보기에 언급된 정보의 결정적 주체인 'primary groups'에 대한 언급이 누락되었으므로 오답이다.

다른 방식으로 paraphrase 하기

As ① primary groups not only <u>give members a sense of their unity which is very important for social solidarity</u>, but also serve as transmitter, interpreter and mediator of cultural patterns in a society, ② <u>they are deemed as bridges which connect individuals with the larger social group</u>.

→ ② Primary groups help social solidarity between individuals and the larger society, by ① <u>heightening the sense of unity</u> and preserving a society's cultural patterns.
→ ② Primary groups contribute to social solidarity through ① <u>the development in the sense of unity</u> and the preservation of cultural patterns in a society.

원문의 접속사 'as'가 이끄는 종속절(①)은 '~이기 때문에'의 의미를 갖고 있는 접속사 'as'를 통

REVIEW TEST [DAY 26-30]

해 주절(②)의 내용의 근거 또는 방법을 언급하고 있음을 알 수 있으므로 paraphrase 할 때에는, '(제 1차 집단의 두 가지 역할을) 통해' 라는 의미를 갖는 전치사 'through'를 사용하여 구의 형태로 언급할 수 있으며, 이 과정에서 원문의 종속절에서 동사의 형태로 서술된 'primary groups'의 두 가지 기능을 보기에서는 전치사 'by'를 사용하여 동명사의 형태로 서술하였다면, 재진술 문장에서는 명사의 형태로 언급하여 품사를 바꿈으로써 문장을 재구성할 수 있음도 항상 염두에 두도록 한다.

16. Substances which modify their chemical and physical characteristics as the ambient climatic conditions fluctuate tend to be piled up on the ground in a systematic way over the long term, which furnishes comprehensive information concerning how the climate has gone through principal changes over hundreds or even thousands of years.

   (A) As substances change their chemical and physical properties depending on climatic changes, they are deposited in an unexpected way, making it difficult to observe natural climatic variability over time.
   (B) Changes in chemical and physical properties of substances according to climate enable the substances to be systematically deposited, providing a better understanding of fluctuations in the climate.
   (C) It might be much easier to get a massive amount of information about changes in chemical and physical characteristics of substances unless temperature variations influenced their systematic changes.
   (D) Information on changes in chemical and physical characteristics of substances with the climate prevents meteorologists from securing substantial evidence of slow changes in systematically deposited substances.

해설 정답 (B)

① Substances (which modify their chemical and physical characteristics as the ambient climatic conditions fluctuate) tend to be piled up on the ground in a systematic way over the long term, ② which furnishes comprehensive information concerning how the climate has gone through principal changes

over hundreds or even thousands of years.
→ ① (Changes in chemical and physical properties of substances according to climate) enable the substances to be systematically deposited, ② providing a better understanding of fluctuations in the climate.

원문의 문장을 크게 ①과 ②의 두 부분으로 나누고, 이 두 부분 사이의 의미 관계가 순접 관계임을 명확하게 이해하였는지를 평가하고자 하는 문제이다. 원문의 ①은 특정 물질의 특징에 대해 서술하고 있으며 이 특징 때문에 ②의 결과를 얻을 수 있음을 언급하고 있다. 원문에서는 이를 나타내기 위해 관계대명사 계속적 용법을 활용하여 관계 대명사 which가 앞 절의 전체 내용을 받고 그 관계대명사절의 주어의 역할을 함을 알 수 있다. 여기에서 관계대명사 which는 and this와 같은 의미를 갖는다고 보면 무방하다. Paraphrase 할 때에는, 원문 ①의 주어인 'substances'를 재진술 문장에서는 동사의 목적어의 자리에 놓고 그 물질의 특징을 언급하는 관계대명사절 'which modify ~ conditions fluctuate'을 재진술 문장의 주어의 자리에 두어 강조함으로써 문장을 재구성 할 수 있다. 이 과정에서는 동사 'enable'의 특징을 잘 알고 있어야 문장 안에서 적절한 활용이 가능함을 기억해 두도록 한다. 원문 ②의 부분은 ①의 결과 또는 ①에 의해 얻게 되는 이점을 언급하고 있으므로 원문에서의 관계대명사 계속적 용법 대신에 앞 절의 결과를 나타내기 위해 종종 사용되는 현재 분사 구문을 활용하여 간단하게 재구성 할 수 있다. 문장을 재구성할 때에 기억해야 할 것은 기본적으로 동의어 또는 동의어구의 사용, 품사 바꾸기, 주어 바꾸기, 단문의 복문 또는 복문의 단문 전환 등과 같은 paraphrase를 위한 다양한 방법들이 한 문장 안에서 단편적으로가 아니라 복합적으로 활용되어야 한다는 점이며 이것이 자유자재로 이루어질 때 문장에 대한 이해도도 높아지며 명확한 문장의 재진술도 가능하게 된다.

오답의 근거

(A) As substances change their chemical and physical properties depending on climatic changes, they are deposited in an unexpected way, (making it difficult to observe natural climatic variability over time).
→ 원문에서는 '기후 변화에 따라 화학적 물리적 특성을 바꾸는 물질'은 'in an unexpected way'가 아니라 'in a systematic way'로 퇴적된다고 하였으므로 반대로 진술된 보기는 틀린 내용이며, 보기의 괄호 안의 내용은 원문의 관계대명사절 ②의 내용과 완벽하게 반대되는 내용을 언급하고 있으므로 이 또한 틀린 내용으로 오답이다.

(C) It might be much easier to get a massive amount of information about (changes in chemical and physical characteristics of substances) unless temperature variations influence their systematic changes.
→ 보기의 밑줄 친 부분의 정보는 '기후 변화에 따라 물질의 화학적 물리적 특성의 변화'하기 때문에 '날씨 변화에 대한 정보를 얻을 수 있다'라고 언급한 원문의 내용에 대치되는 내용으로 틀린 내용이며, 원문의 관계대명사절 ②에 따르면 보기의 괄호 안의 '물질의 화학적 물리적 특성의 변화에 대한 정보'가 아니라 '날씨의 변화에 대한 정보'를 얻을 수 있는 것이므로 이 또한 틀린 내용으로 오답이다.

(D) Information on changes in chemical and physical characteristics of substances with the climate prevents meteorologists from securing

REVIEW TEST [DAY 26-30]

substantial evidence of slow changes in systematically deposited substances.
→ 보기의 밑줄 친 부분의 정보는 원문의 관계대명사절 ②를 통해 추론할 수 없는 언급되지 않은 내용으로 오답이다.

다른 방식으로 paraphrase 하기

① Substances (which modify their chemical and physical characteristics as the ambient climatic conditions fluctuate) tend to be piled up on the ground in a systematic way over the long term, ② which furnishes comprehensive information concerning how the climate has gone through principal changes over hundreds or even thousands of years.

→ ① As (substances change their chemical and physical properties in response to climatic changes), they are deposited systematically, ② contributing to a better understanding of climatic variability over time.

원문의 ①은 관계대명사절 'which modify ~ conditions fluctuate'을 활용하여 'substances'의 특징을 기술함으로써 절에서 다소 긴 주부('substances which ~ conditions fluctuate')의 형태를 보여주는데, 이를 paraphrase 할 때에는 원문의 주부를 접속사 'as'가 이끄는 하나의 절로 풀어서 재구성할 수 있고, 원문 ①의 술부('tend to ~ over the long term')는 재진술 문장에서 주절의 형태로 놓일 수 있다. 이 과정에서 원문 ①의 하나의 절은 재진술 문장에서처럼 두 개의 절로 재구성 될 수 있다. 또한 이 과정에서 원문 ①의 절의 형태를 취하고 있는 'as the ambient climatic conditions fluctuate'는 재진술 시 'in response to climatic changes'와 같이 구의 형태로 재구성 될 수 있다.

→ ① (As a result of changes in chemical and physical characteristics with the climate, systematically deposited substances) ② present substantial evidence of climate changes.

원문의 ①의 주부에서 'substances'를 수식하는 관계대명사절의 내용은 'as a result'를 활용하여 구의 형태로 전환될 수 있으며 원문의 ①의 술부가 되는 '체계적으로 퇴적되는 경향이 있다'는 문장의 의미상 주요 내용이므로 강조를 위해 재진술 문장의 주어의 자리에 놓을 수 있다. 이 과정에서 원문의 ①의 술부는 명사 'substances'를 수식하는 형용사의 형태, 즉 'systematically deposited'로 품사를 바꾸어 재진술 될 수 있다. 또한, 원문 ②의 관계대명사절의 형태로 언급된 정보는 재진술 시에 위와 같이 문장의 술부의 형태로 놓여 문장을 좀 더 간략하게 할 수 있다.

주제별 표현

Anthropology 인류학

aboriginal [æbərídʒənəl] 원주민의, 토착민의, 원시의
adaptive [ədǽptiv] 적응하는
adjustment [ədʒʌ́stmənt] 조절, 적응, 순응
animism [ǽnəmìzəm] 애니미즘, 정령 숭배
antiquity [æntíkwəti] 고대
aristocrat [ərístəkræ] 귀족
ape [eip] 유인원
biological anthropology 생물학적 인류학
bohemian [bouhíːmiən] 인습에 얽매이지 않는 사람
chieftain [tʃíːftən] (부족의) 족장
clan [klæn] 씨족 사회
class struggle 계급 투쟁
custom [kʌ́stəm] 풍습
depredation [déprədèiʃn] 약탈
descendant [diséndənt] 자손, 후손
epic [épik] 서사시
folk story (= folk tale) 민간 설화
forebear [fɔ́ːrber] 선조, 조상
hereditary peer 세습 귀족
holocaust [hάləkɔ̀ːs] 대학살
hominoid [hάmənòid] 유인원
Homo erectus 직립원인, 호모 에렉투스
indigenous [indídʒənəs] 토착의, 그 지역 고유의
juxtaposition [dʒʌ̀kstəpəzíʃən] 병렬, 병치
labyrinth [lǽbərìnθ] 미궁, 미로
legend [lédʒənd] 전설
legitimism [lídʒitimizəm] 정통주의
medieval [mèdiíːvəl] 중세의
matrilineal system 모계제도
monarchy [mɔ́nərki] 군주제
myth [miθ] 신화
mythology [miθάlədʒi] 신화

nomadic [noumǽdik] 유목민의
ominous [άmɪnəs] 불길한
organism [ɔ́ːrgənɪzəm] (유기적 조직으로서의) 사회
patriarchy [péitriaːki] 가부장제
patrician [pətríʃən] (고대 로마의) 귀족
persist [pə(ː)síst] 잔존하다
phenomena [finάmənə] 현상
plebeian [pləbíːən] (고대 로마의) 평민, 서민
pluralism [plúərəlizəm] 다원론
progenitor [proudʒénitə] 조상, 선조, 원종
regime [reiʒíːm] 통치방식, 체제
restoration [rèstəréiʃən] 복원, 회복
retaliation [ritæliéiʃən] 앙갚음, 보복
sanctuary [sǽŋktjuəri] 성역, 신성한 장소
status [stéitəs] 신분
tribe [traib] 부족
turmoil [təːmɔil] 소란, 소동, 소용
weaver [wíːvə] 직조공, (천 등을) 짜는 사람
worship [wə́ːʃip] 예배, 숭배

Archaeology 고고학

artifact [άːtifækt] 인공 유물, 공예품
authentic [ɔːθéntik] 진품의, 진짜의
Bronze Age 청동기 시대
chronology [krənάlədʒi] 연대기, 연료
class warfare 계급 투쟁
date [deit] 연대를 추정하다
deform [difɔ́ːrm] 변형시키다
digging [dígiŋ] 발굴
dolmen [dóulmen] 고인돌
engrave [engréiv] (금속, 돌 등에) 새기다
excavate [ékskəvèit] 발굴하다
excavation [ékskəvèiʃn] 발굴, 출토품
feudal age 봉건시대

flowering [fláuəriŋ] 번영, 개화기
fossil [fásl] 화석
fragment [frǽgmənt] 조각, 파편
glacial epoch 빙하기
haft [hæft] 손잡이
hierarchy [háiərá:rki] 계급 제도
Ice Age 빙하시대
implement [ímpləmənt] 도구
Invincible Armada 무적함대
Iron Age 철기 시대
mammoth-tusk 맘모스 어금니
Mesolithic [mèzəlíθik] 중석기 시대의
mummy [mʌ́mi] 미라
mound [maund] 고분
Neolithic [nì:oulíθik] 신석기 시대의
origin [ɔ́:rədʒin] 기원
Paleolithic [pèiliəlíθik] 구석기 시대의
Pleistocene Epoch 홍적세
polish [póuliʃ] 마모시키다
pottery [pátəri] 도자기
prehistoric [prì:histɔ́rik] 역사 이전의, 선사 시대의
prehistoric times 선사시대
prehistory [prì:hístəri] 선사시대사
primeval [praimí:vəl] 원시의
primitive [prímətiv] 원시시대의
primitive people 원시인
pristine [prísti:n] 원시시대의
relics [réliks] 유물
remains [riméinz] 유물
rise and fall 흥망성쇠
ruins [rú:ins] 유적
sampling [sǽmpliŋ] 표본추출
scraper [skreipə(r)] 긁어 내는 도구
Scythian [síθiən] 스키타이(의)
shard [ʃa:rd] (도자기 등의) 파편
site [sait] 유적지
skeletal [skélətl] 해골의, 골격의

specimen [spésəmən] 표본
Stone Age 석기 시대
stratum [stréitəm] (고고학상의) 유적층
stratigraphy [strətígrəfi] 층위, 층위학
unearth [ʌnə́:rθ] 발굴하다
unprecedented [ʌnprésədəntɪd] 전례 없는
ups and downs 영고성쇠, 흥망성쇠

Architecture 건축학

architect [á:rkitèkt] 건축가
architectural acoustics 건축음향학
asymmetrical [èisimétrikəl] 비대칭의, 불균형의
Baroque style 바로크 양식
beam [bi:m] 대들보
block [bla:k] 건축용 석재
blueprint [blú:prɪnt] 설계도
brick [brɪk] 벽돌
building material 건축자재
building permit 건축 허가
building site 건축 부지
Building Standards Act 건축 기준법
capital [kǽpitl] 기둥머리, 주두
cellar [sélə(r)] 지하실, 저장실
column [káləm] 기둥
construction bid 건설 입찰
Corinthian [kərínθiən] 코린트식
corridor [kɔ́:ridər] 복도, 화랑
coverage [kʌ́vəridʒ] 건폐율
decoration [dèkəréiʃən] 장식
den [den] 서재, 작업실
design criteria 설계 기준
dome [doum] 둥근 천장
domestic architecture 주택
Doric [dɔ́(:)rik] 도리아식
durability [djùərəbíləti] 내구력, 내구성
eaves [i:vz] 처마

447

edifice [édəfis] 대건축물
erection [irékʃn] 건축
façade 파사드, 건물의 정면
ferroconcrete [fèroukánkri:t] 철근 콘크리트
fireproof [faɪərpru:f] 방화의, 내화성의
fire-resistance 내화성
fixture [fíkstʃər] 설치물, 고정물
floor area ratio 용적률
floor plan 평면도, 설계
frame [freim] 뼈대, 구조, 골조
geological survey map 지질 조사도
Gothic style 고딕 건축 양식
hand-chiseled 손으로 깎은
hand-hewn 손으로 깎은
impulsive load 충격 하중
insulating material 단열재
Ionic 이오니아식
lay out 설계 도면을 그리다
parlor [pá:rlər] 객실, 거실
patio [pætiou] 옥외 테라스
pillar [pílər] 기둥, 지주
plane geometry 평면 기하학
porch [pɔ:rtʃ] 베란다, 현관
profile [próufail] 측면도
refractory brick 내화 벽돌
scroll [skroul] (석재, 목재의) 소용돌이 장식
seismic technology 내진 공학
shaft [ʃæft] 기둥, 주신
skyscraper [skáiskrèipər] 초고층 빌딩
sound-absorbing power 흡음력
soundproof facilities 방음시설
specification [spèsəfikéiʃən] 설계서
steel frame 철골
stone building 석조 건물
stress-strain diagram 응력 변형도
structural iron 건축용 철재
style [stail] (예술작품, 건축 등의) 양식

tenant [ténənt] 거주자
thatch [θætʃ] 초가 지붕
tile [tail] 기와
under construction 건축중인
volumetric method 용적법
walk-up 엘리베이터 없는 빌딩

Art History 예술사

Abstractionism [æbstrækʃən] 추상주의, 추상파
abstract painting 추상화
aesthetic [esθétik] 미적인, 미학의
antique [æntí:k] 골동품
appreciation [əprì:ʃiéiʃən] (작품의) 진가, 이해, 감상
Art Deco 아르데코
artistic style 예술 사조
Art Nouveau 아르누보
Avant-Garde 전위, 선봉, 아방가르드
azure [ǽʒər] 하늘색
brushstroke [brʌʃtròuk] 붓칠
brushwork [brʌʃwə:rk] 화풍, 화법
bust [bʌst] 반신상
caricature [kǽrikətʃùər] 풍자화
carve [ka:rv] 조각하다, 새기다
chiaroscuro [kiá:rəskjú:rou] 명암법
chromatic [kroumǽtik] 색채의
composition [kámpəzíʃən] (미술) 구도
connoisseur [kánəsə:r] (예술품의 감식) 전문가, 감정가
constriction of space 공간의 축소
contour line 윤곽선
copperplate print 동판화
Cubism [kjú:bizəm] 입체파
Dadaism [dá:da:ìzm] 다다이즘
decadence [dékədəns] 타락, 퇴폐
deformation [dì:fɔ:rméiʃən] 변형, 데포르마시옹

emboss [embɔ́s] 도드라지게 새기다
engraving [engréiviŋ] 조각술, 조판술, 판화
Environmental Art 환경 예술
etching [étʃiŋ] 부식 동판술, 에칭(화)
Expressionism [ikspreʃənizəm] 표현파, 표현주의
Fauvism [fóuvizəm] 야수파, 포비즘
figure painting 인물화
fine arts 미술
formative arts 조형미술
fresco [fréskou] 프레스코 화법
Futurism [fjúːtʃərìzəm] 미래파
gallery [gǽləri] 갤러리, 미술관, 화랑
Gothic [gáθik] (건축, 회화 등이) 고딕양식의
handcraft [hǽndkræft] 손으로 만들다
hue [hjuː] 색조
illustrate [íləstrèit] 삽화를 넣다
illustration [iləstréiʃən] 삽화
Impressionism [impréʃənizəm] 인상주의, 인상파
landscape painting 풍경화
limpid [límpid] 투명한
lithograph [líθəgræf] 석판 인쇄(물)
lucent [lúːsnt] 빛나는, 반투명의
luminous [lúːmənəs] 밝은
lurid [lúːrid] 타는 듯이 붉은
luster [lʌ́stər] 광택
manner [mǽnər] (미술, 문학) 형식, 양식
mason [méisən] 석공
master [mǽstər] 명인, 거장
modernist [mádərnist] 현대주의자, 현대주의의
monochrome [máːnəkroum] 단색화
motley [mátli] 잡색의
mural painting 벽화
oil painting 유화
Op Art 착시현상을 이용한 현대 예술양식
Performance Art 행위 미술

piece [piːs] 작품
pigment [pígmənt] 안료, 그림 물감
plaster cast 석고상
Pointillism [pwǽntəlìzəm] (신인상파가 쓴) 점묘화법
Pop Art 팝아트
portrait [pɔ́ːrtrit] 인물화, 초상화
Postimpressionism [pòustimpréʃənìzm] 후기인상주의
Postmodernism [pòustmádərnìzm] 후기모더니즘
profile [próufail] 측면도
relief carving 부조
rendering [réndəriŋ] 표현
reproduction [rìːprədʌ́kʃən] 복제품
retouch [riːtʌ́tʃ] 손질하다
Rococo [ròukəkóu] 로코코 양식
school [skuːl] (학)파
sculptor [skʌ́lptər] 조각가
sculpture [skʌ́lptʃə(r)] 조각
statue [stǽtʃuː] 조각상
still-life painting 정물화
Surrealism [səríːəlizəm] 초현실주의
Symbolism [símbəlizəm] 상징파, 상징주의
symmetry [símətri] 대칭, 균형
tempera [témpərə] 템페라 화법
three dimensional artwork 조형물
transparent colors 투명 그림물감
vandal [vǽndəl] 예술품 피괴자
vantage point 관점
wash drawing 담채 풍의 수채(화), 수묵화
watercolor [wɔ́ːtərkʌ̀lər] 수채 물감
watercolor painting 수채화
wood carving 목각(술)
woodprint [wúdprìnt] 목판화

Astronomy 천문학

aerospace [éərouspeis] 항공우주(산업)
air resistance 공기 저항
antimatter [ǽntimætə(r)] 반물질
apogee [ǽpədʒìː] 원지점
application satellite 실용 위성
asteroid [ǽstərɔ̀id] 소행성
asteroid belt 소행성대
astrology [əstrálədʒi] 점성학
astronaut [ǽstrənɔ̀ːt] 우주 비행사
astronautics [æ̀strənɔ́ːtiks] 우주 항공학
astronomer [əstránəmər] 천문학자
atmosphere [ǽtməsfiər] 대기
atmospheric pressure 기압
axis [ǽksis] 축
balloon satellite 기구 위성
blackout [blǽkaut] (대기권 돌입시 등의) 통신 두절
blast-off (로켓, 미사일의) 발사
booster rocket 보조추진로켓
broadcasting satellite 방송 위성
carrier rocket 운반 로켓
celestial body 천체
celestial sphere 천구
circumlunar flight 달 궤도 비행
cluster [klʌ́stər] 성단
combustion chamber (로켓의) 연소실
comet [kámit] 혜성
concentration [kànsəntréiʃən] 농도
condense [kəndens] 응축 (하다)
congeal [kəndʒiːl] 응고하다, 응결하다
constellation [kànstəléiʃən] 성좌, 별자리
eccentricity [èksentrísəti] 이심률
ecliptic [iklíptik] 황도
equinox [íːkwənáks] 추분, 춘분
friction [fríkʃən] 마찰
galactic nebular 은하성운
galaxy [gǽləksi] 은하, 은하수, 은하계
gravitational [græ̀vətéiʃənl] 인력의, 중력의
gravity [grǽvəti] 중력
heat wave 열파
heavenly body 천체
HST 허블우주망원경
Internal combustion engine 내연소기관
interstellar matter 성간물질
Jupiter [dʒúːpitər] 목성
launch [lɔːntʃ] 발사하다
leap year 윤년
luminous [lúːmənəs] 빛을 내는
lunar eclipse 월식
magnetic storm 자기 폭풍
Mars [maːrz] 화성
mass [mæs] 질량
Mercury [mə́ːrkjuri] 수성
meteor [míːtiər] 유성, 운석
meteorite [míːtiəràit] 운석
naked eye 육안
nebular [nébjulər] 성운
Neptune [néptjuːn] 해왕성
neutron star 중성자별
observatory [əbzǽːrvətɔ̀ːri] 관측소
orbit [ɔ́ːrbit] 궤도; ~을 궤도를 그리며 돌다
perigee [péridʒìː] 근지점
planet [plǽnit] 행성
Pluto [plúːtou] 명왕성
Polestar [póulstàːr] 북극성
proton [próutan] 양성자
pulsar [pʌ́lsaːr] 펄서
red giant star 적색 거성
repulsion [ripʌ́lʃən] 척력
revolution [rèvəlúːʃən] 혁명
rotation [routéiʃən] 자전
satellite [sǽtəlàit] 위성, 인공위성
Saturn [sǽtərn] 토성

solar eclipse 일식
solar system 태양계
spacecraft [speiskræft] 우주선
stellar [stélər] 별의
sunspot [sʌ́nspát] 흑점
supernova [sjùːpərnóuvə] 초신성
supergiant star 초거성
telemetry [təlémətri] 텔레미터법, 원격측정법
telescope [téləskòup] 망원경
the Polaris 북극성
thunderstorm [θʌ́ndərstɔ̀ːrm] 뇌우
trade wind 무역풍
track [træk] 궤도, 추적하다
transparency [trænspéərənsi] 투명도
Uranus [júərənəs] 천왕성
Van Allen Radiation Belt 밴앨런복사대
variable star 변광성
Venus [víːnəs] 금성
vessel [vésəl] 우주선
weather phenomenon 기상현상
weightlessness 무중력상태
white dwarf star 백색왜성
wind velocity 풍속

Biology 생물학

adaptation [ædəptéiʃən] 적응
aerobic [ɛəróubik] 유산소이, 호기성의
agility [ədʒíləti] 민첩성, 명민함
anaerobic [ǽnəròubɪk] 무산소의, 혐기성의
anabolism [ənǽbəlìzm] 동화 작용
amino acid 아미노산
atavism [ǽtəvìzm] 격세유전
building block 기초 단위, 구성물
catabolism [kətǽbəlìzm] 이화 작용, 이화 작용
chromosome [króuməsòum] 염색체
class [klæs] (분류학상의) 강

conjugation [kándʒəgèiʃn] 접합
crust [krʌst] 껍질, 갑각
culture [kʌ́ltʃər] 배양, 재배, 사육
cytology [saitálədʒi] 세포학
cytoplasm [sáitouplæ̀zm] 세포질
DNA 디옥시리보핵산
dominant [dámənənt] 우성의
enmity [énməti] 적의, 불화
enzyme [énzaim] 효소
family [fǽməli] (동물의 분류에서) 과
ferment [fəːrment] 효소, 발효
fermentation [fə̀ːrmentéiʃən] 발효 (작용)
genetic [dʒənétik] 유전의
gene pool 유전자 풀
genus [dʒíːnəs] 속
heredity [hərédəti] 유전형질
homeostasis [hóumioustéisis] 항상성
hybrid [háibrid] (동물의) 잡종
inactivity [inæktivəti] 무활동, 휴지
kingdom [kíŋdəm] 계
membrane [mémbrein] 세포막
metabolism [mətǽbəlìzm] 신진대사
metaplasm [métəplæ̀zm] 후형질
microbe [máikroub] 미생물
mutation [mjuːtéiʃn] 돌연변이
natural enemy 천적
natural selection 자연선택
natural death 자연사
naturalist [nǽtʃərəlist] 박물학자, 자연주의자
nervous system 신경계
niche [nitʃ] 적소, 서식지
nucleic acid 핵산
nucleus [njúːkliəs] 핵
orderr [ɔ́ːrdə] (동물 분류상의) 목
organism [ɔ́ːrgənìzm] 유기체, 생물체
osmotic pressure 삼투압
recessive [risésiv] 열성의

451

phylum (division) [fáiləm] 문
protein [próuti:n] 단백질
protoplasm [próutouplæzəm] 원형질
sense [sens] 감지하다
species [spí:ʃi(:)z] 종
symbiotic [sìmbaiátik] 공생하는
trait [treit] 형질
taxonomy [tæksánəmi] 분류, 분류법(학)
tissue [tíʃju:] (생물) 조직
vacuole [vǽkjuòul] 액포
variety [vəráiəti] (유전적 차이에 의한) 변종
yeast [ji:st] 효모

Botany 식물학

absorb [æbsɔ́:rb] 섭취하다
aerial plant 식물학
annual ring 나이테
anther [ǽnθər] 꽃밥
arbor [á:rbər] 나무
bark [ba:rk] 나무껍질
bloom [blu:m] 꽃
bough [bau] 나뭇가지
bouquet [boukéi] 꽃다발
burgeon [bə́:rdʒən] (초목의) 싹, 싹트다
cactus [kǽktəs] 선인장
carbon dioxide 이산화탄소
carpel [ká:rpəl] 암술 잎
cellulose [séljəlòus] 섬유소
chlorophyll [klɔ́:rəfil] 엽록소, 엽록체
colony [káləni] 군생
conifer [kóunəfər] 침엽수
corolla [kərálə] 꽃부리
deciduous tree 낙엽수
dominant [dámənənt] 우성의
efflorescence [èflourésns] 개화
epiphyte [épəfàit] 착생식물

evergreen tree 상록수
feral [fíərəl] 야생의
fern [fə:rn] 양치류
fertilization [fə́:rtəlizéiʃən] 수정
fibrous roots 수염뿌리
flowery [fláuəri] 꽃이 많은
foliage [fóuliidʒ] 잎
fungus [fʌ́ŋgəs] 균, 진균식물
hydrotropism [haidrátrəpìzəm] 굴수성
generic [dʒənérik] 속의, 일반적인
germinate [dʒə́:rmənèit] 발아하다, 싹이 나다
glucose [glú:kous] 포도당
graft [græft] 접붙이기, 접지
gravitropism [grǽvətróupizəm] 굴중성
greenhouse [grí:nhàus] 온실
habitat [hǽbətæt] (식물의) 자생지
hermaphrodite [hə:rmǽfrədàit] 양성화, 자웅동체, 암수한몸
hollow [hálou] 속이 텅 빈
husk [hʌsk] 과일이나 땅콩의 마른 껍질
insectivore [inséktəvɔ̀:r] 식충 동물
intake [ínteɪk] 섭취
ivy [áivi] 담쟁이 덩굴
juicy [dʒú:si] 즙이 많은
kernel [kə́:rnəl] (씨앗의) 알맹이, (과실의) 인
liana [liánə] 덩굴식물
lichen [láikən] 지의류, 이끼
lumber [lʌ́mbər] 재목
lush [lʌʃ] 무성한, 우거진
maize [meiz] 옥수수
marshland [ma:rʃlænd] 습지
meadow [médou] 목초지
mistletoe [mísltòu] 겨우살이
mushroom [mʌ́ʃru(:)m] 버섯, 급속히 커지다
native [néitiv] 원산의, 토종의, 자생의
nectar [néktər] 과즙, 화밀, 꽃 속의 꿀
ovary [óuvəri] 씨방

perennial [pəréniəl] 다년생의 (식물)
petal [pétl] 꽃잎
photosynthesis [fóutousínθəsis] 광합성
phototropism [fóutoutróupizəm] 굴광성
pigment [pígmənt] 색소
pollination [pálənèiʃən] 수분 (작용)
pollen [pálən] 꽃가루
proliferous [proulífərəs] (식물이 가는 줄기로) 번식하는
prune [pruːn] (나무를) 전지하다, (가지를) 잘라내다
rampant [rǽmpənt] 울창한
resin [rézin] (나무의) 진, 송진
sap [sæp] 수액, (식물의) 액즙
sapling [sǽpliŋ] 어린 묘목
seedling [síːdliŋ] 묘목, 어린 나무
sepal [síːpəl] 꽃받침 조각
shed [ʃed] (잎, 씨 따위를) 떨구다
spore [spɔːr] 포자, 홀씨
sprout [spraut] (식물의) 싹, 싹이 나다
stamen [stéimən] (식물) 수술
starch [staːrtʃ] 전분, 녹말
stem [stem] 줄기
stigma [stígmə] 암술머리, 주두
stoma [stóumə] (식물의 잎, 줄기에 있는) 기공
submerge [səbməːrdʒ] 물 속으로 잠기다
sucker [sʌkər] (식물의) 흡지, 흡근
taproot [tǽpruːt] 곧은 뿌리
tentacle [téntəkəl] 촉모, 섬모
thorn [θɔːrn] (식물의) 가시, 가시가 있는 관목
timber [tímbər] 목재, 재목
transpiration [trænspəréiʃən] 증산작용
tropism [tróupizəm] (식물의) 굴성, (생물의) 향성
trunk [trʌŋk] (나무) 줄기
turf [təːrf] 잔디
underbrush [ʌ́ndərbrʌʃ] (큰 나무의 밑에 자라는) 덤불
vegetation [védʒətèiʃən] 식물, 초목

vein [vein] 엽맥
weed [wiːd] 잡초
wilt [wilt] 시들다
wither [wíðər] 시들다

Chemistry 화학

acceptor [ækséptər] 수용체
acid [ǽsid] 산
additive [ǽdətiv] 첨가제
alchemy [ǽlkəmi] 연금술
alkalinity [ælkəlínəti] 알칼리성
alloy [ǽlɔi] 합금
aluminum [əlúːmənəm] 알루미늄
amylum [ǽmələm] 녹말
boiling point 비등점
brine [brain] 식염수
cadmium [kǽdmiəm] 카드뮴
capillarity [kæpəlǽrəti] 모세관 현상
carbohydrate [káːrbouháidreit] 탄수화물
carbon [káːrbən] 탄소
catalyst [kǽtəlist] 촉매
catalyze [kǽtəlàiz] 촉매 작용을 하다
chemical action 화학 작용
chemical element 원소
chemical equation 화학 방정식
chemical reaction 화학 반응
chemical symbol 화학 기호
colloid [kálɔid] 콜로이드
combustion [kəmbʌ́stʃən] 연소
composition [kàmpəzíʃən] 합성, 성분
compound [kəmpáund] 화합물, 혼합물
concentration [kànsəntréiʃən] (용액의) 농도, 농축
condense [kəndéns] 농축하다
content [kəntént] 함유량
coolant [kúːlənt] 냉각제

453

corrode [kəróud] 부식되다
crude [kruːd] 가공하지 않은
crystal [krístl] 결정(체)
decomposition [dìːkampəzíʃən] 분해
deposit [dipázit] 침전물, 퇴적물
diffusion [difjúːʒən] 확산
dilution [dilúːʃən] 희석
element [éləmənt] 원소
evaporation [ivæpərèiʃən] 증발
exothermic [èksouθəˊːrmik] 발열의, 발열성의
explosively [iksplóusivli] 폭발적으로
fat [fæt] 지방
freezing point 어는점, 빙점
gas/liquid/solid 기체/액체/고체
generate [dʒénərèit] 산출하다, 만들어내다
helium [híːliəm] 헬륨
hydrochloric acid 염산
hydrogen [háidrədʒən] 수소
incandescent [ìnkəndésənt] 백열의, 백열광을 내는
ingredient [ingríːdiənt] (혼합물의) 성분
inject [indʒékt] 주입하다
inorganic compounds 무기화합물
insoluble [insáljubəl] 용해되지 않는
isotope [áisətòup] 동위원소
lead [liːd] 납
liquefaction [lìkwifækʃən] 액화, 용해
lukewarm [lúːkwɔ̀ːrm] (온도가) 미지근한
manganese [mǽŋɡənìːz] 망간
matter [mǽtər] 물질
melting [méltiŋ] 용해
melting point 융(해)점, 녹는점
molecular [moulékjulər] 분자의
moldy [móuldi] 곰팡이 낀
neutralize [njúːtrəlàiz] 중화하다
nitrogen [náitrədʒən] 질소
osmosis [azmóusis] 삼투, 삼투성

oxide [áksaid] 산화물
oxidizing agent 산화제
oxidize [áksədàiz] 산화하다
oxygen [áksidʒən] 산소
periodic table 주기율표
phosphate [fásfeit] 인산염
plate [pleit] 도금하다
property [prápərti] (어떤 물건 고유의) 특성, 특질
purify [pjúərəfài] 정제하다
react [riːækt] 반응하다
reactant [riæktənt] 반응체
reagent [riːéidʒənt] 시약
reducing agent 환원제
reduction [ridʌˊkʃən] 환원(법)
replacement [ripléismənt] (다른 원자로 바꾸는) 치환
saturation [sætʃərèiʃən] 포화, 포화 상태
silicon [sílikən] 규소
solidification [səlìdəfikéiʃən] 응고
solute [sáljuːt] 용질
solution [səlúːʃən] 용액
solvent [sálvənt] 용매
starch [staːrtʃ] 녹말
steam [stiːm] 수증기
sublimation [sʌ̀bləmèiʃən] 승화
sulfuric acid 황산
thermometer [θərmámitər] 온도계
tin [tin] 주석
uranium [juəréiniəm] 우라늄
vapor [véipər] 수증기
vaporization [vèipərizéiʃən] 기화
variable [véəriəbəl] 변수
viscous [vískəs] 점착성의
volume [váljuːm] 체적
zinc [ziŋk] 아연

Communication 커뮤니케이션

agenda [ədʒéndə] 의제, 안건
analog transmission 아날로그 전송
caption [kǽpʃən] 사진 설명문
circulation [sə̀ːrkjəléiʃən] 발행부수
columnist [kǽləmnist] (신문) 특별 기고가
Commercial Message (C.M) 광고, 방송
correspondent [kɔ̀ːrəspándənt] 특파원
coverage [kʌ́vəridʒ] 보도, 취재
critic [krítik] 비평가
deadline [dedlain] 마감시간
digital broadcasting 디지털 방송
direct broadcasting service 위성방송서비스
editor [édətər] 편집자, 논설위원
editorial [èdətɔ́ːriəl] 논설 (위원)
electronic conference 전자 회의
erroneous report 오보
exclusive [iksklúːsiv] 독점 기사, 특종
extra [ékstrə] 호외
high frequency 고주파
feature [fíːtʃər] 읽을 거리
feature syndicate 기사 제공 업체
follow-up 속보, 후속 기사
foreign dispatch 외신
forum [fɔ́ːrəm] 공공 토론
freedom of the press 출판, 보도의 자유
frequency [fríːkwənsi] 주파수
journalist [dʒə́ːrnəlist] 신문, 잡지 기사
lead [liːd] (신문기사의) 첫머리, 톱기사
Morse code 모스 부호
multiplex broadcasting 다중 신호
optical communication 광 통신
optical fiber 광섬유
optical transport network 광 전송망
optical wireless 광 무선통신
panel discussion 공개 토론회
press censorship 신문 검열
quotation [kwoutéiʃən] 인용
reflectivity [rìːflektívəti] 반사율
resolution [rèzəlúːʃən] 해상도
satellite network 인공위성 통신망
scoop [skuːp] 특종기사
telegraphy [təlégrəfi] 전신
wireless data communication 무선 데이터 통신

Computer Science 컴퓨터 공학

access time 접속에 걸리는 시간
assembler [əsémblər] 어셈블러
(명령을 기계어로 전환하는 프로그램)
binary code 이진 부호
capability [kèipəbíləti] 용량
capacity [kəpǽsiti] 용량
Central Processing Unit (CPU) 중앙 처리 장치
code [koud] 암호
compatible [kəmpǽtəbl] 호환성이 있는
computer specialist 컴퓨터 전문가
configuration [kənfìgjuréiʃən] (컴퓨터의) 환경 설정
freeware [fríːweə(r)] 프리웨어
hex code 십육진 부호
Integrated Circuit (IC) 집적회로
information retrieval 정보 검색
laptop computer 노트북 컴퓨터
memory bank 기억 장치
memory chip 메모리칩
memory unit 기억장치
microchip [máikroutʃip] 마이크로칩,
micro millennium 마이크로 시대
microcomputer center 컴퓨터 센터
microprocessor [máikrouprásesər] 마이크로 프로세서
mouse [maus] 마우스

455

Office Automation (OA) 사무 자동화
Operating System (OS) 운영체계
optical memory 광 메모리
peripheral device 주변 장치
portable [pɔ́ːrtəbəl] 들고 다닐 수 있는
retrieval system 정보검색시스템
runtime [rʌ́ntaim] (프로그램의) 실행시간
store up 저장하다
terminal [tə́ːrmənəl] 단말기
throughput [θruːput] 작업량, 처리량
transistor [trænzístər] 트랜지스터(증폭장치)
volatile [vɔ́lətàil] 휘발성의
wetware [wetweər] (컴퓨터의 소프트웨어를 고안해 내는 인간의) 두뇌

Economics 경제학

a state of boom 호황
advance [ædvǽns] 선불하다, 가불하다
annuity [ənjúːəti] 연금
appraise [əpréiz] 평가견적, 값매기다
appropriation [əpròupriéiʃən] 횡령, 도용
assess [əsés] (세금, 벌금을) 정하다
auction [ɔ́ːkʃən] 경매
audit [ɔ́ːdit] 회계 감사
avocation [ævoukéiʃən] 부업
bankruptcy [bǽŋkrʌptsi] 파산
bargain [báːrgən] 매매계약, 거래, 특가품
barter [báːrtər] 물물교환(하다)
bidding [bídiŋ] 입찰
bill [bil] 어음, 증서
bill of debt 약속어음
bill of dishonor 부도어음
black ink balance 흑자
blue chips 우량주
bond [band] 채권
bottom line of budget 예산의 최저절감

budget [bʌ́dʒit] 예산
buoyant [bɔ́iənt] (시세가) 오름세의
bust [bʌst] 파산시키다
bystander [báistændər] 방관자
cession [séʃən] (권리의) 양도
check and balance 견제와 균형
clearing house 어음교환소
commodity [kəmádəti] 상품, 필수품
competitive bidding 경쟁입찰
consolidation [kənsálədèiʃən] 합병
counterfeit [káuntərfit] 가짜의, 모조의
covenant [kʌ́vənənt] 계약, 계약 조항
currency [kə́ːrənsi] 통화, 유통
current price 시가
declare [dikléər] 과세금을 신고하다
deficit [défəsit] 적자
deflation [difléiʃən] 통화수축
demand [dimǽnd] 수요
depreciation [dipríːʃièiʃən] 가치 하락
depression [dipréʃən] 불황, 불경기
detriment [détrəmənt] 손해, 손실
devaluation [diːvæljuèiʃən] 평가 절하
due [djuː] 지불되어야 할
economic depression 경제공황
endorse [endɔ́ːrs] (어음, 증권에) 배서하다
equilibrium [ìːkwəlíbriəm] 균형, 안정
expansionary policy 경기부양책
exploitation [èksplɔitéiʃən] 착취
extravagance [ikstrǽvəgəns] 낭비, 사치(품)
facilities 공공 편의시설
fiasco [fiǽskou] 대실패, 큰 실수
fiat money 불환 화폐
fiscal [fískəl] 국고의, 재정상의
fiscal year 회계연도
fluctuation [flʌ́ktʃuèiʃən] 변동
forge [fɔːrdʒ] 위조하다
frugality [fruːgǽləti] 검소

functionalism [fʌ́ŋkʃənəlizm] 기능주의
fund [fʌnd] 기금, 자금, 공채, 국채
futility [fjuːtíləti] 무익, 무가치
gains [geins] 수익, 수익금
generalization [dʒénərəlàizéiʃən] 일반화
glut [glʌt] 공급 과잉
gratuitous [grətjúːətəs] 무료의
gratuitous conveyance 무상양도
Gross National Product (GNP) 국민총생산
financial crisis 재정위기, 금융위기
incorporation [inkɔ́ːrpərèiʃən] 합병
increment [ínkrəmənt] 이윤
inflation [infléiʃən] 통화 팽창, 물가 상승률
installment [instɔ́ːlmənt] 분할 불입금
interest [íntərist] 이자
interest rate 금리, 이율
inventory [ínvəntɔ̀ːri] 목록, 재고품
levy [lévi] 부과하다, 징수하다
liquidate [líkwidèit] (부채를) 갚다, (회사가) 파산하다
mass-produce 대량생산하다
mergers & acquisitions (M&A) 기업의 인수 및 합병
monetary system 통화제도
monopoly [mənápəli] 독점, 전매
monopoly and oligopoly 독과점
moratorium [mɔ̀ːrətɔ́ːriəm] 모라토리움, 지불유예
mortgage [mɔ́ːrgidʒ] 저당(잡히다)
national treasury 국고
objectivity [ábdʒiktívəti] 객관성
oligopoly [áligápəli] 과점, 소수 독점
operating cost 운영비, 경상 경비
output [áutpùt] (일정 기간 동안의) 생산고
panic [pǽnik] 공황
paper money 지폐
paper note 지폐

passbook [pǽsbuk] 은행통장
pecuniary [pikjúːnièri] 금전상의
pension [pénʃən] 연금
population density 인구 밀도
preferential [prèfərénʃəl] 우선권을 주는, 특혜를 주는
price fluctuation 물가 변동
profligacy [práfligəsi] 낭비, 대량
property [prápərti] 재산
proprietary name 특허 등록명, 상표명
public utilities 공익시설
realism [ríːəlìzəm] 현실주의
recall [rikɔ́ːl] 회수하다
recession [riséʃən] 불경기, (일시적) 경기후퇴
recruit [rikrúːt] (조직, 기업 등의) 새로운 구성원
reimbursement [rìːimbəːrsmənt] 상환, 변제
relief work 실업대책 사업
retail [ríːteil] 소매
revaluation [rìːvæljuéiʃən] 평가절상
revenue [révənjùː] 세입
rush [rʌʃ] 주문쇄도, 대수요
security [sikjúəriti] 담보, 보증(물)
shinplaster [ʃínplǽstər] 소액 지폐
shutdown [ʃʌ́tdaun] (공장 등의) 일시 폐쇄, 휴점
skyrocket [skáirakit] (물가가) 치솟다
slump [slʌmp] (물가가) 폭락하다, 불황
small and medium enterprises 중소기업
smuggle [smʌ́gəl] 밀수하다, 은닉하다
speculate [spékjəlèit] (주시, 토지 등에) 투기하다
stagnation [stægnéiʃən] 경기침체하의 인플레이션
stipulate [stípjəlèit] 약정하다, 계약하다
stocktaking [stɔ́kteikiŋ] 재고조사
subsidy [sʌ́bsidi] (국가의) 보조금
stock [stɔk] 주식
stocks and bonds 유가증권
subcontract [sʌbkántrækt] 하청 (계약)
supply [səplái] 공급

swap [swap] 물물교환하다
tariff [tǽrif] 관세
tender [téndər] 입찰(하다)
the black-ink balance 흑자
the trade imbalance 무역 불균형
trade cycle 경기순환
transaction [trænsǽkʃən] 거래, 상거래
tycoon [taikúːn] 재벌, 기업계의 거물
underpopulated [ʌndərpápjuleìtid] 인구 밀도가 낮은
Value Added Tax (VAT) 부가가치세
voucher [váutʃər] 영수증, 전표
welfare [wélfɛər] 복지
wholesale [houlseil] 도매

Ecology 생태학

acid rain 산성비
alpine [ǽlpain] 높은 산의
aquatic [əkwǽtik] 물속의
biodiversity [báioudivə́ːrsəti] 생물다양성
biomass [báioumæs] (특정 지역내의) 생물량
biome [báiəum] 생물군계
biosphere [báiəsfiər] 생물권
catastrophe [kətǽstrəfi] 대재해, 파멸
chemosynthesis [keməusínθəsis] 화학 합성
conservationist [kánsəːrvéiʃənist] (자연환경 등의) 보호론자
consumer [kənsúːmər] (생태계의) 소비자
cycle of material 물질순환
decay [dikéi] (식물, 동물 등의 조직이) 썩다
decomposer [dìːkəmpóuzər] 분해자(박테리아, 균류 등)
deforestation [diːfɔ̀ːristeiʃən] 삼림 파괴, 삼림 벌채
desertification [dizə̀ːrtəfikéiʃən] 사막화
ecological efficiency 생태 효율

ecological niche 생태적 지위
ecosystem [ékousístəm] 생태계
elevation [èləvéiʃən] 고지, 고도
emission [imíʃən] 방출, 배출
endangered species 멸종위기의 동식물
energy flow (생태계의) 에너지 흐름
fauna [fɔ́ːnə] 동물상
filter [fíltər] 여과하다
flora [flɔ́ːrə] 식물상
food chain 먹이 사슬
food web 먹이 그물
garbage [gáːrbidʒ] 쓰레기
hectare [héktɛər] 헥타르
industrial waste 산업 폐기물
landfill [lǽndfil] 쓰레기 매립지
noxious [nákʃəs] 유해한, 유독한
oil spill (해상의) 석유 유출
overpopulation [òuvərpapjuléiʃən] 인구 과잉
ozone hole 오존 구멍
PCB 폴리 염화 비페닐
permafrost [pə́ːrməfrɔ̀ːst] 영구동토
photochemical smog 광화학 스모그
purification [pjùərəfikéiʃən] 정화
rain forest 열대 우림
reclamation [rèkləméiʃən] 재개발, 개간
recycle [riːsáikəl] 재활용하다
replant [rìːplǽnt] 다시 심다, 고쳐 심다
reprocess [rìːpráses] 재생하다, 재가공하다
reservoir [rézərvwáːr] 저수지
salvage [sǽlvidʒ] 해난 구조, 폐품 회수
soil contamination 토양 오염
terrestrial [təréstriəl] 육지의
tract [trækt] 토지의 넓이, 지역
untreated [ʌntríːtid] 처리되지 않은, 정화되지 않은
valley [vǽli] 골짜기
vegetation [védʒətèiʃən] 식물, 초목
waste water 폐수

water pollution 수질 오염
watershed [wɔ́:tərʃed] (강의) 유역
wetland [wétlænd] 습지
wildlife [wáildlaif] 야생 동물
woodland [wúdlænd] 산림지대의

Energy 에너지

alternative energy 대체에너지
blackout [blǽkaut] 정전
byproduct [báiprɑdəkt] 부산물
chamber [tʃéimbər] (엔진의) 공기실, 방
clean energy 청정에너지
crude oil 원유
daylight saving time 일광절약시간, 서머타임
deplete [diplí:t] 압축하다
diesel [dí:zəl] 경유
electricity [ilèktrísəti] 전력, 전기
energy conservation 에너지 절약
energy consumption 에너지 소비
energy-efficient 에너지 효율이 높은
energy resources 에너지 자원
enrich [enrítʃ] (동위 원소 등을) 농축하다
extract [ikstrǽkt] 추출하다, 뽑다
fossil fuel 화석연료
gasoline [gǽsəlì:n] 휘발유
gas station 주유소
generator [dʒénərèitər] 발전기
harness [há:rnis] (자연력을) 이용하다
hydroelectric power plant 수력발전소
kerosene [kérəsì:n] 등유
LNG 액화천연가스
LPG 액화석유가스
maintenance [méintənəns] 유지 (관리)
mine [main] 채굴하다
natural resources 천연자원
nuclear power 원자력

oil drilling 석유 시추
oil field 유전
oil-producing country 산유국
oil refinery 정유공장, 정유소
oil-tanker 유조선
petroleum [pətróuliəm] 석유
pipeline [páiplain] 송유관
power plant 발전소
power supply 전력 공급
quest [kwest] 탐색, 추구
reserve [rizə́:rv] (석탄, 석유, 천연가스 등의) 매장량
reserve power 예비전력
reservoir [rézərvwá:r] 매장 지역, 저수지
site-specific 특정 장소에 설치하기 위해 제작된
tidal power plant 조력발전소
renewable [rinjú:əbl] 재생 가능한
renewable energy 재생에너지
solar energy 태양에너지
sustainable [səstéinəbl] (자원이) 지속 가능한
synthetic fuel 합성연료
thermal [θə́:rməl] 열의
thermal power station 화력발전소

Engineering 공학

abrasion [əbréiʒən] 마모, (물리적) 부식
accelerator [æksélərèitər] 촉진제
advanced materials 신소재
aircraft [éərkræft] 항공기
application [æplikéiʃən] 용도
artificial gene 인공 유전자
artificial heart 인공심장
artificial organs 인공장기
automatic control 자동제어
bionics [baiániks] 생체공학
biotechnology [báiouteknálədʒi] 생명공학
breakthrough [bréikθrù:] 돌파, 타결

459

compression [kəmpréʃən] 압축, 응축
conductor [kəndʌ́ktər] 전도체
conduction [kəndʌ́kʃən] 전도
conduit [kándjuit] 도관
control system 제어방식
conveying machinery 운반기계
corrosion [kəróuʒən] (화학적) 부식
cure [kjuər] 경화하다, 가황하다, 경화
elastic [ilǽstik] 탄성의, 신축성이 있는
factory automation (FA) 공장자동화
galvanic [gælvǽnik] 전류를 발생시키는
galvanic cell 갈바니 전지
Gantt chart 간트 도표(프로젝트 일정 등을 도표로 표시하는 것)
grounding [gráundiŋ] 접지(어스)공사
insulation [ìnsəlèiʃən] 절연, 단열, 보온
laminate [lǽmənèit] 얇은 판자 조각, 합판
leakage [líːkidʒ] 누출, 누전
mechanical engineering 기계 공학
metallic material 금속 재료
mixture [míkstʃər] 혼합물
mold [mould] 틀, 주형, 거푸집
natural gas 천연가스
non-conductive 비전도s
nuclear engineering 원자력 공학
obsolete equipment 노후설비
pathfinder [pǽθfaindər] 선구자
petrochemical industry 석유화학산업
pilot [páilət] 시험적인
pneumatic [njumǽtik] 기체의, 공기의 압축에 의한
polymer [páləmər] 고분자, 중합체
polymer chemistry 고분자화학
precision machine 정밀 기계
propulsion [prəpʌ́lʃən] 추진, 추진력
prototype [próutoutàip] 시제품, 원형
radio [réidiòu] 무선의, (통신을) 무선으로 보내다

reception [risépʃən] 수신
refraction [rifrǽkʃən] 굴절
reinforcing [rìːinfɔ́ːrsiŋ] 강화
remote control 원격조정
resin [rézin] 수지, 합성수지
rubber [rʌ́bər] 고무
scramble [skrǽmbl] (도청방지를 위해) 주파수를 바꾸다
shape memory alloy 형상 기억 합금
soldering [sádəriŋ] 땜질
superconductor [súːpərkəndʌ́ktər] 초전도체
synthetic fiber 합성섬유
synthetic rubber 합성고무
steel [stiːl] 철강
teleprinter [téləprìntər] 전신타자기
tensile [ténsəl] 장력
thermosetting [θəːrmosétiŋ] 열경화성의
thermosetting resin 열경화성수지
thrust [θrʌst] 추력
transistor [trænzístər] 트랜지스터, 증폭장치
transmission [trænsmíʃən] 송신, 전송
tuning [tjúːniŋ] 동조, 조율
vulcanization [vʌ̀lkənàizeiʃn] 가황, 경화
welding [wéldiŋ] 용접

Entomology 곤충학

ant [ænt] 개미
antenna [ænténə] 더듬이
beetle [bíːtl] 투구풍뎅이, 딱정벌레
bumblebee [bʌ́mblbì] 뒁벌
butterfly [bʌ́tərflài] 나비
camouflage [kǽmuflàːʒ] 위장
caterpillar [kǽtərpìlər] 애벌레
centipede [séntəpìːd] 지네
chrysalis [krísəlis] 번데기(집)
cicada [sikéidə] 매미

cockroach [kákròutʃ] 바퀴벌레
cocoon [kəkúːn] 누에고치
coloration [kʌ̀ləréiʃən] (생물의) 천연색
compound eye 복안
deformed [difɔ́ːrmd] 변형된, 불구의
dragonfly [drǽgənflai] 잠자리
drosophila [drousáfilə] 초파리
endoskeleton [éndouskélətn] 내골격
ensnare [ensnéər] 덫으로 잡다
excrete [ikskríːt] 분비하다
exoskeleton [èksouskélitn] 외골격(갑각류의 겉껍질)
feed on ~을 주식으로 하다
firefly [fáiərflai] 반딧불이, 개똥벌레
flagelliform [flədʒéləfɔ̀ːrm] 편모모양의
flea [fliː] 벼룩
fly [flai] 파리
fruit fly 광대파리
gland [glænd] 내분비샘, 선
grasshopper [grǽshápər] 여치, 메뚜기
hive [haiv] 벌집
honeybee [hʌ́nibìː] 꿀벌
imago [iméigou] 성충
inedible [inédəbl] 먹을 수 없는
infest [infést] (해충이나 병이) 만연하다
infestation [ìnfestéiʃən] (기생충의) 체내 침입
insect [ínsekt] 곤충
insecticide [inséktəsàid] 살충제
insectivorous [insektívərəs] 벌레를 먹는
ladybug [léidibʌg] 무당벌레
larva [láːrvə] 애벌레, 유충
leaf-cutter ant 가위개미
locust [lóukəst] 메뚜기
mandible [mǽndəbəl] 위턱, 큰 턱
mayfly [méiflai] 하루살이
metamorphosis [mètəmɔ́ːrfəsis] 변태
misshapen [mísʃéipən] 기형의

mite [mait] 응애, 진드기
mosquito [məskíːtou] 모기
moth [mɔ(ː)θ] 나방
parasite [pǽrəsàit] 기생충
pest [pest] 해충
proboscis [proubásis] (곤충의) 주둥이, 입
pupa [pjúːpə] 번데기
pupate [pjúːpeit] 번데기가 되다
sac [sæk] 주머니, 낭
scale [skeil] (나비 날개 등의) 인분, 비늘
segment [ségmənt] 부분, 단편
sensor [sénsər] 감각기관
spider [spáidər] 거미류
spinneret [spínərèt] 방적돌기
spiracle [spáiərəkl] (곤충의) 숨구멍, 기문
strand [strænd] 한가닥
suck [sʌk] 빨다
termite [təːrmait] 흰개미
thornbug [θɔːrnbʌg] 가시벌레
tiger moth 불나방
treehopper [triːhɔ́pər] 뿔매미
wasp [wasp] 장수말벌
worm [wəːrm] (지렁이 등의) 연충

Environmental Science 환경학

anemometer [ænəmámitər] 풍력계
acid dust 산성진
air rain 산성비
air pollution 대기 오염
atomic energy 원자력
biphenyl [baifénl] 비페닐
bleacher [blíːtʃər] 표백제
bulwark [búlwərk] 방벽, 방어물
carcinogenic [káːrsənoudʒénik] 발암성의
car exhaust 배기가스
catastrophic [kætəstráfik] 재앙적인

conservationist [kánsəːrvéiʃənist] 자연보호론자
contamination [kəntæmənèiʃən] 오염
countermeasure [káuntərméʒər] 대응책
depletion [diplíːʃən] (자원) 고갈
detergent [ditə́ːrdʒənt] 세제
ecocide [íːkousàid] 환경 파괴
emission control 배기가스 규제
endangered [endéindʒərd] (동식물이) 멸종위기에 처한
environmental watchdog 환경감시단체
environmentalist [invàiərənméntlist] 환경보호론자
environment assessment 환경영향평가
exhaust [igzɔ́ːst] 배기가스
expedition [èkspədíʃən] 탐사, 탐험
fresh water 담수, 민물
fertilizer [fə́ːrtəlàizər] (화학) 비료
generation [dʒènəréiʃən] 세대
global warming 지구 온난화
greenhouse effect 온실효과
groundwater [gràundwɔ́ːtər] 지하수
heavy metal 중금속
industrial waste 산업 폐기물
lead poisoning 납중독
natural resource 천연자원
noise pollution 소음 공해
nuclear waste 핵폐기물
ocean current 해류
ozone hole 오존 구멍
peril [pérəl] 위험
photochemical smog 광화학 스모그
plastic bag 비닐봉지
plight [plait] 곤경
pollutant [pəlúːtənt] 오염 물질
profound [prəfáund] 깊은
public hazards 공해

purify [pjúərəfài] 정화하다
radioactive waste 방사성 폐기물
recycled paper 재생지
red tide 적조
reserve [rizəːrv] 지정 보호지역, 비축하다
sewage [súːidʒ] 하수
shallow [ʃælou] 얕은
sick house syndrome 새집증후군
toxic waste 유독성 폐기물
traffic jam 교통 체증
waste disposal 폐기물 처리
wastewater [wéistwɔ́ːtər] 폐수
water quality 수질
water-soluble [wɔ́ːtərsàljubl] 수용성의
wilderness [wíldərnis] 황야
wildlife animal 야생 동물

Film 영화

adaptation [ædəptéiʃən] 각색
avant-garde [əváːntgáːrd] 전위적인, 전위
blockbuster [blɔ́kbʌstə(r)] 블록버스터
box office 매표소, 흥행성적
brightness [bráitnis] 명도
casting [kæstiŋ] 배역
censorship [sénsərʃip] 검열
cinematic [sìnəmǽtik] 영화의
cinematograph [sìnəmǽtəgræf] 영사장치
close-up 근접 촬영
commentary [káməntèri] 논쟁, 논평, 주석
computer graphics 컴퓨터그래픽
continuity [kàntənjúːəti] 촬영 대본, 콘티
critical [krítikəl] 비평가의, 평론가의
criticism [krítisìzəm] 비평, 평론
derive from 각색하다
dissolve [dizálv] 디졸브, 오버랩
documentary film 기록영화

double-exposure shot 이중노출화면
dramatist [drǽmətist] 극작가
dramatize [drəmǽtaiz] 드라마로 만들다
echo [ékou] 흉내내다, 반향하다
fade [feid] 서서히 사라지다
filmmaker [fílmméikər] 영화제작자, 영화회사
film director 영화감독
first run 개봉
first run theater 개봉관
flicker [flíkər] 명멸현상, 영상의 깜빡임
full shot 전사
fuzzy [fʌ́zi] 흐린, 선명하지 않은
horror [hɔ́ːrər] 공포영화
hype [haip] 지나친 영화선전
independent film 독립영화
kinetoscope [kinétəskòup] 에디슨이 발명한 영사기
magnetic sound recording 자기녹음
medium shot 중간 원경
metol [míːtal] 형상할 때 사용하는 용액
montage [mantáːʒ] 몽타주(합성 사진), 필름편집
motion picture 영화
nouvelle vague 누벨바그, 새물결
optical illusion 착시현상
personality star 개성파 배우
preview [príːvjùː] 시사회, 시연
prop [praːp] 소도구, 소품
puff [pʌf] 과장되거나 부풀린 칭찬
range [reindʒ] 카메라 피사체 간의 거리
rating [réitiŋ] (관람) 등급
release [rilíːs] (영화 등을) 개봉하다
rerelease [rìːrilíːs] (영화 등을) 재개봉하다
restricted [ristríktid] 17세 미만은 부모 동반이 필요한 (R)
running time 상영시간
scenario [sinéəriòu] 영화각본
scenery [síːnəri] 무대장치, 배경

score [skɔːr] (영화의) 배경음악
set designer 무대감독
shot [ʃat] 화면
silent film 무성영화
sound track 영화음악
stop-action 순간정지의
subtitle [sʌ́btáitl] 영화 자막, 부제
synchronous recording 동시 녹음
talking picture 발성영화
technique [tekníːk] 기법
ticket agency 예매소
usher [ʌ́ʃər] (극장의) 안내원
visual effects 특수효과

Geography 지리학

archipelago [áːrkəpéləgòu] 군도
bluff [blʌf] (바다나 강가의) 절벽
canal [kənǽl] 운하
canyon [kǽnjən] 협곡
cape [keip] 해각, 곶
cavern [kǽvərn] 큰 동굴
cliff [klif] 절벽
coast [koust] 해안, 연안
compass [kʌ́mpəs] 나침반
delta [déltə] 삼각주
estuary [éstʃuèri] 강어귀
eutrophic lake 부영양호
flood plain 범람원
freshwater lake 담수호
geographical [dʒìːəgrǽfikəl] 지리학적인
geyser [gáizər] 간헐천
gorge [gɔːrdʒ] 골짜기
GPS 위성위치확인시스템
highland [háilənd] 고지
hot spring 온천
inland river 내륙 하천

463

lagoon [ləgúːn] 석호
landmass [lǽndmæs] 광대한 토지, 대륙
latitude [lǽtətjùːd] 위도
longitude [lándʒətjùːd] 경도
magnetic north 자북
meander [miǽndər] 곡류
Northern Hemisphere 북반구
pass [pæs] 고개
peninsular [pinínsələr] 반도
plateau [plætóu] 고원
ridge [ridʒ] 산맥, 산등성이
rotational axis 지축
rugged [rʌ́gid] (지형이) 험준한
sand dune 사구, 모래언덕
swamp [swamp] 늪, 소택
tributary [tríbjətèri] (강의) 지류
the North Pole 북극
true north 진북
waterfall [wɔ́ːtərfɔ̀ːl] 폭포
watershed [wɔ́ːtərʃed] 하천유역, 분수령

Geology 지질학

active volcano 활화산
antarctic [æntáːrktik] 남극의
Antarctica [æntáːrktikə] 남극대륙
alluvial [əlúːviəl] 충적토의
arctic [áːrktik] 북극의 (the Arctic: 북극)
aurora [ərɔ́ːrə] 극광, 오로라
brine [brain] 소금물, 염수
bulge [bʌldʒ] 융기(하다)
chasm [kǽzəm] (땅, 바위 등의) 크게 갈라진 틈
chronological [krànəládʒikəl] 연대순의
correlation [kɔ̀ːrəlèiʃən] (층위의) 대비
corrosion [kəróuʒən] 부식, 침식
colliery [káljəri] 탄갱, 탄광
crater [kréitər] 분화구

cross-section 횡단면
crude oil 원유
crust [krʌst] 지각
crystallize [krístəlàiz] 결정화하다
deposit [dipázit] 퇴적시키다, 침전시키다
dormant volcano 휴화산
earthquake [ə́ːrθkwèik] 지진
earth's axis 지축
epicenter [épisèntər] 진앙, 진원지
erosion [iróuʒən] 침식
fault [fɔːlt] 단층
geologist [dʒìːálədʒist] 지질학자
geophysics [dʒíːəfíziks] 지구물리학
geyser [gáizər] 간헐온천
glacier [gléiʃər] 빙하
gorge [gɔːrdʒ] 골짜기
granite [grǽnit] 화강암
iceberg [áisbəːrg] 빙산
igneous rock 화성암
inlet [ínlèt] 후미, 강 어구
lava [láːvə] 용암
lava bed 용암층
law of superposition 지층누중의 법칙
limestone [láimstoun] 석회암
lithification [lìθəfikéiʃən] 석화작용
magma [mǽgmə] 마그마
mantle [mǽntl] 맨틀
marble [màːrbl] 대리석
mason [méisən] 석수
mass [mæs] (흙, 얼음, 구름의) 밀집체
meander [miǽndər] 굽이쳐 흐르다
mercury [məˊːrkjuri] 수은
metamorphosis [mètəmɔ́ːrfəsis] 변형 (작용)
mineral [mínərəl] 광물, 광석, 무기물
molten [móultn] 용해된, 녹은
natural levee 자연제방
Pangaea [pændʒíːə] 판게아

petrifaction [pètrəfǽkʃən] 석화작용, 석화물
plate [pleit] 석판, 지각을 구성하고 있는 암판
plate tectonics [pleit] 판구조론
plutonic rock 심성암
Richter scale 지진계의 눈금, 진도, 척도
rift [rift] 단층
river basin 유역
sand dune 사구
sediment [sédəmənt] 퇴적물
sedimentary rock 퇴적암
sedimentation [sèdəməntéiʃən] 퇴적 작용
seismic intensity 진도
slope [sloup] 비탈, 경사면
stalactite [stǽləktàit] 종유석
stalagmite [stəlǽgmait] 석순
stratify [strǽtəfài] 층을 형성하다
stratum [stréitəm] 지층
subfrigid [sʌbfrídʒid] 아한대의
submarine ridge 해저산맥
subterranean river 지하천
subtropical [sʌbtrápikəl] 아열대의
supercontinent [súːpərkántənənt] 초대륙
tectonic plate 지각의 플레이트
terrane [təréin] 지층, 암층
transformation [trænsfərméiʃən] 변형
tremor [trémər] 진동
trench [trentʃ] 해구
unconformity [ʌnkənfɔ́ːrməti] (지층의) 부정합
upheaval [ʌphíːvəl] 융기
uplift [ʌplíft] 융기
upwarp [ʌpwɔ́ːrp] 곡륭, 배사
volcanic ashes 화산재
volcanic eruption 화산 폭발, 분화
volcanic zone 화산대
wear away/down/off/out 마멸하다
weather [wéðər] 풍화시키다

Health Science 건강의학

administer [ədmínistər] 투약하다
aftereffect [ǽftərifékt] 여파, 후유증
anatomy [ənǽtəmi] 해부학
anesthesia [ænəsθíːʒə] 마취
anesthetic [ænəsθétik] 마취제
antibiotic [æntibaiátik] 항생 물질의
antibody [ǽntibádi] 항체
antidote [ǽntidòut] 해독제
antiseptic [æntəséptik] 방부제, 소독약
athlete's foot 무좀
barren [bǽrən] 불임의
belly [béli] 배, 복부(abdomen)
biovular twins 이란성 쌍둥이
bleeding [blíːdiŋ] 출혈
brain death 뇌사
brain fag 신경 쇠약
bronchi [bráŋkai] 기관지
caesarean section 제왕 절개 수술
carrier [kǽriər] 보균자
cerebellum [sèrəbéləm] 소뇌
cerebral [sérəbrəl] (대)뇌의
cerebral death 뇌사
chest [tʃest] 가슴뼈 주위의 가슴
choke [tʃouk] 숨이 막히다
chronic [kránik] 만성의
circulatory system 순환기
coagulation [kouǽgjəlèiʃən] (혈액의) 응고
coma [kóumə] 혼수 상태
complexion [kəmplékʃən] 안색
constipation [kánstipeiʃən] 변비
contagious [kəntéidʒəs] 전염성의
delivery [dílivəri] 분만, 출산
dermatology [dəːmətálədʒi] 피부과
diagnose [dáiəgnəuz] 진단하다
diagnosis [dáiəgnousis] 진단

diarrhea [dàiərí:ə] 설사
diet therapy 식이요법
disinfect [dìsinfékt] 소독하다
dose [dous] (약의) 1회 복용량
dyspepsia [dispépʃə] 소화불량
early detection of cancer 암의 조기발견
endoscopy [endáskəpi] 내시경 검사
epidemic [èpədémik] 전염병, 유행병, 역병
euthanasia [jù:θənéiʒiə] 안락사
gastric ulcer 위궤양
hereditary [hərédətèri] 유전(성)의
Human Immunodeficiency Virus (HIV)
인체 면역 결핍 바이러스
Hygiene [háidʒi:n] 위생학
hypnosis [hipnóusis] 최면
indigestion [ìndidʒéstʃən] 소화불량
internal medicine 내과
intoxication [intáksikèiʃən] 중독
latency period 잠복기
leprosy [léprəsi] 문둥병
malnutrition [mæ:lnju:tríʃən] 영양 실조
marrow [mǽrou] 골, 골수
medical certificate 진단서
membrane [mémbrein] 막
narcotic [nɑ:rkátik] 마취제
narcotism [nɑ́:rkətìzm] (마취 따위에 의한) 혼수
상태
nausea [nɔ́:ziə] 구역질
nursing staff 간호진
obesity [oubí:səti] 비만
obsession [əbséʃən] 강박 관념
obstetrics and gynecology 산부인과
ophthalmology [áfθælmálədʒi] 안과
orthopedics [ɔ̀:rθoupí:diks] 정형외과
otolaryngology [óutoulæriŋgá:lədʒi] 이비인
후과
paralysis [pərǽləsis] 마비

pediatrics [pediatrics] 소아과
pharmaceutical [fá:rməsú:tikəl] 조제의, 약학
의, 약제(사)의
plague [pleig] 역병
plastic surgery 성형 외과
recurrence [rikə́:rəns] 재발
respiratory [réspərətɔ̀:ri] 호흡의
saliva [səláivə] 침
sedative [sédətiv] 진정제
segregation [ségrigèiʃən] 격리, 분리
sex reversal 성전환
sore [sɔ:r] 상처, 종기, 아픈, 부은
sperm [spə:rm] 정자
sputum [spjú:təm] 가래, 타액
sterilization operation 불임 수술
stethoscope [stéθəskòup] 청진기
strain [strein] 피로, (심신의) 긴장
surgical instruments 수술도구
syncope [síŋkəpi] 졸도, 기절
tranquilizer [trǽŋkwəlàizər] 진정제
transfusion [trænsfjú:ʒən] 수혈
transplantation [trænsplǽnteiʃən] 이식 (수술)
ulcer [ʌ́lsər] 궤양
vaccination [vǽksənèiʃən] 예방 접종
vaccine [vǽksi(:)n] 백신
vegetable [védʒətəbl] 식물 인간
vertigo [və́:rtigòu] 현기증
ward [wɔ:rd] 병동, 병실
wisdom tooth 사랑니

Law 법학

accessory [æksésəri] 방조범
accuse [əkjú:z] 고소하다, 고발하다
Act [ækt] 법령, 조례
agreement [əgrí:mənt] 협정, 협약
amnesty [ǽmnəsti] 특사, 사면

arbitrator [áːrbitrèitər] 중재자
appeal [əpíːl] 항소하다, 상고하다
arrest warrant 체포영장
arson [áːrsn] 방화죄
autopsy [ɔ́ːtapsi] 부검, 검시
bail [beil] 보석(금)
blackmail [blǽkmeil] 공갈죄
bug [bʌɡ] 도청하다
bylaw [báilɔː] 규약, 회사내규
capital punishment 사형
civil law 민법
civil suit 민사 소송
code [koud] 법전, (사회의) 규범
commit [kəmít] 저지르다
complaint [kəmpléint] (민사의) 고소
confinement [kənfáinmənt] 금고형
conspiracy [kənspírəsi] 불법공모, 음모
constitution [kánstətjúːʃən] 헌법
contingency [kəntíndʒənsi] 우발적 사건
conviction [kənvíkʃən] 유죄의 판결
courtroom [kɔ́ːrtrum] 법정
criminal [krímənl] 범죄자
criminal law 형법
criminal suit 형사 소송
cross-examine (증인에게) 반대 심문하다
custody [kʌ́stədi] 구류형
death penalty 사형
default [difɔ́ːlt] 채무불이행, (법정에의) 결석
defense [diféns] 변호, 답변(서)
detention [diténʃən] 구류형
double jeopardy 일사부재리의 원칙
due process 적법절차
embezzle [imbézl] 횡령하다
enforce [enfɔ́ːrs] 집행하다, 시행하다
ex-convict [èkskánvikt] 전과자
execution [èksikjúːʃən] 사형집행, 강제집행
false charge 무고

felony [féləni] 중범죄
fine [fain] 벌금형
fraud [frɔːd] 사기죄
guilt [gilt] 유죄
hearing [híəriŋ] (법정에서의) 청문회
homicide [háməsàid] 살인죄
illegal [ilíːɡəl] 불법의
implication [implikéiʃən] 연루, 연좌
imprisonment [imprízənmənt] 금고형
indict [indáit] 기소하다, 고발하다
iniquity [iníkwəti] 불법행위, 죄
injustice [indʒʌ́stis] 부정, 불공평
innocence [ínəsns] 무죄
interrogation [intérəgèiʃən] 심문
jeopardy [dʒépərdi] (피고의) 유죄가 될 위험성
judge [dʒʌdʒ] 판사
judicial [dʒuːdíʃəl] 사법의
jury [dʒúəri] 배심(원단)
larceny [láːrsəni] 절도죄
lawsuit [lɔ́ːsúːt] 소송
lawyer [lɔ́ːjər] 변호사
life imprisonment 종신형
lose a suit 소송을 취하다
manipulate [mənípjulèit] 조작하다
misdemeanor [misdimíːnər] 경범죄
monetary penalty 벌금형
mute [mjuːt] (피고가) 묵비권을 행사하는
outlaw [áutlɔː] 상습범
penal [píːnəl] 형법의, 형벌의, 형사상의
petition [pitíʃən] 소장
perjury [pə́ːrdʒəri] 위증죄
plaintiff [pléintif] 원고
plea [pliː] 항변, (피고의) 답변
precedent [présədənt] 판례
principal [prínsəpəl] 정범, 주범
probation [proubéiʃən] 보호관찰
procedure [prəsíːdʒər] 소송절차

prosecution [pràsikjúːʃən] 기소, 고발
prosecutor [pràsikjùːtər] 검사
rape [reip] 강간죄
robbery [rábəri] 강도죄
search warrant 가택수색영장
sentence [séntəns] (형사상) 판결, 선고, 형벌
sexual harassment 성희롱
sue [suː] 제소하다
summon [sʌ́mən] 소환하다
suspect [səspékt] 용의자
suspended sentence 집행유예
suspicion [səspíʃən] 혐의
take the Fifth 묵비권을 행사하다
testimony [téstəmòuni] 증언
the judicature [dʒúːdikèitʃər] 사법부
verdict [vəːrdikt] (배심원이 판사에게 제출하는) 평결
violate [váiəlèit] 위반하다, 강간하다
warrant of attorney (소송) 위임장
warrant of attest 체포영장
witness [wítnis] 증인
writ [rit] 영장, 공문서

Linguistics 언어학

accent [ǽksent] 강세, 어조, 말투
accentuation [æksèntʃuèiʃən] 억양(법)
articulation [aːrtìkjuléiʃən] 조음
bilingual [bailíŋgwəl] 이중 언어의
classical diction 고전적 어법
cognate [kágneit] 어원이 같은, 동족어
cognition [kagníʃən] 인지
collocation [kàləkèiʃən] 연어, 말의 배열
colloquial [kəlóukwiəl] 구어의, 일상 회화의
complex word 합성어
conjugation [kàndʒəgèiʃən] 어형변화
contraction [kəntrǽkʃən] 축약
derivative [dirívətiv] 파생어

ellipsis [ilípsis] 생략, 생략 부호
etymology [ètəmálədʒi] 어원학
explosion [iksplóuʒən] (폐쇄음의) 파열
fricative [fríkətiv] 마찰음
homograph [háməgræf] 동형이의어
homonym [hámənìm] 동음이의어
homophone [háməfòun] 동음어
jargon [dʒáːrgən] 전문용어, 특수용어
language acquisition 언어 습득
lexicon [léksəkən] 어휘, 어휘 목록, 사전
linguist [líŋgwist] 언어학자
linguistic competence 언어능력
linguistic relativism 언어상대성이론
linguistic universalism 언어보편성이론
morpheme [mɔ́ːrfiːm] 형태소
morphology [mɔːrfálədʒi] 형태론, 어형론
narration [næréiʃən] 화법
nonverbal [nánvəːrbəl] 비언어의
oral cavity 구강
philology [filálədʒi] 문헌학, 언어학
phoneme [fóuniːm] 음소, 음운
phonetic alphabet 발음 기호
phonetics [fənétiks] 음성학
phonology [fənálədʒi] 음운론
predicate [prédikit] 술부
prefix [príːfiks] 접두사
prescriptive grammar 규범 문법
prolonged sound 연음
prosody [prásədi] 운율
rhetorical [ritɔ́(ː)rikəl] 수사학의
semantics [simǽntiks] 의미론
semivowel [sémiváuəl] 반모음
sign [sain] 기호, 암시
silent [sáilənt] 묵음의
speech organ 발음 기관
structural linguistics 구조주의 언어학
suffix [sʌ́fiks] 접미사

syntax [síntæks] 구문론, 통사론
three diphthong 삼중 모음
transformational grammar 변형 문법
generative grammar 생성 문법
unstressed syllable 비강세 음절
vernacular [vərnǽkjələr] 자국어

Literature 문학

abridge [əbrídʒ] (서적, 이야기 등을) 요약하다
allegory [ǽləgɔ̀ːri] 풍유, 우화
alliteration [əlítərèiʃən] 두운(법)
allusion [əlúːʒən] 암시
annotation [æ̀nətèiʃən] 주석
anonymous [ənánəməs] 익명의
anthology [ænθáləʤi] 명시 선집, 시집
archaic [aːrkéiik] (말이나 어법이) 고어체인
archetype [áːrkitàip] 전형, 원형
authenticity [ɔ̀ːθentísəti] 출처가 분명함, 진정함
authorship [ɔ́ːθərʃip] 원작자임, 저자
autobiography [ɔ̀ːtəbaiágrəfi] 자서전
bibliography [bìbliágrəfi] 저서 목록, 서지학
biography [baiágrəfi] 전기
catharsis [kəθáːrsis] 카타르시스
censorship [sénsərʃip] 검열
chronicle [kránikl] 연대기
civilized [sívəlàizd] 문명화된, 세련된
cliché [kli(ː)ʃéi] 판에 박은 문구, 진부한 표현
commentator [kámənteitər] 주석자
comparative literature 비교문학
compendium [kəmpéndiəm] 개요, 개론
copyright [kápirait] 판권, 저작권
crib [krib] 표절(물)
cynicism [sínisìzm] 냉소주의
decadence [dékədənsi] 타락, 퇴폐
deconstruction [dìːkənstrʌ́kʃən] 탈구축, 해체 비평

denouement [deinúːmənt] (소설, 희곡의) 대단원
derivative verse 파생적인 운문
dialect [dáiəlèkt] 방언, 사투리
dialectic [dàiəléktik] 변증법
draft [dræft] 초안, 초고
elegy [éləʤi] 애가, 비가, 엘레지
empiricism [empírəsìzəm] 경험주의
epic [épik] 서사시
epigram [épigræm] 경구, 풍자시
epitome [ipítəmi] 요약
eulogy [júːləʤi] 찬사, 칭송
excerpt [éksəːrpt] 인용구, 발췌
existentialism [èɡzisténʃəlizm] 실존주의
fable [féibl] 우화
fairy tale 동화
fiction [fíkʃən] 소설
flowery [fláuəri] 미사여구를 쓴
folklore [fóuklɔːr] 민간 전승, 민속(학)
genre [ʒáːnrə] 장르
gloss [glɔːs] 주석, 해설
hue and cry 고함 소리, 심한 비난
innuendo [ìnjuéndou] 암시, 풍자
installment [instɔ́ːlmənt] (연재물의) 1회분
irony [áirəni] 빈정댐, 풍자, 반어, 빗댐
libel [láibəl] 비방하는 글
light literature 대중문학
literacy [lítərəsi] 읽고 쓰는 능력
lyric [lírik] 서정시의, 서정적인
macabre horror 섬뜩한 공포
materialism [mətíəriəlizm] 유물론
metaphor [métəfɔ̀ːr] 은유
metaphysical [mètəfízikəl] 형이상학의
narrative [nǽrətiv] 이야기, 소설
ode [oud] 송시
orthography [ɔːrθágrəfi] 철자
paradox [pǽrədàks] 역설, 패러독스
paraphrase [pǽrəfrèiz] 바꾸어 말하다, 바꾸어

말하기

parody [pǽrədi] 패러디, 풍자적으로 개작하다
piracy [páiərəsi] 저작권 침해, 도용
pirate [páiərət] 저작권 침해자
plagiarism [pléidʒiərìzəm] 표절
plagiarize [pléidʒiəràiz] 도용(표절)하다
poem [póuəm] 시
poet [póuit] 시인
posthumous [pástʃuməs] 사후의,
proofread [prúːfrìːd] 교정보다
prose [prouz] 산문
protagonist [proutǽgənist] (소설, 희곡의) 주인공
pseudonym [súːdənim] 익명, 필명, 가명
punctuate [pʌ́ŋktʃuèit] 돋보이게 하다, 구두점을 찍다
recite [risáit] 낭독하다, 암송하다
revise [riváiz] 교정하다, 수정하다
rhetoric [rétərik] 수사학, 수사법
rhyme [raim] 각운
royalty [rɔ́iəlti] 인세, 저작권사용료
satire [sǽtaiər] 풍자, 풍자문학, 풍자작품
setting [sétiŋ] (소설, 희곡의) 배경
stenography [stənágrəfi] 속기
sonnet [sánət] 소네트(14행시)
stereotype [stériətàip] 상투적인 문구, 고정 관념
structuralism [strʌ́ktʃərəlizm] 구조주의
style [stail] 문체
stylist [stáilist] 문장가, 명문가
subscribe [səbskráib] 정기 구독하다
syllabus [síləbəs] 개요, 강의시간표
synopsis [sinápsis] 줄거리
terse [təːrs] (문체, 표현이) 간결한
verse [vəːrs] 운문
version [vəːrʒən] 번역(서)
wit [wit] 기지, 위트

Mathematics 수학

addition [ədíʃən] 덧셈
algebra [ǽldʒəbrə] 대수학
algorithm [ǽlgərìðəm] 연산(법)
arc [aːrk] 호, 포물선
arithmetic [əríθmətik] 산술
calculation [kælkjuléiʃən] 계산
calculus [kǽlkjuləs] 미적분학
central angle 중심각
circle [sə́ːrkl] 원
circumference [sərkʌ́mfərəns] 원주, 원둘레
cone [koun] 원뿔
count [kaunt] 계산하다
convergent [kənvə́ːrdʒənt] 한 점에 모이는
cube [kjuːb] 세제곱
cylinder [sílindər] 원기둥
decimal [désəməl] 소수
decimal system 10진법(체계)
degree [digríː] 각도
diagonal (line) [daiǽgənəl] 대각선, 사선
diameter [daiǽmitər] (원, 구체 등의) 지름, 직경
division [divíʒən] 나눗셈
dozen [dʌ́zn] 12 (의)
ellipse [ilíps] 타원
equation [i(ː)kwéiʒən] 방정식
even number 짝수
figure [fígjər] 도형, 숫자
fraction [frǽkʃən] 분수
function [fʌ́ŋkʃən] 함수
geometry [dʒiːámətri] 기하학
heptagon [héptəgàn] 칠각형
hexagon [héksəgàn] 육각형
imaginary number 허수
level [lévəl] 수평의
matrix [méitriks] 행렬
minus [máinəs] ~을 뺀, 마이너스의

multiplication [mʌltəplikéiʃən] 곱셈
octagon [ɔ́ktəgənˋ] 팔각형
odd number 홀수
par [pɑːr] 등가, 동등, 동위
parabola [pərǽbələ] 포물선
parallel [pǽrəlèl] 평행의
parallelogram [pærəléləgræm] 평행사변형
pentagon [péntəgàn] 오각형
periphery [pərí:fəri] (원, 곡선 등의) 둘레
perpendicular [pəˋːrpəndíkjələr] 수직의, 직각으로 교차하는
plus [plʌs] ~을 더한, 플러스
prism [prizəm] 각기둥
probability [prábəbíləti] 확률
pyramid [píræmìd] 각뿔
quadrangle [kwádræŋgl] 사각형
radius [réidiəs] 반지름
real number 실수
reckon [rékən] 계산하다
rectangle [réktæŋgl] 직사각형
rhombus [rámbəs] 마름모
sector [séktər] 부채꼴
set [set] 집합
subtraction [səbtrǽkʃən] 뺄셈
sphere [sfiər] 구
square [skweər] 제곱, 정사각형
statistics [stətístiks] 통계학
tImes [taimz] ~을 곱하여
trapezoid [trǽpəzɔid] 사다리꼴
triangle [tráiæŋgəl] 삼각형
variable [véəriəbl] 변수
vertical [vəˊːrtikəl] 수직의
width [widθ] 넓이

Marine Biology 해양 생물학

abysmal [əbízməl] 심해의

algae [ǽlgə] 조류
aquanaut [ǽkwənɔ̀ːt] 해저 탐험가
aquarium [əkwéəriəm] 해양 수족관
bay [bei] 만
buoy [búːi] 부표
cape [keip] 곶
carp [kɑːrp] 잉어
clam [klæm] 대합조개
crustacean [krʌstéiʃən] 갑각류 동물
culture pond 양식지
dorsal fin 등지느러미
ebb [eb] 썰물
eddy [édi] 소용돌이
fishery [fíʃəri] 어업, 수산업
flipper [flipə(r)] 물갈퀴
herring [hériŋ] 청어
lobster [lábstər] 바다가재
nekton [néktən] 유영 동물
otter [átər] 수달
phytoplankton [fáitouplǽŋktən] 식물성 플랑크톤
plankton [plǽŋktən] 플랑크톤
sardine [sɑːrdíːn] 정어리
seal [síːl] 바다표범
squid [skwid] 오징어
starfish [stɑːrfiʃ] 불가사리
strait [streit] 해협
the silver carp 붕어
undercurrent [ʌ́ndərkəˋːrənt] (해류의) 저류
zooplankton [zòuəplǽŋktən] 동물성 플랑크톤

Medical Science 의학

acquired [əkwáiərd] 후천성의
amnesia [æmníːʒə] 기억 상실, 건망증
anemia [əníːmiə] 빈혈
arthritis [ɑːrθráitis] 관절염

asthma [ǽzmə] 천식
brain storm 정신착란
breast cancer 유방암
bruise [bruːz] 타박상, 멍
cardiac [káːrdiæk] 심장(병)의
cataract [kǽtərækt] 백내장
depression [dipréʃən] 우울증
diabetes [dàiəbíːtis] 당뇨병
gastric ulcer 위궤양
glaucoma [glɔːkóumə] 녹내장
heart attack 심장마비
hepatitis [hèpətáitis] 간염
high blood pressure 고혈압
hygienics [hàidʒiéniks] 위생학
hyperopia [háipəróupiə] 원시
insomnia [insámniə] 불면증
internist [intəːrnist] 내과의사
leukemia [luːkíːmiə] 백혈병
manic depression 조울증
measles [míːzlz] 홍역
mental illness 정신질환
myopia [maióupiə] 근시
neuralgia [njuərældʒə] 신경통
neurosis [njuəróusis] 노이로제
onset [ɔ́nset] 발병, 징후
pain reliever 진통제
painkiller [péinkílər] 진통제
panacea [pænəsíːə] 만병통치약
phobia [fóubiə] 공포증
physician [fizíʃən] 외과
pneumonia [njumóunjə] 폐렴
polio [póuliòu] 소아마비
prescription [priskrípʃən] 처방전
progressive [prəgrésiv] 진행형의
psychiatry [saikáiətri] 정신과
psychopath [sáikoupæθ] 정신병자
recuperate [rikjúːpərèit] (병에서) 회복하다

regressive [rigrésiv] 퇴행성의
remedy [rémədi] 치료
scurvy [skəːrvi] 괴혈병
smallpox [smɔ́ːlpaks] 천연두
sneeze [sniːz] 재채기
sore throat 인후염
surgeon [səːrdʒən] 외과의사
surgery [səːrdʒəri] 외과, 수술
trauma [trɔːmə] (정신적) 충격, 외상
tuberculosis [tjubəːrkjəlóusis] 결핵
stroke [strouk] 뇌졸증

Meteorology 기상학

air current 기류
air mass 기단
anorexia [ænəréksiə] 거식증
anticyclone [ǽntisáikloun] 고기압
arid [ǽrid] 건조한, 불모의
atmosphere [ǽtməsfiər] 대기
atmospheric pressure 기압
autumnal equinox 추분
avalanche [ǽvəlæntʃ] 눈사태
barometric pressure 기압
below freezing 영하
blast [blæst] 돌풍
bleak [bliːk] (날씨, 바람이) 매섭게 찬
blizzard [blízərd] 눈보라
bulimia [bjuːlímiə] 폭식증
Celsius [sélsiəs] 섭씨
chilly [tʃíli] 으슬으슬 추운
climate [kláimit] 기후
cloudburst [kláudbəːrst] 갑작스런 호우
cold front 한랭전선
condense [kəndéns] 응축하다
continental climate 대륙성 기후
cyclone [sáikloun] 사이클론

damp [dæmp] 습한
deluge [déljuːdʒ] 대홍수
dense [dens] 밀도가 높은
desert climate 사막 기후
dew [djuː] 이슬
downfall [dáunfɔːl] 강우, 강설
downpour [dáunpɔːr] 큰 소나기, 호우
dreary [dríəri] 을씨년스러운
drizzle [drízl] 이슬비
droplet [draplit] 작은 물방울
drought [draut] 가뭄
equinox [íːkwənáks] 주야 평점시, 춘분, 추분
evaporate [ivǽpərèit] 증발하다
fallout [fɔ́ːlaut] 낙진
Fahrenheit [fǽrənhàit] 화씨
flood [flʌd] 홍수
fog [fɔ(ː)g] 안개
forecast [fɔ́ːrkæst] 예상, 예보
frigid [frídʒid] 얼어붙을 듯이 추운
frost [frɔːst] 서리
funnel cloud 깔대기 모양의 구름
gale [geil] 강풍
glacial epoch 빙하기
glacier [gléiʃər] 빙하
gust [gʌst] 돌풍
hail [heil] 우박
hailstorm [héilstɔːrm] 우박을 동반한 폭풍
halcyon [hǽlsiən] 온화한, 평온한
haze [heiz] 아지랑이
heat wave 열파
highland climate 고산성 기후
high pressure 고기압
humidity [hjuːmídəti] 습기, 습도
hurricane [həːrəkèin] 대폭풍, 허리케인
icecap [áiskæp] 만년설
inclement [inklémənt] (날씨가) 험한, 혹독한
inclement weather 악천후

interstellar matter 성간물질
inundation [ínəndèiʃən] 범람, 침수
inverted [invəːrtid] 거꾸로 된, 역의, 전도된
lightning rod 피뢰침
meteorologist [mìːtiərálədʒist] 기상학자
mission [míʃən] 우주 비행 계획, 임무
mist [mist] 연무, 엷은 안개
moisture [mɔ́istʃər] 습기, 수분
monsoon climate 계절풍 기후
oceanic climate 해양성 기후
overcast [óuvərkæst] 아주 흐린
parched [paːrtʃt] (땅 등이) 바짝 마른
polar climate 극지적 기후
precipitation [prisìpətéiʃən] 강우, 강우량, 강설량
pressure [préʃər] 압력, 기압
scorching [skɔːrtʃiŋ] 몹시 뜨거운
serene [siríːn] 화창한
shiver [ʃívər] 추위로 떨다, 전율하다
shower [ʃáuər] 소나기
sleet [sliːt] 진눈깨비
snowstorm [snóustɔːrm] 눈보라
soaked [soukt] 흠뻑 젖은
solidify [səlídəfài] 굳다, 응고하다
spring equinox 춘분
sprinkle [spríŋkl] 가랑비
squall [skwɔːl] 돌풍, 스콜
stuffy [stʌ́fi] 통풍이 안 되는, 무더운
subarctic climate 아한대 기후
subtropical climate 아열대 기후
sultry [sʌ́ltri] 후덥지근한
summer solstice 하지
sweltering [swéltəriŋ] (숨이 막힐 정도로) 무더운
temperate climate 온대성 기후
tempest [témpist] 폭풍우, 폭설
thunderstorm [θʌ́ndərstɔːrm] 천둥 번개를 동반한 폭우
tornado [tɔːrnéidou] 대선풍

torrential rain 호우
torrid [tɔ́ːrid] 타는 듯이 뜨거운
track [træk] 추적하다, 찾아내다
trade wind 무역풍
trade wind 무역풍
trough [trɔ(ː)f] 기압골
tropical climate 열대성 기후
typhoon [taifúːn] 태풍
warm front 온난전선
water particle 물의 미립자
Weather Bureau 기상청
westerlies 편서풍
wind chill (factor) 체감기온
wind direction 풍향
wind velocity 풍속

Music 음악

accompaniment [əkʌ́mpənimənt] 반주
acoustics [əkúːstiks] 음향학
ad lib 즉흥 연주
anthem [ǽnθəm] 성가, 송가
appreciation [əpriːʃiéiʃən] (예술품의) 평가, 이해
aria [áːriə] 오페라 등의 반주 있는 독창곡
arpeggio [aːrpédʒiòu] 화음을 빨리 연속적으로 연주하기
arrange [əréindʒ] 편곡하다
arrangement [əréindʒmənt] 편곡
ballad [bǽləd] 민요
beat [biːt] 박자
bow [bou] (현악기를) 연주하다
brass [bræs] 금관악기
cacophony [kækáfəni] 불협화음
chamber music 실내악
choir [kwáiər] 합창단
chord [kɔːrd] 현, 화음
chromatic [kroumǽtik] 반음계의

clef [klef] 음자리표
compose [kəmpóuz] 작곡하다
composer [kəmpóuzər] 작곡가
composed [kəmpóuzd] 침착한, 차분한
composition [kámpəzíʃən] (음악) 작곡
concertgoer [kánsə(ː)rtgóuər] 음악 애호가
concerto [kəntʃértou] 협주곡
concord [kánkərd] 화성
concours [kaŋkúər] 경연, 콩쿠르
conductor [kəndʌ́ktər] 지휘자
conservatory [kənsə́ːrvətɔ̀ːri] 음악학교, 예술학교
contralto [kəntrǽltou] 여성 최저음
counterpoint [káuntərpɔ̀int] 대위법
duet [djuét] 이중창, 이중주
dynamic mark 셈여림표
ensemble [aːnsáːmbl] 2부 이상의 합창(곡)
enthusiasm [enθjúːziæzəm] 열정
execution [èksikjúːʃən] 연주솜씨
fiddle [fídl] 바이올린
field holler (흑인의) 노동요
fingering [fíŋɡəriŋ] 운지법, 운지 기호
folk tune 민요
harmonious [haːrmóuniəs] 협화음의, 화성의
harpsichord [háːrpsikɔ̀ːrd] 하프시코드(건반 악기)
improvisation [impràvəzéiʃən] 즉흥 연주
instrument [ínstrəmənt] 악기
inventiveness [invéntivnis] 독창성
lyric [lírik] 가사
major [méidʒər] 장조 음계의
march [maːrtʃ] 행진곡
marine band 해군 군악대
masterpiece [mǽstərpìːs] 명작, 걸작
melody [mélədi] 선율, 가락
minimalism [mínəməlizm] 최소 악기편성
minor [máinər] 단조 음계의
motif [moutíːf] 주제

movement [múːvmənt] 악장
musical literature 음악 서적
musical notation 기보법
national anthem 국가
note [nout] 음표, 음조
octave [áktiv] 음역
opera [ápərə] 오페라
opus [óupəs] 음악 작품
oratorio [ɔ̀(ː)rətɔ́ːrìou] 성담곡
orchestra [ɔ́ːrkəstrə] 관현악
overture [óuvərtʃər] 서곡, 전주곡
percussion [pərkʌ́ʃən] 타악기
performance [pərfɔ́ːrməns] 연주
philharmonic [filhɑːrmánik] 교향악단(의)
phonograph record 음반
piece [piːs] 작품
pluck [plʌk] (현악기를) 타다, 뜯다
polyphony [pəlífəni] 다성음악
prelude [préljuːd] 서막
read music 악보를 읽다
recital [risáitl] 독주회
recorder [rékərdər] 피리(옛날 플루트의 일종)
refrain [rifréin] 후렴(구)
rehearsal time 연습 시간
resident [rézidənt] 전속의
rhythm [ríðəm] 장단
rhythm and blues 리듬 앤 블루스(R&B)
scale [skeil] 음계
score [skɔːr] 악보
side-blown 옆으로 부는
single note (음악에서) 하나의 음
solemn [sáləm] 장엄한
solemnity [səlémnəti] 엄숙, 장엄
strike [straik] (음, 악기 등을) 때려서 울리다
string [striŋ] (오케스트라의) 현악기
string quartet 현악 4중주
symphony [símfəni] 교향악

synthesizer [sínθəsàizər] (소리) 합성장치
tempo [témpou] 속도
threnody [θrénədi] 비가, 애가
timbre [tímbər] 음색
tone [toun] 음조, 음색
tone-deaf 음치의
tune [tjuːn] 음조, 선율
undertone [ʌ́ndərtoun] 저음
upbeat [ʌ́pbiːt] 여린박, 약박
variation [vèəriéiʃən] 편곡, 변주
vocal [vóukəl] 음성의
vocalization [vòukəlaizéiʃən] 발성법
wind instrument 관악기
woodwind [wúdwind] 목관악기
word [wəːrd] 가사

Oceanography 해양학

Antarctic Ocean 남극해
Arctic Ocean 북극해
Atlantic Ocean 대서양
circulation [sə̀ːrkjuléiʃən] 순환
continental shelf 대륙붕
counterclockwise [kàuntərklakwàiz] 반시계 방향으로
current [kə́ːrənt] 조류, 흐름
downwelling [dáunwèliŋ] 용하, 하강류
drift [drɪft] 떠다니다, 표류하다
gyre [dʒaiər] 회전, 소용돌이
Indian Ocean 인도양
mooring [muəriŋ] 계류, 정박
Northern Hemisphere 북반구
ocean floor 해저
Pacific Ocean 태평양
peak [piːk] 꼭대기
photic zone (해면 아래의) 투광대
plain [plein] 평평한

ridge [ridʒ] 능선, 산마루 융기 부분
saliferous [səlífərəs] 염분을 함유하는, 염분이 생기는
salimeter [sælímitər] 염도계
salinity [səlínəti] 염분, 염도
seamount [síːmàunt] 해산
submarine valley 해저 협곡
submersible [səbmə́ːrsəbl] 잠수할 수 있는
tidal energy 조수 에너지
tidal wave 해일
tide [taid] 조수
topography [toupágrəfi] 지형학, 지형도
trench [trentʃ] 해구
thermocline [θə́ːrməklàin] (수온이 급격히 변하는) 변온층
tsunami [tsunáːmiː] 해일, 쓰나미
upwelling [ʌ́pwèliŋ] (심해수 등의) 용승
valley [vǽli] 골짜기
wave [weiv] 파도
whirlpool [wə́ːrlpùːl] 소용돌이

isolation theory 격리설
Jurassic period 쥐라기
kill off 멸종시키다
law of inheritance 유전법칙
mammoth [mǽməθ] 맘모스
ornithology [ɔ̀ːrnəθálədʒi] 조류학
progenitor [proudʒénətər] (생물학적) 선조, (동식물의) 원조
progeny [prɔ́dʒəni] 후손, 자손
pterosaur [térousɔːr] 익룡
resemble [rizémbl] 닮다
rib [rib] 갈빗대
sebaceous gland 피지선
skeleton [skélətn] 뼈대, 골격
speciation [spìːʃiéiʃən] 종의 형성
tail vertebra 꼬리 척추골
tusk [tʌsk] (코끼리 등의) 엄니
trilobite [tráiləbàit] 삼엽충
wishbone [wíʃboun] 위시본, 차골

Paleontology 고생물학

ammonite [ǽmənàit] 암모나이트
anachronism [ənǽkrənìzəm] 시대착오, 연대의 오기
ancestral [ænséstrəl] 조상의
archaeopteryx [àːrkiáptəriks] 시조새
archive [áːrkaiv] 고문서, 고문서에 관한
burial site 매장지, 무덤
cuneiform [kjúːniəfɔ̀ːrm] 설형문자(의)
date [deit] 연대를 추정하다
degeneration [didʒènəréiʃən] 퇴화
evolution theory 진화론
feature [fíːtʃər] 특징
fossil organisms 고생물
hieroglyph [háiərəglìf] 상형 문자

Philosophy 철학

analogy [ənǽlədʒi] 유추, 유추법
antecedent [æntəsíːdnt] 전제의, 가정의
association [əsòusiéiʃən] 연상, 관련
conclusion [kənklúːʒən] 결론
conjecture [kəndʒéktʃər] 유추
connotation [kánoutéiʃən] 함축, 내포
contradiction [kántrədíkʃən] 모순, 자가당착
counterargument [káuntərá:rgjəmənt] 반박, 반론
deduction [didʌ́kʃən] 연역법
denotation [dìːnoutéiʃən] 외연, 명시적 의미
determinism [ditə́ːrmənìzm] 결정론
dialectic [dàiəléktik] 변증법
dichotomy [daikátəmi] 이분법
empiricism [impírəsìzm] 경험론

empiricist [impírəsIst] 경험론자
epistemology [ipìstəmálədʒi] 인식론
fallacy [fǽləsi] 논리적 오류
gist [dʒist] 요지
hedonics [hi:dániks] 쾌락론
humanism [hjú:mənizəm] 인본주의, 휴머니즘
humanitarianism [hju:mænitéəriənìzm] 인도주의
hypothesis [haipáθəsis] 가설, 가정
idealism [aidí:əlìzəm] 관념론
ideology [àidiálədʒi] 이데올로기, (사회, 정치적) 이념
implication [ìmplikéiʃən] 암시, 함축
inconsistency [ìnkənsístənsi] 모순
induction [indʌ́kʃən] 귀납법
inference [ínfərəns] 유추
materialism [mətíəriəlizəm] 유물론
middle [mídl] 중명사
ontology [antálədʒi] 존재론
pantheism [pǽnθìizəm] 범신론
paradigm [pǽrədàim] 전형, 패러다임
parallelism [pǽrəlelìzəm] 평행, 병행론
pessimism [pésəmìzəm] 염세주의, 비관주의
positivism [pázətivìzəm] 실증주의
premise [prémis] 전제
proposition [pràpəzíʃən] 명제
reasoning [rí:zəniŋ] 추리, 추론, 논증
skepticism [sképtəsìzm] 회의론
skeptic [sképtik] 회의론자
sophism [sáfizm] 궤변(법)
sophist [sáfist] 궤변론자, (고대 그리스의) 철학자
statement [stéitmənt] 진술, 주장
stoicism [stóuisìzm] 스토아 철학, 금욕
structuralism [strʌ́ktʃərəlìzm] 구조주의
substance [sʌ́bstəns] 본질, 실체
syllogism [sílədʒìzəm] 삼단논법
term [tə:rm] 명사

theism [θí:izəm] 유신론
undistributed [ʌndistríbju:tid] 부주연의
utilitarianism [ju:tìlətéəriənìzəm] 공리주의

Physics 물리학

application [æplikéiʃən] 응용, 적용
accelerated velocity 가속도
action and inaction 작용과 반작용
alternating current 교류
amplitude of vibration 진폭
ammeter [ǽmmì:tər] 전류계, 암페어계
anaclastic [ænəklǽstik] 굴절의
annihilation [ənáiəlèiʃən] 소멸
anode [ǽnoud] 양극
buoyancy [bɔ́iənsi] 부력
capillarity [kæpəlǽrəti] 모세관 현상
cathode [kǽθoud] 음극
centrifugal force 원심력
centripetal force 구심력
charge [tʃa:rdʒ] 충전, 전하
concave lens 오목 렌즈
conduction [kəndʌ́kʃən] 전도
conductor [kəndʌ́ktər] 도체
convex lens 볼록 렌즈
critical mass 임계량
density [dénsəti] 밀도
deposit [dipázit] 침전하다
deviation [dì:viéiʃən] (광선의) 굴곡, 평향
diameter [daiǽmitər] 직경, 지름
direct current 직류
discharge [distʃá:rdʒ] 방전
dynamics [dainǽmiks] 역학
elasticity [ilæstísəti] 탄성
electrode [iléktroud] 전극
electromagnetic wave 전자기파
electron [iléktran] 전자

electronics [ilèktrániks] 전자공학
fission [fíʃən] (원자의) 핵분열
flexibility [flèksəbíləti] 신축성, 유연성
fluctuation [flʌ́ktʃuèiʃən] 파동
fluid [flúːid] 유동체, 유체
force [fɔːrs] 힘
free fall 자유낙하
freezing point 빙점
friction [fríkʃən] 마찰
fusion [fjúːʒən] 융합
generate [dʒénərèit] 발전하다
generator [dʒénərèitər] 발전기
hydrodynamics [háidroudainǽmiks] 유체역학
inertia [inə́ːrʃiə] 관성
infrared rays 적외선
kinetic energy 운동에너지
lever [lévər] 지렛대
magnetic field 자기장
magnetic force 자력
magnetism [mǽgnətìzəm] 자력
malleability [mæliəbíləti] (금속의) 가단성
mass [mæs] 질량
mechanical energy 역학적 에너지
mechanics [məkǽniks] 역학
melting point 융해점
meson [mézan] 중간자
molecule [máləkjùːl] 분자
neutralize [njúːtrəlàiz] 중화하다
neutron [njúːtran] 중성자
optics [áptiks] 광학
pendulum [péndʒuləm] 진자, 추
potential energy 위치에너지
pressure [préʃər] 압력
proton [próutan] 양성자
quantum [kwántəm] 양자
radiant energy 복사 에너지

radiation [rèidiéiʃən] 방사, 복사선
radius [réidiəs] 반경, 반지름
reduction [ridʌ́kʃən] 환원, 환산
reflection [riflékʃən] 반사
refraction [rifrǽkʃən] 굴절
resonance [rézənəns] (장의) 공진, 공명
semiconductor [sèmikəndʌ́ktər] 반도체
sound wave 음파
specific gravity 비중
strain [strein] 변형, 당김, 찌그러짐
surface tension 표면 장력
symmetrize [símətràiz] 대칭이 되게 하다
terminal [təːrmənəl] (전자의) 단자, 전극
the theory of relativity 상대성 이론
torsion [tɔ́ːrʃən] 염력, 비트는 힘
universal gravitation 만유인력
ultraviolet rays 자외선
vacuum [vǽkjuəm] 진공
velocity [vəlásəti] 속도
vibration [vaibréiʃən] 진자의 진동
visible rays 가시광선
voltage [vóultidʒ] 전압
voltmeter [vóultmìːtər] 전압계
volume [váljuːm] 체적
wavelength [wéivlèŋkθ] 파장

Physiology 생리학

abdomen [ǽbdəmən] 배, 복부
abortion [əbɔ́ːrʃən] 낙태
acute [əkjúːt] 급성의
ambidextrous [æmbidékstrəs] 양손잡이의
antibiotic [æntibaiátik] 항생물질, 항생물질의
antiseptic [æntəséptik] 방부제, 소독약, 살균된
aorta [eiɔ́ːrtə] 대동맥
artery [áːrtəri] 동맥
biological clock 생체시계

birth control pill 피임약
bleeding [bli:diŋ] 출혈
bosom [búzəm] 가슴
bowel [báuəl] 장
breast [brest] 가슴
brain-washing 세뇌
bronchus [bráŋkəs] 기관지
cerebellum [sèrəbéləm] 소뇌
cerebrum [sérəbrəm] 대뇌
circulatory organ 순환기
contagion [kəntéidʒən] 전염, 감염
contraceptive (pill) [kántrəséptiv] 피임약
corporal [kɔ́:rpərəl] 육체의
cranium [kréiniəm] 두개골
denture [déntʃər] 틀니, 의치
disorder [disɔ́:rdər] 장애, 가벼운 병
epidermis [èpədə́:rmis] 외피, 표피
esophagus [isáfəgəs] 식도
excrement [ékskrəmənt] 배설물
fast [fæst] 단식하다
fit [fit] 발작
germ [dʒə:rm] 세균
heartbeat [há:rtbi:t] 심장의 고동
hypnosis [hipnóusis] 최면
immunity [imjú:nəti] 면역
influenza [ìnfluénzə] 독감
inoculate [inákjuleit] 예방접종하다
intake [inteɪk] 섭취량
intestine [intéstin] 창자
joint [dʒɔint] 관절
kidney [kídni] 신장, 콩팥
large intestine 대장
lethargy [léθərdʒi] 혼수 상태, 무기력
limb [lim] 팔, 다리, 날개
liver [lívər] 간
lymphatic [limfǽtik] 임파선
mammary [mǽməri] 유방의

marrow [mǽrou] 골수
migraine [máigrein] 편두통
miscarriage [miskǽridʒ] 유산
nasal [néizəl] 코의
nostril [nástrəl] 콧구멍
skull [skʌl] 두개골
ointment [ɔ́intmənt] 연고
ovary [óuvəri] 난소
palliate [pǽlièit] (증상만) 완화시키다
pancreas [pǽŋkriəs] 이자, 췌장
pregnancy [prégnənsi] 임신
regimen [rédʒəmən] 식이요법
respiratory organ 호흡기
sanitary [sǽnətèri] 위생적인
secrete [sikrí:t] 분비하다
sex reversal 성전환
side effect 부작용
small intestine 소장
spinal cord 척수
spine [spain] 척추
sputum [spjú:təm] 가래
stomach [stʌ́mək] 위
surfeit [sə́:rfit] 과식
symptom [símptəm] 증상
syncope [síŋkəpi] 기절
thyroid gland 갑상선
transfusion [trænsfjú:ʒən] 수혈
vaccinate [vǽksənèit] 예방접종하다
vein [vein] 정맥
wisdom-tooth 사랑니

Politics 정치학

abolition [æbəlíʃən] (법률, 제도, 조직 등의) 폐지
abstention [æbsténʃən] 기권
address [ədrés] 연설(하다)
aide [eid] (대통령의) 보좌관, 조력자

airspace [éərspèis] 영공
appointment [əpɔ́intmənt] 임명
autarchy [ɔ́ːtɑːrki] 독재권
authority [əθɔ́ːrəti] 당국
autonomy [ɔːtánəmi] 자치(권)
ballot box 투표함, 무기명 투표
bicameral [baikǽmərəl] 상하양원제의
bureaucracy [bjuərákrəsi] 관료정치
by-election 보궐선거
cabinet [kǽbənit] 내각
campaign [kæmpéin] 선거운동
candidate [kǽndidèit] 후보자
canvass [kǽnvəs] (선거 전) 여론조사, 유세(하다)
communism [kámjunìzm] 공산주의
Congress [káŋgris] (미국) 국회
consul [kánsəl] 영사
debate [dibéit] 토론하다
delegate [déligət] 대의원, 대표자
demagogue [déməgàg] 선동 정치가
democracy [dimákrəsi] 민주주의
deputy [dépjuti] 대리인
frontier [frʌntíər] 국경
hard-liner 강경파
hegemony [hidʒéməni] 헤게모니, 지배권
impasse [ímpæs] 난국, 곤경
inaugural [inɔ́ːgjərəl] 취임연설, 취임식의
inaugurate [inɔ́ːgjərèit] 취임식을 거행하다
independent [ìndipéndənt] 무소속 국회의원
official [əfíʃəl] 공무원
opposition party 야당
oppression [əpréʃən] 억압
ouster [austə(r)] 추방, 축출
parliament [páːrləmənt] (영국) 의회
petition [pətíʃən] 탄원, 청원
plurality [pluərǽləti] 과반수
political impasse 정치적 난국
publicize [pʌ́bləsàiz] 공표하다

protocol [próutəkɔ̀ːl] 의정서, 조약
poll [poul] 투표 결과
ratify [rǽtəfài] 비준하다
referendum [rèfəréndəm] 국민투표
rehabilitation [rìːhəbìlətèiʃən] 복위, 복직
riot [ráiət] 폭동, 분규
secession [siséʃən] 탈당
senator [sénətər] 상원의원
sovereignty [sávərənti] 주권
stalemate [stéilmeit] 교착상태, 궁지
status quo 현상
stopgap [stá:pgæp] 임시방편, 미봉책
subject peoples 피지배 민족
suffrage [sʌ́fridʒ] 참정권
summit conference 정상회담
the House 상원, 하원
totalitarianism [toutælitéəriənìzm] 전체주의
unanimous [juːnǽnəməs] 만장일치의
vote [vout] 투표

Psychology 심리학

abnegation [æ̀bnigèiʃən] 금욕, 극기
awareness [əwéərnis] 자각
consumer psychology 소비심리학
drive [draiv] 동기, 동인
ego [íːgou] 자아
egocentrism [ìːgouséntrizm] 자기 중심성
egoism [íːgouìzm] 이기주의
extrovert [ékstrəvə̀ːrt] 외향적인 사람
feedback [fíːdbæk] 반응, 의견
frustration [frʌstreiʃən] 좌절
hang-up 콤플렉스, 심적장애
identity crisis 자기 정체감의 위기
inconsistency [ìnkənsístənsi] 모순
instinct [ínstiŋkt] 본능
introvert [íntrəvə̀ːrt] 내성적인 사람

motivation [mòutəvéiʃən] 동기, 주기
negative reinforcement 부정적 강화
nonverbal communication 비언어적 의사소통
norm [nɔːrm] (행동의) 기준
pedagogue [pédəgàg] 교육자, 교사
repression [ripréʃən] 억압, 억압 본능
resistance [rizístəns] 반감
self-fulfillment 자기 충족
stereotype [stériətàip] 고정관념
stimulus [stímjələs] 자극
therapy [θérəpi] 요법

Religion 종교

advent [ǽdvent] 그리스도의 강림, 도래
Adventism [ǽdventìzm] 그리스도 재림설
archbishop [aːrtʃbíʃəp] 대주교
apocalypse [əpákəlìps] 계시, 묵시
apostle [əpásl] 사도
atheism [éiθiìzəm] 무신론
atheist [éiθiist] 무신론자
Baptist Church 침례교
blasphemy [blǽsfəmi] 신성모독
Buddhism [búːdizəm] 불교
Buddhist [búːdist] 불교신자, 불교도
cardinal [káːrdənl] 추기경
Catholicism [kəθálisìzm] 카톨릭교, 천주교
chapel [tʃǽpəl] 예배당
Christianity [krìstʃiǽnəti] 그리스도교, 기독교
circumcision [sèːrkəmsíʒən] 할례
clergyman [kləːrdʒimən] 성직자
Confucianism [kənfjúʃənìzm] 유교
convert [kənvəːrt] 개종자, (그리스도교로) 개종시키다
deification [dìːəfəkéiʃən] 신격화, 신성화
denomination [dinàmənéiʃən] 종파
diabolism [daiǽbəlìzm] 악마주의

disciple [disáipl] 제자, 사도, 신봉자
doom [duːm] 최후의 심판, 파멸
doomsday [dúːmzdèi] 최후의 심판날
Easter [íːstər] 부활절
eschatology [èskətálədʒi] 종말론
heterodox [hétərədáks] 이단의, 이교의
Hindi [híndiː] 힌두교의
Hinduism [híndùːizəm] 힌구교
immolation [ímələièʃən] 제물, 희생
infidel [ínfədl] (그리스도교의) 불신자, 이교도
Islam [ísləːm] 이슬람교
Judaism [dʒúːdiìzm] 유대교
karma [káːrmə] 인연, 업보
malediction [mæ̀lədíkʃən] 저주, 악담, 욕
martyr [máːrtər] (기독교의) 순교자
martyrdom [máːrtərdəm] 순교
mass [mæs] (로마 카톨릭교) 미사
meditation [mèdətéiʃən] 명상
minister [mínistər] 목사, 성직사
mission [míʃən] 선교하다, 성령을 보냄
missionary [míʃənèri] 선교사
monotheism [mánəθiːìzm] 일신교
Muslim [mʌzlim] 이슬람교도
New Testament 신약성서
nirvana [niərváːnə] 열반
Old Testament 구약성서
omnipotence [amnípətəns] 전능
orthodox [ɔ́ːrθədák] 정통(파)의
pagan [péigən] 무종교자, 비기독교도
parish [pǽriʃ] 교구
persecution [pə̀ːrsikjúːʃən] 박해
piety [páiəti] 신앙심
pilgrim [pílgrim] 성지순례자
pious [páiəs] 독실한
polytheism [páliθiːìzm] 다신교
primitive religion 원시종교
profane [prəféin] 불경스러운

Protestantism [prátəstəntìzm] 신교
providence [právədəns] 신, 섭리
province [právins] (교회, 수도회의) 관구
rabbi [rǽbai] (유대교의) 지도자, 율법학자
redemption [ridémpʃən] 구원
reincarnation [rìːinkáːrneiʃən] 윤회, 환생
religious cult 사이비 종교
religious dispute 종교 분쟁
ritual [rítʃuəl] 종교적 의식
salvation [sælvéiʃən] 구원, 구세주
samsara [səmsáːrə] 윤회
sanctity [sǽŋktəti] 신성, 존엄
Satanism [séitənìzəm] 사탄주의
sermon [sə́ːrmən] 설교
spell [spel] 주문, 마법, 마력
spirit [spírit] 영혼
synagogue [sínəgàg] 유대교 사원
the Lord [lɔːrd] 주, 그리스도
the Resurrection [rèzərékʃən] 그리스도의 부활
theology [θiːálədʒi] 신학

Sociology 사회학

adolescence [ædəlésns] 청춘기, 사춘기
adoption [ədápʃən] 양자 결연
alienation [éiljənèiʃən] 소외
alimony [ǽləmòuni] 별거수당, 이혼수당
altruism [ǽltru(ː)ìzəm] 이타주의
average life expectancy 평균 예상수명
bastard [bǽstərd] 사생아
benediction [bènədíkʃən] 축복기도, 감사기도
break up 이혼하다, 해산하다
bureaucracy [bjuərákrəsi] 관료제
bureaucrat [bjúərəkræt] 관료주의자
bystander [báistændər] 방관자
census [sénsəs] 인구조사
charity [tʃǽrəti] 자선

civic movement 시민운동
climacteric [klaimǽktərik] 갱년기(의)
collective behavior 집단 행동
community [kəmjúːnəti] 공동체, 지역 사회
concentrate [kánsəntrèit] 집중하다
congestion [kəndʒéstʃən] 혼잡, 과잉
consensus [kənsénsəs] 합의
consort [kánsɔːrt] (통치자의) 배우자
contrariety [kántrəráiəti] 모순점, 불일치
cultural bias 문화적 편견
delinquency [dilíŋkwənsi] 비행, 범죄
demography [dimágrəfi] 인구통계학
denomination [dinámənèiʃən] 명명, 명칭
disorder [disɔ́ːrdər] (사회적, 정치적) 불온, 소동
divorce [divɔ́ːrs] 이혼하다
engagement [engéidʒmənt] 약혼
ethnic [éθnik] 민족의
evolution [èvəlúːʃən] 발전, 진전
exodus [éksədəs] 이주, 이동
expansive [ikspǽnsiv] 확장해 가는, 거대한
explosion [iksplóuʒən] 폭발
fiancé [fiːɑːnséi] 약혼자
go-between 중매인
half brothers 이복형제
heyday [héidei] 전성기
hymn [him] 찬송가
illegitimate [ilidʒítəmət] 서출의, 사생아의
immigrate [ímgrèit] 이주하다
infancy [ínfənsi] 유아, 유년
infrastructure [ínfrəstrʌ̀ktʃər] 하부구조, 사회기반시설
institution [ìnstətjúːʃən] (사회) 제도, (공공) 시설
juvenile [dʒúːvənl] 청소년
juvenile delinquency 청소년 범죄
juvenile delinquent 비행 청소년
kinship [kínʃip] 친족관계, 혈족관계
lineage [líniidʒ] 부족, 종족, 혈통

longevity [lanʤévəti] 장수, 수명
metropolitan [mètrəpálitən] 대도시의
norm [nɔːrm] 규범
outer city 외곽 도시
overpopulation [óuvərpápjəleíʃən] 인구과잉
pedigree [pédəgriː] 가계, 계보
peer group 동료집단
penal [píːnəl] 형법의, 형사상의
penalty [pénəlti] 형벌, 벌금
precocious [prikóuʃəs] (어린이가) 조숙한
prosperity [praspérəti] 번역, 풍요
public facilities 공공 편의시설
public utilities 공익사업
public works 공익사업
relocation [rìːloukéiʃən] 이주
resident [rézidənt] 거주민
satellite [sætəlàit] 위성도시
senescent [sənésnt] 노화, 늙어가는
senile [síːnail] 노인, 노년기의
separation [sèpəréiʃən] (부부) 별거
sibling [síbliŋ] 형제, 자매
skyscraper [skáiskrèipər] 초고층 건물
smuggle [smʌgl] 밀수하다
social behavior 사회적 행동
social integration 사회통합
social security 사회보장제도
strike [straik] 동맹파업
suit [suːt] 소송, 단원
testament [téstəmənt] 유서, 유언(장)
throng [θrɔ(ː)ŋ] 군중
uproar [ʌ́prɔːr] 소란, 소동
walkout [wɔ́ːkaut] 동맹파업

U.S. History 미국사

armed conflicts 무력충돌
armistice [áːrməstis] 휴전, 정전

anecdote [ǽnikdòut] 일화, 기담
annex [ənéks] (영토 등을) 병합하다
anomaly [ənáməli] 변칙, 예외
artillery [aːrtíləri] 포병, 포, 대포
baron [bǽrən] (지방) 호족
benefactor [bénəfæktər] 후원자
bonanza [bounǽnzə] 일확천금, 노다지
bootlegging [búːtlègiŋ] 주류 밀매, 밀조, 밀수
cavalry [kǽvəlri] 기병대
carnage [káːrnidʒ] 대학살, 살육
carpetbagger [káːrpitbægə(r)] 남북전쟁 후 이익을 노리고 남부로 건너온 북부 출신자
captive [kǽptiv] 포로, 사로잡힌
casualty [kǽʒuəlti] 사상자(수)
cavalry [kǽvəlri] 기병대
circuit court 순회 재판소
colonist [kálənist] 식민 이주자, 개척자
colonization [kálənizéiʃən] 식민지화
commoner [kámənə(r)] 평민
consolidate [kənsálədèit] 강화하다
Convention [kənvénʃən] 협정, 관습
covered wagon (초기 개척자들이 사용한) 포장마차
crusade [kruːséid] (개혁, 박멸 등의) 운동
Declaration of Independence 독립선언서
disarmament [disáːrməmənt] 군비감축, 무장해제
dismemberment [dismémbərmənt] (국토 등의) 분할
doctrine [dáktrin] 교의, 주의
drift [drift] 표류하다
(the) Dust Bowl 미국 중남부의 대초원 지대
early settlers 초기의 정착민들
electoral college 선거인단
Emancipation Proclamation 노예 해방 선언 (1963)
famine [fǽmin] 기근, 굶주림
Federal Court 연방법원

Federal government 미국연방정부
federalism [fédərəlìzm] 연방주의
feudalism [fjúːdlìzm] 봉건주의
flowering [fláuəriŋ] 전성기, 개화기
framer [fréimər] 입안자, 고안자
greenback [gríːnbæk] 미국 지폐
hardship [háːrdʃip] 역경, 고난
imperialism [impíəriəlìzəm] 제국주의
Independence Day 미국의독립기념일
Indian reservation 인디언 보호 거주지
Indiscriminate [ìndiskrímənət] 무차별의, 닥치는 대로의
infant nationhood 신생국
institution [ìnstətjúːʃən] 제도, 관습
integration [ìntəgrèiʃən] 통합, 인종 차별 폐지
itinerant preacher 순회 설교사
Jim Crow laws (흑인에 대한) 인종 차별 정책
July Fourth 미국 독립 기념일
Lewis and Clark 태평양 연안에 도달한 탐험가
life annuity 종신연금
Louisiana Purchase 루이지애나 구입지
massacre [mǽsəkər] 대량학살
Mexican War 멕시코 전쟁
migrate [máigreit] 이주하다
minority [minɔ́ːrəti] 소수민족
monarchy [mɑ́nərki] 군주제, 군주정치
monument [mɑ́njumənt] 기념비, 기념관
musket [mʌ́skit] 구식 소총
muckraker [mʌ́krèikər] 추문 폭로자
pasture [pǽstʃər] 목초지
patent [pǽtənt] 특허(권)
peer [piər] 귀족, 상원의원
persecute [pə́ːrsikjùːt] 박해하다
philanthropist [filǽnθrəpist] 박애주의자, 자선가
Pilgrim Fathers 청교도단
plantation [plæntéiʃən] 대농장
privilege [prívəlidʒ] 기본적인 인권

promulgate [prɑ́məlgèit] (법률, 명령 등을) 공포하다
provision [prəvíʒən] 조항, 규정
Pulitzer Prize 퓰리처상
Puritan [pjúərətn] 청교도
Quaker [kwéikər] 퀘이커교도
racial discrimination 인종차별
ranch [ræntʃ] 목장
ratify [rǽtəfài] 비준하다
redemptioner [ridémpʃənə(r)] 무임 도항 이주자
renewal [rinjúːəl] (도시 등의) 재개발, 일신
Representative [rèprizéntətiv] 하원의원
rifle [ráifl] 소총
Roaring Twenties 격동의 20년대
segregation [ségrigèiʃən] 격리, 인종 차별
settlement [sétlmənt] 정착지
slavery [sléivəri] 노예제도
Spanish-American War 미서전쟁(1899)
steel magnate 철강왕
submarine [sʌ́bmərìːn] 해저의
suppression [səpréʃən] 탄압, 억압
Supreme Court 대법원
Shutter's Mill 셔터즈밀
the Amendments [əméndmənt] (미국 헌법의) 수정 조항
the American Revolution 미국 독립 전쟁
the Bill of Rights 권리장전
the Capitol [kǽpitl] 미국 국회의사당
the Civil War 미국 남북 전쟁
the Confederacy [kənfédərəsi] 남부연방
the Dust Bowl (가뭄, 지나친 경작으로 인한) 건조지대
the Great Depression 대공황
the prohibition law 금주법(1820~33)
the Reformation [rèfərméiʃən] 종교개혁
the Union [júːnjən] 북군
thrall [θrɔːl] 노예, 노예 상태

transcontinental railroad 대륙 횡단 철도
trial and error 시행착오
truce [truːs] 휴전, 정전
unconstitutional [ʌnkanstitjúːʃənl] 위헌의
upheaval [ʌphíːvəl] (사상, 사회 등의) 격변, 동란
uprising [ʌ́pràiziŋ] 폭동, 반란
wagon train 큰 짐마차 떼, 포장마차 떼

Zoology 동물학

aestivate [éstəvèit] 하면하다, 여름잠을 자다
alteration of generations 세대교번
altricial [æltríʃəl] 만성의
amphibian [æmfíbiən] 양서류
animal kingdom 동물계
antelope [ǽntəlòup] 영양
arachnid [ərǽknid] 절지동물 중 거미류
arthropod [áːrθrəpád] 절지동물
asexual reproduction 무성생식
assimilation [əsíməlèiʃən] 동화작용
beak [biːk] (새의) 부리
bear [bɛər] (여성, 암컷이 아이를) 낳다
bill [bil] (새의) 부리
biped [báiped] 2족 동물
breed [briːd] (동물이) 번식하다
bug [bʌg] 갑충류(딱정벌레, 개똥벌레 등)
burrow [bə́ːrou] 숨다, 파고 들다
camouflage [kǽməflàːʒ] 위장하다
capture [kǽptʃər] 포획하다
carnivore [káːrnəvɔ̀ːr] 육식동물
carnivorous [kaːrnívərəs] 육식성의, 식충성의
carrion [kǽriən] 썩은 고기
chambered [tʃéimbərd] 실이 있는
chordate [kɔ́ːrdeit] 척색동물
claw [klɔː] 발톱
coelenterate [siːléntərèit] 강장동물(해파리, 말미잘 등)

cold-blooded 냉혈의
colloid [kálɔid] 콜로이드, 교질
colony [káləni] 집단, 군집
culture [kʌ́ltʃər] 배양
cyclostomata [sáikloustóumətə] 원구류
den [den] 굴, 우리
descend [disénd] ~의 계통을 잇다
dormant [dɔ́ːrmənt] 잠자는, 동면의
echinoderm [ikáinədə̀ːrm] 극피동물
egg cell 난자, 난세포
evolve [iválv] 진화하다
fend [fend] 방어하다, ~을 부양하다
finch [fintʃ] 되새류
fish [fiʃ] 어류
flock [flɔk] 집단
game [geim] 사냥감
genetics [dʒənétiks] 유전학, 유전적 특길
habitat [hǽbətæt] 번지지, 서식지
hatch [hætʃ] (알, 병아리를) 까다, 부화하다
herbivore [hə́rbəvɔ̀ːr] 초식동물
herbivorous [həːrbívərəs] 초식의
herd [həːrd] 무리, 떼
hibernation [háibərnèiʃən] 동면, 겨울잠
hindfoot [haindfut] 후족부, 뒷발
insectivore [inséktəvɔ̀ːr] 식충동물
invertebrate [invə́ːrtəbrət] 무척추동물
lair [lɛər] (짐승의) 굴, 집
lay [lei] (알을) 낳다
leathery [léðəri] 가죽 같은
live off ~에 기생하다
lizard [lízərd] 도마뱀
mammal [mǽməl] 포유동물, 포유류
marsupial [maːrsúːpiəl] 유대류
mate [meit] 짝을 짓다
metamorphosis [mètəmɔ́ːrfəsis] 변태, 변형작용
mollusk [máləsk] 연체동물

moose [muːs] 무스, 말코손바닥사슴
nocturnal [naktə́ːrnl] 야생성의
nutrient [njúːtriənt] 양분, 영양소
offspring [ɔ́(ː)fsprìŋ] 자식, (동식물의) 새끼
omnivore [ámnivɔ̀ːr] 잡식동물
omnivorous [amnívərəs] 잡식성의
pant [pænt] 헐떡거리다
parasite [pǽrəsàit] 기생동물
paw [pɔː] (동물의) 발
pigmentation [pìgməntéiʃən] 색소형성
plant kingdom 식물계
precocial [prikóuʃəl] 조성성의
predator [prédətər] 약탈자, 육식동물
prey [prei] 먹이, 희생자
primate [práimeit] 영장류
proboscis [proubásis] (코끼리 같은 동물의) 코
quadruped [kwádrupèd] 4족동물
reproduce [rìːprədjúːs] 번식하다
reproduction [rìːprədʌ́kʃən] 생식, 번식
reptile [réptail] 파충류
respiration [rèspəréiʃən] 호흡작용
rodent [róudnt] 설치류
ruminant [rúːmənənt] 반추동물
scavenger [skǽvəndʒə(r)] 썩은 고기를 먹는 동물
scrap [skræp] 먹다 남은 것, 찌꺼기
secretion [sikríːʃən] 분비 (작용)
shell [ʃel] (알 등의) 껍데기, (동식물의) 외피
soft tissue 부드러운 조직
sponge [spʌndʒ] 해면동물
survival of the fittest 적자생존
swoop [swuːp] 급습하다
tentacle [téntəkl] (동물의) 촉수, 더듬이
torpid [tɔ́ːrpid] (동물이) 동면, 휴면하고 있는
ungulate [ʌ́ŋgjulət] 유제 동물
vertebrate [və́ːrtəbrèit] 척추 동물